Work, Family,
and Religion
in Contemporary
Society

Work, Family, and Religion in Contemporary Society

edited by
Nancy Tatom Ammerman
and Wade Clark Roof

Routledge ■ New York & London

Published in 1995 by
Routledge
29 West 35 Street
New York, NY 10001

Published in Great Britain in 1994 by
Routledge
11 New Fetter Lane
London EC4P 4EE

Printed in the United States of America.

Library of Congress Cataloging-in-Publication Data

Work, family, and religion in contemporary society /
Nancy Tatom Ammerman and Wade Clark Roof, editors.
    p.   cm.
    "Papers grew out of a consultation that was held in October,
1988, in Amherst, Massachusetts."
    Includes bibliographical references and index.
    ISBN 0-415-91171-0 (cloth) — ISBN 0-415-91172-9 (pbk.)
1. Church work with families—United States—Congresses.
2. Family—United States—Religious life—Congresses.
3. Christianity—United States—20th Century—Congresses.
I. Ammerman, Nancy Tatom.   II. Roof, Wade Clark.

BV4438.W67   1995   94-33979
277.3'0829—dc20   CIP

CONTENTS

ACKNOWLEDGMENTS

This collection of essays grew out of a consultation that was held in October, 1988 in Amherst, Massachusetts. At that time many of the people who have essays in the present volume came together to think about issues on family and religion. Our concern was to explore changing patterns of work, family, and faith across religious traditions, and the responses of religious institutions to these changes. That initial discussion provided a basis for the essays found here. Additional contributors were subsequently asked to prepare essays on selected topics that emerged in our thinking over the next several years. Along the way, many of the essays were presented at the meetings of the Society for the Scientific Study of Religion in special sessions on family and religion. To those who contributed to all of these discussions, we owe our thanks.

We are also grateful to the Lilly Endowment, Inc. for funds making the consultation possible, and for support of the research reported in these essays.

Nancy Tatom Ammerman
Wade Clark Roof
June, 1994

Introduction

Old Patterns, New Trends, Fragile Experiments

Nancy Tatom Ammerman
and Wade Clark Roof

O ne of the promising developments of the early 1990s is the mounting chorus of voices in support of family issues—concerns such as child care, working parents, parental leave, and support services for families. This new consciousness about family needs has been fostered in part by high levels of divorce, domestic crisis and abuse, and teenage pregnancies, combined with a growing sense that even seemingly stable families face unprecedented difficulties. Striking evidence that a new consciousness was emerging came in 1991. A new alliance was formed, comprised of well-known liberals and New Right conservatives, who chose to overlook the issues on which they were divided in order to take a public stand on behalf of the family concerns where they were in agreement.[1]

This new concern for the American family is encouraging for several reasons. First, it suggests a new realism about families and their needs in the late twentieth century. While this does not mean an end to the "cultural wars," particularly over controversial issues like abortion and homosexuality, it does signal a significant level of concern and agreement among Americans of opposing ideologies. Neither the pessimistic view that families are all falling apart nor the blind optimism that fails to see any problems is acceptable. The fact is that families, in one form or another, are central in the lives of Americans; people want to protect them. Surveys continue to show that the overwhelming majority of Americans continue to value what families can provide—love, emotional support, nurturance. Even when married people are asked if they would remarry their spouses, more than three-fourths say yes.[2] The problems facing families today are real, but family life as such is not disappearing.

Second, a new image of family is emerging that is more flexible and more adaptable. Behind the new realism drawing together people of differing persuasions is a model of family that is appealing, in part, because it combines seemingly contradictory elements. Arlene Skolnick writes:

> The New American Dream mixes the new cultural freedoms with many of the old wishes—marital and family happiness, economic security, home ownership, education of children. But the new dream is more demanding than the old, and even the basics—a secure job, a home, health care, education—are becoming more difficult to achieve. The new life course has more twists and turns than it did in the past; it offers greater opportunities for autonomy, but greater risks of loneliness. Further, even the middle class faces more travails than in the past: divorce, time pressures, and the dilemmas of raising children in a world that has grown more dangerous, competitive, and uncertain.[3]

The "new cultural freedoms" to which Skolnick refers are rooted in the experiences of the 1960s and 1970s. During those years of cultural upheaval, there were sweeping changes in marriage and family values. Women moved into the workplace, dual-career marriages became more common, and of course the sexual revolution led to changes in sexual mores, to the empowerment of women, and to new ways for men and women to relate to one another. For many, career took precedence over family, resulting in a "postponed generation" putting off marriage and children until later. Especially for a younger generation of Americans growing up at the time—the so-called baby-boomers—the new values were widely embraced. Terms like the "new morality" and "lifestyle" became a common part of the vocabulary among those for whom choice and self-expression were taken for granted. While much that is remembered about the 1960s and 1970s has long since passed, still many values from that period are now a permanent part of our culture—among others, greater tolerance of those who are different, concern for the individual, and gender equality.[4] Now, in the 1990s, there is a trend away from the more extreme expressive individualism of that earlier era and toward greater attachment to family and to others. The "ethic of commitment" which Daniel Yankelovich foresaw a decade ago appears now to have come into its own—emphasizing a greater connectedness with people, institutions, places, nature.[5]

Why this shift today? A major reason is that many in the baby-boom generation are now rearing children—and thus are confronted with the responsibilities which come with parenthood. There is considerable awareness, too, that preoccupation with the self has its limits: genuine personal fulfillment lies in discovery of a vital balance between self and concern for others. That is, through their attachments to others and commitments to worthy causes, people find meaning and satisfaction in their own lives.

Yet as Skolnick points out, this is not a return to the old traditional values. The Ozzie and Harriet family of the 1950s is gone forever, now replaced by a wide array of many differing types of marital and parent-child arrangements, all recognized in a pluralistic society as deserving of being called "family." It is a new era when women enjoy more freedom to choose whether to work or to stay at home as wives and mothers. Although women are still entering the labor force in greater numbers each year, the birthrate has actually begun to increase again, and child-centered values seem to be replacing adult-centered values. For increasing numbers of couples, there is shared responsibility at home and a redefinition of marriage and parenting. There appears to be a growing concern for finding fulfillment within the home and greater attention to "quality" of relationships and deeper personal values such as intimacy, warmth, and sharing.[6]

This new mix of values has its counterpart in the workplace. A recent book title describing today's younger corporate executives—*The New Individualists*[7]—sums up what is happening in the workplace. Paul Leinberger and Bruce Tucker argue that the generation after the "organization man" is less conforming, and holds to a more psychologized conception of individualism—a change from a socially formed, highly internalized self to a more subjective, highly expressive self. Young executives, for example, look upon work as an opportunity to be creative, a place where they can develop their potential. Yet they also are concerned about family life, and how work and family can mesh together. They judge the merits of their work not just in terms of pay or how they "feel" about it, but also on the basis of whether it conflicts with family values. They like to "network," because it offers a chance to cultivate social relationships—in keeping with similar values at home. Today's corporate managers see themselves as embedded in relationships and commitments that make them who they are—and family is high on that list of relationships.

In the workplace generally, movement is toward more decentralized structures, greater participatory decision-making, the inclusion of women into leadership positions, more flexible hours and work rules, more leisure activities, facilities for physical exercise, child care and parental leaves. Family is no longer something left behind with a kiss at the door.

This *does not* mean, however, that women and men are now overwhelmingly in egalitarian marriages and satisfying careers. Most of the women who are in the paid labor force are in monotonous, low-wage, sometimes hazardous jobs. Many are heads of household, not providing a second paycheck. While increasing numbers of women may be working either for fulfillment or to pursue a career, that is clearly not the norm. Even when women work full-time, most still define their primary roles as wife and mother.

Their husbands often agree. Men still see home as the place where they get supported and nurtured. While they are at work, they think about family less than do women. And when they are at home, they do much less of the housework and child care than do women.[8] And not surprisingly, working men are more satified with their marriage and family life than are working women. Whether the household is headed by a single man, a single woman, a two-paycheck couple, or a dual-career couple, there is still household labor to be done and the rewards of nurture and intimacy to be had. Who does what labor and who gets what reward, however, is very much up for grabs.

Whether out of "new freedoms" or out of economic necessity, the last generation has seen the balance between work and family life dramatically shifting. People have different sets of involvements, different schedules, different relationships, different resources. That shifting and complex network of activity and resources is spilling over into every other area of people's lives. It is affecting the economy on both the employment and consumption ends—witness the appearance of "family friendliness" ratings of corporations and the growth of catalog shopping.

Likewise, the religious landscape is undergoing its own changes. The changing ethos of values and commitment and greater sense of choice that characterized family life have engulfed not just work but also religion. With this "new voluntarism" and a shifting from collective-expressive to individual-expressive values[9], there is greater freedom to make religious decisions on the basis of personal preferences and needs. For some people, this new freedom leads to religious indifference and a secular outlook; for others, to "religion *à la carte*" and pastiche styles of belief and practice that draw from a variety of religious and spiritual resources; and for still others, it leads to a more conscious, personally responsible type of commitment to a church, synagogue or mosque.[10] Greater choice need not undermine religious loyalties; it can actually enhance greater clarity of commitment.

As a result of greater choice, parishes and congregations themselves are taking on distinctive identities as they come to reflect the preferences of their members. Denominational labels may mean less in identifying a church or synagogue than the particular worship styles, programs, and mission activities created by those who have chosen it. And chief among the things that characterize congregations is the relationship they have developed with the families—of all shapes and sizes—that fill their pews. Congregations can take on a variety of family-related identities. They may become known as "traditional family" bastions, or places open to gay and lesbian persons, or supporters of women's rights or great places for kids—or some combination thereof.

What is becoming increasingly clear is that the cultural trends we have described are influencing not just families, but the entire nexus of work, family, and religion. The links among all three institutions are in process of redefinition. To state this is not just to argue, as sociologists are prone to do, that the parts of a society are interrelated. Rather, it is to suggest that, in an age of greater choice and reorienting of self in relation to other attachments—to work, to religious community, to family—all become more fluid and adaptable.

This new context of work, family, and religion must be understood against the backdrop of broader changes that have structurally altered how these institutions relate to one another today. The old patterns have been described by cultural historians and sociologists as having divided life fairly neatly (at least for the middle class) into public and private spheres. Work, politics, and men belonged in the public sphere; home, faith, and women belonged in the private sphere.[11] Functionalist sociologists like Talcott Parsons saw this division of labor as ingeneous—instrumental needs got taken care of in one place, expressive needs in another.[12] For an economy and a government to run smoothly, homes and faith communities were needed to instill values in their individual worker-citizens, and to bind up the wounds of those injured by the calculations of the public arena.[13] Social psychologists looked at what sorts of values were being taught by parents, and discovered that they did indeed serve the needs of the economy well. Working-class families were teaching their children to be disciplined and obedient, while middle class and professional families were encouraging autonomy and creativity.[14]

At least through the 1950s, churches themselves seemed to assume this social division of labor. A 1937 book called *Family and Church*[15] exhorts pastors to help families to have healthy relationships and foster psychological well-being. It notes that work-related problems like mobility or financial strain can have an impact on families, but that the family should be a haven from such strains. The church, for its part, should be a facilitator of that role. The book also exhorts families to be diligent in the religious training of their children, and in maintaining devotional activities in the home. Like a similar book written two decades later, the picture is of mutual "back-scratching" between home and church. That later study, by Fairchild and Wynn,[16] recognizes that there are increasing signs of ill-health among families—juvenile delinquency, divorce, and the like (and there are hints that the real problem may be mothers who work), but there is little expectation that any fundamental realignment is underway. The expectation remained that religion and child-rearing were connected to each other, and that both were women's work. Congregations existed in part to help families do their jobs, and families were expected to support in their homes the work and worldview of the congregation. The public world of labor force and economy was an occasional intrusion, largely alien to the world of family and faith kept alive by the work of women.

But today, the work of women is expended in both "public" and "private" domains. No single factor has been more responsible for shifts in the relationships among work, family, and religion than the massive entry of women into the workforce. By the mid-1970s, well over half the women under fifty-five were in the paid labor force.[17] In the next decade and a half, employment rates essentially doubled. By 1990, among white women, seventy percent were employed at least part-time; indeed, over forty percent of all mothers with children at home were employed full-time.[18] Women were clearly no longer "confined" to the private sphere; families were adjusting to new configurations of time, money, and child-rearing; and if congregations were paying attention, they noticed that shifting family and work patterns had changed who sits in their pews and when.

Many congregations, however, were not paying attention as family life changed around them. Both their programming and the image they projected reinforced the notion that "family" (meaning married couples with children) and "religion" go together. The old norms in American culture predicted that married women, especially with children, were both less likely to be in the labor force than single women, and more likely to be affiliated and active in religious organizations. Married men are *more* likely to be in the labor force than single men, and more likely to be religiously affiliated. The norm seemed to be that being religious went along with getting married, having a single-earner household, and having children. The corollary, then, was that those who are not "families" in that traditional sense do not belong in congregations. Consider the following bits of evidence:

- Women who have no religious affiliation have the highest rates of labor force participation.[19]
- College women who claim to be feminists, according to one study, almost never attend religious services.[20]
- Canadians with no religious preference have the most egalitarian marriages, the lowest fertility, and the highest divorce rates.[21]
- Men with no religious affiliation do better as custodial parents than men involved in religious institutions.[22]

Those bits of evidence paint a picture of pushes and pulls between religion and people in nontraditional families.

The changing alignments of work, family life, and religion—organized and otherwise—are the subject of this book. In Part I, we will assess the trends. Just how many women are working? Does the relationship between "traditional family" structure and religious participation still hold? Has the baby-boomer generation returned to religious participation? Or are the changes in work and family structure eroding the traditional core of the churches and synagogues, with no other demographic core emerging in their wake? Papers in this section sort out the trends, some exploring patterns for the society as a whole (and thus across faith traditions) and others in particular religious constituencies.

In the opening essay, Penny Marler argues that Protestant churches do indeed remain wedded to a nostalgia for a traditional family structure that is no longer dominant. She offers evidence from an ethnographic study of a Congregationalist church in Connecticut, along with a national survey of seventy-two Protestant congregations, and national survey data from Gallup and others. She documents that churches are getting their "market share" of traditional families and older singles, but are losing younger singles and other nontraditional households. "Other family" and "nonfamily" are the two household types growing fastest in the U.S. population, and they are ill-represented in church memberships. Those who are in church are older, empty-nest couples, and widow(er)s, along with families that look like the "parents with kids" of yore. She shows, in fact, that Protestant church membership has varied with the proportion of such "traditional" families in the U.S. population. "From the fifties peak, the proportion of married persons with children in the U.S. population began to decline. This group was 40% of American households in 1970, 31% in 1980, and 26% in 1990." And Protestant church membership has declined in parallel fashion.

She argues, however, that churches are kept alive by a kind of symbiosis between their young families and the older persons who remember when *they* were attending church with their families. At the church she calls Briarglen, programming is shaped by a younger cohort of families with children, who "consume" what suits them, and an older generation of empty nesters, who remember how it used to be and are willing to "produce" the programming to support these young families. The problem, of course, is that this generation is not really like the last, nor is it assured that they will take over the "producer" role of the older generation when they reach that age.

Just what this generation is really like is the subject taken up by Wade Clark Roof and Lyn Gesch in the next chapter. Working from a major study of the "baby-boom" generation, they ask whether and how the emphasis on individual choice has affected this generation's relationship to religious institutions and practices. They find that the principle of individual choice is now prevalent even inside the family, with nearly half the baby boomers saying family members should choose for themselves about religious matters, rather than necessarily attending together as a family.

This emphasis on choice is tied in predictable ways to people's work and family experience. Women who work full-time are more likely to be individualists than women who do not, and people without children are more proindividualist than parents. Emphasis on choice is also prevalent in divorced and blended families. The individualists, Roof and Gesch find, grew up in more permissive homes, and do not think it is particularly important to pass religious values on to children. Most dropped out of religious participation in their teen and young adult years, and have not returned. Roof and Gesch wonder about this de-emphasis on religious instruction of children—religious individualists seem not so much interested in facilitating an informed choice as simply disinterested in any institutional form of religion at all. Theirs is a more privatized faith, perhaps expressed in other small-group activities, such as Twelve-Step groups.

In contrast, people who think families should attend church together are much more likely to be religiously involved. People who dropped out as youth, but who hold that attitude, have a religiously active spouse, and have children, have returned to participation at a ninety percent rate. Individualists with religiously active spouses and children have returned only at a forty-one percent rate. The link between family and religion is alive and well, then, but only for a specific segment of the population with traditional views about family participation and traditional family structures to match.

While each of these studies has posited that women who work full-time are less religiously active than other women, the relationship between women's labor force participation and their religiosity is hardly straightforward. Using nearly twenty years of surveys from the General Social Survey, Bradley Hertel takes up the task of untangling that relationship. He takes into account that the relationship may be different for people with different family and work statuses and for different aspects of religiosity. But like all the other studies, he finds that both marriage and having children are positively related to all measures of religiosity for both men and women. Again, the link between "traditional family" and religiosity seems alive and well.

But is this affected by labor force participation? He notes that the "social class hypothesis" says that higher occupational status leads to more religious participation, meaning that people in the labor force ought to participate more. But the "workforce hypothesis" says increasing labor force participation leads to less religious participation. What he discovers is that the patterns for single women and for married men tend to support the former: the more involved in the labor force they are, the more they participate in both secular and religious organizations. That full-time employed women are less religiously active than part-time employed women suggests that there is some truth to the "workforce hypothesis" for them. In addition, the husbands of full-time employed women are less involved than the husbands of non- or part-time employed women. The strains of two-job households may be taking a toll on participation. Still, even when employed, married women are more involved than any other group, especially when they have school-aged children. They seem to join when the children are born, but not go regularly until they are older.

Hertel also uses this extended data set to examine differences among cohorts—preboomer, boomer, and postboomer—and across time. For each of these groups, he looks at how attendance differs by cohort, full-time employment, and employment of spouse. For all three broad groups there has been a steady increase in religious commitment. However, much of that increase has been offset by the fact that earlier birth cohorts were more religious than persons born more recently. Women's employment has had a greater impact on religious involvement for boomers and postboomers. These patterns lead Hertel to conclude that the implications of married women's employment for the future of organized religion are greater than has generally been recognized in past research. There are, in addition, larger cultural forces shaping the patterns of work, family, and religion.

One of those forces is the feminist movement itself. Women simply expect different things today from earlier generations, and those expectations have an impact on work, on families, and on religion. Lyn Gesch looks at the same General Social Survey data to see just what that impact may be. She compared women with egalitarian ideals to women with traditionalist ideals. It should not surprise us by now to find that the former are much less conventionally religious than the latter. They also have less conventional families. Women with traditionalist ideals, in contrast, are less likely to be in the labor force and more likely to be in conservative congregations. They come disproportionately from an older, less-educated cohort that is disappearing in the face of younger, well-educated women with egalitarian ideals. And it is these attitudes, Gesch finds, more than actual work force participation, that affect religious participation. There are curious hints in her findings, however, hints about the private religiosity of women who have shunned public, institutional forms of religious involvement.

The one place we should find the link between "traditional" family values and religion especially strong is among various conservative groups. While surveys rarely classify people with much precision, the diverse groups that have found their way into various surveyer's "conservative" category are distinctive in their family patterns.

- They have the lowest divorce rates of any religious group.[23]
- They have the lowest rates of female labor force participation.[24]
- They have the highest fertility rates.[25]
- They have the most conservative attitudes on gender roles.[26]

The ethos in many conservative churches is strongly supportive of traditional male-provider/female-homemaker families, and that ethos is strong enough to show up in survey results like these. However, what does not show up are the subtle negotiations that surround family life even here.[27] Those who study conservative groups closely soon discover both that the "new freedoms" have found their way into these communities as well,[28] and that "traditional" norms can be readily adapted to serve the needs of women.[29]

Charles Hall's chapter in this book looks carefully at those work and family negotiations among religious conservatives. Because he used data from a poll conducted by *Christianity Today*, he can be confident that the women he studied define themselves within the conservative milieu. He discovered that their religious beliefs do influence what they think women ought to be doing, and that, in turn, affects their labor force participation. However, other factors intervene as well. Having preschool children and a husband with more income made working less likely. Even here, there appear to be countervailing pressures on the "traditional" family.

The picture that emerges throughout these chapters, then, is of a continuing tie between "traditional families" and conventional religious participation. In Marler's words, "as the family goes, so go the churches." However, the picture on the same page is of increasingly diverse family forms, with fewer "traditional families" in the population. A younger generation may be returning to religious participation, but its experiences of individualism and feminism continue to place barriers between it and much of organized religion. It seems likely that some of this survey evidence hints at a kind of mutual exclusion going on between conservative religionists and people committed to new patterns of family and work. It may be that many congregations have actively promulgated family values that have pushed nontraditional members out.[30] Catholics and Mormons who have been divorced, for instance, are less likely to attend church than are their coreligionists who have not violated that particular church teaching.[31]

But the extremes of disenchantment do not tell the whole story. What people are experiencing in their work and family life—whether traditional or nontraditional—cannot be disconnected from the sorts of religious communities they are choosing.[32] Between the secularist family innovator at one extreme and the conservative religious traditionalist at the other are vast portions of the U.S. population.[33] For them, *both* faith and new forms of work and family are realities, both autonomy and commitment are values to be cherished.[34]

What does not yet show up in national surveys are the experiments cropping up throughout American religious life. Despite its image as an unchanging institution, American religion has begun to absorb these work and family changes. In the mid-1980s, Steven Hart asked Lutherans about the changes they had noticed in their congregations.[35] They noted, of course, that more of their women members were working. They also noted more single parents and more divorces, as well as more single people and marrieds without children. They regretted the loss of female volunteer time, but they were glad for the new skills and experience women were bringing into their churches. They were also glad for the presence of more family diversity, noting that it had helped to make them more open and tolerant of different lifestyles.

Faced with more working women, probably the most common response of religious organizations has been to start a day-care center. A 1983 study estimated that as many as fifty percent of the nation's day-care centers are housed in churches.[36] Most of those congregations are just landlords, but others provide religious instruction along with care. For many, this endeavor may be more of a ministry to people outside the congregation than a response to members' needs. The study found, for instance, that church-run centers are more likely to serve low-income populations than are other kinds of centers.

Inside the congregations, the changes induced by new work and family realities have included the rise of women clergy, inclusive language, new forms of religious education, and altered weekly schedules. Many Protestant churches now have singles ministries; Catholic parishes are developing marriage enrichment programs; Jewish congregations, including the Orthodox, have found ways to integrate working and career women into their activities.[37] Indeed, in this era of change, religious groups have often been an arena in which cultural experimentation of all sorts has happened. In Part II of this volume, we take up the everyday, on-the-ground patterns now emerging in faith communities around this country. Our approach differs from that of theorists of a previous generation, who looked upon these institutions as functionally integrated around a common set of values. Rather than value consensus we assume—in keeping with the mounting concerns today about family issues—that cultural change is more common than cultural continuity, and that the altered worlds of work and family have created new "meaning space" with profound religious and spiritual implications. As old institutional patterns give way, there are new and innovative experiments in reconnecting faith, family, and work in ways more responsive to the needs of people and their life situations. In Catholic parishes, in liberal Protestant and conservative Protestant congregations, in Jewish synagogues, in Muslim mosques, one finds attention today to similar concerns. What follows in Part II are "reports" on some of the experiments and conversations now underway.

The first is a report that reflects the kinds of rethinking theologians are doing. Protestant theologian Don Browning begins this section with a proposal for how Christian churches *ought* to respond. What we need, he says, is a new family ethic based on "equal regard." Neither the old neo-orthodox ethic of self-sacrifice nor the hedonist ethic of self-fulfillment will do; both autonomy and commitment are essential. "You shall love your neighbor as yourself." Such an ethic answers the concerns of feminists who reject the self-sacrifice churches have imposed on them. And it answers the concerns of those who worry about the long-term future of an ethic of self-fulfillment. Browning argues that mainline Protestant churches have been scared into thinking that emphasis on the family is "private" and therefore to be eschewed in favor of a "public" ministry. They have therefore let the conservative churches do the family talk. He notes, however, that issues related to the family are very public, bringing individuals and churches into contact with public agencies and public action.

Nowhere is the link between family and public life more apparent than in the African-American community. Cheryl Townsend Gilkes writes in her chapter that black churches have always tied work and family to the church and public life. Today, however, they are faced with the twin dilemmas of an increasingly imperilled group of "truly disadvantaged" persons largely alienated from the church, and another group that has benefited from the changes in the last generation and may also be alienated from black church and community. She notes: "It is possible to read the history of the African-American experience as a succession of dislocations affecting the relationship between work and family."

Among the churches that seem to be working best in the face of this crisis are a growing number of "megachurches"—the churches of "what's happening now." These churches bring together comfortable, middle-class persons with the truly disadvantaged. They emphasize Afrocentrism, and provide structures of support for men, women, and families. They stand in contrast to older, more traditional, black churches that are confronting the same family crises behind a veil of quiet respectability.

Gilkes points out that in confronting this crisis, black churches have a rich heritage to call on. Throughout slavery and the oppression of racism, churches have helped people define and sanctify their unions, care for their children, mourn their losses. The church served as extended family in times when blood families were precarious, cooperating especially in the socialization of children. Drawing on that family-church heritage will be critical as black churches continue to search for new ways to make the connections.

Making connections between church and public life is also the task being undertaken by a church in Atlanta. This mainline Protestant congregation, described by Joe Reiff in his chapter, was brought back from near-death by an influx of baby-boomers, who are now asking hard questions about what it means for them to be involved in the institutional life of a church. As a theologian, Reiff is interested in what their dilemmas can teach the churches. He says they have to begin by pondering: "What *is* the nature of the church and its relationship to the world in these days? What role can the church and its adult members play in both the nurture of its children in the faith and the equipping of those children for present and future Christian vocation, mission and ministry?" Again, the answering of these questions takes us into the world of theologians who are taking new work and family patterns seriously.

There are multiple public arenas to which this congregation and its children are seeking to relate. First, the congregation itself must be recognized as a public arena. But they are also seeking to find links to a larger public discourse, and to the public issues that define the common good and establish our solidarity with the whole human community, especially those at the bottom. Issues about work and politics are as much a part of congregational concern as issues about parenting and spirituality. By seeing children as a gift to the entire community, not just to their parents, children are treated as full participants in the effort to address these publics. They are shaped by their participation in the congregation and in its discourse and solidarity. Being accepted as members of the congregation helps them to grow their roots. Both parents and church are engaged in helping the child get a critical consciousness about the culture that surrounds them.

Such a critical consciousness is also the central ingredient in the particular issue examined by Sister Mary Johnson. A married person with children and a high-paying job in a defense-related industry would—given the old patterns—suggest a good "traditional family" church participant. However, for some people, religious organizations and religious faith have meant a radical alteration in that work-family-church pattern. Johnson has studied adults for whom religion and family helped to shape a major life change—leaving a job in the defense industry. "For all nineteen respondents, it [religion] helped to create the doubts they had about their jobs, motivated them to act, and served to confirm their definition of the situation." She takes us through their stages of leaving—from doubting, to seeking alternatives, to a turning point, and finally out. This chapter makes explicit what has been implicit in the previous three—when religious organizations are willing to breech the line between public and private, real change may result, both for individuals and for the larger institutions of which they are a part.

Especially important in the process of seeing the connections between faith and work, according to Johnson, were nonparish religious organizations—Pax Christi and the like. While Reiff and Gilkes are describing parish-based efforts to reknit work, family, and religion, Johnson's work suggests that other religious organizations may sometimes fill the gaps left by parishes that insist on remaining detached from public issues. A wide array of groups at the margins of institutional religious life are described in the chapters by D'Antonio, Wright, and Neitz that follow.

William D'Antonio surveys the variety of small groups that are springing up within the Catholic Church, groups that meet in homes, schools, and parish halls, groups that meet with and without the presence of a priest, but groups that attempt to provide a forum in which work, family, and public issues can be brought into dialogue with faith. Intentional Eucharistic Communities are lay-run groups for whom the eucharist is central as an expression of and impetus to their involvement in service to the world. They are relatively autonomous in governance, but the church itself has sponsored a variety of other groups as part of other outreach and renewal efforts. These groups are related to changes brought by Vatican II and to the increasing educational levels of American Catholics, but there were even precursors before 1960. They seem to reflect both the democratic instincts of much of the American church and the efforts of faithful people to place faith in the real context of their lives. Now the question is how the presence of such groups will change the church.

The "house church groups" studied by Stuart Wright also exist in a variety of relationships with otherwise organized religion. Some are wholly independent creations, while others are intentional efforts at church growth undertaken by innovative congregations. He argues that all these groups are an effort to "dedifferentiate," to get home, work, and faith back together in an intimate community. They get around the boomer generation's distrust of institutions, are mobile and flexible, and provide support to families and a context in which to discuss work and vocation. Like D'Antonio's Catholic groups, they are egalitarian and participatory.

Slightly further outside the domain of traditional religion is the group studied by Mary Jo Neitz. Called "Limina," its leaders have adapted many of the liturgical resources of their Catholic memories into ritual expressions of the lives of very contemporary women. They also draw on a wide range of ritual and symbols from ancient Celts and indigenous peoples from throughout the world, with the resulting mix falling somewhere between the reforms of those who attempt to stay inside the church and the radical practices of others who embrace witchcraft and goddess worship. What the group accomplishes, Neitz argues, is a public expression of the work women do throughout their lives, work that contributes to the common good of the household and beyond. And in so doing, they enact new definitions for the relationship between work, family, and faith.

Just as many women have found the images and rituals of the churches and synagogues disconnected from their experience, so have many couples who experiment with new ways of combining work and family life. Faith, says William Johnson Everett, is about what we care most about. When we change our work and family patterns, we inherently reshape our faith, he says. Couples who work together, then, are challenging the fragmentation of the modern world and may be reshaping images of the right ordering of life that will have implications for religion itself. They are disproportionately likely to be nontraditionally religious. The more egalitarian they are, the more "spiritual" and less orthodox their religious images, and the less involved in religious institutions they are. They seem to be inventing new religious and spiritual patterns out of a "perception that churches exist more to pass on traditional values to the next generation than to help today's adults, especially couples, invent new patterns for their lives."

And so we return to the dilemma of institutional religion. Its strength for over a century has been its tie to the socialization of children. As people marry and produce offspring, they have been more likely to align themselves with religious organizations and values. That pattern seems clearly still in place, even for the baby-boom generation.

However, changes are afoot. Both inside and outside traditional religion there is experimentation going on. Inside, theologians are calling for a new family ethic that takes the individualism of the boomers seriously, but calls them to balance that quest with a commitment to "equal regard." Inside, congregations—black, white, and integrated—are tackling public issues that arise out of the crises faced by neighborhood, family, and nation. They are rejecting the notion that being a "family church" means being quietly private and irrelevant. They are creating programs and structures that enable congregants to engage each other in a "mediating structure," where persons in all their complexity encounter the public world in all its complexity.

On the margins of traditional religion, even more experimentation is happening. Thousands of small religious groups are springing up, often to fill a void left by ordinary congregations. From Catholic RENEW groups, to Protestant house churches, to Limina, people are creating spaces in which to reunite the pieces of life fragmented by modernization. These groups unite work and family concerns in a religious context apparently without requiring that the people in them belong to "traditional families."

The essays in this book document both the dilemma—the traditional link between organized religion and one increasingly less prevalent kind of family—and efforts at moving beyond our current impasse. The experiments we describe here are still precarious, and may be crushed under the weight of tradition in both religion and economy. But the cries of concern about family life have reached the ears of church and industry alike. It is clear that the years ahead will bring increasing efforts to provide a more viable institutional structure surrounding American families. The days when business could ignore families and churches could take them for granted are over. What this book attempts to show is that millions of Americans are already facing this dilemma with both courage and creativity. We are remaking our lives.

NOTES

1. Steven A. Holmes, "Unlikely Union Arises to Press Family Issues," *New York Times*, May 1, 1991, p. A–12.
2. Louis Harris, *Inside America* (New York: Vintage Books, 1987).
3. Arlene Skolnick, *Embattled Paradise: The American Family in an Age of Uncertainty* (New York: Basic Books, 1991), p. 220.
4. For a discussion of these changes as they affected religion and family, see

William V. D'Antonio, "Family Life, Religion, and Societal Values and Structures," and Barbara Hargrove, "The Church, the Family, and the Modernization Process," in William V. D'Antonio and Joan Aldous, eds., *Families and Religions: Conflict and Change in Modern Society* (Beverly Hills: Sage Publications, 1983).

5. Daniel Yankelovich, *New Rules: Searching for Self-Fulfillment in a World Turned Upside Down* (New York: Random House, 1981).

6. Barbara Defoe Whitehead makes these arguments in "A New Familism?" *Family Affairs* 5, No. 1–2 (Summer 1992).

7. Paul Leinberger and Bruce Tucker, *The New Individualists: The Generation after the Organization Man* (New York: Harper, 1991).

8. Joseph H. Pleck, *Working Wives/Working Husbands* (Beverly Hills, CA: Sage Publications, 1985). See also Uma Sekaran, *Dual-Career Families* (San Francisco: Jossey-Bass, 1986), and Arlie Hochschild (with Anne Machung), *Second Shift* (New York: Viking, 1989).

9. Wade Clark Roof and William McKinney, *American Mainline Religion: Its Changing Shape and Future* (New Brunswick, NJ: Rutgers University Press, 1987), and Phillip E. Hammond, *Religion and Personal Autonomy: The Third Disestablishment in America* (Columbia, SC: University of South Carolina Press, 1992).

10. See Wade Clark Roof, *A Generation of Seekers: The Spiritual Journeys of the Baby Boom Generation* (San Francisco: Harper SanFrancisco, 1993). Also see Penny Long Marler and David A. Roozen, "From Church Tradition to Consumer Choice: The Gallup Surveys of the Unchurched American," in David A. Roozen and C. Kirk Hadaway, *Church and Denominational Growth* (Nashville: Abingdon Press, 1993), pp. 253–277.

11. Ann Douglas is among the many authors to document the nineteenth-century shifts that put this split in place. See her *The Feminization of American Culture* (New York: Knopf, 1977).

12. Talcott Parsons, "The American Family: Its Relation to Personality and to the Social Structure," in *Family Socialization and Interaction Process*, eds. T. Parsons and R.F. Bales (New York: Free Press, 1960), pp. 3–33.

13. John Wilson, *Religion in American Society* (Englewood Cliffs, NJ: Prentice-Hall, 1978).

14. David C. McClelland, *The Achievement Motive* (New York: Irvington, 1976).

15. Lewis J. Sherrill, *Family and Church* (New York: Abingdon, 1937).

16. Roy Fairchild, and John C. Wynn, *Families in the Church: A Protestant Survey* (New York: Association, 1961).

17. R. E. Smith, "The Movement of Women into the Labor Force," in *The Subtle Revolution: Women at Work*, ed. R. E. Smith (Washington: Urban Institute, 1979), pp. 1–20.

18. Bradley Hertel, "Gender, Religious Identity, and Work Force Participation," *Journal for the Scientific Study of Religion* 27, No. 4 (1988), pp. 574–592.

19. Mary Y. Morgan, and John Scanzoni, "Religious Orientations and Women's Expected Continuity in the Labor Force," *Journal of Marriage and the Family* 49 (1987), pp. 367–379. See also Holley Ulbrich and Myles Wallace, "Women's Work Force Status and Church Attendance," *Journal for the Scientific Study of Religion* 23 (1984), pp. 341–350.

20. Sheila K. Korman, "The Feminist: Familial Influences on Adherence to Ideology and Commitment to a Self-Perception," *Family Relations* 32 (1983), pp. 431–439.

21. Tim B. Heaton, and Marie Cornwall, "Religious Group Variation in the Socioeconomic Status and Family Behavior of Women," *Journal for the Scientific Study of Religion* 28, No. 3 (1989), pp. 283–299.

22. Geoffrey L. Greif and Alfred Demaris, "Single Fathers with Custody," *Families in Society* 71, No. 5 (1990), pp. 259–266.

23. Tim B. Heaton, and Kristen L. Goodman, "Religion and Family Formation," *Review of Religious Research* 26, No. 4 (1985), pp. 343–359.

24. *Ibid.*

25. J. P. Marcum, "Explaining Fertility Differences Among U.S. Protestants," *Social Forces* 60 (1981), pp. 532–543. See also William D. Mosher and Gerry E. Hendershot, "Religious Affiliation and the Fertility of Married Couples," *Journal of Marriage and the Family* (1984).

26. Bradley R. Hertel, and Michael Hughes, "Religious Affiliation, Attendance, and Support for 'Pro-Family' Issues in the U.S.," *Social Forces* 65 (1987), pp. 858–882.

27. Nancy T. Ammerman, *Bible Believers: Fundamentalists in the Modern World* (New Brunswick, NJ: Rutgers University Press, 1987).

28. Judith Stacey, *Brave New Families* (New York: Basic Books, 1990). See also Lawrence Iannaccone and Carrie A. Miles, "Dealing with Social Change: The Mormon Church's Response to Change in Women's Roles," *Social Forces* 68, No. 4 (1990), pp. 1231–1250.

29. See Elizabeth Brusco, *The Household Basis of Evangelical Religion and the Reformation of Machismo in Colombia*, unpublished Ph.D. dissertation, City University of New York, 1986; also Pauline Turner, "Religious Aspects of Women's Role in the Nicaraguan Revolution" in Yvonne Haddad and Ellison Findly, eds., *Women, Religion and Social Change* (Albany: State University of New York Press, 1985).

30. For an evaluation of this debate, see E. Wilbur Bock and M. L. Radelet, "The Marital Integration of Religious Independents: A Reevaluation of its Significance," *Review of Religious Research* 29, No. 3 (1988), pp. 228–241.

31. On Catholics, see J. McCarthy, "Religious Commitment, Affiliation, and Marriage Dissolution," in *The Religious Dimension*, ed. Robert Wuthnow, (New York: Academic, 1979). On Mormons, see Philip R. Kunz and Stan L. Albrecht, "Religion, Marital Happiness, and Divorce," *International Journal of Sociology of the Family* 7, No. 2 (1977), pp. 227–232.

32. Barbara Hargrove makes this point in her *The Sociology of Religion*, 2nd

edition (Arlington Heights, IL: Harlan Davidson, 1989).

33. Further evidence of this large middle between the two extremes is found in Merlin B. Brinkerhoff and Marlene M. Mackie, "Religious Denominations' Impact on Gender Attitudes: Some Methodological Implications," *Review of Religious Research* 25, No. 4 (1984), pp. 365–378.

34. William V. D'Antonio, "The Family and Religion: Exploring a Changing Relationship," *Journal for the Scientific Study of Religion* 19, No. 2 (1980), pp. 89–104.

35. Stephen Hart, "Religion and Changes in Family Patterns," *Review of Religious Research* 28, No. 1 (1986), pp. 51–70.

36. Sylvia Hewlett, A. S. Ilchman, and J. J. Sweeney, *Family and Work: Bridging the Gap* (Cambridge, MA: Ballinger, 1986).

37. See Lynn Davidman, *Tradition in a Rootless World* (Berkeley: University of California Press, 1991).

I

Assessing the Trends

2

Lost in the Fifties

The Changing Family and the Nostalgic Church

Penny Long Marler

This chapter explores family structure change in America from the fifties to the present, nostalgia about the family as a cultural response, and the effects of both factors on the church. Largely due to the available data, the focus is on white Protestants. We will look at family structure change via U.S. Census data, poll data, and a 1986 nationwide congregational survey. Yet the key for interpreting such change lies in the experiences of those who negotiate church, work, and family on a daily basis. Woven in the demographic data and congregational research are the stories of members from one church, Briarglen United Church of Christ, near Springfield, Massachusetts.[1] Throughout, Christopher Lasch's twin notions of nostalgia and memory are employed to probe the interplay of family fiction and family reality. The resulting portrait is variegated and dynamic: the family in the contemporary Protestant church is both a family of memory—an "ex-family" church—and a "traditional family preserve."

Traditional nuclear families continue to be drawn to the church, but their lifestyles and expectations have changed. And some nontraditional families (older empty-nesters and widowed persons) continue to support traditional family values and programming, albeit through fifties lenses. In a world of multiplying options and consumer-based choice, these two groups continue to choose church because it meets their respective needs. The resulting market niche for the church is shrinking and aging.

BACKGROUND OF THE RESEARCH

Peter Berger once suggested that the family *and* the church are the remaining mediating structures for intimacy and community in the modern world.[2] This logic leads to three powerful, if misleading, conclusions: one, that modernity is necessarily destructive of community; two, that larger, cultural reorganizing processes have not already permeated these sectors; and three, that the family and the church provide sanctuary—if not protection—from the negative consequences of change. Indeed, on the other side of the tumultous sixties, self-interested seventies, and gratuitous eighties, the formula is quite seductive (as, for example, Lasch's "haven in a heartless world"[3]). What has proved most enticing is the compounded image: the family *in* the church.

Attention to the family is widespread. Slogans are fashioned around a family church concept, like "Mt. Zion Baptist, the Family Church" or "Briarwood Presbyterian, Concord Height's Family Church." Denominations and local churches sponsor a host of marriage and parenting seminars, from "Marriage Encounter" to "Systematic Training for Effective Parenting."[4] James Dobson's "Focus on the Family" series draws thousands, and his videotapes are popular fare for adult education classes in both mainline and evangelical churches.[5] The explicit message is that the family is important, and on that few church leaders disagree. The sometimes more subtle message is not, however, about the importance of family but about its definition. Typically, a "family church" motto is illustrated by the conjoined figures of two adults and one or two children and a cross.

Over the past decade, a full-scale family debate has erupted between conservatives and liberals. Conservatives point to the "breakdown" of the traditional family as a signal of and precursor to the moral deterioration of America. As a result, conservative politicos within and outside the church press for a "return" to the family structures (and values) of earlier times, notably the 1950s.[6] Liberals view the origins and consequences of family change differently. Family change, they argue, is the result of a number of societal forces with both negative and positive effects. On the negative side, economic stagnation and workplace inequities—more than a failure of moral nerve—put inordinate pressure on all families. On the positive side, the loosening of social and legal sanctions around marriage and divorce has freed some individuals *from* abusive and destructive nuclear family arrangements and others *to* pursue intimate, family relationships in other, nontraditional forms (including same-sex partnerships). This has led some mainline denominations to condemn traditional "family idolatry" and officially sanction nontraditional family forms.[7]

However, in the absence of aggressive adult evangelism, most mainline congregations still depend on the nurturance and confirmation of children for their survival. When those children depart during their teen years, congregational inertia is propped up by declarations like: "Our children will come back to church when they settle down, get married, and have their own children." In this way, the more traditional, nuclear family remains an abiding concern.

However idealized at present, the notion of a "family church" has basis in fact. The fifties were a statistical anomaly, providing the largest proportional pool of married couples with children in American history.[8] Church membership grew so rapidly that the fifties have been designated—arguably—as a "religious revival."[9] In tandem, churches developed largely successful emphases for youth and their families that set the patterns for today's expectations.

Convictions that church is the (nuclear) family place run deep. That *was* the experience of this generation and their parents. Older members and empty-nesters wistfully recall large confirmation classes and active youth groups. One longtime lay leader at Briarglen United Church of Christ outside Springfield, Massachusetts, observes: "My warmest memories of the church are times when families are together. You don't see that as much any more; the youth group is small, and you hardly ever see teenagers at worship. I've been told that a lot of people just drop their children off for church school and don't stay. Times are different."

What are the likely effects of continued disjuncture between past ideals and present reality? Significantly, these data show that, despite traditional family rhetoric, church members have responded to larger change processes in surprising ways. As is often the case, changes in cultural symbols and their meanings lag behind structural adaptations.[10]

ABDICATING MEMORY: NOSTALGIA, FAMILY, AND THE CHURCH

Christopher Lasch has recently defined nostalgia as the abdication of memory.[11] Functionally, nostalgia provides a temporary buffer against cultural upheaval and the dislocating effects of social change. The nostalgic perspective "freezes the past," and so avoids confrontation with the changing realities of the present. While memory embraces the past in order to understand and inform the present, nostalgia dwells in an idealized past—by definition unattainable—and disparages the present.

Lasch traces the nostalgic impulse in America to nineteenth century Romanticism. The rapid pace of social change associated with industrialization, immigration, and surging population growth occasioned a period of unprecedented nostalgia for the simplicity and purity of agrarian life. Popular literature, particularly poetry, was sprinkled with pastoral allusions. Typically, the nostalgic genre vilified the accouterments of "city life." Modernity or "progress" was viewed as destructive of the pastoral ideal.[12]

The intrusion of city and industry into the agrarian frontier led to new constellations of family, work, and church. Work and home became increasingly differentiated. For the main, men were guardians of the workplace. Women—and ministers—became the guardians of the home which included the nurturance and moral education of children.[13] Sentimentalized in home and hearth, the traditional family was a ready vessel for earlier agrarian nostalgia.

Interestingly, the divergence of the home and work spheres contributed another highly sentimentalized image: the male hero.[14] A carryover from the rugged adventurer of the Western frontier, the man was the only family figure who received a blessing for leaving home and hearth through the world of work. The masculine image stood for the questing, expansive individualism of America, and feminine images reflected nurturing, conservative, and socializing impulses.[15] Not paradoxically, both images were considered essential to combat the moral and spiritual onslaught of modernity. Working men needed the restorative haven of home; women, children, and church were expected to benefit from the new resources (knowledge and technology) that those who braved the world of work could supply.[16]

By the early twentieth century, the focus of American cultural nostalgia shifted away from the vanishing frontier to small-town life. Sentimental images of small-town America abound in twentieth century literature. At the center of those scenes is the family and the church. Home and hearth, in themselves, could no longer guarantee adequate moral and physical protection from the secular (and dangerous) urban workplace. The small town provided a necessary buffer zone: it was the perfect place to "raise the kids."[17]

Indeed, the symbols of American cultural nostalgia changed as the locus of threat shifted. Agrarian expanse was threatened by encroaching settlements; then, networks of small towns retreated in the face of sprawling industrial centers. Wartime brought a further threat. While men left home for military quests, women stayed behind to "man" needed industry. The number of women in the workforce accelerated significantly during and after the Second World War.[18] At the same time, the number of family units almost trebled.[19] The two dynamics began to work together—and the reality of one was exaggerated in the wake of the threat posed by the other.

The rift between work and home widened as more and more women went to work. In response, the focus of American nostalgia shifted to the smallest unit of community life: the home. "Donna Reed," "Father Knows Best," "Leave It To Beaver" and other family sitcoms became popular television images. Nuclear family harmony, however, did not hold the spotlight long. The sixties witnessed teenage antiestablishment rebellion, the seventies, a soaring divorce rate, and the eighties, a dramatic increase in single parenthood. The semiofficial guardians of home and hearth, Protestant clergy, decried family disruption. Such rhetoric in the name of "traditional values" was also enjoined by neoconservative politicos as part of a populist backlash against liberalism in the early eighties.[20] Both groups interpreted family change as a direct threat to the moral fabric of America.[21] Indeed, if church membership was any measure of that seamless cloth, then something was certainly amiss. For nearly two decades following the pew-packed fifties and early sixties, American Protestantism suffered dramatic declines.[22] By earlier standards, the family and the church were in trouble. The fortunes of the church seemed irrevocably tied to that fundamental unit.

In sum, from pastoral scenes to Rockwellian images to family sitcoms, Americans have displayed their common concerns about change and its meaning. Nineteenth century yearnings for the farm where home and work melded were quelled, as Americans became comfortable with the myriad opportunities of an industrializing nation. Small-town nostalgia faded as improved education and transportation opened the larger world to village teens. Yet that larger world proved dangerous and unstable in the face of sixties' upheaval and seventies' self-absorption. By the eighties, the dramatic family structure changes of the previous decades could no longer be ignored. So, with memories of the family fifties lingering in the collective American mind, the nostalgic impulse refocused on home and hearth.

American nostalgia has deep roots in the late nineteenth century, when traditional family roles were upset and recast. Indeed, these yearnings for an idealized past find their clearest voice in what Swidler has called "unsettled periods," that is, times when the society undergoes rapid and widespread demographic, economic, and/or political change. While nostalgia for traditional structures may be functional in times of upheaval—because it provides recognizable and comfortable lenses for viewing and responding to change—it becomes dysfunctional in more settled times. When social and cultural lifeways have been reshaped, there is less need for obscurantist devices. Then, memory—not nostalgia—may be recovered, and the present freed from a sentimentalized past.

FAMILY PORTRAITS: THE FIFTIES TO THE PRESENT

The contemporary family/church dynamic in white American Protestantism is a product of the tense relationship between nostalgic family image and family reality. The following sections address family change—and perceptions of family change—in American society and the church from the fifties to the present. Then, the varied tastes and activities of present-day Protestant families are examined. The research itself is an exercise in sharpening memory and refocusing nostalgia, and the results provide intriguing departures from and continuities with previous interpretations of the family in the church.

An American Family Album: The Postwar Picture

Recent demographic data illustrate the extent of family structure change since the pew-packed fifties. According to the U.S. Census Bureau, at the close of the fifties almost half of all households consisted of married couples with children.[23] By 1990, a little over a quarter were made up of two parents and their children—a twenty percentage point decline in the overall share of the U.S. household structure in thirty years.

The proportion of U.S. households that consists of married couples only, however, has remained virtually stable. So where has the differ-

FIGURE 1
The Changing Structure of Households in the United States

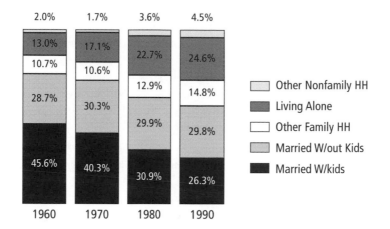

ence been made up? In two areas: in the rise of "other family house-holds"—mostly single-parent families—and the increase in "nonfamily" households.

While single-parent households have increased their share of the overall household "market" by four percent, the nonfamily category has increased by fifteen percentage points. In fact, in 1990 there were about 27.3 million nonfamily households, representing almost three of every ten households. The largest category of nonfamily households are persons "living alone." This type has nearly doubled since 1960. Those living alone include two major subgroups: never-married young adults (eighteen to twenty-four) and widowed, elderly women (sixty-five and over).

Demographers and social scientists are having much conversation at present about the increase in "premarital residential independence"—that is, the numbers of young adults who are leaving home to establish their own households prior to marriage. This trend has generally been pushed by the increase in the numbers of youth pursuing college educations, but such an interim phase of independence from a family group has broader implications for future family patterns. Young adults who live "on their own" for a period of time prior to marriage are less bound by the traditional conventions of their families of origin. They marry later than their parents, delay parenthood and have fewer children, go to church less often than their parents, and in general, hold less traditional social and political views.[24]

Elderly, widowed women living alone also experience role transition. Widowed women face the unwanted, but unavoidable, dissolution of their once-traditional families. First, they lose the active role of "mother" when their children grow up, move away, and perhaps, start their own families. Second, they lose their status as "wives" through the death of their husbands. Their family is fragmented; for the first time in many of their lives, they are alone.[25]

The resulting picture is startling: by 1990, no single category of household structure dominates, and the "nonfamily" category represents about thrity percent of the whole. The traditional family of the fifties is no longer the sociological norm. The family today is pluriform.

Interestingly, not only has the proportion of traditional families decreased, but they have also become smaller. The average number of children per family has dropped, from 2.34 in 1960 to 1.81 in 1988. Further, fewer children per family, more single-parent families, and larger numbers of people living alone contribute to the decline in household size. In 1960, the average household size was 3.33; by 1990, the average was 2.63.[26] Concurrently, natural webs of intimate social relationships are limited. With the breakdown of the extended family, cross-generational relationships are also less available.[27] And even in more traditional families, other demographic factors are at work which change traditional patterns of family life.

Fewer and fewer mothers stay at home to "raise the kids." Primarily driven by a stagnant economy, the proportion of married women with children in the labor force has increased dramatically.[28] Since 1960, the number of working moms with preschool children has doubled; the number of working moms with children of six to seventeen is about one and a half times larger. The fifties' picture of the traditional family with a stay-at-home mom has been shattered: only a quarter of all households contain a married couple with children; and in over half of those, the mother goes to work.[29]

Other disruptive factors for the modern family are separation, divorce, and remarriage. Between 1950 and 1981, divorces increased from 385,000 to 1.2 million annually, and the divorce rate more than doubled. Since 1981, the divorce rate has leveled—yet still remains high. Another trend that has changed the configuration of American family life is a marked increase in the number of children born to unmarried mothers. In 1960, one in twenty births was to an unmarried mother. In 1987, the statistic was one in four.[30] Overall, a high divorce rate and an increase in out-of-wedlock births have resulted in a rise in single-parent families. Between 1960 and 1990, the percentage of chil-

FIGURE 2

The Changing Age Structure of the United States: Children and Older Adults

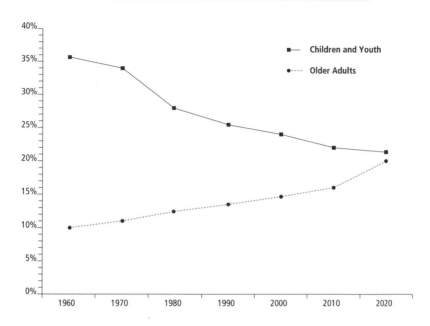

dren living with one parent—usually the mother—increased from nine to tcwnty-two percent.[31] Family disruption has become the norm rather than the exception.

What is the future of the family on the U.S. demographic horizon? There is little reason to believe that a return to a traditional family-centered culture is likely, at least not for the *next* thirty years. At least for that period, the aging of the baby boom, as well as their pluriform family structures, will continue to make an impact. In fact, demographers project that by 2020 the proportion of the American population under age eighteen and over sixty-five will converge at the same level: twenty percent.[32]

As the population ages, the proportion of married couples with children will continue to decline. At the same time, the proportion of married couples without children is projected to increase.[33] Older empty-nested couples will predominate as the baby boom moves into retirement. The changing tastes, needs, and demands of the fifties family cohort will continue to shape American culture for the foreseeable future.

Even the recent "echo boom" will not affect the overall decline in the proportion of nuclear families. While the boomlet has caused an unex-

FIGURE 3

Married With and Without Children: Percentage of All Married Households

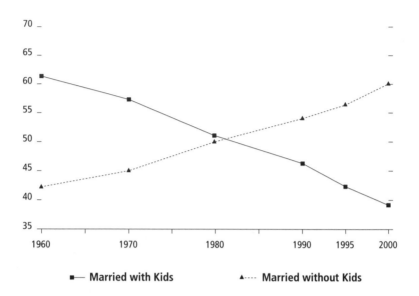

● — Married with Kids   ▲···· Married without Kids

pected rise in the birthrate, it is not expected to affect the continued decline in traditional family units. Indeed, recent demographic reports indicate that the boomlet occurred because "women were having more children, not because more women were having children."[34]

Divorce, marital infertility, and longer periods of singlehood will continue to contribute to the number and variety of nontraditional families.[35] Sizable numbers of married couples will choose to remain childless. Likewise, the loosening of traditional values and sanctions will encourage alternative families, including persons who choose lifelong single status or other committed relationships outside heterosexual marriage.[36] As a result, families without children and nonfamily households will likely increase over the next several decades.

While the tendency towards pluriform family styles may be linked to the loosening of traditional family values, another pressure is at work which encourages dual career families and the constitution of nonfamily households: sheer economics. As the population ages, this factor will continue to affect the fortunes of the American family. In fact, without drastic changes in work and retirement practices and compensation patterns, approximately thirty percent of Americans will be economically dependent by 2020. The coming strains on the overall economy will not encourage larger families or stay-at-home parents.

Church and Family from the Fifties to the Present

How do families in the country at large compare to families in the church? While available survey data from the fifties to the present is hardly perfect, a consistent picture does emerge. In a 1952 national survey of Episcopalian parishes, little over fifty percent of church members were married with children.[37] In an analysis of the 1960 National Election Survey, Roozen reports the percentage of respondents with children among all Protestant church attenders at forty-two percent—which is very close to the distribution of this family type in the general population[38]

In response, the Protestant church actively promoted and programmed for the traditional family. Bible-related materials for the home (and hearth) were developed and utilized by eleven major Protestant denominations representing thirty-five million consitutents.[39] On the basis of a number of indices, Fairchild and Wynn determine that the fifties represented a marked advance over the forties in the incidence of "the family going to church together, the reading of the Bible at home, and saying grace at meals."[40] Even from partial accounts, the fifties' church was a traditional family church.

From that fifties peak, the proportion of married persons with children in the U.S. population began to decline. This group was forty percent of American households in 1970, thirty-one percent in 1980, and twenty-six percent in 1990. In a parallel development, the proportion of Protestant church attenders who were married with children also declined.[41] The demographic trends that have altered the shape of American family life have also altered the contours of the Protestant churchgoing population.

Interviews with thirty-six Briarglen church leaders illustrate the survey trends well. Laity tell story after story about moving to the community and joining the church "with my family" or "to be together as a family." A chronological and demographic accounting is especially instructive. Three cohorts of today's key leaders at Briarglen joined, respectively, in the late twenties and thirties with an average of three or more children; in the fifties and early sixties with an average of two or more children; and in the mid-seventies with one to two children. A handful of present leaders joined in the mid-eighties with an average of one to two children.

Similarly, the program history of Briarglen reflects a societywide decrease in the numbers and size of family units and stay-at-home moms. Older members fondly recall building the "new parish house" to accomodate the growing church school. They reminisce about churchwide family suppers and the annual Mother-Daughter Banquet. At the same time, longtime members worry about the now-declining youth program and the cancellation of the churchwide Harvest Supper. Older laity are concerned about the "new generation's" diminishing interest in women's groups and Mother-Daughter events "because of all those working women." And while Briarglen members and leaders see themselves as a "family church," this image is severely strained by growing numbers of empty-nested families, retirees, and widow(er)s. A new member at Briarglen observed: "I've heard it said that in the most prominent church[es] all the heads are gray—that there are very few young people. Those churches are dying out…this is something that this church has to focus on."

Snapshots: The Church and the Contemporary Family

The contrast between nostalgia and reality can be seen even more vividly when we compare the types of families present in a group of today's Protestant congregations with the family structures in the population at large.[42] In a 1986 survey of seventy-two Protestant congregations (sixty-two "mainline" and ten "evangelical"), and a survey of Briarglen United Church of Christ, the emerging family portrait stands in sharp contrast to the larger American population.[43] In only one category—married persons with children under eighteen—does the proportion in these congregations mirror the proportion in the general population.

The distribution of nontraditional families in these Protestant congregations is quite unlike the general population. The churches report more married persons without children and fewer singles. This difference however, is even more dramatic when examined by age. While the Protestant churches seem to be holding their share of the overall nuclear family market, the character of that segment is strikingly different. In the seventy-two-congregation group, the proportion of middle-aged married persons with children outdistances the general population by almost twenty percentage points. Further, there are fewer younger marrieds with children in the Protestant church survey group.

The church population is, in fact, much older than the general population. Seventy percent of the married persons without children in the surveyed congregations are over fifty-five. Single adults also tend to be older than singles in the general population. Indeed, Protestant respondents are disproportionately older empty-nesters, retirees, and widow(er)s. Young singles and younger to middle-aged married persons without children are grossly underrepresented in the church. Again, the Briarglen congregation presents a more dramatic picture. Despite a

FIGURE 4

Marital Status and Children: U.S. Population Compared to Churches

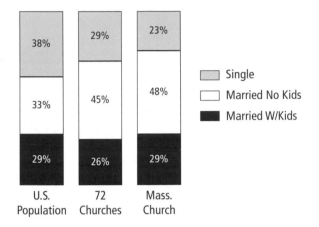

Single
Married No Kids
Married W/Kids

Percentage of U.S. Population or Church
Married with Children under 18

FIGURE 5

Married With Kids by Age: U.S. Population Compared to Churches

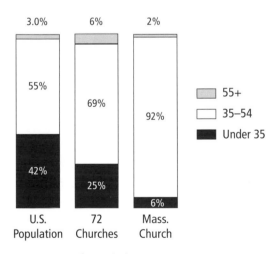

55+
35–54
Under 35

Percentage of Married Persons
with Children under 18

FIGURE 6

Married, No Kids by Age: U.S. Population Compared to Churches

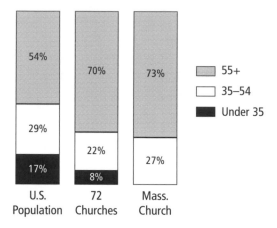

**Percentage of Married Persons
without Children under 18**

FIGURE 7

Age Distribution of Singles: U.S. Population Compared to Churches

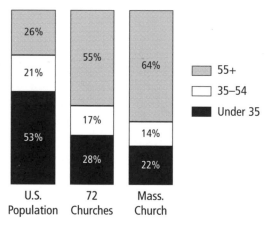

Percentage of Singles in Age Group

"family church" self-perception, Briarglen is an aging church made up of nontraditional families—empty-nesters and older single adults. In fact, the church's leadership consists of almost equal numbers of middle-aged traditional *and* older nontraditional family members.[44]

The demographic picture constructed so far suggests that the white Protestant church is perceived as a "family church." But what does that really mean? In the fifties and early sixties, a "family church" meant, simply, lots of nuclear families. In the nineties, a "family church" may mean something else altogether.

THE CHURCH AS A TRADITIONAL FAMILY PRESERVE

The church is still a place where traditional families gather. Surprisingly, churches have managed to maintain their share of this family type. In contrast to complaints that "we aren't attracting young families the way we used to," churches appear to draw married persons with children in the same proportions as their distribution in the general population.

Yet contemporary families differ from fifties' families in several ways. First, more couples are remarried, and rearing blended families.[45] Second, considerably more mothers work part- or full-time.[46] Finally, contemporary families seem to expect different things from the church from their fifties and sixties counterparts. Initial findings from interviews at Briarglen United Church of Christ suggest that younger, traditional families are consumers of church programs, while older, ex-families provide institutional commitment, support, and a familial identity.

In the remaining sections, these two preliminary conclusions are explored further. First, the suggestion that the fortunes of the church are closely tied to those of the traditional family is tested by replicating and extending Nash's analysis of denomination and U.S. population change.[47] Second, the premise that contemporary church members—particularly traditional families—take an explicit consumer stance to the church is examined through analysis of the seventy-two-congregation and Briarglen surveys.

As the Family Goes…

Based on a case study of another New England congregation, Nash and Berger suggested that the source of the fifties' religious revival was an increase in the number of children *and* in the number of family units.[48] Several years later, Nash constructed a statistical test of these findings, utilizing annual measures of church membership as well as U.S. population statistics, including overall population change, number of families, and families with children under eighteen. The resultant correlation between families with children and church membership was very high (.99). Thus, Nash concluded that the test yielded "positive results," and that "church affiliation does rise (and fall) in association with the number of American families with children."[49]

Hadaway and Marler replicated and extended Nash's original statistical test.[50] Correlating annual statistics for church membership from *The Yearbook of American and Canadian Churches*[51] and U.S. Census data for overall population, families with children, and the birthrate from 1950 to 1988, we found that the strongest correlate of church membership was indeed the number of families with children. The bivariate correlation was .98, and it remained high (.72) when controlling for the effects of the overall population and the birthrate.

While families with children remained the best predictor of church membership over the entire period, separate analyses on the Nash test period, 1950 to 1966, and the later time period, 1967 to 1988, yielded different findings.[52] The variable that contributed most to predicting church membership during the first period, the "boom years" for American denominations, was sheer population change. By contrast, fluctuations in the numbers of families with children contributed most to church membership variation during the "bust years" for the church. It seems, after all, that the fifties' revival was spurred more by increased numbers of children than by family units *per se*.

Replicating the Nash analysis reinforces the suspicion of a strong tie between the fortunes of the family and those of the church. Two further analyses of a subsample of Protestant denominations tended to confirm that finding: among other demographic changes, fluctuations in the number of nuclear family units remained the best predictor of Protestant church membership since 1950.[53] Finally, in an analysis of the effect of family formation on patterns of Protestant church attendance, Chaves concluded that "religion in the U.S., at least in its Protestant churchly form, is carried by a household type perhaps as much as by a particular socio-economic class, status group, or geographical region."[54] As the family goes, so goes the church?

Little wonder the traditionally white Protestant denominations bemoan the "demise of the family." For the past forty years, church growth and decline has hinged on the respective fortunes of that unit. Still, the impact of the nuclear family is more complex than simple supply concerns. Demand, the other side of the consumer equation, has shaped family behavior in relation to the church in equally important ways.

The Traditional Family: From Pillar to Consumer

The seventy-two congregations surveyed in 1986 were asked about involvement in the organization and worship life of the church.[55] In comparing the church participation of people from different types of families, we found no significant differences. Forty-one percent of singles, forty-four percent of married persons without children, and forty-five percent of married persons with children were highly involved in the church. Moderate involvement was reported by about thirty-five percent of all married member types and thirty-seven percent of singles; and low levels of involvement range from nineteen percent percent for traditional and twenty-one percent for nontraditional family members.[56]

Briarglen respondents showed a similar pattern. On a measure of worship attendance, no difference was found between members of traditional families and those in nontraditional families. Again, the Briarglen sample is a very active group. Seventy-three percent of married members with children attend at least two to three times a month; sixty-five percent of married persons without children attend at that rate; and for single members, the figure was seventy-four percent Apparently once members are "selected in," family type matters very little in terms of participation.

If levels of involvement do not vary, where do the differences occur for white Protestant churchgoers of differing family types? As suggested in the previous historical overview, the *perception* of the family in the church may be an important key. Indeed, the most striking finding in the seventy-two-congregation and Briarglen surveys is the fact that respondents in nontraditional families are more likely to view the church "as one large family," while younger respondents from traditional families are more inclined to see the church as a "loosely knit association of individuals and groups."[57]

At Briarglen, when married persons with children talk about family, they describe *their* families and families like them. They are drawn to Briarglen because of what the church offers for families with children: a lively church school, a creative children's minister, and a variety of special activities, including choir, handbells, family events, and children's communion in the early service.

When singles and married couples without children describe Briarglen, they also engage in family-talk. Most are older members—empty-nesters or widow(er)s—and their families are primarily families of memory. These members attend and participate because of "what the church *has meant* to me and my family." Interestingly, despite their large numbers, many of Briarglen's older members are hesitant to push for additional ministry time or money. The church administrator observed:

> It's frustrating. If you ask most of the older members about their own needs
> and interests, they'll say they are not important. They still insist that the
> church's money should go to young people and their families. It's hard to
> change that mind-set.

Whether Briarglen's members are part of an intact family at present or
not, their primary orientation and commitment are to the family in the
church.

Nontraditional family members constitute a kind of ex-family cohort
or *family residue*. This defining characteristic is more an issue of a past
family identity than present family demography. Empty nesters and
widow(er)s were once heads of traditional families highly integrated
into the life of the church. They recall—often with tears—times when
"the church" responded to a family crisis with a "great, big bouquet" or
"meals for a week"; when "my daughter was married and my granddaughter was baptized"; when "my twins preached on Youth Sunday";
or when "the whole family was together for Christmas services."[58] The
church has been a vital part of their family life, and they remain committed to maintaining that legacy.

The tendency of this family residue to sentimentalize the family in
the church is seen most clearly in their attitudes about the youth program at Briarglen. Nostalgia for the large, active youth group "we used
to have" is widespread. In interviews, older members consistently linked
church growth and vitality to the presence and activity of youth. One
elderly widow concluded: "Well, you see it's the youth program that is
the key. If you're going to have a growing church, you've got to bring in
the youth." In fact, in the seventy-two-congregation survey, older singles joined younger and middle-aged nuclear families in targeting
"Christian education for children and youth" as a church task that
"needs to be strengthened."[59]

Middle-aged members—especially those who were very active when
they were youth in the fifties and early sixties—also view a large youth
program as essential. A physician and newly active committee member
at Briarglen reflected on his own "blind spots":

> I've always assumed that what this church needed was a big youth center
> like the one my church had back in North Carolina when I was growing
> up. But when I think about my daughter, I realize that that's just not true
> for her. I just didn't think.

Fully socialized at the pinnacle of the baby boom's church-going years, this layman has admittedly viewed the role of the church through fifties-tinted glasses. These sentimental lenses tend to obscure current family structure and lifestyle realities.

Fifties' lenses continue to color program concerns at Briarglen. Despite the fact that the proportion of families with children and youth in the Briarglen community declined from the seventies onward,[60] youth programs remained a top priority for church expenditures. Still, these programs failed to attract the large numbers of the past. Briarglen's most recent associate minister for youth—who is not a product of the fifties' family boom—observed:

> Most of the activities for youth over the past several years have drawn fewer kids than most people would like. I think, though, that we've been successful in putting the emphasis more on quality than quantity. Still, not everybody would agree.

More recently, the congregation's leadership decided that efforts to reach youth and their parents are still "not enough."

Younger parents at Briarglen are less concerned that youth groups are small. They expect high-quality programming for their children. As a consequence, a smaller-sized program with a full-time, paid minister and a generous program budget is considered satisfactory.[61]

While members across family types in both surveys are involved, their perceptions of the family and the church are very different. Significant differences between the responses of traditional and nontraditional family members surfaced on a number of items concerning organization and program life. Younger to middle-aged members of traditional families are more interested in adult education programs dealing with marriage, the family and parenting; in assistance with their own spiritual development; in the availability of pastoral counseling for members; and in worship development and leadership as a priority for the pastor. Middle-aged to older members of nontraditional families are more concerned about stewardship emphases at the church; about the pastor's involvement in the local community; about the world mission of the church; about social action and advocacy; about the availability of adult education groups/programs; and about pastoral outreach to members in their homes.[62]

Again, the two varying perspectives are rooted in a divergent identity. Members of traditional families in the seventy-two- congregation survey were more likely to respond that "our church is primarily oriented to

serving its members"; while members of nontraditional families reported that "our church is primarily oriented to serving the world beyond its
membership."[63] Members of traditional families are consumers: they are
interested in programs/services that will benefit "me and others like
me." Members of nontraditional families see themselves as "producers"
more than consumers. They are committed to involvement for the sake
of others—although this commitment is not as altruistic as it seems.
Perceptions of church programming for traditional families are based
on memories of what was good about their own families' church life.

Fortunately, the consumer group within the church—the intact, traditional family—is one of the constituencies that the producer group
cares about, works for, and is committed to. In this sense, the two divergent perspectives serve each other's interests. Preserving the family in
the church is an extension of the activist stance of older members in
nontraditional families. Self-preservation suits younger traditional families in a world where multiple organizations continually vie for their
time, attention, and resources.

The older family residue is made up of what Lyle Schaller calls the
"pillars of the church."[64] These longtime church activists tend to be
institutional loyalists. As evidenced by continuing volunteer commitment and financial support, these members tend to be optimistic about
the institution itself. Schaller adds that such loyalty can be both a help
and a hindrance. Institutional loyalty can retard organizational innovation and is antithetical to a consumer mind-set. Schaller contends that,
freed from the nostalgic constraints of such institutional loyalty, the new
generation of church laity are less convinced by many taken-for-granted
procedures and programs.

The answers of older nontraditional-family respondents reflect their
involvement in and loyalty to the congregation. They are significantly
more likely than younger traditional-family people to say that "members are well-informed" about committee goings-on; that the "community is well-informed" about church activities; that "lay leaders are
provided training"; that "the theological and biblical implications of
important decisions are explicitly discussed"; and that "cooperative projects" with other churches are "highly valued."[65] While Briarglen's
younger leadership is quick to criticize traditional organizational practices, older leadership—the family residue—is equally ready to defend
any perceived criticisms of the church.

The divergence between traditional and nontraditional family members clearly reflects the dominance of older persons in decisions and
planning of the church. However, it is wrong to conclude that nontra-

ditional family members in the church are a homogenous group. Indeed, they are not. When the tastes and opinions of nontraditional family members in the seventy-two congregations are analyzed *by age*, younger and older cohorts differ significantly on a wide range of items.[66] Again, institutional tradition and loyalty predominate among older members, while personal needs and interests dominate among the younger ones.

For example, *young* married persons without children want more "emphasis on worship that deepens my experience of God"; pastoral attention to "spiritual development" and "personal counseling"; adult education programs, including Bible study and marriage and family seminars; "new services and liturgies" that mark life cycle transitions; and pastoral involvement in providing worship "sensitive to the needs" of the congregation. By contrast, *older* marrieds without children are more positive about the organizational characteristics of their churches. They are more likely to feel that the church engages in regular self-study; to agree that they get "support for trying new things"; to report that leadership is provided adequate training; and to feel that morale is high or that they are "excited" about the future of the congregation. Older empty-nesters are more likely to view the church as "one big family"— and interestingly, they are more likely than younger marrieds without children to agree that the pastor should "support Christian education for children and youth."[67]

Younger and older singles in the seventy-two-congregation survey displayed almost identical divergence on the same issues as younger and older marrieds without children. However, there were some very intriguing differences in the tastes and opinions of these singles over against the other nontraditional group. In addition to variance over organizational characteristics, spiritual development concerns, and congregational identity, younger and older singles expect clearly different things from worship. Younger singles are less satisfied with worship overall. Specifically, younger singles are less satisfied with the music, and they desire sermons that are "provocative," "comforting," and that "touch on my everyday life." Older singles (mostly widowed persons) are very satisfied with worship and prefer sermons with "scholarly illustrations." Younger singles express more interest in fellowship groups and athletic groups and clubs. Finally, while older singles are more likely to say that the pastor should "support the world mission" of the church, younger singles are more likely to value organizing advocacy groups to "support the disadvantaged."[68]

Among other things, the wide differences across both age and family type present significant program challenges for the church. Attracting and holding such diverse constituencies demands incredible creativity and flexibility. Indeed, as the following section demonstrates, the traditional family appears to be a much easier group for the contemporary Protestant church to target, plan for, and satisfy.

While traditional families differed significantly from married persons without children and from singles, they themselves are a remarkably *homogenous* group. Even when compared across age categories, nuclear families want and expect similar things. Out of over 150 opinion items, the only significant differences between older and younger members of traditional families occurred on two worship items. Younger marrieds feel that children need to be more involved in the worship service, and—not so paradoxically for young parents with kids—the same group wants more time for silent prayer and meditation.

These differences reflect different levels of involvement. Younger marrieds with children are less involved than older traditional family members. For example, thirty-six percent of younger traditional family respondents in the seventy-two-congregation survey were highly involved in church; by contrast, forty-eight percent of middle-aged and fifty-four percent of older traditional family respondents were highly involved. Similarly, younger traditional families at Briarglen attended worship as often as older groups—but they held fewer leadership positions. Since worship is the primary channel of participation for younger marrieds with children, it is not surprising that they have stronger feelings about what happens in that context.

Older married persons with children, like older empty-nesters, tend to fill more active, producer roles in the church while younger marrieds with children are more passive consumers. As Hoge and Carroll[69] suggest, younger married couples may be less involved in church because of the time pressures imposed by the needs and demands of younger children.[70] This may be particularly true for dual career families. A thirty-eight-year-old father at Briarglen, whose son is in junior high, talks about his earlier noninvolvement in more general terms: "We've just been back in the church a few years. You know, there was a period of time in my life when other things just seemed more important—and pressing—it was harder to keep involved." Now, this lay member is a regular player on the church softball team; he also coaches younger children.

Regardless of family type, younger Protestant cohorts approach the church differently. For older members, factors such as institutional tradition and denominational loyalty dictate involvement; for younger members, personal tastes and more immediate needs shape church choices. And there is good evidence that the source of these differences is cultural, not simply developmental. In an analysis of two national surveys—one conducted in 1957 and the other, a replication in 1976—Verhof, Douvan, and Kulka document a shift from a socially integrated to a more personal or individuated paradigm for structuring well-being among Americans. This observed change includes: the erosion of role standards for decision-making; an increased focus on self-expressiveness and self-direction in social life; and a shift in concern from social organizational integration to interpersonal intimacy.[71] Marler and Roozen found a similar shift among Protestant church attenders in a comparison of the 1978 and 1988 Gallup Unchurched American surveys. For liberal and conservative Protestants, involvement is increasingly determined by "church consumerism" factors, like the perceived warmth of a congregation, more than by traditional religious beliefs or social background factors.[72]

Summarily, a very particular family dynamic is in operation in contemporary Protestant church life. First, this modern church is still very much a family church. In fact, in the face of culturewide family fragmentation, the church has remained surprisingly able to attract and hold traditional families. Second, at least part of the reason the contemporary church continues to draw this family type is the church's continuing focus on traditional families. Third, the fact that the white Protestant church seems to have great difficulty attracting and holding younger singles and married persons without children merely reinforces the traditional family church ethos. That ethos is intensified by the ex-family character of many Protestant congregations.

If these statistics are at all indicative, the present Protestant church is operating off an existent family residue. This nostalgic and increasingly aging cohort presents both an impediment to and an opportunity for the family in the church. This older faction serves as an impediment insofar as it resists innovation and change (in the family and in the church). On the other hand, these empty-nesters and widow(er)s represent an opportunity, in that they remain committed to the religious education of children and the moral nurturance of their families. In addition, the church remains an important religious touchstone for the now-grown-up and often scattered children of this family residue. For whether their grown children have moved away in physical distance or in commitment, the church remains a place where the "family can gather together," at least for Christmas, Easter, weddings, or funerals.

FAMILY THEORIES REVISITED

How do the findings of this study relate to past theories of family involvement in the church? And what are its implications for building new insights about the American family/church dynamic? Perhaps the most debated family theory vis-à-vis religious participation is family surrogate theory. It was originated by Glock, Ringer, and Babbie,[73] and has been reexamined over the years with mixed results.[74] In essence, the theory states that the church tends to attract persons deprived of family linkages who, by consequence, seek to "complete" their family status through church involvement. As one of the few available voluntary organizations that include and involve persons of all ages and family states, the church becomes a natural locus for sating familial urges.

Thus, Glock, Ringer, and Babbie label singles and married persons without children as "incompletes," in contrast to complete or "intact" families: married persons with children under eighteen. It is interesting to note that the very designations, complete and incomplete, reflect the influence of idealized notions of the traditional, nuclear family. Not surprisingly, findings that nontraditional family members were very involved in the church—compounded by images of incompleteness—led to theoretical hypotheses about deprivation.

Indeed, family surrogate theory is linked to psychosocial assumptions about deprivation. The presumption is that increased involvement is associated with familial neediness. Christiano effectively tested and refuted the deprivation theory.[75] He was also unable to replicate Glock, Ringer, and Babbie's earlier finding that persons from "incomplete" families tended to be more involved in the church. Age and sex, Christiano reports, are the most important predictors of involvement.

The data in this chapter are both consistent and at odds with former theories and tests of theories. The data provide evidence for family surrogate theory, but only insofar as it is measured by the involvement of members from nontraditional families. Briarglen's empty-nested couples and older single adults are very involved in the church. However, most link their activity to a deep, personal commitment based on a history of church participation that began as a family endeavor—not to feelings of deprivation in the absence of nuclear family involvement. Members' support of family-oriented programs is an extension of how they conceive the role of the church. As one layman put it: "Briarglen is a very family-oriented church. It's a place for children to learn about Christ and a place where the family comes together."

As Christiano suggests, and these demographic patterns indicate, age seems to be an important factor in relation to church involvement. And as Hoge and Carroll found, older couples with children—in contrast to their younger counterparts—exhibit increased involvement with the church.[76] Although there is reason to infer some developmental effect from such findings, that is, that moving from singlehood to marriage, and on to child-rearing increases the chances that individuals will become involved or reinvolved in church, the present survey analysis seems to suggest that the link may be related more to programmatic emphases within congregations that are driven primarily by changing cohort experience. Indeed, Christiano's findings on the importance of age in determining church involvement may say more about differing cohort experience than anything else. The older people of the next generation may not look like the older people of today. Christiano himself suggests this possibility.

For example, the Glock, Ringer, and Babbie study would have included a sample with histories of family and church involvement different from the Christiano study or the present survey groups. In the case of the Episcopalian survey, it must be remembered that the adult cohorts surveyed around 1952 were largely shaped by a world in turmoil: the First World War, the Great Depression, and the Second World War. In fact, in a group interview at Briarglen, an older layman told this story with tears in his eyes:

> When my wife and I moved to [the community] forty-four years ago, we didn't know a soul. Right after we moved, my in-laws lost a son at Omaha Beach. And somehow—I don't even know how they knew—four or five people from [Briarglen] church made meals and brought them over for a week. The church meant everything to us. It is important to think of this.

In that context, Glock's comfort thesis might more readily explain the presence and activity of "incomplete" family members in the church.

In the 1971 survey, Christiano included yet different family and non-family cohorts. By the early seventies, the American church population was in a statistical valley—and by this time, the intact families of the fifties and early sixties were moving toward the empty-nest stage. If church involvement in the fifties is a factor in later attendance patterns, then individuals over thirty at that time might be expected to attend and participate at higher levels than younger persons. Indeed, that is what Christiano found.

In the sample Christiano analyzed, younger respondents who experienced adolescence in the mid- to late sixties were less active or were nonmembers. During that period, the church, like the larger culture, was in considerable flux. Those who "stuck with the church" were not looking for comfort, so much as staying with something that was familiar. In fact, if Hadden is correct, church members at the time were more likely to be in conflict with their leadership than comforted by them.[77] Indeed, in conversations about church conflict, Briarglen members continually point to a late-sixties' controversy with an associate pastor who spoke out on civil rights and the Vietnam War. So, it is reasonable to assume that habit, more than comfort, may have encouraged continued church involvement. Further, since hardier habits tend to develop over time, the increasing significance of age in the 1971 sample is expected.

If habit reinforced through years of church involvement compelled those who stayed in Protestant churches when others were breaking their ties, then Christiano's findings about the decreased involvement of young singles and older widowed persons is interpretable. Habitual behavior is not easily broken. Only extremely disruptive life crises loosen the ties of taken-for-granted regular activity. This is especially the case when life changes not only disrupt present activities but are also perceived to alter radically future lifestyle patterns. Then everything, including church involvement, is up for grabs. Such may have been the case for younger respondents more directly affected by the countercultural movement and the Vietnam War. A similar case might be made for older women and men in the transition to widowhood.

Given varied cohort experiences, the divergences between Glock, *et al.*, and Christiano's findings become intuitively clearer. Granted, as Christiano explains, the two studies employed surveys of different constituences (denomination versus national poll) and utilized varying methods. These differences alone could account for opposed findings. Still, placing the findings of the two studies in a larger historical frame, differences become less problematic, more interpretable. For in spite of sampling and analytic differences, one fact remains: the relation between the family and the church is hardly static. Thus, contemporary constellations of family and church are expected to produce a unique family/church dynamic.

This certainly seems to be the case. The contemporary family/church relationship is uniquely influenced by both old and new dynamics. The nuclear family boom of the fifties, the neoconservative political resurgence of the eighties, the culturewide expansion of a consumer mindset, and an increasingly aging population become indispensable keys for understanding the current situation. Add a century-long American penchant for sentimentalizing home and hearth, and the result is the preservation of a dwindling traditional family cohort in a largely ex-family church.

Older members—the family residue—are clearly interested in the preservation of the institution. Nostalgic images of the family in the church still play in their conversations and in their decision-making. Because of the importance of the church for their families, these older members remain committed to the family in the church. Younger members in traditional families are interested in being served. Increasingly, they are drawn to churches that meet their perceived needs and those of their children. Both groups continue to choose church not for comfort or out of habit, but because of the myriad possible activities and organizations that are available to them. The church continues to offer something that they value, need, and/or want.

CONCLUSION

How can this story of family and church be summarized? And what are the implications for the church family of the future? I would like to turn my original analysis on its head, and begin with insights about contemporary family/church reality. Lasch has said that: "Memory calls up actions and events; it seeks to reconstruct what happened."[78] As already suggested, this research is an exercise in sharpening memory. As such, it illumines the obfuscating function of nostalgia—a subject to which I will return shortly.

First, *contemporary family structure has changed dramatically over the past forty years*. The dominance of the traditional family, as a proportion of all households, has fallen sharply. The result, which is hardly news at all, is a pluriform family structure—and an aging one. The baby boom will continue to shape the demography and tastes of the family. As this large cohort ages, the ex-family character which already dominates white Protestantism will also define American culture.

Second, *despite considerable family disruption, the white Protestant church has managed to attract and hold its market share of traditional families*. Perhaps the most remarkable finding in this research is the fact that the fortunes of the church seem so closely tied to those of the family unit. Nash and Berger and the follow-up study by Nash were on the right track, tying the supply of family units to growth in church membership. However, the data presented here indicate that their interpretation was slightly off. The rising birthrate in the fifties did seem to fuel overall church growth; so, in that sense a "little child [did] lead them." However, both for Protestants in the fifties and for church membership in general from the fifties to the present, fluctuations in the number of family units are determinative. What is the implication? Protestant churches attract traditional families, and as the proportion of that unit has declined, the church has "preserved" a commensurately shrinking number. The good news is that something about Protestant churches draws traditional families; the bad news is that as their market share of the U.S. population decreases, it is very likely that a similar pattern will be reflected in the churches.

Third, *the family structure of the Protestant church is primarily composed of two rather complimentary cohorts: people who are in traditional families and those who used to be*. Older empty-nesters and widowed persons largely make up a fifties' *family residue*. This very visible segment in many white Protestant churches maintains a sentimentalized familial identity and a related commitment to the traditional family in the church. In addition, this ex-family cohort maintains considerable institutional loyalty: they support the church for the church's sake. "New" traditional family members share older members' commitment to the traditional family. However, they are less likely to view the church itself as an extended traditional family. These traditional families choose the church for their sake and the sake of their children.

Fourth, *while the traditional family cohort is a very homogeneous group, younger families seem to be the most avid consumers—and the most reluctant producers*. These data underline the fact that younger traditional families expect to be served by the church rather than to serve. To some degree, this may be a function of having younger children on top of juggling dual careers. On the other hand, it is equally likely that this group—lacking a personal legacy of involvement in the active youth programs of the fifties and early sixties—carries little sense of a "group loyalty" that crosses the boundaries of other age and interest groups in the church. Consumerism, a culturewide organizing principle, characterizes the dominant style of this group. Other family types also exhibit a consumer approach to the church through intense involvement, specific interest group concerns, and a more-or-less critical appraisal of overall institutional functioning. However, younger traditional families seem to share not only a consumer style, but also consumer *values*.

Fifth, *the primary groups that are left out of the contemporary Protestant church are those that are gaining increasing shares of the family household market*. Singles, especially younger singles, and younger to middle-aged couples without children are gravely underrepresented in the white Protestant church. Some might well argue that this has always been the case. Yet, even if that is true, the lack of these nontraditional family types in the church is a serious issue. Indeed, it might be argued that in its nostalgia for the traditional family, the Protestant church has claimed a narrowly circumscribed market niche for itself, almost by default. The result is an identity and a program that implicitly or explicitly appeal to one kind of family type in both its present and past forms. In fact, when an aging group of institutional loyalists is matched with younger traditional family consumers, the result is a fairly happy niche of persons with "like interests" if not "like minds." Loyalty to the social group (the church family of the past) and consumer self-interest for one kind of group (the traditional family of the present) lead to lack of vision, interest, or flexibility to reach out to other family types.

Sixth, *these data emphasize the possibilities for a synthesis of theoretical insights to interpret complex family/church reality*. At any one time, the Protestant church includes a number of family and ex-family cohorts. In the end, it is the unique interaction of these various age and interest groups that colors and contours the contemporary family/church reality. Engaging, then, theoretical memory rather than nostalgia, it is possible to embrace past insights, and to view the family today as a rich constellation of persons whose primary ties to the church were forged in and through a variety of cultural crises.

Finally, what about American cultural nostalgia? What implications may be drawn from this study about the function of "family fiction" in shaping contemporary church reality? A further insight from Lasch is helpful here:

> Nostalgia evokes the past only to bury it alive. It shares with the belief in progress, to which it is only superficially opposed, an eagerness to proclaim the death of the past and to deny history's hold over the present. Those who mourn the death of the past and those who acclaim it both take for granted that our age has outgrown its childhood. Both find it difficult to believe that history still haunts our enlightened, disillusioned maturity. Both are governed, in their attitude toward the past, by the prevailing disbelief in ghosts.[79]

That is, those who "mourn the death of the past"—those who sentimentalize fifties' family reality—share a common, fallacious stance toward history with those "who acclaim it"—those who want to move beyond the traditional family, and especially traditional family values.

Truly embracing memory means, simply, embracing diversity—not the adoption of the dominant (demographic) family structure of the moment. Indeed, consumerism as an organizing principle *does* provide programmatic answers to the question of pluriform families. Many independent and innovative congregations have responded to diverse family constituencies by multiplying program options.

But what about institutional loyalty? Does increased church consumerism necessarily dilute the power of the once-valued social ties of congregational life? And further, do Americans need (whether they know it or not) such intimate connections? Two alternatives come to mind. First, in the face of family fragmentation, there may be precedent for self-consciously programming to "make family" in contemporary Protestant congregations.[80] That is, congregations might seriously institute cross-generational programming that brings disparate family "pieces" together and makes past family nostalgia fodder for creative, present, family memory. This alternative builds on the ex-family character of white Protestantism—and extends it.

Another alternative is to abandom the assumption that churches "ought" to operate at all like extended families. This alternative embraces more positive interpretations of American individualism. A socially vacuous "Sheilaism" (the individual inner voice dubbed a religion by Sheila, an interview subject in *Habits of the Heart*)[81] is not the only logical outcome of individualism, after all. As a form of individualism, increasing church consumerism emphasizes freedom of choice and diversity. "Choice" includes both the choice to participate as well as the choice not to participate. And if persons choose to participate, there are additional choices about "how"—under what conditions—they will participate. The strategic response is specialized and personalized programming. In the church choice, program is product.[82] As such, church programming itself must diversify to fit the interests and needs of a variety of family types.

In either case, this research offers hope and a warning. Change is occurring in the church, as witnessed by the continued inclusion of traditional families with very contemporary tastes—and the commitment to those families exhibited by the older, loyal family residue. Unfortunately, the "missing families"—mostly nontraditional—continue to "take their business elsewhere." Clearly, while bowing to the critical contributions of traditional families, past and present, congregations must cast their nets farther and more conscientiously. Otherwise, contemporary white Protestantism may be forever "lost in the fifties." Given the realities of an aging population and a shrinking traditional family base, it is clear that a future mired in the past is really no future at all.

NOTES

1. I worked with "Briarglen" (not its real name) from 1989 through 1991 in a long-range planning process. In addition to gathering data through the Parish Profile Inventory, I met with several focus groups and conducted numerous individual interviews with staff and lay members.

2. Peter L. Berger, "In Praise of Particularity: The Concept of Mediating Structures," in Facing Up to Modernity: Excursions in Society, Politics, and Religion (New York: Basic Books, Inc., 1977), pp. 130–147.

3. Christopher Lasch, *Haven in a Heartless World: the Family Besieged* (New York: Basic Books, 1977).

4. David Mace and Vera Mace, "The Marriage Enrichment Movement: Its History, its Rationale, and its Future Prospects," in *Toward Better Marriages: The Handbook of the Association of Couples for Marriage Enrichment (ACME)*, eds. L. Hopkins, *et al.* (Winston-Salem, NC: Assn. of Couples for Marriage Enrichment, 1978).

5. Melinda Bollar Wagner, *God's Schools: Choice and Compromise in American Society* (New Brunswick, NJ: Rutgers University Press, 1991).

6. Timothy LaHaye, *The Battle for the Family* (Old Tappan, NJ: Fleming H. Revell, 1982).

7. See Janet Fishburn, *Confronting the Idolatry of Family: A New Vision for the Household of God* (Nashville, TN: Abingdon, 1991); and Barbara Hargrove, "Family in the White American Protestant Experience," in *Families and Religions*, eds. William D'Antonio and Joan Aldous (Beverly Hills, CA: Sage, 1983).

8. Paul Glick, "American Household Structure in Transition," *Family Planning Perspectives* 16 (1984), pp. 205–211.

9. Among sources on the religious situation in the 1950s, see Will Herberg, *Protestant, Catholic, and Jew* (Garden City, NJ: Doubleday and Company, 1955); Dennison Nash, "A Little Child Shall Lead Them: A Statistical Test of an Hypothesis that Children Were the Sources of the American 'Religious Revival,'" *Journal for the Scientific Study of Religion* 7 (1968), pp. 238–240; Seymour M. Lipset, "Religion in America: What Religious Revival?" *Columbia University Forum* 11, No. 2 (Winter 1965); and Charles Glock and Rodney Stark, *Religion and Society in Tension* (Chicago, IL: Rand, McNally and Company, 1965).

10. Ann Swidler, "Culture in Action: Symbols and Strategies," *American Sociological Review* 51 (1986), pp. 273–286.

11. Christopher Lasch, *The True and Only Heaven: Progress and its Critics* (New York: W.W. Norton, 1991).

12. See Lasch, *The True and Only Heaven*, pp. 87ff, for a review of nineteenth century literature that emphasizes pastoral images over against the urban—including lengthy excerpts from Wordsworth.

13. See Barbara Welter, "The Cult of True Womanhood: 1820–1860," in *The American Family in Social-Historical Perspectives*, ed. M. Gordon (New

York: St. Martin's Press, 1973); and Ann Douglas, *The Feminization of American Culture* (New York: Knopf, 1977).

14. Billie J. Wahlstrom, "Images of the Family in the Mass Media: an American Iconography?" in *Changing Images of the Family*, eds. V. Tufte and B. Myerhoff (New Haven, CT: Yale University Press, 1979).

15. John Demos, "Images of the American Family, Then and Now," in *Changing Images of the Family*, eds. V. Tufte and B. Myerhoff, (New Haven, CT: Yale University Press, 1979).

16. Kirk Jeffrey, "The Family as Utopian Retreat from the City: The Nineteenth-Century Contribution," in *The Family, Communes, and Utopian Societies*, ed. S. TeSelle (New York: Harper and Row, 1972); and Barbara Laslett, "The Family as a Public and Private Institution: An Historical Perspective," *Journal of Marriage and the Family* 35 (1973), pp. 480–492.

17. Again, for a rather extensive review of this literature, see Lasch, *The True and Only Heaven*, pp. 105ff. Lasch's primary examples include works by Thornton Wilder, Theodore Dreiser, Sinclair Lewis, and Zona Gale.

18. U.S. Bureau of the Census, Special Demographic Analysis, CDS–80–8, *American Women: Three Decades of Change* (Washington, D.C.: U.S. Government Printing Office, 1984).

19. U.S. Bureau of the Census, Current Population Reports, Series P–20, No. 447, *Household and Family Characteristics: March 1990 and 1989* (Washington, D.C.: U.S. Government Printing Office, 1990a).

20. See Lasch, *The True and Only Heaven*, pp. 512ff; and Jeffrey Hadden, "Televangelism and the Mobilization of a New Christian Right Family Policy," in *Families and Religion: Conflict and Change in Modern Society*, eds. W. D'Antonio and J. Aldous (Beverly Hills, CA: Sage Publications, 1983).

21. James Davison Hunter, *American Evangelicalism: Conservative Religion and the Quandary of Modernity* (New Brunswick, NJ: Rutgers University Press, 1983).

22. Penny Marler and Kirk Hadaway, "New Church Development and Denominational Growth (1950–1988): Symptom or Cause?" in *Research in the Social Scientific Study of Religion*, vol. 4, eds. M. Lynn and D. Moberg, (Greenwich, CT: JAI Press, 1992).

23. U.S. Bureau of the Census, Current Population Reports, Series P–20, No. 106, *Household and Family Characteristics: March 1960* (Washington, D.C.: U.S. Government Printing Office, 1960); and Census, *Household and Family Characteristics: March 1990 and 1989*.

24. Linda Waite, Frances Goldscheider, and Christine Witsberger, "The Development of Individualism: Non-Family Living and the Plans of Young Men and Women," *American Sociological Review* 51 (1986), pp. 541–554; Calvin Goldscheider and Francis Goldscheider, "Moving Out and Marriage: What Do Young Adults Expect?" *American Sociological Review* 52 (1987), pp. 278–285; Frances Goldscheider and Celine Lebourdais, "The Falling Age at Leaving Home, 1920–1979," *Sociology and Social*

Research 70 (1986), pp. 99–102; Calvin Goldscheider and Frances Goldscheider, "Ethnicity, Religiosity, and Leaving Home: The Structural and Cultural Basis of Traditional Family Values," *Sociological Forum* 3 (1988), pp. 525–547; and Penny Marler, "Churches must 'Make Family' in 90s," *The Witness* 74 (1992), pp. 6–9, 16.

25. Helen Lopata, "The Social Involvement of American Widows," *American Behavioral Scientist* 14 (1970), pp. 41–57.

26. U. S. Census, *Household and Family Characteristics*.

27. Diane Pancoast, "A Network Focus for Family Ministry," in *The Church's Ministry with Families*, eds. D. Garland and D. Pancoast (Dallas, TX: Word Publishing, 1990).

28. Suzanne Bianchi, "America's Children: Mixed Prospects," *Population Bulletin* 45, No. 1 (June 1990) (Washington, D.C.: Population Reference Bureau, Inc.).

29. U.S. Bureau of the Census, *The Statistical Abstract of the United States: 1990*, 110th Edition (Washington, D.C.: U.S. Government Printing Office, 1990b).

30. Bianchi, "America's Children."

31. U. S. Census, *Household and Family Characteristics*.

32. U.S. Bureau of the Census, Current Population Reports, *Projections of the Population of the United States by Age, Sex, and Race: 1988 to 2020* (Washington, D.C.: U.S. Government Printing Office, 1988).

33. Thomas Exter, "Demographic Forecasts: Married with Kids," *American Demographics* 55 (February 1990).

34. "Marketing Tools Alert," *American Demographics* 1 (July 1990).

35. Wendy Baldwin, and Christine Nord, "Delayed Childbearing in the U.S.: Facts and Fictions," *Population Bulletin* 39, No. 4 (1984) (Washington, D.C.: Population Reference Bureau); also Bianchi, "America's Children."

36. Goldscheider and Goldscheider, "Ethnicity, Religiosity and Leaving Home."

37. Charles Glock, Benjamin Ringer, and Earl Babbie, *To Comfort and to Challenge: A Dilemma of the Contemporary Church* (Berkeley, CA: University of California Press, 1967).

38. David A. Roozen, *Church Attendance from a Social Indicators Perspective: an Explanation into the Development of Social Indicators of Religion from Existing National Data*, Unpublished dissertation (Atlanta, GA: Emory University, 1979).

    Demographic family types in the two studies reported here were available by marital status only, not by family households. The 1960 Census percentage of family *households* (married with kids) was 45.6% and of married *persons* (with kids), 43%. See note 41 for further explanation.

39. Roy Fairchild and John C. Wynn, *Families in the Church: A Protestant Survey* (New York: Association, 1961), p. 50, n 61 lists the following denominations: American Baptist, Church of God, Congregational-

Christian, Disciples of Christ, Evangelical and Reformed, Lutheran Church—Missouri Synod, Methodist, Protestant Episcopal, Southern Baptist, United Lutheran, and United Presbyterian.

40. Fairchild and Wynn, *Families in the Church*, pp. 36–37.

41. James A. Davis and Tom Smith, *General Social Surveys, 1972–1990*, Machine-readable data file (Chicago, IL: National Opinion Research Center, 1990).

42. As marital status categories—rather than family household types—are the bases for analyzing responses by family type, comparative data from the general population are also computed in this way (See U.S. Bureau of the Census, Current Population Reports, Series P–20, No. 445, *Marital Status and Living Arrangements: March 1989* (Washington, D.C.: Government Printing Office, 1990c). Two items are of note. First, all "single" categories are again collapsed without regard to the presence of children. In the case of the general population, this category included approximately 12% single parents with children under 18. Second, the proportion of households (married couples with children under 18) and the proportion of nuclear families by marital status categories are slightly different. This difference is expected given the entirely different bases for dividing the data and calculating percentages. Still, overall proportional relationships between family types calculated by household or marital status categories remain.

Family type categories in both church-based surveys included: married with children under 18; married without children under 18, and single (including "single, never married," "widowed," "divorced," and "separated"). As the primary line of analysis concerns traditional families, the combined characteristics of *married* and *children* are the most critical indices. Therefore, singles were grouped regardless of the presence of children. Further, single parents constitute extremely small proportions of the churched population in the surveys analyzed: 1% of the Briarglen survey (N = 306) and 2.6% of the 72-congregation survey (N = 1491).

43. A 1986 survey conducted by Hartford Seminary sampled membership of 72 Protestant congregations: 18 congregations were clustered around Louisville, Kentucky; 13 around Durham, North Carolina; 16 around Hartford, Connecticut; 5 around Rochester, New York; 8 around Chicago, Illinois; and 12 around Indianapolis, Indiana. Sixty-two "mainline" congregations included: 15 United Church of Christ, 20 Presbyterian, 17 Methodist, 7 American Baptist, and one each of Episcopal, Disciples, and Mennonite. Ten "evangelical" congregations included: 9 Southern Baptist and one Church of Christ.

A random sample of membership in each congregation completed a version of Hartford Seminary's "Church Planning Inventory" which contained over 150 opinion items on tasks of the church, organizational characteristics, congregational identity, tasks of the pastor, size and condition of facilities, Christian education for children, youth programs, adult education and small group programming, worship, community and social involvement, stewardship development, evangelism, and religious beliefs. Items measuring church participation and a number of demographic attributes were also included. Data utilized in the present analysis are from a 20% sample of the individual respondents, 1491 cases out of a total of 6,736.

Members of a United Church of Christ congregation in suburban Springfield, Massachusetts were also surveyed. Church Planning Inventories were made available to the entire Briarglen congregation through a telephone and survey delivery campaign. The resident membership of Briarglen (over confirmation age) is about 600. Of these, 306 persons completed the survey, for a return rate of 52%. A demographic analysis of the sample showed that respondents attend worship at least twice a month and are on one or more committees (60%); 50% are over the age of 55; and 86% have lived in the community for 10 years or more.

44. The vast majority of Briarglen's traditional family members falls in the 35 to 54 age group for several reasons: 1) Briarglen church is located in a small New England town cum upper middle-class bedroom community. The community attracts more settled, upper-elite, one-career and professional two-career families. Both categories of respondents are older and have fewer children, later in life. 2) Briarglen's survey group is weighted toward those most active in congregational life. Given previous findings that married persons with school-aged children tend to have increased church involvement, the high proportion of Briarglen respondents in this age group and family type is expected. (See Dean Hoge and Jackson Carroll "Determinants of Commitment and Participation in Suburban Protestant Churches," *Journal for the Scientific Study of Religion* 17 (1978), pp. 107–127; Bernard Lazerwitz, "Some Factors Associated with Variation in Church Attendance," *Social Forces* 39 (1961), pp. 301–309; and Jackson W. Carroll, and David A. Roozen, *Religious Participation in American Society: An Analysis of Social and Religious Trends and Their Interaction*, Multilith (Hartford, CT: Hartford Seminary Foundation, 1975). Larger numbers of "older baby-boomers" also fit more recent research substantiating a trend toward increased church attendance among this cohort (David A. Roozen, William McKinney, and Wayne Thompson, "The 'Big Chill' Generation Warms to Worship: A Research Note," *Review of Religious Research* 31, no. 3 (1990), pp. 314–322. 3) the paucity of active younger marrieds at Briarglen is particularly noteworthy. As Hoge and Carroll suggest, the demands of younger children may discourage active adult involvement in the church.

45. Marilyn Ihinger-Tallman and Kay Pasley, *Remarriage* (Newbury Park, CA: Sage Publications, 1987).

46. U.S. Census, *American Women...*

47. Nash, "A Little Child Shall Lead Them...."

48. Dennison Nash and Peter Berger, "The Child, the Family, and the 'Religious Revival' in Suburbia," *Journal for the Scientific Study of Religion* 2 (1962), pp. 85–93.

49. Nash, "A Little Child Shall Lead Them...."

50. Kirk Hadaway and Penny Marler, "A Retest and Extension of Nash's 1968

'A Little Child Shall Lead Them,'" unpublished manuscript (Hartford, CT: Hartford Seminary, 1990).

51. Constant H. Jacquet, Jr., ed., *The Yearbook of American and Canadian Churches*, yearly edition (Nashville, TN: Abingdon Press, 1990).

52. The items in this data set are by their very nature collinear—that is, separately, they constitute several points along the same straight line. Regression analysis, then, of disparate collinear items presents the problem of multicollinearity. As expected, multiple regression analyses with these data yield large standard errors and high adjusted R^2s. Still, as C.E.V. Leser has observed, multicollinearity is "less serious when the objective of prediction of the dependent variable is stressed" (See *Economic Techniques and Problems*, Griffins' Statistical Monographs and Courses (London: Griffin, 1969). Predictions may be very stable, despite large standard errors. Iterations of items in the data set provide a helpful indication of the likely stability of predictions via regression coefficients. In the case of the Marler and Hadaway analysis ("New Church Development and Denominational Growth (1950–1988): Symptom or Cause?" in *Research in the Social Scientific Study of Religion*, vol. 4, eds. M. Lynn and D. Moberg, (Greenwich, CT: JAI Press, 1992), iterated forward regression sequences revealed little change in the effect of the main predictor variable.

53. Fourteen Protestant denominations were selected, and their total memberships as reported in the *Yearbook* were summed on an annual basis from 1950 to 1988. The Protestant denominations included eight "mainline" groups (The Disciples of Christ; The Church of the Brethren; The Episcopal Church; The Evangelical Lutheran Church in America; The Presbyterian Church, USA; The Reformed Church in America; The United Church of Christ; and The United Methodist Church) and six "evangelical" bodies (The Assemblies of God; The Church of God, Anderson, Indiana; The Church of the Nazarene; The Lutheran Church, Missouri Synod; The Seventh Day Adventist Church; and The Southern Baptist Convention). Then, this representative figure for Protestant membership was correlated with the U.S. population, families with children, and the birthrate for the same period. The strongest correlation, again, was between church membership and families with children (.90)—even when controlling for population and the birthrate, the correlation remained strong (.76).

Stepwise regressions were performed with the 14-denomination subsample for the "boom" and "bust" years, as in the Nash retest. As opposed to the larger sample, regression analyses for the 2 periods yielded similar results: the strongest predictor among Protestants remained families with children.

54. Mark Chaves, "Family Structure and Protestant Church Attendance: The sociological basis of cohort and age effects," *Journal for the Scientific Study of Religion* 30 (1991), pp. 501–515.

55. Involvement was calculated by summing reponses to worship attendance (from "none" to "four times a month or more"—options coded 1–6) and committee or other organization membership (from "none" to "four or

more"—options coded 1–5). Low involvement was defined by a total of 2–6; moderate involvement, 7–8; and high involvement, 9–11.

56. Interestingly, no significant differences in involvement were found between married couples when both were employed, and married couples when only one spouse was employed. The "traditional" pattern, with one full-time, working spouse and one stay-at-home spouse did not result in increased church activity.

57. Respondents chose a response from a 7-point scale ranging from: "Our congregation feels like one large family" to "Our congregation feels like a loosely knit association of individuals and groups." The correlations between family type and the family identity item were -.07 for the 72 congregation survey and -.24 for the Briarglen survey. Both were significant (p <=.01).

58. These responses were gleaned from semistructured interviews with over sixty laypeople at Briarglen, ranging in age from 15 to 85, representing new members, youth, young families with children, church school teachers, empty-nesters, single adults, senior adults, Social Concerns Board members, church staff, and trustees.

59. Respondents identified "tasks of the church" that they "would most like to see strengthened" for "the sake of [their] own personal involvement in [their] congregation." The two highest priorities for married persons with children were: "helping members deepen their personal and spiritual relationship with God" (23.6%), and "providing Christian education for children and youth" (12%). Singles' highest priorities included the same two items: deepening their spiritual relationship (19.6%) and providing Christian education for children and youth (9.8%).

60. U.S. Bureau of the Census, "1980 Demographic Profile Report," National Planning Data Corporation, Online Demographic Data Management and Reporting System, Ithaca, NY, 1980.

61. In a focus-group interview with young couples with children, the primary concern was: "how to keep youth coming to church after confirmation." When they talked about stewardship and fund-raising, they suggested a "family picnic" rather than the "fancy dinner the church sponsored before." They felt that "education of parents" was the key to involving youth and children, and when they talked about "local mission," the emphasis was on "getting kids involved in small projects like Habitat." They felt that the church had "resources that haven't even been tapped yet," and that it "does a great job" with families.

62. Correlations between these items and family type were significant <=.01.

63. Respondents chose a response from a 7-point scale ranging from: "Our church is primarily oriented to serving its members" to "Our church is primarily oriented to serving the world beyond its membership." The correlations between family type and this identity item were .064 for the 72 congregation survey (p<=.01).

64. Lyle Schaller, "The Disappearing Pillars," *Net Results* 7 (February, 1991), p. 8.

65. Correlations of these items with family type are all significant (p <=.01).

66. When analyzing data from the surveys by family type and age, the following groupings were utilized: 1) "younger, under 35"; 2) "middle-aged, 35–54"; 3) "older, 55 and over."

67. Correlations of married persons without children under 18 by age with the items noted are all significant (p <=.01).

68. Correlations between singles by age and the items noted were significant (p <=.01).

69. Hoge and Carroll, "Determinants of Commitment."

70. Steven L. Nock and Paul Kingston, "Time with Children: The Impact of Couple's Work-Time Commitments," *Social Forces* 67 (1988), pp. 59–85. See also Hertel's chapter in this volume.

71. Joseph Verhof, Elizabeth Douvan, and Richard Kulka, *The Inner American: A Self-Portrait from 1957 to 1976* (New York: Basic Books, 1981), especially p. 529.

72. Penny Long Marler and David Roozen, "From Church Tradition to Consumer Choice: The Gallup Surveys of the Unchurched American," in *Church and Denominational Growth*, eds. David Roozen and C. Kirk Hadaway (Nashville, TN: Abingdon Press, 1993).

73. *To Comfort and to Challenge.*

74. See, for example, Hoge and Carroll, "Determinants of Commitment"; Charles W. Hobart, "Church Involvement and the Comfort Thesis in Alberta," *Journal for the Scientific Study of Religion* 17 (1974), pp. 107–127; Dean Hoge and David Roozen, "Research on Factors Influencing Church Commitment," in *Understanding Church Growth and Decline: 1950–1978*, eds. Dean Hoge and David Roozen (New York: Pilgrim Press, 1979); Dean Hoge and David Polk, "A Test of Theories of Protestant Church Participation and Commitment," *Review of Religious Research* 21 (1980), pp. 315–329; Wade Clark Roof and Dean Hoge, "Church Involvement in America: Social Factors Affecting Membership and Participation," *Review of Religious Research* 21 (1980), pp. 405–426.

75. Kevin Christiano, "Church as a Family Surrogate: Another look at Family Ties and Church involvement," *Journal for the Scientific Study of Religion* 25 (1986), pp. 339–354.

76. Hoge and Carroll, "Determinants of Commitment."

77. Jeffrey Hadden, *The Gathering Storm in the Churches: The Widening Gap Between Clergy and Laymen* (Garden City, NJ: Doubleday, 1969).

78. *The True and Only Heaven*, p. 104.

79. *Ibid.*, p. 118.

80. Marler, "Churches Must 'Make Family.'"

81. Robert Bellah, *et. al.*, *Habits of the Heart: Individualism and Commitment in American Life* (Berkeley: University of California Press, 1985).

82. Marler and Roozen, "From Church Tradition."

3

Boomers and the Culture of Choice

Changing Patterns of Work, Family, and Religion

Wade Clark Roof and Lyn Gesch

F ew would dispute that decision-making within the family has greatly changed in recent decades: young Americans today choose to marry, and if married, whether to have children, and how many children, and whether to remain married. Many women enter into careers previously not open to them, others choose to stay at home as wives and mothers, and their spouses accommodate them and their choices in ways that would have shocked earlier generations of Americans. Indeed, choice in the sense of increased options—that is, differing ways in which people can live and relate to one another—is as taken for granted today as was the 1950s expectation that men would be breadwinners and women housewives. The "Ozzie and Harriet" families of that era have been replaced with a variety of family styles, each with a differing calculus of how family, work, and everyday life fit together. Television programs of recent years illustrate such diversity, including, of course, "Murphy Brown," with a single woman who chooses to keep her child—a choice assailed by then-Vice President Dan Quayle in 1992 for its lack of "family values."

Television is a mirror of contemporary change, and in its portrayal of family life we see the extent to which families are shaped by individual needs, preferences, and circumstances. No doubt the large postwar, baby-boom generation—seventy-five million strong—has reshaped American culture. The baby-boomers grew up in a time of major gender-role, family, and lifestyle changes, and the freedom they enjoyed has come to be widely accepted throughout the society, among the younger "busters" following them and among even older age cohorts. What this generation has done amounts to a transformation of the most intimate realms of life—endowing sexuality, family, and lifestyle with greater choice and options, extending to these realms the very same operative principles that have long characterized the public spheres.

All of this has led to much concern, over the past couple of decades, about the culture of choice and related themes of self-absorbing individualism and self-centeredness. During the 1970s, there was discussion of the "me generation," with its emphasis upon turning inward and exploring the self. "Narcissistic" and "self-fulfilling" were adjectives much in vogue. Then in the 1980s, came the "decade of greed," with concerns of materialism and making money. Along with it came a new set of social labels, such as "Yuppies" and "Dinks" (dual income, no kids), to characterize, however inaccurately, the young boomer population. Books like Bellah and associates' *Habits of the Heart* focused attention on how individualism may be eroding American social life with an excessive emphasis upon self-interest and self-absorption, and a corresponding lack of concern for others and for give and take in social life.[1] Many commentators worry that this culture of choice is seriously undermining our capacity for commitment to one another, thus threatening the very basis of institutional life. Even if we are not alarmed by this possibility, the fact is that all our social institutions, not just the family, are caught up in, and influenced by, a fierce devotion to individual freedom.

Religion is no exception. Especially since the time of the Reformation, Western religion has stressed concepts of freedom of conscience and adult commitment, thus often putting strains on family loyalty. Trends have been in the direction of dissolving ascriptive group loyalties in favor of autonomous and independent decision-making. The historic drift has been toward greater voluntarism in matters of faith. Talcott Parsons called this the working out of the "Protestant principle," in which "the individual is bound only by responsible personal commitment, not by any factor of ascription."[2] With its great religious pluralism, America, especially, has been and continues to be a fertile ground for nurturing religious voluntarism. This is seen in a denominational approach to religion, in a strong evangelical impulse urging responsible individual choice, and in the close affinities among religious and secular values, such as individual achievement, equality, competition, and personal freedom.[3]

Americans are deeply committed to the principle of religious choice. Gallup polls have found that eighty-one percent agree that "one should arrive at his or her own religious beliefs independent of a church or synagogue," and seventy-eight percent agree that "one can be a good Christian or Jew without attending a church or synagogue." The overwhelming majority of the population—both inside and outside the churches—holds to privatized views on religion. Even among American Catholics, with their strong tradition of ecclesiastical authority, trends toward greater freedom of conscience and personal responsibility have, in the years since Vatican II, been quite swift. In religious as well as moral values and practices, young Catholics are moved less and less by exhortations from the church (couched as obligations), more and more by their own consciences. Whether Catholic, Protestant, Jewish, or whatever, the highly privatized, personally expressive mode of religion is a contemporary American cultural form. The epitome of this form is perhaps Sheila Larson, a nurse interviewed by Bellah and associates. She describes her faith ("my own little voice") as "Sheilaism." Phrased in the language of sociology, and in keeping with the long-term Western trend described by numerous theorists, the shift broadly in American culture has been away from religion as collective-expressive toward more individual-expressive forms.[4]

While religion has become a matter of choice, it has not always been a choice to be exercised within the family; within this realm, more so than in any other, the norms of religious individualism were held at bay. But this is now less true. Both institutions are subject to individualistic trends. The cultural forces of both utilitarian individualism and expressive individualism, to cite Bellah and associates' distinction, function to reorient institutional attachments. Utilitarian or economic factors reshape family and religion around instrumental values, with the result that both become largely removed from the public realm and invested with greater meaning in the "private" realm; expressive or subjective factors enhance the role of choice and concern with individual needs and preferences. The result is a major shift in the "religion and family connection."[5]

FINDINGS FROM A RECENT SURVEY

To what extent has contemporary individualism invaded religious thinking within the family? How important is it to have and celebrate a common faith within families? Or is it now accepted that individuals within families will simply make decisions about religion on their own? To get some answers, we turn to an analysis of data from a survey of baby-boomers, the generation of young adults born between 1946 and 1964 who make up roughly one-third of the American population.

In this survey, funded by the Lilly Endowment, Inc. and conducted in 1988 and 1989, a subsample of 536, boomers selected from a total sample of 1599 telephone interviews in the four states of California, Massachusetts, North Carolina, and Ohio, were asked: "Is it important to you to attend church/synagogue as a family, or should family members make individual choices about religion?" The responses show that the boomers are split right down the middle on this issue: fifty-five percent answered that it was important to attend as a family, and forty-five percent said family members should make their own choices. The split is roughly the same in all four states, with the family stance somewhat stronger in North Carolina (sixty-two percent) and weaker in Massachusetts, where a majority (fifty-one percent) actually endorses the more individualistic approach toward religion. On the basis of these clear-cut patterns, we draw a distinction within the boomer generation between "religious individualists" who insist on each person making his or her own decision about religious involvement, and "family attenders," who feel that families as a unit should make such decisions.

As a check on this single-item measure, we examined whether the two groups it identified—religious individualists and family attenders— differed on whether children should be allowed to make their own decisions about attending church or synagogue. Forty-one percent of the religious individualists, but only seven percent of the more traditional family attenders, said yes to this very pointed, forthright question. We also looked for differences on other, related, survey questions. The

TABLE 1

Indicators of Religious Individualism

	Family Attenders	Religious Individualists
1. An individual should arrive at his or her own religious beliefs independent of any church or synagogue	68%	87%
2. A person can be a good Christian/Jew without attending church/synagogue	83	94
3. Church is something freely chosen by each person rather than passed on from generation to generation	54	73

results are shown in Table 1. The item correlates as expected with these questions, all taken from other studies that have explored levels of religious individualism or personal autonomy in American society.[6] Hence it seems reasonable to conclude that our measure is a valid index of religious individualism in the family context.

SOCIO-DEMOGRAPHIC PROFILES

Who are the people described here as "religious individualists"? And who are the "family attenders," those who look upon church as a family matter? We look briefly at the socio-demographic profiles of these two constituencies. Here we emphasize their differences of background and of experience, recognizing of course that they also have similarities arising out of a common boomer culture.

Two factors especially influence the boomers' norms of religious individualism within the family: work and family type. People who work full-time, especially women, are much more likely to be religious individualists. Women working full-time, no matter what their marital and family status, are more individualist-oriented than either the part-time employed or housewives (see Table 2). Single men are highly individualist, with childless married men only slightly less so. The divorced and separated, both male and female, are understandably inclined in this direction. Clearly, the most important family factor is parenthood. Those with children are far less likely to endorse individual norms, and

TABLE 2

Religious Individualism by Work and Family Types

Work Status	Family Type	%	N
Females:			
Full-time	Single, no children	38	(29)
Full-time	Married, no children	81	(16)
Full-time	Married, with children	45	(65)
Full-time	Divorced/separated, with children	46	(35)
Part-time	Married, with children	24	(37)
Housewives	Married, with children	24	(46)
Males:			
Full-time	Single, no children	64	(45)
Full-time	Married, no children	61	(28)
Full-time	Married, with children	32	(114)
Full-time	Divorced/separated, with children	84	(19)

to favor family norms of churchgoing. Whereas eighty-one percent of married working women without children and sixty-one percent of married working men without children are religious individualists, only forty-five percent of working mothers and thirty-two percent of working fathers are so inclined.

What about social class and occupations? We might expect to find that a lot of yuppielike boomers and middle-class, career-oriented types would be more individualistic in their religious views than working-class boomers. But this turns out not to be the case. First, there are far fewer yuppie types than we might think. And second, boomers in clerical, service, and other lower-paying jobs are slightly more individualistic in their religious views than are their better-paid cohorts. More of the individualists are in service and clerical jobs, even though their educational levels tend to be about as high as the family attenders. A great number of religious individualists have scaled-down expectations of future success. They tend to be liberal politically and morally. Many are divorced or separated, and are single parents or childless; only a third of them live in two-parent families with children. Many of them now have older children, already in or approaching the teen years.

Compared to the family attenders, religious individualists remember being less close to their parents when they were growing up. They grew up in more permissive homes, where their parents were not very strong church attenders. Individualists are less embedded in social networks today. They tend to have fewer close friends living in the same area, fewer freinds of the same national or ethnic background, and fewer friends who attend a church or synagogue regularly. In addition, many of them agonize over their personal needs and potential possibilities. In some respects, they resemble those Daniel Yankelovich identified some years ago as "strong formers"—people who are deeply concerned about their own personal self-fulfillment and personal growth.[7]

In contrast, traditional family attenders are more likely to be well-established career types with higher incomes. A majority are professionals and managers. Twice as many of the women are housewives. They are more conservative politically and morally. Two-thirds are in two-parent families with children—Norman Rockwell's idealized picture of the American family. Fewer of them are divorced or separated today. Most are in their first marriages, and in marriages which, on the average have lasted longer than those of their individualist counterparts. Sixty-one percent presently have young children, indicating that parenthood was postponed during their early adult years.

They grew up in more demanding homes, and had parents who were more likely to attend religious activities. They had closer family ties and report happier childhood experiences. Relatively speaking, they are far more likely today to be socially involved—in both organizations and informal activities. They appear to be more content with their lives. As a population, they resemble those in Yankelovich's study who are settled into stable commitments to family, work, friends, and community. They retain more traditional values, including "a moderate commitment to the old self-denial rules, even as they struggle to achieve some measure of greater freedom, choice, and flexibility in their lives."[8]

RELIGIOUS TRADITIONS AND PERSONAL AUTONOMY

Our interest lies in the impact of this style of individualism on religion generally, so we begin with a look at the religious traditions themselves. It was expected that levels of religious individualism within the family would vary across the major religious families that are found in the United States. Liberal Protestantism encourages the autonomy of the individual in matters of religious belief and practice; and in contrast, conservative Protestantism places much greater stress upon family solidarity and conformity to traditional family and religious values. Roman Catholicism has emphasized family and traditional values, but since Vatican II in the 1960s, many young Catholics have come to emphasize the role of conscience as the final arbiter in moral and religious

TABLE 3

Religious Individualists by Religious Tradition

	%	N
Roman Catholic	42	176
Conservative Protestant	35	153
Mainline Protestant	44	105
Jewish	41	23
No Religious Preference	83	52

decisions. Jews also emphasize conscience and the importance of the believer making his or her own decisions.

The patterns of religious individualism among Protestants are in keeping with our expectations, with a 9-point spread between mainliners (forty-four percent) and conservatives (thirty-five percent). Catholics fall between the two Protestant groups, at forty-two percent. Jews are very similar—forty-one percent. The small group of religious "nones," or those with no religious preference, are highly individualistic—eighty-three percent. Thus it is clear that, while family-centered religious values predominate in the major religious traditions, there are sizable groups within each—from a third to well over two-fifths—who take an autonomous, deeply personal approach to religion, even within the family. As an ideology, individualism is deeply embedded in both the family and religion in American society; and is gradually but unmistakably reshaping the way these two institutions relate to each other.

Another measure of the individualism of this cohort is the extent to which they have dropped out of organized religion. Although ninety percent claimed to have been involved in Sunday School and congregations while they were growing up—as high a rate as any generation before them—by their late teens and early twenties many had dropped out of the churches and synagogues. Growing up in a time of widespread social and cultural upheavals—the era of the Vietnam War, of assassinations of national leaders, and of youthful protests—in what amounted to a major revolt against the cultural and religious establishment, large numbers abandoned the religious institutions in which they had been reared. Some experimented with new religious movements, a few joined communes, but by far most of them simply dropped out, joining the ranks of the religiously disaffiliated.

Figures in Table 4 show just how many dropped out for a period of two years or more—more than half of all Protestants (mainline and con-

TABLE 4

Patterns of Loyalty to Religious Traditions

Institutional Attachment	Mainline Protestant		Conservative Protestant		Catholic	
	1	2	1	2	1	2
	N=57	N=49	N=103	N=50	N=61	N=75
Loyalist	45%	25%	43%	22%	58%	16%
Dropped Out	55	75	57	78	42	84
Of these: %Who Have Returned:	65	14	72	24	52	27

1 = Family Attenders
2 = Individual Attenders

servative) and Catholics.[9] We do not know how these figures compare with previous generations, but they strike us as very large. Clearly it is the religious individualists who dropped out in greater numbers.

Striking, too, are the subsequent patterns for dropouts—whether they later returned to active participation in a congregation, or have remained uninvolved. Here again, the distinction between family attenders and religious individualists helps in uncovering crucial differences. For all three religious communities, a majority of those for whom it is important to attend as families has returned to active involvement. Among individualists, however, the comparable figures are astounding. The vast majority of the individualist dropouts are *still* inactive: eighty-six percent among the mainline Protestants, seventy-six percent among conservative Protestants, and seventy-three percent among Catholics. Both the cultural differences among boomers and the strong force of family norms upon religious belonging are apparent in these numbers. The pattern is similar across all major religious traditions. Those who think families should attend religious services together were more likely to stay involved throughout their young adult years, and far more likely to return, if they dropped out. Those who think each family member should make independent decisions are more likely to decide to leave entirely, and far less likely to return.

BOOMERS AND THE LIFE CYCLE HYPOTHESIS

More insight into the "return to religion" phenomenon is gained by looking at three major variables known to have an influence upon young adults in the direction of greater religious involvement—marriage, influence of a spouse, and children. It has often been pointed out that Americans are religiously involved as children, often drop out in adolescence and early adulthood, but then return to greater religious involvement once they have married, settled down, and have children. Norms of parental responsibility are especially strong, encouraging young adults with children to live up to their roles as parents. Taken as a whole, marriage, a religiously active spouse, and parental responsibility all amount to a strong set of influences leading those with religious roots to reclaim their heritage, and to begin anew the pattern of religious socialization with their children.[10]

It turns out that the distinction between "family attenders" and religious individualists is crucial as a precondition for these influences. Among those who hold that families should attend a church or synagogue together, sixty-six percent of those who are married have returned to active religious involvement. With the addition of a religiously active spouse, religious involvement increases to eighty-four percent. If there are children as well, the figure reaches even higher to ninety percent. However, for those who favor individual choices within the family, the figures are very different. Among those who are married, twenty-four percent have returned, which increases to thirty percent with a religiously active spouse, and finally to forty-one percent with the presence of children. The old life cycle pattern of religious involvement holds best for those who still adhere to conventional family norms about religion; it does not hold very well for those high in personal autonomy. Those boomers most influenced by the events and upheavals of the 1960s and 1970s, and who were jarred out of a collective-expressive mode and into an individual-expressive mode of identity, continue to be much less responsive to traditional role expectations about religion.

These results raise questions about the adequacy of the old life cycle hypothesis about the religious return of young adults. For some boomers, the life cycle pattern clearly holds; for others, there is little evidence of it. Cultural shifts in the relation of individuals to religious institutions and of the declining importance of religious belonging are also factors in the experience of this generation. In some respects, these are more significant than the life cycle and role changes themselves.

MIXED FAITHS AND BLENDED FAMILIES

Two other important changes characterizing boomers are the large number of mixed-faith marriages, and an increase in what is now called "blended families." Both are problematic for traditional family and church ties: mixed-faith (for example, Jewish-Catholic or Protestant-Catholic) marriages are characterized by high levels of tension surrounding religious matters and reduced levels of religious involvement; and blended families are complex, divorce-extended families, which in many respects are resourceful and adaptable as families go, but not without religious strains.[11] As both types of family contexts have become more common for young adults, shifts in the "religion and family connection" have followed.

Our survey shows that individual choice in religion varies both with the incidence of mixed-faith marriages and with the number of marriages: choice becomes more important in marriages where the partners come from differing religious backgrounds and in second, third, or subsequent marriages (see Table 5). No doubt, individual choice in religious matters is very functional for families where more than one faith is represented and/or children have differing backgrounds and parent-child relationships. Choice minimizes tensions over religious disputes. Whether the tension is between spouses of different faiths, or the result of demands from ex-spouses about the religious rearing of children, choice helps sustain often fragile families.

TABLE 5
Marriages and Faiths, Individual Choice, and Religious Socialization of Children

	Individual Choice in Religion	Children go to Sunday School	Religious Training "Very Important"
Same Faith, First Marriage (N=170)	27%	76%	72%
Same Faith, Second Marriage or more (N=41)	40	58	66
Mixed Faith, First Marriage (N=71)	44	58	46
Mixed Faith, Second Marriage or more (N=25)	60	48	48

But equally important, we found that the family types with the highest levels of emphasis on choice have the lowest levels of emphasis on the religious training of children and the lowest levels of children's actual involvement in religious activities. People in those family contexts where choices about religious issues are both necessary and difficult are less likely to follow the customary norms of passing on their religious views to their children. A major link in the religious transmission process is thus broken. As the norms of religious individualism have invaded the family, the likelihood that families will be the carriers of religious loyalties across generations is greatly diminished.

DIFFERING RELIGIOUS STYLES

Boomers today are characterized generally by two, differing, religious styles, one described simply as "religious" and the other "spiritual." The distinction is very real to members of this generation. To be religious conveys an institutional connotation, prescribed rituals, and established ways of believing; to be spiritual is more personal and experiential, and has to do with the deepest motivations of life for meaning and wholeness. The first is "official" religion, standardized, and handed down by religious authorities; the second is "unofficial," highly individualistic, religion "à la carte" as Reginald Bibby puts it.[12] To many boomers, the religious and the spiritual have become disjointed, out of sync with one another in a world where institutions often seem cut off from people's inner feelings and experiences. Worse still, just going through the motions of religious involvement, if it is empty of meaning, smacks of hypocrisy to many who have felt estranged from institutions and activities that, in their judgment, lack authenticity and credibility.[13]

As shown in Table 6, there is a close linkage between the family attenders and traditional religious styles. Compared with religious individualists, family attenders believe more in God, pray more frequently, are stronger church or synagogue members, and say grace at meals more often. Those who are Christian tend to hold a view of Jesus as a caring Shepherd, and insist that a person should "stick to a faith" rather than "explore many differing traditions." This pattern of conventional beliefs, practices, and views is not surprising, especially the long-standing symbolic significance to family life of prayer and grace at meals.

Religious individualists, on the other hand, favor exploring religious alternatives; and those who are Christians are drawn to images of Jesus as "liberator" and "challenger." Many of them are oriented to social justice causes, which in turn often places them in some conflict with the more conventional institutional belongers. They hold to a more expansive style of religious commitment, open and ready to enlarge their experiences, believing that faith—like life—is best thought of as a journey, a process rather than a finished product. If they relate at all to traditional belief systems and religious communities, it is in a somewhat detached manner, simply because they are less likely to commit themselves to the point of being controlled by any one way of believing. Consequently, many combine Judeo-Christian beliefs with reincarnation, astrology, and other "New Age" beliefs and practices such as communicating with the dead, exploring psychic powers, and meditating. Many see no inconsistency whatsoever in such syncretism, arguing as did one person we interviewed that he was "primarily Catholic." While telling us that he attends Mass weekly, he said he also belongs to an ecumenical prayer group, and frequently worships at a local evangelical church. This *pastiche* style of religiosity is common, and obviously takes many combinations; what distinguishes it is not any particular constellation of elements—whether liberal or conservative, contemporary or ancient—but the openness and readiness with which it is practiced.

TABLE 6
Religious Styles for Family Attenders and Individual Attenders

	Family Attenders (N=281)	Individual Attenders (N=234)
Definitely believes in God	89%	71%
Prays frequently	80	48
Member of church/synagogue	77	39
Says grace at meals	73	43
View of Jesus (asked only of Christian respondents):		
Shepherd	78	58
Liberator/Challenger	13	31
One should:		
Explore many traditions	49	73
Stick to one faith	40	17
"New Age" beliefs:		
Reincarnation	23	35
Astrology	21	33
Meditation	11	17
Communication with dead	20	27
Psychic powers	63	77

VIEW OF CONGREGATIONS

One crucial way in which the culture of choice operates on religion today has to do with the way in which boomers look upon religious congregations. Already we have seen that individualists are inclined to see the church as something "freely chosen by each person," rather than as something "passed on from generation to generation." Ascriptive loyalties have come under fire, as people have demanded that they be able to make their own decisions about religion. Moreover, as Phillip E. Hammond has argued, the *meaning* of religious involvement itself has undergone a change with increased personal autonomy. His point is that with the exercise of greater choice has come a shift in the meaning of the church in people's lives—away from being collective-expressive to being more individual-expressive.[14] In other words, church has more to do with personal needs and preference, and less to do with social background and group identity.

Using our distinction between family attenders and religious individualists, it should follow that the latter are more likely to hold individual-expressive views of the church. That this is very much the case is evident from a battery of questions, all aimed at deciphering various aspects of how people look upon religious institutions (see Table 7). Here we see that boomers generally look upon church as "something you do if it meets your needs," rather than as a "duty and obligation," but the figures are even more pronounced for the religious individualists—ninety percent of them opting for the more personalized language of needs. The individualists are less inclined to look upon the church as a way of becoming established in the community, and more likely to see the morality espoused by churches and synagogues as restrictive. They are more likely to advance the view that "people have God within them, and hence, churches aren't really necessary." This last item is particularly revealing: one half of the religious individualists holds to a deeply mystical conception of the Deity, and seemingly, a privatized faith largely cut off from, and presumably not dependent upon, organized religion. Though often having little or nothing to do with churches or synagogues, significant numbers of them report belonging to small gatherings, such as Twelve-Step groups, sharing groups, Goddess worship groups, women's groups, and men's groups, that allow them to share their lives and concerns in intimate, and yet often anonymous settings.

Many of the returnees—those who dropped out of congregations but have come back—bring with them a culture of choice which sets them apart from the loyalists. Typically caught up more in the trends toward greater moral freedom and personal autonomy, the returnees speak a

TABLE 7
View of Church

	Family Attenders (N=281)	Individual Attenders (N=234)
Going to church is:		
a duty and obligation.	21%	5%
something you do if it meets your needs.	66	90
Being a church member is an important way to become established in a community.	72	54
The rules about morality preached by churches and synagogues today are just too restrictive.	28	46
People have God within them, so the church isn't really necessary.	16	49

different language from the loyalists, a language more like that of the religious individualists: they speak of "getting my needs met," of "spiritual growth," of "exploring faith," of "working on" aspects of the self, drawing off themes found in both journey theology and recovery theology today. Spirituality is at the center of this more individual-expressive vocabulary. Indeed, we may go so far as to say that spirituality is one of the fundamental concerns that drive some boomers back to congregations. They look for settings that strike them as honest and authentic; for congregations where the concerns for self and for others mesh; where they can receive but also give. They want to do so in hands-on activities, be it in an evangelical-organized abortion counseling center, or on behalf of a social justice cause in a mainline Protestant, Catholic, or Jewish congregation. Denominational heritage is relatively unimportant: far more important is a place where they can find what *they* are looking for. The shift in the meaning of church does not imply that it loses all collective-expressive relevance. Rather, for those who return to religious congregations, belonging to a group or identifying with a cause can take on collective meaning but in a new context—one of individual choice, defined by the participants themselves.[15]

IMPLICATIONS FOR FAMILY, WORK, AND RELIGION

As we have seen from this overview, contemporary cultural trends of individualism and personal autonomy have important consequences for religious meaning and belonging. But what about the larger institutional connections of work, family, and religion? Are there any new, emerging patterns for the future? Several implications would seem to follow.

Family Dynamics

Families are, to use Peter Berger's phrase, "plausibility structures," in the sense that what happens within them affects people's own individual lives and view of the world.[16] Doing religious things together, grace at meals for instance, traditionally has been seen as a source both of family togetherness and of support for individual faith. With higher levels of individualism and personal autonomy within the family, these patterns all change. Religion gets removed from the "family" sector to the "individual" sector—and in the process its role and significance within the family are greatly altered.

One very subtle change, for example, has to do with the influence of spouses. In our analysis of the correlates of religious involvement for boomers, whether or not the spouse is actively involved in a congregation turns out to be one of the strongest predictors. It is true as well that, among those who look upon church or synagogue as a family matter, the influence of spouse is much greater (three times greater, in fact). Obviously religious individualism works against this intrafamily influence, and erodes what has been, and for traditional churchgoers still is, a significant force in bringing families into congregations as functioning units. In the emerging new culture, spouses do play a role, but it is less that of moral and religious guardian of the family, as was often the case in the past, and increasingly that of a mutual inquirer and seeker, in a quest for a faith that "fits" their own lives and family situations.

Plural Lives and Plural Families

With increasing numbers of working women, single-parent families, people remaining single for longer periods of their lives, and perhaps more childless couples, the structural supports for religious individualism within the family appear to be well in place for the future. Lives have become more pluralized in the sense of greater individuality and alternative styles, and so, also, have family patterns. This being the case, congregations will succeed best not by attempting to defend "traditional family" styles, but by providing ministries to singles and divorced groups, and by exploring ways to serve working and career women.

Boomer women do not relate as well as did their mothers to old-style women's organizations in churches; they find these groups often out of touch with their experiences in the contemporary world, and no longer in keeping with their definitions of gender space. Many of the career women and single parents in the Lilly survey, while expressing a reluctance to get involved in the programs that churches typically offer them, at the same time showed considerable interest in religious and spiritual possibilities, and especially in small groups.

The relation of congregations to families might be seen along a gradient, ranging from "social control" at one end to "social support" at the other. "Control" typically means holding up the old normative model of the family as the standard against which all others are judged. "Support" conveys the recognition of a variety of family forms, and relating to each of them in helpful and sustaining ways. Boomers are attracted more to those congregations which emphasize social support and nurturance, which help people to realize their human potential, and which, as D'Antonio says, "draw out the love and caring features of religious teachings."[17]

Plural Theology

As we have seen, both mixed faiths and blended families have an impact upon religious individualism, and in a manner that is unlikely to be modified anytime soon. The impact has to do not just with ideology or outlook. For example, the children of boomers will know less about religious traditions in the years ahead than probably any generation in recent American history. They will have heard about many religions but not know much about any of them. It may be that they will know more about non-Western faiths than about historic Judeo-Christian teachings. In any case, the opportunity for congregations will lie in relating to people in their everyday circumstances, and in recognizing that mixed faiths and blended families are not anomalies, but the way in which many families now know about religion in a global world. Congregations will have to confront the challenge of dealing creatively with religious pluralism and maybe even espousing a theology of religious syncretism.

In sum, the cultural changes in the direction of greater religious individualism within families pose far-reaching changes in the relations of work, family, and religion, yet at the same time open up new challenges for congregations to relate to the individual-expressive aspects of personal identity. Perhaps it is better to view these changes less as a corrosion of old institutions, and more as a possibility for new institutional forms. Contrary to stereotypes, boomers are not opposed to serious commitment, but they do insist that the causes and activities to which they give themselves give expression to their deepest understandings of who they are and of their more cherished relationships—in love, in work, in everyday life.

The real challenge, of course, lies in religious institutions' willingness to move beyond old conceptions of how work, family, and religion fit together, and open themselves up to new possibilities. This will require on the part of congregations a stance of flexibility and adaptation—a willingness to change as institutions—rather than expecting that boomers will change to fit them. As institutions they must break out of their own cultural captivity and search for ways to give expression to more meaningful relationships between people's work lives and family lives and the unities rooted in spiritual experience. Those congregations that can meet the challenge, can accept the boomer culture as it is, and can see in it new possibilities for organizing life in all its beauty and brokenness, may actually find in this generation a source of life and spiritual renewal for themselves.

NOTES

1. Robert Bellah, *et al.*, *Habits of the Heart: Individualism and Commitment in American Life* (Berkeley: University of California Press, 1985).
2. Talcott Parsons, "Christianity and Modern Industrial Society," in *Sociological Theory and Modern Society* (New York: Free Press, 1967), p. 413.
3. Barbara Hargrove, "Family in the White American Protestant Experience," in *Families and Religions*, eds. William D'Antonio and Joan Aldous (Beverly Hills, CA: Sage, 1983); and Wade Clark Roof and William McKinney, *American Mainline Religion: Its Changing Shape and Future* (New Brunswick, NJ: Rutgers University Press, 1987).
4. Phillip E. Hammond, *Religion and Personal Autonomy: The Third Disestablishment in America* (Columbia, SC: University of South Carolina Press, 1992); and Bellah, *et al.*, *Habits of the Heart*.
5. Darwin L. Thomas, ed., *The Religion and Family Connection: Social Science Perspectives* (Provo, UT: Brigham Young University Religious Studies Center, 1988).
6. George Gallup, *The Unchurched American* (Princeton: Princeton Religion Research Center, 1978); and Hammond, *Religion and Personal Autonomy*.
7. Daniel Yankelovich, *New Rules: Searching for Self-Fulfillment in a World Turned Upside Down* (New York: Random House, 1981), pp. 58–62.
8. Yankelovich, *New Rules*, p. 90.

9. There were too few Jews in our sample for a meaningful comparison here.

10. Robert Wuthnow, *Experimentation in American Religion* (Berkeley: University of California Press, 1978), pp. 137–139; and W. Widich Schroeder, "Age Cohorts, the Family Life Cycle, and Participation in the Voluntary Church in America: Implications for Membership Patterns, 1950–2000," *Chicago Theological Seminary Register* 65 (Fall 1975).

11. Judith Stacey, *Brave New Families* (New York: Basic Books, 1990).

12. Reginald W. Bibby, *Fragmented Gods* (Toronto: Irwin, 1987).

13. Wade Clark Roof, *A Generation of Seekers* (San Francisco: Harper, 1993).

14. Hammond, *Religion and Personal Autonomy*.

15. R. Stephen Warner, "Work in Progress toward a New Paradigm for the Sociological Study of Religion in the United States," *American Journal of Sociology* 98, No. 5 (March 1993), pp. 1044–1093.

16. Peter L. Berger, *The Sacred Canopy* (New York: Doubleday, 1967).

17. William V. D'Antonio, and Joan Aldous, *Families and Religions: Conflict and Change in Modern Society* (Beverly Hills: Sage Publications, 1983), p. 106.

4

Work, Family, and Faith

Recent Trends[1]

Bradley R. Hertel

I t is clear that the relationship between work and family has changed significantly over the last half century, especially with the increasing numbers of women entering the paid labor force. What is much less clear is the impact these changes are having in the area of religious belief and participation. In an earlier paper, I explored the relationship among gender, religious identity, and level of participation in the workforce.[2] An interesting and unexpected finding was that single men and women who were religious dropouts had strikingly similar workforce participation, but were very different from people of the same sex with other religious and family statuses. Compared with other men, single apostate males showed *lower* levels of participation in the workforce. Single apostate females, on the other hand, showed *higher* participation than any other group of women, bringing them into close comparison with the single men who had, like them, left the religious affiliation of their childhood for no affiliation at all. These findings for marital status no doubt reflect differences in the importance of the breadwinner role: single men have fewer dependents, may feel less pressure to work full-time, and are unconnected with organized religion, while single women are more in need of employment than married women. However, the parallel pattern for apostasy and employment is by no means intuitively obvious. These findings strongly suggest that movement away from traditional roles in marriage and religious involvement may be part of a larger pattern that includes rejection of still other gender values and roles. Those outside the traditional institutions of family and religion—men and women—may be less likely to uphold the pre-Second World War division of labor that saw men working outside the home and women largely confined to home duties.

The present study further explores the relationship between gender, work, and religion by focusing on ways in which Americans' religiosity is shaped by family life and work experiences. The erosion in membership and attendance among mainline Protestants and Catholics, and the steady influx of women into the workforce since the Second World War across faith traditions are two important changes in American society whose possible relationship has been the subject of a growing number of studies in recent years.[3]

Social scientists have developed a number of hypotheses for understanding the impact of work and occupations on religious participation. The *social class hypothesis* of Demerath and Fukuyama holds that, compared with the lower classes, the upper classes are more inclined to participate in organized religion. Religious participation is an expression of social status and economic security. This hypothesis is rooted in Troeltsch's church-sect distinction, which in turn is widely understood to have derived from Weber's distinction between the priest, who preserves an established religious tradition, and the prophet, whose innovative message challenges the status quo.[4]

The underlying meaning of the link between social class and participation in organized religion has been called into question, however, by research showing that much of this link can be explained by the high involvement of the upper classes in voluntary associations *in general*.[5] Conceivably, gains in social class are likely to be followed by greater involvement in a wide range of voluntary associations—service clubs, political parties, churches—not necessarily by increased religiosity measured in terms of more private matters, such as belief and prayer.

The social class hypothesis was developed at a time when gender differences in religion and other social institutions were quietly ignored by society and by scholars as well. Consequently, although the hypothesis was not explicitly stated in terms of men, there is reason to believe that its early proponents had men in mind. In more recent years, women's participation in many aspects of society, including work and religion, has received increasing attention from social scientists.

The growing interest in women in the workforce has been accompanied by a growing number of studies supporting another hypothesis about the relationships between religion and work: The *workforce hypothesis* predicts that employment *discourages* participation in organized religion, and that gender differences in religiosity are due at least in part to differences in workforce participation. As part of his well-known thesis that privately held "invisible" religion is replacing organized religion in Western society, especially among young, urban, college-educated persons, Luckmann succinctly states the workforce hypothesis: "The degree of involvement in the work processes of modern industrial society correlates negatively with the degree of involvement in church oriented religion."[6]

On the basis of his extensive review of the literature, deVaus provides numerous possible explanations of the workforce hypothesis:

(1) Compared with the unemployed, employed persons have less time that they can spend in organized religion.
(2) Women, especially those who are not employed, may feel left out of society and turn to organized religion for comfort.
(3) The competitive values fostered by participation in the workforce may discourage workers from participating in organized religion.
(4) Individuals not in the workforce may be insulated from secularization as a result of their having fewer contacts with workers undergoing secularization.[7]

To test this hypothesis, deVaus analyzed General Social Science (GSS) data for national random samples of Americans interviewed between 1972 and 1980. He concluded against the workforce hypothesis for both men and women. Instead, he found support for the social class hypothesis, but only for men. For them, level of participation in the workforce (unemployed, part-time, full-time) as well as education and occupational prestige were found to be positively related to church and synagogue attendance. The more firmly a man had established himself in the status hierarchy through education and full-time employment in a prestigious job, the more he attended religious services. For women, no clear pattern emerged between attendance and level of involvement in the workforce. Later summarizing these findings, deVaus and McAllister observed, "in the United States...workforce participation does not appear to affect female religious orientation."[8] Similarly, in her study of gender, work, and attendance in Canada, Gee found some support for the social class hypothesis and, as in deVaus's study, this support was appreciably stronger for men than for women.[9]

Old patterns do not disappear quickly. Discernable links between participation in the workforce and in organized religion are still largely links between the status and religious participation *of males*. It is possible, however, that women in America are at a crossroads in which the impact on religion made by social class—as defined in terms of their husbands' education, occupation, and income—is giving way to a new era in which women's religiosity is coming to be affected more by their own, increased, workforce participation. For women, the patterns described by the social class hypothesis may have been offset by a growing relevance of the workforce hypothesis but not yet replaced by new patterns. Such a turning point and offsetting crosscurrents would account for deVaus's finding support for neither hypothesis for American women.

There is some evidence, in fact, that the link between social class and religion is declining in general. Roof and McKinney have concluded that nonaffiliation is no longer clearly associated with low levels of education and status. They report a decline in attendance among the college-educated. Whereas at midcentury, better-educated Americans were decidedly more inclined to attend religious services, by the late 1980s there were only "slight differences in participation across education levels."[10]

A recent study in Australia has helped to shed new light on the relationships among work, family, and religion. DeVaus and McAllister found that gender differences in religiosity can be accounted for in part by women's lower workforce participation. They concluded: "Females who work full-time are less religious than their counterparts who are full-time housewives"[11] This was the case with four measures of religiosity—attendance, commitment, belief, and religious experience. These findings imply that no single explanation of the workforce hypothesis can account for its relevance to Australian society. If the temporal demands of employment—rather than shifts toward secular worldviews—were largely responsible for lower attendance, we might expect to find work to have resulted in reduced attendance but not necessarily reduced levels of belief and religious experience of working women. And if external employment erodes religiosity through modernization of worldviews, we might expect to find lower belief among working women but not necessarily lower attendance.

It may be that the various explanations of the workforce hypothesis—time constraints, secularization, and differences in need for social interaction—are each relevant for different segments of the population or at different stages in the withdrawal from organized religion. The forces that affect belief may not be the same as those that affect attendance. Different forces may be at work among part-time workers and full-time ones. The variables that separate nonattenders from attenders may be different from those that affect levels of participation among those who attend. And these factors may combine with each other in a variety of ways. For example, some unemployed women may be regular attenders with secular worldviews; on entering the workforce these women might be ideologically predisposed to reduce their level of attendance and might choose to do so after taking on the demands of a full-time job. For other women, these changes may occur in reverse order: employment may result in tighter schedules, lower attendance and less re-enforcement of traditional beliefs and values, the end result being secular worldviews.

We have hints in the research already available that fine-tuning of predictions will be necessary if we are to understand the relationship between religion and workforce participation. For instance, in Gee's study, *among attenders*, workforce participation did decrease women's religious participation, a finding that stands in contrast to deVaus's study—that included nonattenders. Perhaps the forces at work among attenders are different from those at work among nonattenders. While deVaus described his findings as showing no relationship between American women's workforce participation and their attendance of religious services, strictly speaking, he found no *monotonic* relationship. Women with part-time jobs showed higher levels of attendance than women with either full-time jobs or no jobs.[12] Previous studies suggest that no simple work-religion hypothesis will do. There may well be a threshold in workforce participation for married women, after which what begins as a positive relationship between work and religious attendance reverses, so that further increases in hours worked result in decreased attendance.

And what about the impact of children? DeVaus and McAllister looked for but found no gender differences in the impact of child-rearing on religiosity. This finding is somewhat surprising, in that women have traditionally been the chief child-rearers and men the chief breadwinners: movement of women into the workforce could be expected to have resulted in changes in the salience of women's identity with motherhood and, in turn, might have affected the links between parenthood and religiosity. The present study will further explore the relevance of parenthood to religiosity.

TESTING THE WORKFORCE AND SOCIAL CLASS HYPOTHESES
Time of Study and Source of Data
This report is based on data from the 1972 through 1990 *General Social Surveys*, which were conducted each year of that period except 1979 and 1981 by the National Opinion Research Center (NORC).[13] This is a particularly appropriate period for our purposes, because women's movement into the workforce and from part-time to full-time jobs continued throughout this period not only for women in general (Figure 1) but for married women including mothers (Figure 2). Further, as deVaus showed, a great deal of the decline in attendance among women between the Second World War and 1980 occurred after 1972.[14] The GSS data provide opportunity to study much of the post-Second World War period, including the years of particularly rapid decline in attendance and membership.

There are still other reasons for using GSS data to address the questions of the present study. One is the opportunity to replicate deVaus's study using the GSS data for the surveys to which he had access, 1972 through 1980, as well as for the more recent decade. Second, data for a common set of questions for nearly twenty consecutive years make it possible to study social change in such a way as to measure cohort effects. A major goal of this study is to determine the influences of the baby boomer generation. The sheer size of the generation of Americans born between 1945 and 1965 may have been the leading factor in the 1950s growth in church and synagogue attendance. At that time, during their childhood, large numbers of baby boomers were at a stage of life that has historically been associated with high levels of participation in organized religion. As Roof and McKinney point out, however, when this segment of the population entered late adolescence and young adulthood—periods that have long been associated with low involvement in organized religion—attendance trends reversed. Not only the

FIGURE 1

Trends in Work Status of White Women, 1972–1990

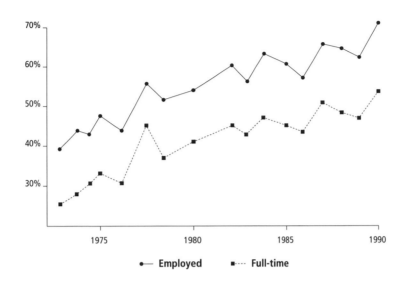

FIGURE 2

Trends in Full-Time Employment of Married White Women, 1972–1990

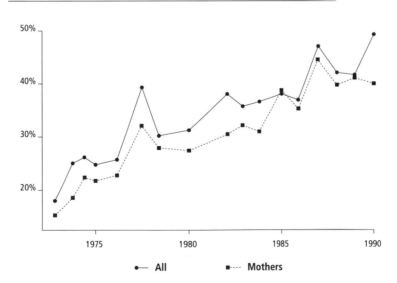

boomers themselves but many of their parents dropped back to lower involvement in organized religion, particularly in mainline denominations. The declines came first in attendance at Sunday School, then in attendance at services, and eventually in membership.[15] Further aging of the baby-boomers quite possibly set the stage for a swing back toward active participation in organized religion.[16] As parents of the next generation, the boomers could lead the way in a return to organized religion prompted by concern that their own children receive religious training. And, say Roof and McKinney, "some are returning to church, although it seems unlikely they will come back in large numbers."[17]

While demographics account for much of the baby-boomers' influence on organized religion in America, this generation has also shaped religion through a distinctive cohort subculture, characterized by tolerance of individual differences and respect for freedom of choice.[18] Recent young adults' acceptance of alternatives in lifestyles and values might make them less inclined to repeat the age-related patterns of attendance and affiliation characteristic of earlier generations. If so, change over the life course in the religiosity of baby-boomers may be more varied and less predictable than for earlier generations. In turn, assessing baby-boomers' impact on overall attendance and on any other aspects of religion in the U.S. may be difficult. Nonetheless, by closely examining the ties between family, work, and religion for multiple generations, we will attempt to learn more about the long-term effects boomers have had on religion in America.

Sample

The present study is confined to white Americans between the ages of twenty-one and sixty-five, who are not widowed, retired, or temporarily unemployed. These restrictions make the analysis comparable with that in deVaus's study,[19] and are desirable for other reasons too. Limiting the study to adults of working age who are not retired reflects our interest in the effects of employment. The small number of temporarily unemployed persons were excluded because of their ambiguous work status. The reality of racial differences are apparent both in the existence of an identifiable black church and in divergent family and employment patterns. Documenting the effects of these differences would require separate analysis of data for blacks and other nonwhites which is well beyond the scope of the present study. Widowed persons have been excluded in order to have a clear distinction between those who are married and those who are unmarried (that is, never married, separated, or divorced). From the seventeen surveys conducted between

1972 and 1990, data for a total of 10,100 to 15,800 individuals have been included in this study; differences are due to variations in the number of years that various measures of religiosity have been included in the General Social Surveys, as well as to variations in response rates to individual questions in each survey.

ANALYSIS

My central concern in this study is the relationship between work and attendance, particularly among women. I wish to reexamine deVaus's conclusion that these are unrelated among American women. Membership in a congregation, strength of religious identity with a church or denomination, and membership in one or more nonreligious voluntary associations will also be studied for possible links to work and family. A battery of measures of religiosity will be used to test the work-force hypothesis so that, if support is obtained, it might be possible to learn more about the ways in which work reduces religiosity. Low rates of regular attendance among full-time workers would provide support for the hypothesis but, without other analysis, might not result in an explanation of why such support was found. If employment encourages more secular worldviews, which in turn lead to declines in numbers of people who regularly attend religious services, then we should also find that employment is related to low membership and low levels of identity with religious organizations.[20] If support for the workforce hypothesis is obtained because workers have little free time, we can expect to find work to be associated with low levels of membership and attendance in all kinds of voluntary associations—religious and secular alike. On the other hand, for secularization to be the underlying cause of support for the workforce hypothesis, we would expect to find that religious membership has declined appreciably more than membership in non-religious organizations. The social class hypothesis will be judged to gain support to the extent that participation in the workforce is found to be positively related to participation in organized religion. While measures of education, occupational prestige, and income would provide more direct measures of social class, these measures are generally positively related to workforce participation, whose effects on religiosity are the focus of this study.

Other Predictors

Religiosity and membership in extrareligious voluntary associations will be examined in terms of their relationships with gender, marital status, number of children, work status, year of interview, birth cohort, and generation effects. To separate the effects of time of study and birth cohort, we have determined the average impact of a one-year increase in year of interview and year of birth on attendance and membership. Then, following guidelines developed by Firebaugh and Davis, we have calculated the total impact of year of birth and interview on religiosity and membership in secular organizations.[21] Details of these procedures will be discussed below.

FINDINGS

We begin by looking at the movement of women into the workforce and into positions of full-time employment. Have women steadily increased their participation in the workforce since 1972? In Figures 1 and 2 we see that the growth in employment and full-time employment of women has been steady throughout the entire period of study. The proportion of white women employed one or more hours a week has approximately doubled, from about thirty-seven percent in 1972 to more than seventy percent by 1990. The proportion of women employed full-time also has doubled, from about twenty-seven percent to fifty-three percent; (see Figure 1). Comparison of Figure 1 for all women and Figure 2 for married women shows that single women continue to be employed at significantly higher rates than married women. However, the rate of increase in full-time employment has been higher for married women: for them, the proportion employed full-time has more than doubled. This is true for all married women, as well as for all married mothers (see Figure 2).

To test the workforce and social class hypotheses, we will start by considering levels of religiosity, without taking changes across the period into account. In Table 1, means for attendance and other measures are presented for men and women, sorted by marital and work status and by number of children. Analysis for men and women was conducted separately. Among the findings:

(1) Marriage is positively related to all three measures of religiosity, but unrelated to membership in nonreligious organizations. Married men and women were found to be decidedly more inclined than their single counterparts to belong to churches and synagogues, to attend religious services, and to have strong religious identities. Each of these relationships was found to be statistically significant at the .001 level (2-tailed test). For both men and women, marital status was found to be unrelated to membership in nonreligious organizations.

TABLE 1

Religion and Voluntary Association Membership by Sex, Work Status, Marital Status, and Number of Children, Controlling for Age, Region and Urban, Whites Only[a]

A. Percent Belonging to a Church or Other Religious Organization, 1974–1990

| Work Status | Single | | Married | |
	Men	Women	Men	Women
Unemployed	19.0	27.0	21.3	40.8
No children	17.5	27.6	19.3	36.1
1-2 children	20.5	27.4	23.0	41.7
3 or more	—	25.2	25.4	50.6
Part-time	24.0	30.6	33.5	47.8
No children	21.8	27.3	35.6	45.0
1-2 children	—	32.0	32.8	46.1
3 or more	—	—	26.2	61.7
Full-time	21.6	33.9	31.9	38.2
No children	19.5	34.1	29.0	32.3
1-2 children	23.5	30.6	33.1	42.8
3 or more	—	26.5	39.4	43.5
ALL	21.8	32.0	31.0	40.8

| | Significant Main and Interaction Effects | |
	Men	Women
MARITAL	***	***
CHILDREN	***	***
WORK	**	**
MARITAL X CHILDREN	N/s	***
CHILDREN X WORK	N/s	*

(2) For both men and women, number of children is also positively related to all three measures of religiosity. Among women, number of children is related to membership in a nonreligious organization as well, but that was not the case for men. In addition, for women only, there is an interaction effect of marital status and number of children for all four measures: for married women, the effect of number of children is clearly to *increase* involvement in religion and secular organizations. For single women, the effects of children are weaker and variable.

That number of children is positively related to married women's reli-

TABLE 1 (continued)

B. Percent Attending Religious Services at Least Once a Week, 1972-1990

Work Status	Single		Married	
	Men	Women	Men	Women
Unemployed	15.0	23.1	21.8	36.0
No children	11.6	23.2	20.9	29.0
1-2 children	16.9	22.8	21.4	38.6
3 or more	—	24.4	28.8	46.0
Part-time	20.8	24.5	22.1	40.1
No children	19.0	21.0	19.4	38.4
1-2 children	14.1	20.7	30.4	37.7
3 or more	—	54.2	14.7	54.2
Full-time	17.7	29.9	25.0	30.4
No children	14.5	30.2	21.8	27.5
1-2 children	19.9	25.2	26.2	32.3
3 or more	19.7	32.3	34.4	33.0
ALL	17.5	28.1	24.7	34.5

	Significant Main and Interaction Effects	
	Men	Women
MARITAL	***	***
CHILDREN	***	***
WORK	N/s	**
MARITAL X CHILDREN	N/s	**
MARITAL X WORK	N/s	***
CHILDREN X WORK	N/s	***

gious membership and participation, regardless of workforce status, recalls other findings on the ways in which married women's lives *do not* change when they enter the workforce. Nock and Kingston found that women's increased participation in the workforce has done little to diminish their role as primary child-rearers.[22] And Huber and Spitze found that external employment of wives had not resulted in major shifts toward equal sharing in housework and decision-making by husbands and wives.[23] Here we find that the more children a woman has, the more involved in religious and secular organizations she is.

Married women's involvement in religion and extrareligious organizations clearly peaks among the part-time employed.[24] This finding suggests that, for many married women, part-time employment repre-

TABLE 1 (continued)

C. Percent Who Strongly Identify with a Church, Denomination, or Other Religious Body, 1974-1990

Work Status	Single		Married	
	Men	Women	Men	Women
Unemployed	26.1	36.8	36.2	45.6
No children	23.8	38.1	39.4	42.4
1-2 children	28.9	36.8	36.3	45.4
3 or more	30.1	33.4	31.6	53.3
Part-time	33.1	38.2	37.3	48.0
No children	33.2	40.8	34.1	50.9
1-2 children	21.3	32.0	44.8	42.8
3 or more	—	44.6	32.6	59.2
Full-time	28.4	40.0	34.0	40.8
No children	25.9	42.5	33.0	38.7
1-2 children	32.6	35.1	33.2	42.6
3 or more	38.0	31.5	41.6	42.7
ALL	27.9	39.5	34.5	44.1

	Significant Main and Interaction Effects	
	Men	Women
MARITAL	***	***
CHILDREN	**	**
WORK	N/s	*
MARITAL X CHILDREN	N/s	**
CHILDREN X WORK	N/s	*

sents a kind of balance between the old norm of women remaining in the home and the new norm of their being employed outside the home.

For men also—regardless of marital status—membership, attendance, and strength of religious identity were found to be similar for the part-time employed as for other men. Gender differences remain, however. Unlike married women, married men are slightly more likely to attend services regularly if they are employed full-time. And—also in contrast to married women—single women and all men are more likely to belong to a secular association the higher their involvement in the workforce. In these respects, men show some support for the social class hypothesis. But it is single women who provide the strongest support for that hypothesis: Their rates of membership, attendance, religious

TABLE 1 (continued)

D. Percent Belonging to a Nonreligious Voluntary Association, 1974-1990

Work Status	Single		Married	
	Men	Women	Men	Women
Unemployed	62.2	43.9	60.6	53.0
No children	65.9	50.2	60.5	45.3
1-2 children	48.3	39.5	62.6	54.3
3 or more	—	38.4	55.8	66.7
Part-time	65.0	63.3	57.0	65.4
No children	68.2	66.2	56.4	59.8
1-2 children	—	57.5	61.8	65.6
3 or more	—	63.7	48.4	78.1
Full-time	71.5	68.2	76.1	62.0
No children	71.8	69.7	75.1	58.8
1-2 children	70.0	62.3	76.5	62.9
3 or more	71.1	64.4	76.6	68.5
ALL	70.6	59.4	73.5	59.2

	Significant Main and Interaction Effects	
	Men	Women
MARITAL	N/s	N/s
CHILDREN	N/s	***
WORK	***	***
MARITAL X CHILDREN	N/s	***
CHILDREN X WORK	N/s	**

a. Analysis excludes persons who are retired, temporarily unemployed, and younger than 21 or older than 65. Findings are not reported for cells containing fewer than 20 cases.

    *   =   significant at .05 level
   **   =   significant at .01 level
 ***   =   significant at .001 level

identity, and membership in secular organizations all increase with increased participation in the workforce. The positive impact of work on religious and nonreligious organizations alike fits Mueller and Johnson's revision of the social class hypothesis. They suggest that class has a positive impact on participation in voluntary associations in general and, therefore, on organized religion.[25]

Qualified support for the work-force hypothesis was obtained for married women as well as for single and married men. However, it is *full-time* employment, not employment *per se*, that appears to discourage religious participation. In that married women, but not men, are also less active in secular organizations if employed full-time, the workforce hypothesis can be said to hold more for them than for any other group. For many married women, the shift to full-time employment may have upset the balance represented by part-time employment. That the workforce hypothesis is supported in part because of time pressures is suggested by full-time-employed married women's reduced levels of membership in religious and nonreligious organizations, and by their markedly lower rate of regular attendance (forty percent for part-time versus thirty percent for full-time employed). However, secularization may also play a role in this decreased religious involvement: Full-time employed married women are much less likely than the part-time employed to be members (thirty-eight percent versus forty-eight percent) but only slightly less inclined than the part-time employed to belong to a nonreligious organization (sixty-two percent versus sixty-five percent). In order to clarify the extent to which support for the workforce hypothesis may be due to secularization from time spent in the work setting, more research is needed on the number and kinds of extrareligious organizations working women are leaving, and which attachments they are preserving.

More research is also needed on the bearing of men's employment on their participation in organized religion. The finding that membership and religious identity are actually higher for part-time than for full-time employed men runs counter to the social class hypothesis. It suggests that, just as married women appear to have experienced disruption of balance in roles, men may also be experiencing tension between an earlier norm based on a link between status and religious participation and new norms linking religious participation with available time. If so, it is likely that the negative impact of work on married men's involvement in organized religion is strongly influenced by the increased workforce participation of their wives. The wealth of data at our disposal make it possible to test this hypothesis. Before doing so, however, we wish to look more at the impact of children on the relationship between work and religiosity.

The relevance of full-time employment and children to involvement in organized religion and extrareligious organizations is the subject of Table 2. Here, these two background characteristics are combined in such a way as to enable us to take ages of children in the household into account. A full-time job and children each represents a demand on one's time, and there is reason to expect that individuals—especially women—who face both of these obligations will be less active in religion and other organizations than those who are either not employed full-time or who are employed full-time but have no children. Young children are likely to be associated with low attendance rates. Once children reach school age, however, there may be a shift from the time pressure of caring for small children to social pressure to provide religious instruction.[26] Meanwhile, parents who have become concerned that their school-aged children receive religious training may increase their own involvement in organized religion.

Recall from Table 1 that involvement in organized religion is lowest for single men, higher for married men, still higher—but only slightly—for single women, and by far the highest for married women. Men are much more likely than women to belong to one or more nonreligious organizations. And, unlike religious organizations, secular organizations attract men more than women, no matter what the marital status. Presence and ages of children clearly affect these relationships, as shown in Table 2. Here, we see that—compared with other married persons—married men and women with full-time jobs and no children are less active in organized religion. For married men, participation in organized religion is lowest among those with no children, and then gradually rises with the arrival and aging of children. For married women, however, presence of young children is related to increased religious membership, but does not result in increased attendance. Instead, for them, the positive impact of children on attendance appears to be delayed until children reach school age. Similarly, married women's identity with religious organizations is lowest among those with only preschool children. Membership in secular organizations is also lowest for married women who are full-time employed and have only preschool children. These findings suggest that the demands of parenting delay the positive impact of parenthood on the religious participation of full-time employed married women until children are of school age.

The pressures of time and social expectations work very differently among single women than among any other group. Compared with single women having children or without a full-time job, those with full-time jobs and no children are the most active in organized religion, and show the highest rate of membership in one or more extrareligious organizations. Like married men, they are more likely to be members of a religious organization than are those who are not full-time employed. These findings provide qualified support of the social class

TABLE 2

Religion and Voluntary Association Membership by Sex, Work Status, Marital Status, and Number of Children, Controlling for Age, Region and Urban, Whites Only*

A. Percent Belonging to a Church or Other Religious Organization, 1974–1990

Work & Children	Single		Married	
	Men	Women	Men	Women
Not fulltime	19.35	27.25	25.75	43.43
Full and no children	19.65	33.57	28.97	32.57
Full and LT 6 years	9.65	33.32	31.56	38.47
Full and LT 6 + older	—	31.91	37.59	45.77
Full and GE 6 only	—	28.59	35.04	43.49

B. Percent Attending Religious Services at Least Once a Week, 1972–1990

Work & Children	Single		Married	
	Men	Women	Men	Women
Not fulltime	15.53	22.18	22.13	38.08
Full and no children	15.11	29.26	21.24	28.05
Full and LT 6 years	8.60	20.27	26.96	26.50
Full and LT 6 + older	26.80	20.17	29.74	34.02
Full and GE 6 only	21.17	25.66	28.65	33.16

C. Percent Strongly Identifying with a Religious Body, 1974-1990

Work & Children	Single		Married	
	Men	Women	Men	Women
Not fulltime	28.63	36.23	36.27	46.88
Full and no children	26.86	41.84	31.56	39.15
Full and LT 6 years	—	39.04	36.11	36.63
Full and LT 6 + older	—	32.01	39.29	43.56
Full and GE 6 only	37.36	33.05	33.91	43.54

D. Percent Belonging to a Nonreligious Voluntary Association, 1974-1990

Work & Children	Single		Married	
	Men	Women	Men	Women
Not fulltime	62.07	49.26	60.09	56.64
Full and no children	70.98	69.48	76.51	59.35
Full and LT 6 years	—	52.16	72.59	54.42
Full and LT 6 + older	—	58.06	74.87	69.37
Full and GE 6 only	72.73	65.19	79.48	65.54

*Analysis excludes retired persons, temporarily unemployed, and younger than 21 or older than 65. Findings are not reported for cells containing fewer than 20 cases. LT = less than; GE = greater than or equal to hypothesis for single women: Their attendance at services is encouraged by full-time employment, but only in the absence of children; for single women with full-time jobs, presence of children is associated with *reduced* attendance at religious services.

The comparatively high levels of involvement in organized religion among single women with full-time jobs and no children contrasts with the low involvement of married women and men with full-time jobs and no children. This involvement may reflect single women's need for social support, and their ability to contribute time and energy to civic pursuits. In contrast, single women *with* children may feel discouraged from participating in religion in part because of time pressures, but possibly economic and social ones as well. By contrast, among married persons of either sex, having children represents conformity to social norms and, in turn, encourages their involvement in religion. The limited sample of single men sorted by ages of children was inadequate for assessing their patterns.

THE EFFECTS OF SOCIAL CHANGE

Having examined the complex ways in which marital status, family status, and workforce participation are interrelated with religious membership, attendance, identification, and nonreligious community memberships, we turn now to consider these relationships over time. Recall that we have data spanning the period 1972 to 1990. The seventeen annual surveys merged into a single data set include responses from people born from 1909 through 1969.[27] To separate the effects of the passage of time from the effects of birth cohort, we have followed guidelines provided by Firebaugh and Davis.[28] Year of study and year of birth will be used to find the rates (raw *betas*, or unstandardized regression coefficients) of change in attendance, membership, and so on, associated with a one-year passage of time or one year's later birth cohort, each controlling for the other.[29]

Firebaugh's and Davis's procedures are well suited for the present study, and will be used to distinguish between change in commitment to religion due to the replacement of older, possibly more conservative, cohorts by new cohorts and society-wide change that cuts across birth cohorts.[30] These cohort and year effects will then be reexamined, after controlling for the work experiences of the individuals in this study, in order to address the question: Do differences in religiosity that can be attributed to the passing of older cohorts and the passing of time disappear when the role of workforce participation is considered? If so, then it is change in workforce participation which accounts for differences between earlier and later birth cohorts, earlier and later years. Alternatively, to the extent that cohort and year effects remain after controlling for employment, these changes are due to other causes.

To move beyond a simple summarizing of cohort and year effects for the arbitrary period 1972 through 1990, we will look for these effects within three generations (that is, "macrocohorts" which are groups of birth cohorts, or "microcohorts"): the *pre-baby-boomers*, born between 1909 and 1945; *early boomers*, born between 1946 and 1957, the year the birthrate peaked; and *late and post-boomers*, born between 1958 and 1969.[31] By sorting the total sample into these three generations and repeating the analysis, we hope to learn whether the impact of time and birth cohort differs from one generation to the next in ways that support the widely held belief that baby-boomers are distinct in values and behavior from other generations.[32]

Roof and McKinney's conclusion that the baby-boomers are distinctive in religiosity provides reason to expect that employment may affect religiosity differently in each of the above broad cohorts. From pre- to early to late and post-boomers, we expect to find successively stronger support for the workforce hypothesis for women. This prediction is based on the reasoning that, compared with the much smaller female workforce in the past, women of later birth cohorts and women interviewed in more recent years are more likely to have experienced conflict between work and religion. Increasing numbers of working women mean that their concerns and constraints gain more currency and legitimacy in the culture. There may be more recognition of their need to cut back on activities, and less social stigma associated with not belonging to a religious organizaion. In addition, rise in the prevalence of female-headed families and of two-earner couples, and the continued income disparity between men and women imply that many women who enter the workforce today are responding more to their financial needs than to ideological changes. Especially if women are being *constrained* to work rather than *choosing* to do so, they may well find themselves with reduced free time and energy, and feel a need to cut back on other activities, including organized religion. In short, one set of temporal constraints may result in others.

The figures in Table 3 are unstandardized regression coefficients, also known as "raw *betas*," indicating the average annual increase or decrease in the percent of respondents who are members, attend regularly, and so on, and the annual change associated with a one-year increase in birth cohort. In other words—looking at column 1 of panel A on membership—taking into account the effect of birth cohort on membership, for

TABLE 3

Unstandardized Regression Coefficients (b) of Religion and Voluntary Association Membership on Year and Year of Birth, Controlling for the Other [odd-numbered columns], as well as Employment, and Spouse's Employment [even-numbered columns] by Marital Status, Sex, and Generation

A. Church Membership

| | Single | | | | Married | | | |
| | Men | | Women | | Men | | Women | |
	(1)	(2)	(3)	(4)	(5)	(6)	(7)	(8)
ALL								
Year	-.291	-.329	.257	.236	.077	.149	.222	.408*
Birth	-.123	-.106	-.309***	-.376***	-.486***	-.481***	-.460***	-.541***
PRE-BOOMERS								
Year	-.681	-.670	.485	.467	-.458	-.350	-.256	-.013
Birth	.071	.023	-.460	-.474	-.339*	-.371**	-.041	-.227
EARLY BOOMERS								
Year	-.403	-.421	.125	.072	.668*	.722*	.944**	1.026***
Birth	-.731	-.725	-.228	-.183	-.295	-.296	-1.469***	-1.397***
LATE & POST-BOOMERS								
Year	.314	.239	-.529	-.589	3.896**	3.869**	3.014**	2.996**
Birth	-.712	-.598	-.684	-.472	-1.930	-1.744	-.592	-.587

TABLE 3 (continued)

B. Church Attendance

	Single				Married			
	Men		Women		Men		Women	
	(1)	(2)	(3)	(4)	(5)	(6)	(7)	(8)
ALL								
Year	-.331	-.334	.321	.294	.423*	.513**	.585***	.713***
Birth	-.152	-.150	-.552***	-.535***	-.316***	-.305***	-.490***	-.495***
PRE-BOOMERS								
Year	-.732	-.724	.947*	.917*	.226	.344	.510*	.600**
Birth	-.329	-.362	-.772**	-.797***	-.156	-.167	-.349**	-.367**
EARLY BOOMERS								
Year	-.353	-.280	-.010	-.073	.841**	.906**	.784**	.882**
Birth	-1.221*	-1.246*	-.198	-.143	-.352	-.380	-1.072**	-.993*
LATE & POST-BOOMERS								
Year	-.196	-.217	-1.525	-1.577	-.367	-.254	.632	.911
Birth	.006	.038	.705	.892	1.773	1.973	-.407	-.609

TABLE 3 (continued)

C. Strength of Religious Identity

	Single				Married			
	Men		Women		Men		Women	
	(1)	(2)	(3)	(4)	(5)	(6)	(7)	(8)
ALL								
Year	-.420	-.424	.423	.418	.587**	.677***	.674***	.759***
Birth	-.005	-.003	-.530***	-.527***	-.309***	-.295***	-.570***	-.574***
PRE-BOOMERS								
Year	-.830	-.821	1.377**	1.376**	.547*	.646**	.470*	.581*
Birth	-.034	-.073	-.811**	-.812**	-.140	-.146	-.510***	-.561***
EARLY BOOMERS								
Year	-.033	-.072	-.021	-.018	.587	.718*	1.113***	1.169***
Birth	-.651	-.638	-.906	-.872	.037	-.078	-0.927*	-0.890*
LATE & POST-BOOMERS								
Year	-2.803*	-2.557*	-2.647*	-2.642*	.004	.193	-.250	.068
Birth	.566	.190	.254	.237	1.409	1.558	-1.317	-1.537

TABLE 3 (continued)

D. Non-Religious Association Membership

| | Single | | | | Married | | | |
| | Men | | Women | | Men | | Women | |
	(1)	(2)	(3)	(4)	(5)	(6)	(7)	(8)
ALL								
Year	.014	-.078	.222	.154	-.027	-.014	-.218	-.148
Birth	-.105	-.064	-.015	.030	-.282***	-.290***	.022	-.075
PRE-BOOMERS								
Year	-.611	-.596	-.168	-.223	-.280	-.182	-.836***	-.732***
Birth	-.226	-.291	.028	-.017	-.075	-.126	.568***	.419***
EARLY BOOMERS								
Year	.277	.005	.606	.427	.577*	.522	1.125***	1.068***
Birth	.966	1.056	-.831	-.676	-1.490***	-1.389**	-1.638***	-1.622***
LATE & POST-BOOMERS								
Year	2.524*	2.525*	.354	.181	2.171	1.793	2.963**	3.011**
Birth	-1.323	-1.325	.445	1.059	-3.198	-3.224*	-3.312**	-3.334**

* = significant at .05 level
** = significant at .01 level
*** = significant at .001 level

successively later years, single men had a membership rate 0.291 percent lower, on average, than for the previous year. Likewise, taking year of survey into account, each later birth cohort of single men had a membership rate 0.123 percent lower, on average, than the previous year's cohort. Figures in the even-numbered columns are for these same variables but with further controls added for workforce participation and, for the married, workforce participation of spouse. Analysis was done separately for single men, single women, married men, and married women. For now we will confine discussion to the odd-numbered columns, and later will consider the employment effects.

By multiplying the rates of change by the relevant number of years, one can arrive at the total change associated with year of study (YEAR) and birth cohort (BIRTH). These figures derived from the rates in Table 3 are presented in Table 4. For example, between 1974 and 1990, membership among single men declined 4.65 percent (column 1 of panel A of Table 4). This figure reflects the 0.291 percent average annual decline reported in Table 3 multiplied by the sixteen years for which that average was found to hold.[33]

Attendance at religious services has declined appreciably since the 1950s. The findings in Tables 3 and 4 provide some understanding of the nature of this decline and, in turn, of the likelihood of a reversal. Examination of congregational membership over time for all single men reveals that for them the decline is attributable to both year and birth cohort. However, when these patterns are reexamined within each macrocohort, we see that for the preboomers the decline is attributable only to year, for early boomers to both, and for late and post-boomers only to cohort. None of these findings is statistically significant, but the large negative coefficients for birth cohort for the early and late boomers point toward the possibility of a long-lasting decline. People born since the Second World War are simply less likely to join religious organizations than are their older counterparts.

As Firebaugh and Davis note, change attributable to cohort replacement[34] tends to be longer lasting than change associated with the societywide trends tapped by year effects. This is because whatever leads a society to move *en masse* in one direction is evidence of potential for broad-based change which in the future could be in the opposite direction; the numerous Republican victories in Presidential elections since the landslide Democratic victory in 1964 illustrate this point. Change that comes about through cohort replacement is more likely to be long-lasting because, in rejecting current societal norms, later-born cohorts show themselves to be more committed to those new values. Thus, in

TABLE 4

Differences in Religion and Voluntary Association Membership Attributable to Year and Year of Birth, Controlling for the Other [odd-numbered columns] as well as for Employment and Spouse's Employment [even-numbered columns] by Marital Status, Sex, and Generation

A. Church Membership

| | Single | | | | Married | | | |
| | Men | | Women | | Men | | Women | |
	(1)	(2)	(3)	(4)	(5)	(6)	(7)	(8)
ALL								
Year	-4.65	-5.26	4.11	3.77	1.23	2.39	3.56	6.53*
Birth	-1.81	-1.55	-5.44***	-5.25***	-7.67***	-7.59***	-7.30***	-8.58***
Fulltime job		3.85		5.96*		7.18*		-5.27***
Spouse fulltime job						-6.36***		12.24***
PRE-BOOMERS								
Year	-10.90	-10.72	7.77	7.48	-7.34	-5.61	-4.09	-.22
Birth	.47	.16	-3.53	-3.65	-2.87*	-3.14**	-.25	-1.41
Fulltime job		9.46		6.91		10.49**		-3.68
Spouse fulltime job						-5.89*		12.07***
EARLY BOOMERS								
Year	-6.44	-6.73	2.00	1.16	10.69*	11.54*	15.10**	16.42***
Birth	.73	-.72	-.46	-.37	-.84	-.85	-4.06***	-3.86***
Fulltime job		.86		5.62		.24		-8.33**
Spouse fulltime job						-7.64		7.24
LATE & POST-BOOMERS								
Year	3.14	2.39	-5.29	-5.89	38.96**	38.69**	30.14**	29.96***
Birth	-4.31	-3.62	-3.33	-2.30	-6.95	-6.28	-2.27	-2.25
Fulltime job		2.61		5.81		2.80		-4.84
Spouse fulltime job						-4.32		8.35

TABLE 4 (continued)

B. Church Attendance

| | Single | | | | Married | | | |
| | Men | | Women | | Men | | Women | |
	(1)	(2)	(3)	(4)	(5)	(6)	(7)	(8)
ALL								
Year	-5.95	-6.02	5.78	5.29	7.62*	9.23**	10.54***	12.83***
Birth	-2.22	-2.19	-9.47***	-9.16***	-5.68***	-5.66***	-9.47***	-9.59***
Fulltime job		.37		7.55**		2.20		-8.42***
Spouse fulltime job						7.74***		4.55*
PRE-BOOMERS								
Year	-13.18	-13.04	17.05*	16.51*	4.07	6.19	9.19*	10.80**
Birth	-2.32	-2.56	-6.60**	-6.81***	-1.51	-1.62	-2.76**	-2.89**
Fulltime job		6.62		11.44**		5.40		-6.00**
Spouse fulltime job						-7.49**		2.57
EARLY BOOMERS								
Year	-6.36	-5.04	-.18	-1.32	15.13**	16.31**	14.11**	15.87**
Birth	-2.74*	-2.79*	-.65	-.47	-1.48	-1.60	-3.52**	-3.25*
Fulltime job		-3.49		6.76		-2.91		-9.62***
Spouse fulltime job						-7.04*		7.16
LATE & POST-BOOMERS								
Year	-1.96	-2.17	-15.25	-15.77	-3.67	-2.54	6.32	9.11
Birth	.04	.23	3.43	4.35	6.38	7.10	-1.56	-2.34
Fulltime job		7.74		5.15		-3.74		-17.89***
Spouse fulltime job						-13.49*		4.64

TABLE 4 (continued)

C. Strength of Religious Identity

| | Single | | | | Married | | | |
| | Men | | Women | | Men | | Women | |
	(1)	(2)	(3)	(4)	(5)	(6)	(7)	(8)
ALL								
Year	-6.71	-6.78	6.76	6.68	9.39**	10.84***	10.79***	12.14***
Birth	-.07	-.05	-7.39***	-7.35***	-4.88***	-4.66***	-9.05***	-9.11***
Fulltime job		.39		1.35		-2.50		-5.62***
Spouse fulltime job						-7.80***		3.02
PRE-BOOMERS								
Year	-13.28	-13.13	22.03**	22.01**	8.75*	10.33**	7.52*	9.30*
Birth	-.23	-.49	-6.24**	-6.24**	-1.18	-1.23	-3.16***	-3.48***
Fulltime job		7.86		.33		3.60		-4.81*
Spouse fulltime job						-6.48**		4.25
EARLY BOOMERS								
Year	-.53	-1.16	.33	-.29	9.39	11.49*	17.81***	18.71***
Birth	-.65	-.64	-1.83	-1.76	.11	-.22	-2.56*	-2.46*
Fulltime job		1.88		4.14		-12.78**		-5.12
Spouse fulltime job						-8.99**		1.91
LATE & POST-BOOMERS								
Year	-28.03*	-25.57*	-26.47*	-26.42*	.04	1.93	-2.50	.68
Birth	3.43	1.15	1.24	1.15	5.07	5.61	-5.06	-5.90
Fulltime job		-8.63		-.46		-7.78		-12.62*
Spouse fulltime job						-16.62*		-5.99

TABLE 4 (continued)

D. Non-Religious Association Membership

	Single				Married			
	Men		Women		Men		Women	
	(1)	(2)	(3)	(4)	(5)	(6)	(7)	(8)
ALL								
Year	.22	-1.24	3.56	2.46	-.44	-.22	-3.50	-2.37
Birth	-1.53	-.93	-.21	.42	-4.46***	-4.59***	.35	-1.18
Fulltime job		9.20**		19.00***		15.36***		4.44**
Spouse fulltime job						-1.32		9.75***
PRE-BOOMERS								
Year	-9.78	-9.54	-2.69	-3.56	-4.48	-2.92	-13.37***	-11.71***
Birth	-1.51	-1.95	.22	-.13	-.64	-1.07	3.53***	2.60***
Fulltime job		12.85*		20.86***		14.93***		4.66*
Spouse fulltime job						-4.36*		7.71**
EARLY BOOMERS								
Year	4.44	.09	9.70	6.83	9.23*	8.36	18.00***	17.09***
Birth	.96	1.05	-1.68	-1.37	-4.27***	-3.98**	-4.52***	-4.48***
Fulltime job		12.98**		19.15***		11.81*		2.87
Spouse fulltime job						-1.01		10.82**
LATE & POST-BOOMERS								
Year	25.24*	25.25*	3.54	1.81	21.71	17.93	29.63**	30.11**
Birth	-8.01	-8.02	2.17	5.16	-11.51	-11.60*	-12.72**	-12.81**
Fulltime job		-.04		16.90**		17.85		7.30
Spouse fulltime job						24.61***		-14.23*

* = significant at .05 level
** = significant at .01 level
*** = significant at .001 level

Roof and McKinney's discussion of the baby-boomers, we find that, despite some shift toward conservatism that normally comes with aging, the baby-boomers remain committed to the tolerance for difference which they displayed as young adults protesting the war in Southeast Asia and rallying for the rights of racial minorities, women, gay and lesbian persons, and for increased protection of the right of free speech.

If trends across birth cohort are the more significant harbinger of long-term change, then the results shown in Table 3 do not bode well for the churches and synagogues. On all three measures of religiosity, each birth cohort is less religious, on average, than those born the year before. (This does not hold, however, for single men's religious identity.) For example, statistically significant declines in membership for successively more recent birth cohorts are found for single women, married men, and married women (see panel A of Tables 3 and 4). In fact, for each of these groups, this decline is significant at the .001 level, and holds after controls for employment. These membership declines are most dramatic among early boomer, married women and, though not statistically significant,[35] among late and postboomer, married men. The movement out of the churches and synagogues exceeds one percent per year for successively older birth cohorts of these women, and approaches two percent per birth cohort year for the men.

However, there has also been proreligious movement during the years of the study. Controlling for birth cohort, these same married, early boomer women and men have, on average, been more likely to join, attend, and identify with religious bodies in each year of the study. For both men and women, the year effect approaches or reaches a one percent increase per year in membership. Moreover, these rates are statistically significant for both women and men. For married, late and post-boomers, the year effects on membership are even larger, with annual increases of three percent for women and nearly four percent for men. Among early boomers, the opposing effects of year and birth cohort also hold for attendance. The increases in religiosity are statistically significant, and are important for their empirical support of the recent perceived return to organized religion.

In light of the opposing time and cohort effects, it is little wonder that there is confusion over trends in membership and attendance. Reversals in year and cohort effects across generations may be evidence of the potential for organized religion to become revitalized in some segments of society, even while apparently waning in society as a whole.[36] Generational differences in year and birth cohort effects for membership and attendance are a further reminder that religion in a modern pluralistic society is too complex and subtle to be fully understood in terms of trends in society as a whole. Instead, regardless of what is happening at a societal level, large segments of society may be moving in an opposite direction.

Determining and interpreting year and cohort effects is further complicated by the fact that age is a third relevant variable, one that we have not included in the analysis. When any two of these three time-related variables is known, the third can be calculated for an individual or an entire sample. This being the case, to bring the third variable into the analysis with the other two would be redundant, and could result in overestimating the total association between the time effects and, say, membership or attendance. This problem is known as "underidentification." As Mark Chaves points out in discussion of Firebaugh's and Davis's procedures, the birth cohort effects may be at least in part *age effects*.[37] The negative impact of birth cohort on all of our measures of religiosity and, to a limited extent, on nonreligious memberships may actually be a *positive* effect of age: successively earlier birth cohorts are, on average, one year older and more likely to fit the profile of active participants in organized religion. This interpretation is supported by further analyses of these data, not included in this report, in which the age and year were used as predictors, instead of birth cohort and year. Similarly, others have found that among early baby-boomers, attendance at religious services is higher among those who are older, married, and have school-aged children.[38]

Trends across macrocohorts provide some basis for optimism for those concerned about the future of organized religion in America. For all four groups—single women, married men, single men and married women—successive birth cohorts of late and post-boomers show either a slowing down or reversal of the early boomer pattern of declining attendance. Moreover, for married, late-boomer men, even though membership has declined across successive birth cohorts, there is a nearly two percent *increase* in attendance associated with each more recent year of birth.

This movement toward the organized religion by married men of recent birth cohorts, coming at a time when more recent cohorts of wives are successively less likely to attend, supports my informal observations of "half-couple" attendance. Some ten to twenty years ago I was struck by the absence of husbands who not long before had regularly attended services with their wives at Lutheran and Presbyterian churches to which I belonged. I thought of the unaccompanied wives as "church widows." But, in the past five or ten years, I have been impressed by the appearance of church widowers, a phenomenon that I believe was a great rarity until very recent times. Even though the return to the pews among later birth cohorts of married, late boomer men is not statistically significant, seen against the backdrop provided by early boomers' attendance patterns, the overall picture for late and post-boomers' attendance across birth cohorts may provide reason for modest hope for organized religion.

For single women the total decline in attendance due to effects of cohort replacement has been the same nine to ten percent as for married women. Like married women, single women show increasing attendance once declines associated with cohort replacement are controlled. These similarities, however, mask large differences between single and married women's attendance patterns that show up when one looks at each generation separately. Among single, preboomer women, the decline in attendance across successive birth cohorts and increase across successive years are roughly twice as large as the same effects for married women. Among early boomers, the large and statistically significant effects in those same directions for married women are absent for single women. And the time effects for single women of the youngest macrocohort are opposite to those of married women. For these youngest single women, there is a decline in attendance associated with year of study, and an increase associated with year of birth.

In attendance trends, late and postboomer, single women show time effects in the same directions as those of married men. More importantly, single women are the most consistent group to show a positive impact of full-time employment on attendance, and are as consistent as married men in showing such a relationship for membership. These patterns, while no basis for sweeping generalizations, are worth noting. We discussed above the apparent fit between the social class hypothesis—which was developed to explain men's religiosity—and the employment and religiosity patterns of single women. It appears that the work experience of single women has about the same impact on attendance as among preboomer, married men, the generation most identified with the "traditional" family.

Among married men born since the Second World War, however, full-time employment is *negatively* related to attendance levels. This is contrary to the social class hypothesis. It suggests that, in earlier times, the positive relationship between social class and attendance among married men may have been due in part to a felt need to represent the family in activities outside the home. As married women have become more active in the workforce, their husbands' position as head-of-house has been weakened, though not greatly. In turn, the work-religion relationship for married men has disappeared for membership, and has become weakly negative for attendance. Further understanding of the social class hypothesis may lie in inquiries into the possible effects on religiosity of being head-of-house.

The one group from which the churches and synagogues can derive the least comfort is single men, the group historically least connected to organized religion. As we saw above, they are the least likely to join, attend, and identify of any of the four broad groups in this study. And membership, attendance, and identification among all single men appear to be declining—due to year as well as birth cohort effects. Most of these effects are too small to be statistically significant, but they add up to almost a five percent drop in membership, a six percent drop in attendance, and a seven percent drop in religious identification over the period studied. However, the rate of decline within this group may be slowing or even reversing. Early boomer, single men had lower rates of attendance due to cohort replacement, but that pattern is absent in the latest generation of single men. Further, the rates of decline in attendance among single men are successively *lower* across successively later generations.

Within the total sample, as well as for each of the three generations, the trends in intensity of religious identity are quite similar to those for attendance. (See panels B and C of Tables 3 and 4). As for attendance, in the total sample, strength of religious identity is positively related to year, but negatively related to birth cohort for single and married women and for married men. This close parallel is as expected, because individuals' tendency to identify with a particular denomination or other religious body is shaped in part by and reflected in their attendance levels. One difference worth noting is the much larger, average, annual declines in religious identity for late and postboomer single men and women. These young, single people seem most affected by the decline in denominationalism of the last two decades.[39] However, even though these findings for religious identity are large, a statistically more significant and more important trend is the declining strength of religious identity across birth cohorts of single and married women and married men. These patterns are clearly tied to the behavioral declines in support of organized religion through membership and attendance.

Trends in membership in nonreligious voluntary associations have been included in this study in order to determine whether declines in participation in organized religion are part of a larger movement away from involvement with groups outside the home and work place. Again, this interest is prompted by earlier research that showed that the link between social class and participation in organized religion is part of a larger pattern of ties between social class and participation in voluntary associations broadly defined.[40]

Nonreligious association membership is examined in terms of whether each individual has *any* such memberships, rather than number of memberships; in this way, the figures in panel D of Tables 3 and 4 can more easily be compared with figures on membership in panel A. Whereas church membership has clearly declined due to reduced participation by later birth cohorts, secular organizations have shown greater resilience. Married men have experienced only a four percent decline in membership in one or more nonreligious organizations due to cohort replacement, and this is the only significant decline in the total sample. In short, nonreligious organizations appear to have fared better than religious ones in retaining their members. The findings also provide some cause for possible concern for the leaders of nonreligious organizations. The cohort replacement effects for married people of the two boomer cohorts reveal statistically significant departures from secular organizations. For the most recent generation, these declines are about twelve percent for both sexes. More than offsetting these declines, at least in the short run, are year effects showing some twenty percent growth in membership for men of the latest generation and thirty percent growth for women. It is possible, however, that there have been reductions in the number of memberships, an issue that goes beyond the scope of the present study. More research is needed on change in *number* and *kinds* of extrareligious memberships.

WORK AND TRENDS IN RELIGION

We turn now to our largest concern, the impact of work on the effects of year, birth cohort, and generation on religion and extrareligious memberships. For their social significance to be understood, time effects ordinarily need to be explained in terms of specific changes undergone by individuals across successive years, birth cohorts, or generations. That is, evidence of social change in one social institution—in the present study, in the declining strength of organized religion—is presumably due not to the mere passage of time, but to change in other social institutions. The question here is whether the declines in religion are due to increases in women's workforce participation.

In Tables 3 and 4, the analysis was done for year and cohort effects alone (odd-numbered columns), and then repeated to take into account the possible relevance of respondents' own workforce participation (whether or not full-time employed) and, for the married, workforce participation of spouse. By and large, even where work does bear significantly on involvement in religious and extra-religious organizations, controlling for work does not greatly affect the year and birth cohort effects. That is, for example, declines in membership and attendance due to cohort replacement are not attributable to *changes* in workforce participation.

Nonetheless, work *does matter* to some of these relationships, particularly for married persons. For example, for the total sample of married women, the small and not statistically significant growth in membership of about 3.6 percent over the years of the study, controlling for the effects of cohort replacement is found to nearly double the figure to 6.5 percent, significant at the .05 level, when their own and their husbands' workforce participation is controlled. That is, were it not for the negative impact of work of married persons, married women would be found to have increased their rates of membership even more than their actual increase in membership. Although to a lesser degree, married persons also show larger annual increases in attendance and religious identity once the effects of work are controlled.

In Tables 3 and 4 *the workforce hypothesis is clearly supported for married women but for no other group*. For single men and women, and married men, in accord with the social class hypothesis, full-time employment is associated with *higher* levels of membership, attendance, and extrareligious memberships than among their unemployed and part-time employed counterparts. By marked contrast, full-time employed married women are about 5.3 percent less likely to be church members, 8.4 percent less likely to attend religious services regularly, and 5.6 percent less likely to strongly identify with a denomination. The negative impact of full-time employment on married women's congregational *membership* is greatest within the early baby-boomer generation. However, the impact of work on their *attendance* is successively higher for each generation: Full-time employed preboomers are 6 percent less likely to attend regularly, early boomers 9.6 percent less likely, and late and post-boomers nearly 18 percent less likely to attend. Similar escalation in the work-related erosion of religiosity is evident in generational differences in strength of religious identity. For preboomers, that effect is -4.8 percent, for early boomers -5.1 percent, and for late and post-boomers -12.6 percent.

As for men and single women, full-time employment among married women actually *encourages* their membership in secular associations. Dropping out of religious participation is evidently not just a matter of time constraints. Since full-time work is associated with higher rates of membership in secular organizations, declines in religious affiliation appear to reflect the declining place of organized religion among the priorities of these working wives.

Whereas full-time work discourages membership, attendance, and religious identity of married women, in general, full-time employment is positively related to religiosity among married men as well as single men and women. For men and single women, these patterns can be interpreted as support for the social class hypothesis.

Organized religion may bear the effects of working wives in both direct and indirect ways. Married women who work full-time are less religiously involved, but so are their husbands—just the opposite of the employment effect for married men. For married women, full-time employment of husbands is associated with increased religiosity and secular membership for the total sample and, for the most part, within each generation. However, for married men, full-time employment of wives is related to a 6.4 percent lower likelihood of membership, a 7.7 percent lower likelihood of attending regularly, and a 7.8 percent lower chance of having strong religious identity. The negative impact of wives' full-time employment on their husbands' involvement in organized religion is consistently present for all three measures of religiosity for all three generations. And the negative impact of wives' employment on husbands' religiosity is as great or greater than the positive impact of husbands' own workforce participation. Further, as among wives themselves, for attendance and religious identity, the negative impact of wives' employment increases across the three generations of this study, so that in the late and postboomer generation, men with full-time employed wives are 13.5 percent less likely to attend regularly and 16.6 percent less likely to have strong religious identities.

These findings show very clearly that, far from having no effect on religiosity, full-time employment for married women discourages their own involvement in organized religion, *and their husbands' involvement.* The implications of these findings for the future of organized religion are not to be underestimated. Recall that Roof and McKinney reported that declines in attendance at Sunday School were followed by declines in attendance at services, which in turn have been followed by declines in membership. It is in all probability the case that the work-related decline in married women's support of organized religion has contributed to the decline in their husband's involvement. The lower levels of membership, attendance, and religious identity of men and women in families in which the wife works full-time may in turn—and probably does—lead those parents to place less emphasis on religious training for their children. If so, then the work-related declines in married women's involvement in religion may impact negatively on the long-term future religious involvement of their children.

CONCLUSIONS

This study was undertaken to investigate the relationships between work, family, and religion among working-aged, white Americans, and trends in those relationships. Some of the findings were not at all surprising: married persons are more religious than single individuals, women more than men, parents more than individuals without children in the home.

The social class hypothesis received little support, and the only clear support came from single women. For them, all three measures of religiosity and membership in extra-religious organizations are positively related with level of participation in the workforce. That the social class hypothesis gained its clearest support from single women is a decidedly unexpected finding, in that the pattern has been associated primarily with married men.

Erosion in organized religion within all four broad groups—married men, single men, married women, and single women—appears to be due more to a rejection of religion by later birth cohorts than to widespread rejection throughout all birth cohorts. In some respects, the early baby boomers are distinctive, but more noteworthy patterns hold across successive generations. Of particular importance is the finding that full-time employment of married women is related to successively larger declines in their own and in husbands' attendance and strength of religious identity. The impact on organized religion of employment of married women provides the clearest support of the workforce hypothesis. *By far the most significant challenge to organized religion lies in the work-related declines in membership and attendance attributable to full-time employment of married women.* Full-time employment of men and women generally encourages their participation and their spouses' participation in extrareligious organizations, but full-time employment of wives very clearly discourages their own involvement, and—in a statistically and otherwise significant finding—discourages their husbands' involvement as well. If more married women become more active in the workforce, there is basis to predict that more of them will become less active in organized religion, and that their husbands, too, are likely to join this exodus. Further, there is reason to believe that future generations of young adults will participate less than today's young adults.

As increased workforce participation of married women leads them and their husbands away from religious participation, their children are undoubtedly less likely than in the past to receive religious training, and are less likely in the future to attend services and join congregations.

While organized religion in America appears likely to face hard times for the foreseeable future, the long-term future cannot be predicted. The negative impact of full-time employment of married women on their support of religious organizations could be slowed down, halted, or even reversed if women's movement into the workforce were to level off—or if congregations were to adapt creatively to their needs. A significant increase in pay equity could lead many married women to drop back from full-time to part-time employment which, again, was found to be positively related to their participation in organized religion. Conceivably, too, the ongoing slow movement toward gender equality in the home could eventually see husbands playing a larger role in the religious socialization of children. If so, fathers might take the lead in returning to the churches and synagogues, and working wives might in turn feel encouraged to join the rest of their family in that return. Still, continuing changes in work and family could result in change in the patterns we have found.

NOTES

1. An earlier version of this paper was presented at the annual meeting of the Society for the Scientific Study of Religion, held in November, 1990, at Virginia Beach, Virginia. I am grateful to Nancy Ammerman for her many helpful comments on drafts of this paper, and to Mark Chaves and Don Luidens for their suggestions. I wish to thank Ruan Hoe and Phyllis Light for preparation of the tables and figures.

2. Bradley Hertel, "Gender, Religious Identity, and Workforce Participation," *Journal for the Scientific Study of Religion* (1988). The study included only white respondents.

3. On declining membership and attendance among Protestants, see Benton Johnson, "Is There Hope for Liberal Protestantism?" in *Mainstream Protestantism: Its Problems and Prospects*, eds. Dorothy Bass, Benton Johnson and Wade Clark Roof (Louisville, KY: Committee on Theological Education of the Presbyterian Church (U.S.A.), 1987), pp. 13–26; also Wade Clark Roof and William McKinney, *American Mainline Religion: Its Changing Shape and Future* (New Brunswick, NJ: Rutgers University Press, 1987); and Wade Clark Roof, "The Third Disestablishment and Beyond," in *Mainstream Protestantism: Its Problems and Prospects*, pp. 27–37. On the Catholic patterns, see Michael Hout and Andrew Greeley, "The Center

Doesn't Hold: Church Attendance in the United States, 1940–1984," *American Sociological Review* 52 (1987), pp. 325–345.

Among the studies of the relationship between workforce participation and religiosity are David A. deVaus, "Workforce Participation and Sex Differences in Church Attendance," *Review of Religious Research* 25, No. 3 (1984), pp. 247–256; and Holley Ulbrich and Myles Wallace, "Women's Work Force Status and Church Attendance," *Journal for the Scientific Study of Religion* 23 (1984), pp. 341–350. DeVaus's study of gender, work, and attendance in American society has led to parallel studies of this relationship in Australia, by David deVaus and Ian McAllister ("Gender Differences in Religion: A Test of the Structural Location Theory," *American Sociological Review* 52, No. 52 (1987), pp. 472–481) and in Canada (Ellen M. Gee, "Gender Differences in Church Attendance in Canada: The Role of Labor Force Participation," *Review of Religious Research* 32 (1991), pp. 267–273), as well as to this research.

4. N.J. Demerath, III, "Social Stratification and Church Involvement: The Church-Sect Distinction Applied to Individual Participation," *Review of Religious Research* 2 (1961), pp. 146–154; N. J. Demerath, III, *Social Class in American Protestantism* (Chicago: Rand McNally, 1965); Yoshio Fukuyama, "The Major Dimensions of Church Membership," *Review of Religious Research* 2 (1961), pp. 154–161. On the church-sect distinction, see Ernst Troeltsch, *The Social Teaching of the Christian Churches*, trans. Olive Wyon (New York: Macmillan, 1931) and Max Weber, *The Sociology of Religion* (Boston: Beacon Press, 1964), see especially p. 46.

5. Charles W. Mueller and Weldon T. Johnson, "Socioeconomic Status and Religious Participation," *American Sociological Review* 40 (1975), pp. 785–800.

6. Thomas Luckmann, *The Invisible Religion* (New York: Macmillan, 1967), p. 30. DeVaus ("Workforce Participation...") cites a number of earlier studies supporting this hypothesis, including Gerhard E. Lenski, "Social Correlates of Religious Interest," *American Sociological Review* 18 (1953), pp. 533–544; David O. Moberg, *The Church as a Social Institution* (Englewood Cliffs: Prentice-Hall, 1962); and Hart M. Nelsen and Raymond H. Potvin, "Gender and Regional Differences in the Religiosity of Protestant Adolescents," *Review of Religious Research* 22 (1981), pp. 268–285. David Martin argues, in *A Sociology of English Religion* (London: S.C.M. Press, 1967), that gender differences in religiosity are due at least in part to differences in workforce participation. Recent research points to an overall increase in individualism and decline in communal commitments. Glenn has reported not only declining religious belief and practice, but declines in political party affiliation, strength of party ideology, and valuation of marital fidelity. See Norval D. Glenn, "The Trend in 'No Religion' Respondents to U.S. National Surveys, Late 1950s to Early 1980s," *Public Opinion Quarterly* 51 (1987), pp. 293–314; and his "Social Trends in the United States: Evidence from Sample Surveys," *Public Opinion Quarterly* 51 (1987), pp. S109–S126.

7. As deVaus ("Workforce Participation," p. 247) notes, the "available time"

and "comfort" explanations come from Charles Glock, Benjamin Ringer, and Earl Babbie, *To Comfort and to Challenge: A Dilemma of the Contemporary Church* (Berkeley, CA: University of California Press, 1967). The "competitive values" and "secularization explanations can be found in Lenski, ("Social Correlates," p. 535) and in J. Milton Yinger, *The Scientific Study of Religion* (New York: Macmillan, 1970).

8. "Gender Differences," p. 480.

9. "Gender Differences in Church Attendance." See especially her findings for education in Table 2 on p. 271.

10. *American Mainline Religion*, p. 115.

11. "Gender Differences," p. 478.

12. "Workforce Participation," p. 251.

13. The General Social Survey data are collected by the National Opinion Research Center at the University of Chicago, and are distributed by the Roper Center for Public Opinion Research at the University of Connecticut, Storrs. A description of the variables on which the analysis for this chapter was based is found in James A. Davis and Tom W. Smith, *General Social Surveys: A Cumulative Code Book* (Chicago: National Opinion Research Center, 1990).

14. "Workforce Participation," p. 248.

15. *American Mainline Religion*, pp. 58–60.

16. Robert Wuthnow suggests, in *The Consciousness Reformation* (Berkeley: University of California Press, 1976), p. 41, that the decline in attendance during the 1960s may have been a "cyclical fluctuation" rather than part of a long-term trend.

17. *American Mainline Religion*, p. 62.

18. *American Mainline Religion*, pp. 60–63. Wuthnow (*The Consciousness Reformation*), p. 38, reports that "large numbers are abandoning the established churches and becoming essentially nonreligious." For figures on this trend, see Glenn, "The Trend" and "Social Trends," and Hertel, "Gender, Religious Identity," p. 580. See also Wade Clark Roof, *A Generation of Seekers: The Spiritual Journeys of the Baby Boom Generation* (San Francisco: Harper SanFrancisco, 1993) and Roof and Gesch's chapter in this volume.

19. "Workforce Participation."

20. In this study, *regular attendance* is defined as at least once a week. Intensity of *religious identity* distinguishes between individuals who strongly identify with a church or denomination and those who do not.

21. Glenn Firebaugh and Kenneth E. Davis, "Trends in Anti-Black Prejudice, 1972–1984: Region and Cohort Effects," *American Journal of Sociology* 94 (1988), pp. 251–272.

22. Steven L. Nock and Paul Kingston, "Time with Children: The Impact of Couple's Work-Time Commitments," *Social Forces* 67 (1988), pp. 59–85.

23. Joan Huber and Glenna Spitze, "Wives' Employment, Household Behaviors, and Sex-Role Attitudes," *Social Forces* 60 (1981), pp. 150–169.

24. This was also deVaus's finding for attendance of women undifferentiated by marital status ("Workforce Participation").

25. In supporting the conclusions of Mueller and Johnson ("Socioeconomic Status"), this finding helps to explain Demerath's ("Social Stratification") and Fukuyama's ("The Major Dimensions") social class hypothesis.

26. J.A. Sweet, "Family Composition and the Labor Force Activity of American Wives," *Demography*, April 1970, pp. 197–198.

27. 1909 through 1969 is the range of birth cohorts available for study *after* eliminating individuals in the total sample who were nonwhite, not of working age, widowed, or temporarily unemployed.

28. "Trends in Anti-Black Prejudice."

29. The total amounts of year and cohort effects can then be calculated by multiplying these rates of change by the number of years associated with each. For the year effects on attendance, that multiplier is 18, the number of one-year steps between 1972 and 1990. For church membership, intensity of religious identity, and membership in nonreligious voluntary associations, the multiplier is only 16, because these variables were not added to the General Social Survey until 1974.

    Measuring the cohort effects is slightly more complicated. Average year of birth for the sample for the earliest survey year is subtracted from average year of birth for the most recent survey to find the total change in birth cohorts represented by the span of the study. The change in birth cohorts would be 18 if the 1990 sample were made up of individuals who each had a counterpart in the 1972 sample born 18 years earlier, but obtaining two such samples with identical age distributions is highly unlikely. Instead, the multiplier indicating number of birth cohorts will invariably be other than a whole integer, because of shifts in the average age of the population and differences across surveys in sampling error.

30. These procedures for assessing the cohort, year, and work effects on religiosity avoid use of five- or ten-year macrocohorts whose arbitrary boundaries can result in underestimation of linear relationships ("Trends in Anti-Black Prejudice," p. 253). However, any longitudinal or quasilongitudinal analysis is limited by the idiosyncracies of the years for which relevant data are available. That is, at a different level, the problem of arbitrariness remains. To illustrate, in the present study, and countless others based on GSS data, 1972 is the starting point simply because that was the year the National Opinion Research Center began this series of surveys.

31. The baby boom is generally regarded as ending with the 1965 birth cohort but, owing to the limited number of people in the General Social Surveys born after that date who otherwise qualify for this study, late and post-boomers were combined into a single group.

32. As noted in Note 30 above, Firebaugh and Davis (p. 253) oppose the conventional practice of calculating means for five- or ten-year aggregates of birth cohorts because this may result in underestimation of linear relationships. The present study addresses this concern by employing regression analysis to look for year and birth cohort effects for all individuals

included in the study, as well as within three substantively defined generations, the pre-, early, and late babyboomers. In this way, the study relies on the regression analysis favored by Firebaugh and Davis but, in modified form, also incorporates the earlier practice of grouping subjects into clusters of birth cohorts.

33. The figures presented in Table 4 are calculated from more digits than shown in Table 3, and therefore differ slightly from exact multiples of 16 or 18 years. And, as noted earlier, the multipliers representing the change in average birth cohort between the earliest and latest years for which data are available are other than whole numbers of years.

34. Firebaugh and Davis, "Trends," p. 268. They explain (p. 253, fn. 2) that cohort replacement means that "the average birth year increases over time in a population as younger members are added and older members are lost."

35. Even a decline in membership as large as 2% per birth cohort was not found to be statistically significant because of the small numbers of late and post-boomers in the total sample.

36. Concurrent resurgence and decline in organized religion is a central theme of Rodney Stark and William Sims Bainbridge in their *The Future of Religion* (Berkeley, University of California Press, 1985).

37. Personal communication, July 22, 1991.

38. David A. Roozen, William McKinney, and Wayne Thompson, "The 'Big Chill' Generation Warms to Worship: A Research Note," *Review of Religious Research* 31, No. 3 (1990), pp. 314–322.

39. In his *The Restructuring of American Religion* (Princeton: Princeton University Press, 1988), pp. 71–99, Robert Wuthnow cites denominations' convergence of values on social issues and other denominations, and increases in denominational switching, as evidence of decline in denominationalism. Decline in importance of religious identity is also suggested by research that shows young Jews to hold images of God that are more similar to those of Christians than the God images held by older Jews (Wade Clark Roof and Jennifer L. Roof, "Review of the Polls: Images of God among Americans," *Journal for the Scientific Study of Religion* 23 (1984), p. 204). Convergence of values and beliefs, however, does not appear to be evidence of an immanent disappearance of denominationalism; other recent research has found that denominations continue to differ on abortion and other family issues in expected directions (Hertel and Hughes, "Religious Affiliation").

40. Mueller and Johnson, "Socioeconomic Status." Our interest in viewing trends in support of organized religion in terms of trends for extrareligious organizations is also prompted by recent research findings on growth in individualism in terms of reduced allegiance to not only organized religion, but political parties (Glenn, "The Trend" and "Social Trends"). It is possible that trends in the strength of organized religion need to be viewed as trends in formal organizations in general.

5

Responses to Changing Lifestyles

"Feminists" and "Traditionalists" in Mainstream Religion[1]

Lyn Gesch

Women's roles in work and family spheres have undergone dramatic changes in the latter part of this century, and there is reason to believe, from previous research, that these changes may have affected women's religious behaviors. First, women who are not in "typical" (two-parent-plus-child) families may be alienated from participation in religious communities dominated by such traditional family groups. Second, several studies have found that high levels of workforce participation limit women's involvement in voluntary activity and expose them to secularizing influences.[2] Yet, overall, women's participation in religion is strong, and, according to Wuthnow, a religiosity gap between the sexes remains consistent over time. He found that forty-six percent of women, compared with thirty-five percent of men, attend religious services regularly; and sixty-six percent (versus forty percent of men) were Bible-readers. These differences, he notes, persisted over a period that saw increasing levels of education and greater rates of participation in the labor force for women.[3]

Although the overall differences between women and men have persisted, and women's rates of religiosity have remained high, not all women are alike. Wuthnow observed that "sharp differences in these levels can be observed...between women with feminist orientations and women with more traditional gender orientations."[4] He is convinced that, with the controversies in mainline churches over the ordination of women, "participation rates in the churches began to divide along lines of how feminist or nonfeminist a person was."[5] He presents survey data that show wide gaps in regular church attendance between feminists and nonfeminists in both Catholic and Protestant churches.[6]

The questions posed in this chapter aim at exploring how feminist and nonfeminist women differ, and how those differences are linked to the work and family situations and the religious involvement of these women. The first objective is to examine how women feel about the roles of wife, divorcee, mother, worker, and homemaker. Second, we will look at how management of these roles and the attitudes women have toward them affect their religious involvement. And third, we will explore the implications of all of this on religious institutions themselves. In examining these differences among women, we will take into account other factors that may shape their experience. We may expect, for instance, that women's attitudes toward their roles, as well as their religious involvement, will vary depending on their age. In addition, differences would be expected along denominational lines, with women in more conservative religious groups differing from those in liberal ones.

What women think about their "proper" roles tends to be closely tied to their actual work and family activities. The sixty-three women Gerson interviewed, for instance, tended to be either traditional and domestic, or nontraditional and nondomestic. Their adult family and work experiences had shaped their gender-role attitudes.[7] In Plutzer's analysis of national survey data, women who were in the labor force had more liberal views on family responsibilities than other women, and divorced women without children had the most liberal views of all.[8] Again, actual work and family experiences appear to be associated with women's attitudes toward gender roles, and both attitudes and behavior have changed dramatically in the last generation.

Meanwhile, most religious institutions are still programmatically oriented toward a traditional family model (as Penny Marler, in this volume, has illustrated), and many are also ideologically supportive of a gender-specific division of labor—male provider and female mother/homemaker.[9] The closer the religious institution is to supporting such "traditional" ideals, the more alien that institution may be for women whose experiences and attitudes do not fit the norm. In the fundamentalist church studied by Ammerman, for instance, "the culture of the congregation establishes only one family structure as normative, and the dominant life experiences of the group reinforce that norm."[10] The importance of family in this church forced those whose family styles deviated from the norm, that is, the divorced, to leave the church rather than feel the pressure of being outside religious standards. In addition, role conflict arose for women in this congregation who, for economic reasons, worked full-time outside the home. The ideal Christian home, in this church's view, should have a full-time mother, yet almost half of the mothers in this study were employed full-time in order to make ends meet. Despite this deviation from the norm, these women remained religiously active, continued to value the ideal, and kept up responsibility for domestic duties in addition to their outside employment.[11]

Family and work situations, then, that do not follow the normative pattern upheld by traditional religious groups present conflict for women, and may result in disengagement from religious institutions. On the other hand, in religious institutions that are more accommodating, conflict can lead to change. In liberal Protestant churches, for instance, feminist women have *higher* rates of participation than traditionalist women, while the opposite is the case in conservative churches.[12]

In this study, assessment of gender-role attitude is based on answers given by white female respondents to the following statements in the 1988 General Social Survey:

1. A working mother can establish just as warm and secure a relationship with her children as a woman who does not work.
2. It is more important for a wife to help her husband's career than have one herself.
3. A preschool child is likely to suffer if her/his mother works.
4. It is better if the man is the achiever outside the home and the woman takes care of the home and the family.

Conceptually, an egalitarian role orientation is one that stresses equality and similarity in the roles of men and women, while a traditional orientation stresses the difference between roles for men and women, with women's lives centered on home and family. Agreement with the last three items (and disagreement with the first) was taken as a traditionalist response, while agreement with the first (and disagreement with the others) was defined as an egalitarian response. Those of the 642 respondents who gave consistently egalitarian responses—25.2 percent—are labeled here "feminists;" those who gave consistently traditional responses—only 8.4 percent—are labeled "traditionalists." The remaining two-thirds gave mixed responses. While those at the poles are the minority, it is these extreme groups who would represent the most support—or challenge—to religious institutions, and they will be, therefore, the focus of this analysis.

On the whole, women with consistently traditional views of gender roles are also firmly entrenched in traditional religious beliefs and active religious participation. They are the women most likely to be church members (eighty percent), to express a firm belief in God (eighty-five percent), have family prayer at meals (sixty-seven percent), and to attend church frequently (sixty-seven percent). Women with egalitarian attitudes, on the other hand, appear to be the least conventionally religious women: fifty-eight percent are church members, fifty-nine percent have firm belief in God, thirty-five percent say meal prayers, and forty-four percent attend church frequently.

Not only are feminists less conventionally religious, their religiosity is also more tolerant and individualistic. Their responses to questions on morality indicate an ambiguous, less punitive orientation. When they are making decisions, they believe it more important to rely on personal conscience than on religious authority. Not surprisingly, they are more likely to view the Bible as having human elements along with the divine. They are more likely than traditionalists to belong to "liberal Protestant" churches, but they tend to rate their denominational identity as weak, especially when compared to the strong denominational identity of their traditionalist counterparts. Many feminists, then, are choosing a path guided more by individual conscience than by institutional religion.

But many feminists *are* still within the churches. In the ranks of women who attend church can be found the full range of attitudes about women's proper roles. Table 1 includes only regular religious attenders, and compares women in "feminist," "moderate," and "traditionalist" subgroups. Feminist religious attenders are no less likely to

TABLE 1

Religious Beliefs, Behaviors, and Attitudes of a Subsample of Women Who Attend Church Once a Month or More, Stratified by Gender-Role Orientation

	Traditionalist N=36	Moderate N=255	Feminist N=70
RELIGIOUS BEHAVIORS			
Belongs to church or synagogue.	86%	88%	84%
Belongs to fundamentalist church.	42%	41%	27%
Belongs to liberal church.	6%	15%	27%
Considers herself strong member of church.	81%	75%	61%
Says prayers at family meals.	75%	72%	51%
RELIGIOUS BELIEF			
Knows God exists and has no doubts.	89%	82%	73%
Feels it's important to believe in God without doubts.	78%	68%	49%
Agrees that the Bible is the actual word of God and is to be taken literally.	66%	50%	30%
Agrees that the Bible is an ancient book of fables recorded by men.	6%	5%	5%
ETHICS AND MORALITY			
Agrees that:			
right and wrong are not usually a simple matter of black and white.	28%	38%	39%
morality is a personal matter.	31%	21%	30%
RELIGIOUS AUTHORITY			
Agrees that:			
one's own personal judgment is important in making decisions.	74%	69%	80%
it's important to follow the teachings of one's church or synagogue.	63%	45%	29%

Source: General Social Survey, NORC, 1988.

belong to a congregation than other women, but they are less likely to consider themselves strong members. Not surprisingly, few of them belong to conservative churches, and they are much more likely than traditionalists to belong to liberal groups. While more than half of feminist attenders say prayers at family meals, that does not match the near unanimity traditionalists have on this practice. While virtually all (eighty-nine percent) traditionalists believe without doubt, doubt is considerably more prevalent among feminists—indeed fewer than half of them think that an undoubting belief is a good thing. Almost no feminists dismiss the Bible as totally human, but they are far less likely than traditionalists to see it as literally true. Indeed on matters of authority, feminists and traditionalists are dramatically different. Feminist attenders are far less likely than traditionalist ones to insist on following religious authorities. While these feminists have made a commitment to certain aspects of religious membership, piety, and belief, their religious beliefs and practices are considerably different from those of their traditionalist sisters.

It should be noted, in fact, that *all* of the traditionalist churchgoers are indeed *church*goers, claiming affiliation with Christian groups, either Protestant or Catholic. Feminists, however, include a small number from non-Christian religions, Jews, and those who claim no religious affiliation. Therefore, questions on the importance of the Bible and the authority of the church have different meaning or no meaning at all to these respondents.

Gender-role attitudes, then, are strongly related to whether and how a woman is religious. However, as was suggested at the beginning, religious patterns—and gender-role attitudes—may be affected by a woman's actual work and family situation, as well. Women in nontraditional roles may believe and act differently from women who meet traditional expectations about family and work.

Indeed, feminist respondents are more likely to have nontraditional families, while traditionalists predominantly have the two-parent-plus-child arrangement. As a group, feminists in nontraditional families tend to be full-time working women under the age of forty-six. In contrast, traditionalists in traditional families are predominantly housewives over the age of fifty-five. This dramatic demographic difference suggests that gender-role attitudes are largely a function of generational cohorts, connected to adult life experiences in time periods when opportunities for women's roles have expanded.

When we compare women in these two groups (see Table 2), we again see real differences in their religious behaviors, beliefs, and attitudes. In fact, there is evidence here that work and family experience intensify the effects of gender-role attitudes. This subgroup of feminists is less likely to attend religious services regularly or be active in church activities than the larger sample of feminists. At the same time, this group of traditionalists attends *more* often and is *more* active than traditionalists in the sample as a whole. Having a traditional family seems to make women with traditional attitudes even more religious, while having a nontraditional family seems to make feminist women even more marginal to organized religious activity.

What is the relative importance, then, of family status to gender-role attitude in influencing religious behavior? A test[13] was made of the strength of gender-role attitude as a predictor of religious activity for all female respondents as a group, holding constant such factors as work and family statuses and demographic characteristics. The results show that both a nontraditional family status and an egalitarian attitude toward gender roles decrease the liklihood of religious involvement. However, gender-role attitude is a stronger predictor of religiosity than is family status.

The importance of family status in influencing religious participation is illustrated by looking at the relative standings of family status groups on average church attendance. With the number "1" representing low church attendance, and "8" high church attendance, the group of respondents with the highest average attendance are those with a traditional family arrangement (4.5). They are followed by widowed respondents (4.1), married, childless respondents (3.9), singles (3.5), and divorced/separated (3.4). The more traditional the family form, the more often women attend religious services.

As we saw above, public and private religious behavior are not affected in the same way. With private religious behaviors scaled from 1 to 6 (low to high involvement), the pattern shifts dramatically for respondents who are divorced or separated. They show the highest average level of devotional behaviors—frequency of prayer, Bible reading, and degree of feeling close to God. While separated and divorced women have the lowest rates of church attendance—lower than widows, married women who are childless, and women with traditional family situations—this same group of women with a nontraditional family form has the highest level of religious involvement in private religious behavior.

These findings are consistent with the suggestion that traditional family situations are most compatible with public religiosity. In addition, these new findings reveal that women with nontraditional families participate strongly on the private level, rather than avoiding religion as an

TABLE 2

Comparison of Two Ideological and Family Status Groups

Feminists In Nontraditional Families N=49	Traditionalists In Traditional Families N=25
CHARACTERISTICS	
65% work full-time	12% work full-time
10% are housewives	64% are housewives
25% are over age 55	56% are over age 55
33% completed some college	24% completed some college
8% advanced degrees	
PUBLIC RELIGIOUS BEHAVIORS	
38% attend church frequently	76% attend church frequently
65% let church attendance lapse as adults	24% let church attendance lapse as adults
27% are involved in church activities	52% are involved in church activities
PRIVATE RELIGIOUS BEHAVIORS	
6% are frequent Bible-readers	40% are frequent Bible-readers
37% say family prayers at meals	72% say family prayers at meals
RELIGIOUS BELIEFS	
65% believe God exists	88% believe God exists
53% think it is very important to believe without doubts	84% think it is very important to believe without doubts
RELIGIOUS ATTITUDES	
25% think it is very important to follow church's teachings	56% think it is very important to follow church's teachings
16% think it is very important to use Bible in making decisions	64% think it is very important to use Bible in making decisions.

Source: General Social Survey NORC 1988.

activity altogether.

While family status makes a real difference in the religiosity of women, the impact of workforce participation is much more ambiguous. In the regression analysis, work status was not a significant predictor of either church attendance or private religiosity. Indeed, when comparing housewives with full-time-employed women, rates of public religious participation are very similar (see Table 3). The effects of

TABLE 3

Religious Participation by Work Status for Women Respondents

	Home Duties	Part-time	Full-time
1. Attends church once a month or more.	52.9%	69.6%	52.6%
2. Holds membership in church or synagogue.	63.0%	70.4%	62.5%
3. Is involved in church activities.	48.0%	48.0%	46.4%
4. Prays once a day or more.	72.6%	64.8%	51.7%
5. Reads Bible.	71.1%	74.7%	61.7%
6. Feels close to God.	89.1%	85.9%	86.3%

Source: NORC General Social Survey 1988.

participation in the workforce are seen, unexpectedly, in private religious behavior. Prayer and Bible-reading decline significantly with increasing levels of workforce participation for women (Table 3). Differences between housewives and full-time workers are measured at 20.9 points for frequency of prayer and 9.4 points for Bible-reading. One might expect declines in public participation because of time constraints; but perhaps time constrains the private life to a greater extent. That these lower prayer and Bible reading participation rates do not reflect a lack of religiosity among working women is supported by the much smaller difference between women in the labor force and those outside it in their reported feelings of closeness to God.

When gender-role orientation is considered along with labor force participation, a telling pattern emerges in this sample. On the whole, eight out of ten feminists are in the labor force, either part-time or full-time, while only two of ten of the traditionalists are nonhousewives; most traditionalists (eighty-two percent) identified themselves as either retired or at work in the home. While it is possible that some women may enter and continue in the workforce as a result of liberating views of women's roles, it is more likely that economic need, job mobility opportunities, and family life cycle considerations influence participation in the labor force.[14] This suggests that women's labor force experience may increase

TABLE 4

Religious Participation of Work Status Groups Stratified by Gender-Role Orientation

	Traditionalist N=54	Moderate N=426	Feminist N=161
Attends church regularly:			
Works full-time:	83%[a]	45%	36%
Home duties:	60%	54%	24%
Participates in church activites:			
Works full-time:	75%	54%	35%
Home duties:	50%	54%	46%
Reads Bible frequently:			
Works full-time:	80%	33%	20%
Home duties:	77%	44%	30%
Knows God exists:			
Works full-time:	100%	63%	59%
Home duties:	88%	76%	72%

Source: NORC General Social Survey 1988.

a. Cell frequencies for traditionalist respondents who work full-time are low—only 6 of 31 traditionalists are in this work category. However, comparative standing to the other groups is relevant for this discussion.

egalitarian attitudes toward gender roles. One view is that the workplace exposes women to different, liberating ideas; however, this assumes housewives lead closeted, unintellectual lives and workplaces are havens for feminists. More likely, women are faced with negotiating (with or without spouse) between work and home lives when child care and housework create "the second shift."[15] This new reality may lead to changing views of gender roles that are grounded in experience.

Can we expect women's contrasting experiences in home and work arrangements to differentially impact traditional religiosity? In Table 4, we see the effects of gender-role attitudes and work status together on religious practice and beliefs. Here, religiosity appears to be more strongly affected by views toward women's roles in work and family than by work status itself. Regardless of their actual work status, women with feminist orientations have the lowest rates of church attendance, church activity, belief in God, and prayer activity. Feminist housewives, who comprise sixteen percent of all feminists in the sample, are no more religiously active than feminist women in the labor force.

Women with different gender role orientations exhibit very different patterns of religious behavior. Not only do women who believe women's roles extend beyond the home show significantly lower levels of both public and private religious behaviors, women who have nontraditional family patterns are isolated from the religious community. Attitudes and family patterns appear to be the key to women's religious participation, especially in public, institutional forms. Participation in the labor force, in itself, is not the primary factor keeping some women away from religious activities. More of the "canvas" that depicts the lives of these women needs to be uncovered.

In considering the implications of these findings for the future of religious organizations, I will look more closely at the groups that claim strong feminist or strong traditional orientations. Women with egalitarian orientations are not staying away from churches altogether, so where are they, and what are they doing?

As noted earlier, feminists represent a much broader range of religious preferences than traditionalists. Feminists who are within mainline Protestantism are likely to be found in liberal churches; while traditionalists are likely to be in fundamentalist churches. In Table 5, these particular locations of feminists and traditionalists are compared. Again we see here the large gaps in age and educational attainment between feminists and traditionalists, which is true for the sample as a whole. While most traditionalists in the sample were born in the Depression era and were adolescents during the years of the Second World War, feminists are the products of the "baby boom," maturing during the turbulent years of social change in the 1960s. For one group, years of economic deprivation and sacrifice influenced their views of life, and, for the other, years of prosperity and personal seeking. The opportunity for higher education and the incentive for personal fulfillment at a time when the Women's Movement was revitalized gave shape for feminists to a judgment of women's relationship to men and to religious institutions that is unseen by the older cohort of traditionalists. The patterns found in this table reveal this different orientation in feminists: lower attachment to the institutional church, as seen in less frequent worship attendance, both past and present, and lower involvement in church activities; less frequent private devotional activity; less certain traditional beliefs; and, more individualistic beliefs in setting the course for one's life.

Secondary analysis of survey data does not allow extensive inference; however, there are some questions that can be raised from these findings about the future of religious organizations. Regarding the cohort

TABLE 5

Comparison on Conventional Indicators of Religiosity of Feminists in Liberal Churches with Traditionalists in Fundamentalist Churches

Feminists In Liberal Churches N=51	Traditionalists In Fundamentalist Churches N=21
CHARACTERISTICS	
39% have traditional families	53% have traditional families
61% have nontraditional families	43% have nontraditional families
10% are housewives	57% are housewives
73% work full-time	14% work full-time
10% are over age 55	57% are over 55
45% are college educated	19% are college educated
PUBLIC RELIGIOUS BEHAVIORS	
57% are church members	85% are church members
30% attend church frequently	67% attend church frequently
69% let church attendance lapse	33% let church attendance lapse
34% are involved in church activities	44% are involved in church activities
PRIVATE RELIGIOUS BEHAVIORS	
8% read Bible frequently	43% read Bible frequently
51% read Bible infrequently	43% read Bible infrequently
20% say prayers at meals	67% say prayers at meals
RELIGIOUS BELIEFS	
43% believe God exists	100% believe God exists
28% think it's important to believe without doubts	91% think it's important to believe without doubts
RELIGIOUS ATTITUDES	
10% think it's very important to follow church's teachings	67% think it's important to follow church's teachings
8% think it's very important to use Bible in making decisions	76% think it is very important to use Bible in making decisions.

Source: General Social Survey NORC, 1988.

difference, it is likely that younger women may have only a limited effect on religious institutions, due to their lower level of involvement. As older women age, the strength of traditionalism in the churches may wane, leaving more room for alienated feminist women to return.

However, while traditional women are very active in fundamentalist congregational life, the lower levels of involvement associated with feminist attitudes may have a negative impact on the vitality of the liberal churches they are more likely to choose. The limited evidence presented here suggests that, while family and church are closely connected for traditionalist women, for feminist women, religious experience is a much more personal and individual matter. If liberal churches expect to attract and keep the commitment of women with nontraditional families and egalitarian views of gender roles, they will probably have to emphasize what this group of women seems to value highly, and that is moral tolerance and openness.

In conclusion, it is apparent that the lasting cultural effects of the civil rights/women's rights/countercultural movements of the 1960s, reported by Roof and McKinney, and the feminism gap among religious women, noted by Wuthnow, are fleshed out in this analysis as well.[16] It was shown here that differences among women reflect the influence of individualistic thinking in the religious sphere. Women who see expansive roles for themselves beyond traditional models apparently extend that privilege to the religious sphere, and expect the same tolerance and openness there. While the rhetoric among political conservatives of returning to "family values" resonates among religious conservatives, feminists are no less concerned about their families than traditionalist women—they simply are more likely to have a different family *structure* within which they are positioned. This places them at different locations within or apart from religious communities, depending on the degree of support their nontraditional lifestyles receive. The challenge to religious institutions is to find ways to respond to the diversity of women's lives.

NOTES

1. Thanks go to Wade Clark Roof and Nancy Ammerman for their guidance and editorial advice in the preparation of this paper.
2. Tim B. Heaton and Marie Cornwall, "Religious Group Variation in the Socioeconomic Status and Family Behavior of Women," *Journal for the Scientific Study of Religion* 28, No. 3 (1989), pp. 283–299; David A. deVaus, "Workforce Participation and Sex Differences in Church Attendance," *Review of Religious Research* 25, No. 3 (1984), pp. 247–256; and David DeVaus and Ian McAllister, "Gender Differences in religion: A Test of the Structural Location Theory," *American Sociological Review* 52, No. 52 (1987), pp. 472–481.

3. Robert Wuthnow, *The Restructuring of American Religion* (Princeton, NJ: Princeton University Press, 1988), p. 226.

4. *Ibid.*

5. *Ibid.*, p. 228.

6. *Ibid.*, p. 229.

7. Kathleen Gerson, *Hard Choices: How Women Decide About Work, Career, and Motherhood* (Berkeley: University of California Press, 1985).

8. Eric Plutzer, "Work Life, Family Life, and Women's Support of Feminism," *American Sociological Review* 53 (1988), pp. 640–649.

9. William V. D'Antonio, "The Family and Religion: Exploring a Changing Relationship," *Journal for the Scientific Study of Religion* 19, No. 2 (1980), p. 91; Nancy T. Ammerman, *Bible Believers: Fundamentalists in the Modern World* (New Brunswick, NJ: Rutgers University Press, 1987), p. 135; and Wade Clark Roof and William McKinney, *American Mainline Religion: Its Changing Shape and Future* (New Brunswick, NJ: Rutgers University Press, 1987), pp. 156, 158.

10. Ammerman, *Bible Believers*, p. 135.

11. *Ibid.*, p. 137.

12. Wuthnow, *Restructuring*.

13. Using multiple regression techniques, two equations were formulated and results analyzed, for the impact of workforce participation, family status, gender-role orientation, education, age, and religious socialization, on church attendance (equation 1), and an index of private religiosity (equation 2; this index scaled frequencies of prayer and Bible-reading, as well as the degree of feeling close to God).

14. Gerson, *Hard Choices*.

15. Arlie Hochschild, *Second Shift* (New York: Viking Press, 1989).

16. Roof and McKinney, *American Mainline Religion*, and Wuthnow, *Restructuring*.

6

Entering the Labor Force

Ideals and Realities among Evangelical Women

Charles Hall

P revious chapters in this volume have offered a variety of portraits of the relationship between religion and family life. Nowhere has the concern for families been more vocal than among conservative religious groups. Conservative protestants have historically favored the idea that women's lives should be principally home- and family-centered. Books on the family written by conservative authors abound with advice such as this:

What is the key to success for a married woman?...it is allowing God to meet her needs through her husband, children and opportunities found through the home.[1]

The maternal role...is the crucial pivot—the foundation upon which both family and society revolve. How women fill that role determines the potential happiness and fulfillment of all of us.[2]

The home is potentially the greatest place for women to be fulfilled.[3]

These statements exemplify the conservative family ideology that has dominated fundamentalism and evangelicalism since the turn of the century. Historically, conservative Protestant groups have opposed the movement of women into the labor force, charging women with the primary responsibility for maintaining a Christian home and raising Christian children.[4] In such circles, this very powerful and effective ideology has prevented many women from even thinking of working outside the home. But is this an ideology of the past? Has not the secularization of society eroded the influence conservative religion once had?

The present study postulates that religion continues to play a significant part in influencing sex-role attitudes and behavior. Of particular interest is whether religion, namely conservative religion, influences the formation of ideals and behavior concerning female family and work roles. By analyzing a survey of 310 conservative Protestant females, we will seek to establish the significance of religion in determining whether or not a woman participates in the labor force. This study suggests that, contrary to the secularization thesis, the economic ideals and behavior of conservative Protestant females are still being influenced by their religion.

THE FORMATION OF GENDER-ROLE IDEALS AND LABOR FORCE BEHAVIOR

Symbolic interactionism provides the theoretical framework for this study.[5] This theory assumes that humans are reflexive, and that our introspection gradually creates a definition of self. It is through introspection that we imagine ourselves as we would "like to be" or as we would "like to act." These imaginations of self reflect our interpersonal concerns, and are idealized and used in forming our identity. It is the identity, or "idealized self," that serves as the primary source of plans of action. The imaginings of what one would like to be and how one would like to act serve as the "rehearsal halls" for actual performance.

Thus, this theoretical model assumes that a good predictor of actual role behavior is the individual's role identity, or "idealized" behavior. How one performs in the rehearsal hall is a good indication of how one will actually perform when the curtain rises. What a woman considers the "ideal" role for her in the family should strongly influence whether she will actually stay at home or enter the labor force. The stronger she holds to that ideal, whether it be traditional or egalitarian, the greater likelihood that her actual behavior will be consistent with those ideals.

Previous research has shown that attitudes about the role of women, and about whether a mother should work, will shape the decision to enter the labor force. Women who define the female role as primarily centered in the home are, in fact, less likely to become involved in paid employment.[6] Conversely, as Scanzoni reports, the greater the "gender role modernity," the more likely a woman is to be employed full-time.[7] Hoffman and Nye suggest that attitudes about children are also important—for example, views about how essential the mother's constant presence is for the child's development.[8]

Based on these past findings, and consistent with the symbolic interactionist perspective, this study will examine whether a woman's "idealized" view of her family role affects whether she will enter the labor force. The more strongly she holds to a traditional ideal, it is hypothesized, the less likely she is to enter the labor force. Likewise, the more strongly she holds to egalitarian[9] ideals, the more likely she is to enter the labor force.

What determines these ideals? What factors determine whether a woman idealizes the traditional role of family caretaker or the egalitarian role of shared family responsibility? Symbolic interactionists believe that ideals are never formed in a vacuum, but are socially constructed in interaction with the situations, experiences, and significant others of the individual. This study will therefore pay attention to both the woman's significant social relationships and to the social situation in which she finds herself—what some symbolic interactionists call social reference relationships and contextual variables.[10] The social reference relationships we will examine are religious beliefs, religious affiliation, and influence of spouse. The contextual variables will include level of education, presence or absence of preschool-aged children, and the economic contribution of the husband. Our theoretical model suggests that each of these external variables will have two kinds of effects—both direct effects on behavior and effects on ideals which, in turn, affect behavior.

Factors to be Examined

Religion. How does religion affect the "idealized" self? Many of our actions are guided by the awareness we have of others' values and their expectations of how we and others ought to behave—what George Herbert Mead called the "generalized other."[11] Religious beliefs and religious groups can play a major role in defining those values and expectations, and thus play a significant part in the formation of the "idealized" self.[12] If the religious community helps to shape the idealized self, then it should shape a wife's ideals about husband-wife roles and motherhood, and ultimately her decision about whether to enter the labor force.[13]

To say that religion helps to shape a woman's sense of the "generalized other," against which she measures her behavior, is not, however, to say what sort of influence religion will have. A number of historians have taken up the task of examining the messages about women's roles that have been communicated in various religious traditions.[14] As social scientists have attempted to assess this relationship between religiosity and sex roles, they have consistently found that the most "religious" women—whether measured by "orthodoxy," congregational membership and participation, or personal devotion—are also the most traditional in their sex-role definitions.[15]

This relationship between religiosity and traditional gender-role attitudes seems to be especially strong in the most conservative churches. In Nancy Ammerman's ethnographic study of a fundamentalist congregation, she observed:

> Southside members come to expect, then, that Christian homes will be headed by a saved man who takes responsibility for the physical, emotional and spiritual needs of the household. By his side will be a saved woman who accepts her role as wife and mother in reverent submission. Ideally, she should spend full time maintaining their home and caring for their children.[16]

Similar results have been found in survey studies. Hesselbart's study, and that by Thornton and Freeman, point out that individuals who are fundamentalist in their religious orientation are more likely than other religious persons to insist that women "stay in their place."[17] Roof and McKinney, in their analysis of data from the General Social Survey, conclude that members of conservative Protestant denominations are the most likely to hold traditional sex-role orientations.[18] As Demmitt explains, "conservative Protestant churches place a high value on the family as the environment for socialization." They believe that social-ization occurs best "when the wife is financially dependent upon the husband so that he is the clear authority figure, and when the wife is committed full-time to overseeing the household and raising the children."[19]

Fundamentalist Protestants, while distinct in their views on gender roles, have certainly not avoided change. In the last two decades, fun-damentalists changed along with the rest of the American population in becoming more egalitarian in their sex-role attitudes, more likely to accept divorce, desirous of smaller families, and the like. However, the extent of the change among religious conservatives is smaller. They are still generally more traditional than other Americans on many aspects of family life.[20] Among the fundamentalists Ammerman studied, a mix of change and tradition was apparent. Their ideals were not always reality. Of the mothers in this church who currently had children under twen-ty-five, only about fifteen percent stayed out of the labor force entirely during their children's growing-up years. Thirty-five percent have worked at jobs that still allowed them to spend most of their time at home, but nearly half of all the mothers were employed full-time out-side the home:

> They continue to hold forth the ideal of full-time motherhood. Cooking, cleaning and child-rearing are the God-given tasks of women. Those who work outside the home define it as an occupation *not* a career. They still see themselves first as wives and mothers. Although they may violate the letter of the rule about working, they by no means violate its spirit."[21]

James Davison Hunter argues that, for evangelicals,[22] the "tradition-al family" has become a symbol of social stability and moral virtue. Hunter catalogs the numerous programs that evangelicals have launched to articulate what the Christian family should be. The prob-lem, says Hunter, is that the family has become so idealized that it has become elevated to unprecedented levels of symbolic importance. It is romanticized:

> The wife's principal responsibility is in the home, serving the needs of her husband and children, transforming the home into a haven…a place of God's peace and warmth and love. She is homemaker in the fullest sense of the word, accountable to her husband and ultimately to God for her per-formance in this role.[23]

Of key interest for Hunter is the younger or "coming generation" of evangelicals. They are caught in the middle, and relate both to the "ideals of the Christian family, publicly advocated by those who supposedly represent them, and to postmodern family patterns developing in the broader culture."[24] For example, thirty-four percent of Hunter's young evangelicals agreed with the statement: "Though it is not always possible, it is best if the wife stays home and the husband works to support the family." This was considerably more than in the secular comparison group, but it was a minority view within the evangelical sample.[25]

The religious beliefs that are of interest here are those that attribute differences in male-female gender roles to the intentions of God. We will test whether women who believe God intended men and women to be equal are also more likely to hold egalitarian ideals regarding work, homemaking, and motherhood. Such ideals should, then, increase the chance that these women will enter the labor force. It should be noted that egalitarian religious beliefs, as applied to male-female roles, are likely to have developed from a less-than-literal view of scripture. Women with such views see the historical context of the scriptures as patriarchal, and accentuate the "spirit" of the message that "in Christ there is no male or female."

Religious beliefs, of course, are usually formed in the context of a religious community. This study will also examine whether religious affiliation has an effect on female ideals and labor force participation. Like ethnic groups and other community groups, religious groups can serve as reference groups. Erskine found that, by providing an evaluative standard for women with regard to employment, reference groups affect women's ultimate decision to work or not to work.[26]

If the church is seen as a reference group, then employment and leadership patterns within the churches ought to serve as a reference pattern for their members. That is, the presence or absence of leadership opportunities for women will directly or indirectly affect gender-role attitudes and employment behavior among the female constituents. Roof and McKinney have observed that churches vary in their views toward women. Some churches, such as Episcopalians, United Church of Christ, Presbyterians and Methodists, have developed policies that have expanded female leadership opportunities to include both ordained and nonordained positions. At the same time, other churches, such as the Nazarenes, Southern Baptists, and Pentecostals, are more restrictive in their views of women in leadership roles.[27] Thus, a woman who is a member of a church where women are permitted to hold positions of leadership at all levels will have a more egalitarian reference group and may have more egalitarian views than women who are in more restrictive environments. The "church" variable used here refers to the religious organization with which the respondent is affiliated, and is a measure of the openness of that organization to female leadership.

Husband's Ideals. A second factor affecting the "idealized" self is the influence of "significant others." Among the most important of those, of course, is a spouse. It is expected that a woman's husband's ideals concerning appropriate family roles will strongly influence her ideals and her decision about whether to enter the labor force. The more egalitarian her husband's ideals concerning work and homemaking roles, the more egalitarian her ideals—and thus her behavior—are likely to be.

Preschool Children. The third factor affecting the "idealized" self of the potentially working woman is the presence or absence of preschool children. Because our culture places child care responsibilities primarily on women, ideals for labor force participation will certainly be different for the woman who has children and for one who does not. These norms are especially strong when the child is quite young. Babies and toddlers require more time than older children, and their care is more crucial, presumably because of their lack of judgment and relatively undeveloped skills.[28] Thus, if a woman has any preschool age children, she may be less likely to have egalitarian ideals regarding work, homemaking, and motherhood.

Level of Education. A fourth factor that must be considered in estimating the likelihood that a woman will be in the labor force is the woman's level of education. We know that having a college degree increases the opportunities of employment for women.[29] Among women twenty-five to fifty-four years of age, with four or more years of college in March 1988, eighty-one percent were in the labor force. Among women of the same age group with less than four years of high school, only fifty-one percent were in the labor force.[30] Women with more education may be more likely to be in the labor force simply because they have increased opportunity.

But they are also likely to think differently about themselves—to have different ideals—due to their experience in educational institutions. Kohn argues that education provides the "intellectual flexibility and breadth of perspective that are essential for self-directed values and orientation."[31] Many have argued that advanced formal education provides a broader, more universalistic set of values that are "less vulnerable to the narrow appeals of intergroup negativism."[32] A more highly educated person is thought to be less conforming, more conscious of equality, and thus more apt to have egalitarian views of male-female roles.

Specifically, several studies have reported that, among women, higher educational levels are associated with more modern, individualistic, egalitarian gender role norms, even to more favorable responses to maternal employment.[33]

Therefore, we will expect that higher levels of formal education will result in more egalitarian, gender-role ideals and a higher likelihood of entering the labor force.

Husband's Income. Finally, a fifth factor to be considered in understanding a woman's decision to enter the labor force is her husband's income. Economic variables are often powerful predictors of behavior. Thus the husband's economic contribution to the household may predict whether the wife will enter the labor force. If the husband makes a sufficient income to support the needs and desires of the family, the wife may be less likely to enter the labor force.

However, there may be countervailing forces at work here. Some literature suggests that being in a higher social class increases egalitarian ideals. Kohn suggests that working class people are more traditional in their general values and experience a greater sex-role division than do middle-class people.[34] It may be, therefore, that higher income makes egalitarian ideals more likely, but does not necessarily increase (and in fact may decrease) the likelihood of participation in the labor force.

In summary, this study attempts to discover whether the above factors significantly influence a woman's decision to enter the labor force. A woman's "idealized" self concerning her role in the family is believed to be the most important factor. Her "idealized" self and ultimately her decision to enter the labor force are influenced by her religious beliefs and church affiliation, her husband's ideals about a woman's role in the family, the presence of preschool children, her level of education, and her husband's income.

Methods

The Sample

Christianity Today is a religious magazine that has traditionally attracted conservative Protestant subscribers. Theologically, subscribers of *Christianity Today* would be labeled evangelical; although some would prefer to be called fundamentalist. For our purposes, the term "conservative Protestants" will be used to describe the population.

In January 1990, *Christianity Today*'s (CT) research department sent a mailed questionnaire to 1,250 CT subscribers who were randomly selected on an "*nth*" name basis from a list of all subscribers.[35] Five hundred nine households mailed back completed questionnaires producing a response rate of forty-one percent. A total of 739 individual responses were received, which included 381 females and 358 males. Since we were interested in explaining female labor force participation, we excluded male respondents. In addition we were only concerned with the views of those females who were married. Thus, our base sample size was reduced to 310 married females.

The Variables

"Female Labor Force Participation" was measured by asking the respondents to check which category best described their employment status: homemaker, employed part-time, employed full-time.

"Wife's Ideals" about her appropriate role in the family were measured by two questions asking her preference concerning what role she would like to play in the family. A third question measured her attitude about whether married women with young children should work. These three questions produced a scale from traditional to egalitarian ideals.

Two questions were used to determine "Religious Beliefs" regarding male-female roles. The first question asked whether she felt God intended males and females to have different roles. The second question asked whether she believes the Bible affirms male headship. These two questions produced a scale of traditional to egalitarian religious beliefs.

The "Church" variable measures how egalitarian her church is. This was determined by asking the respondent to check how many leadership positions in her church were open to females. The more leadership positions open to women, the more egalitarian the church.

"Husband's Ideals" were determined by a question asking his preference for either a marriage where the husband provided for the family and the wife managed the house, or one where both husband and wife worked and shared household tasks. Again, this produced a scale for the husband ranging from traditional to egalitarian ideals.

"Preschool Children" is a measure of whether very young children are present in the home, coded simply "yes" or "no" (a dummy variable).

Finally, the last two variables in the model are "Wife's Education" and "Husband's Income". "Wife's Education" is a measure of the amount of education she has beyond high school. "Husband's Income" is a measure of the total amount of income last year before taxes.[36]

Testing the Model

The relationships among these variables were examined by a method called path analysis. Such a method can provide a useful graphic picture of relationships among several variables. In this case, we were able to test whether the six variables described above have effects on the wife's "idealized" self, and whether those same variables, plus her idealized self, affect her decision to enter the labor force.

Figure I reveals the results of the path analysis. Larger numbers (coefficients) indicate stronger relationships. Positive numbers indicate that, as one variable increases or decreases, the other moves in the same direction; negative numbers indicate the opposite. Only effects found to be "statistically significant" are included in the figure.

In brief, as we predicted, "Wife's Ideals" concerning her role in the family are a strong predictor of whether she enters the labor force (.397). However, only two factors significantly influence those ideals: "Religious Beliefs" (.437) and "Wife's Education" (.151). The egalitarianism of her church, her husband's ideals about a woman's role in the home, the presence or absence of preschool children, and her husband's income had no effect on her ideals.

While the woman's ideals were the single strongest predictor of her decision to enter the labor force, other factors were important, as well. Having preschool children (-.243) and a husband with a higher income (-.251) decreased the likelihood that she was in the labor force, as did belonging to a more egalitarian church (-.150). Her own education, as expected, increased her chances of being in the labor force. Her "Religious Beliefs," while having a strong effect on her ideals, had no direct effect on her decision to enter the labor force. "Husband's Ideals" completely drop out of the model, having no effect on her ideals or her decision to enter the labor force.

Interpreting the Results

What conclusions might be drawn from these results? First, the best predictor of actual role behavior is the individual's role identity or "idealized" behavior. Knowing whether a wife has traditional or egalitarian ideals about family and work roles is the best predictor of female labor force participation.

However, her decisions are also influenced by the constraints and opportunities represented by the presence or absence of preschool children, her own level of education, and her husband's income. If she has at least one preschool child, she is less likely to be in the labor force. The higher her education, the more likely she is to be in the labor force. And as predicted, the higher her husband's income, the less likely she is to be working outside the home. This study confirms the continuing influence of these factors, even among conservative Protestant women whose choices are also shaped by their gender-role ideals.

FIGURE 1

Path Model for Female Labor Force Participation

(with only significant variables and paths indicated)

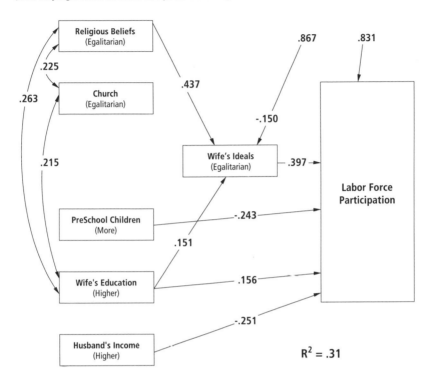

That *both* ideals and other factors affect a woman's decision to enter the labor force may give us some hints about the difficulty of these decisions. While their ideals may lead them in one direction, the reality of their family and economic situation may lead them in another. Future research should address this tension.

The second major point to be noted is that in this sample of conservative protestant women, religious beliefs do strongly influence role identity and "idealized" behavior concerning family roles and motherhood. And by affecting these ideals, religious beliefs indirectly influence female labor force participation.[37] The direct effect of religious beliefs on labor force participation, however, was not supported. Such evidence suggests that conservative religious beliefs about appropriate female family roles do not necessarily translate into behavior consistent with those beliefs. As suggested above, ideals have to be weighed alongside more mundane factors such as income, education, and family structure. In other words, one cannot necessarily predict that strong, conservative, religious beliefs about a woman's role in the family will keep her out of the labor force. Religion is still having an important impact on behavior, but even among these conservative protestants we see evidence of change.

The influence of a woman's religious community (the "Church" variable) turned out to be different from what we expected. It was hypothesized that the more egalitarian her church was, the more likely it was that a woman would be in the labor force. Surprisingly, however, a negative correlation was observed. The more egalitarian her church, the less likely she was to be in the labor force. And there was no relationship between her church's openness to female leadership and her ideals about family roles and motherhood. This result is likely explained by a social class component that was not addressed by this study. Denominations that are more egalitarian in their views toward women also have constituents with higher social and economic status.[38] Another possible explanation is that these women are actually minority voices in otherwise liberal churches. Their ideals are being formed by their own beliefs and not necessaarily by their particular congregation. Further research is needed to untangle these effects.

In summary, religion does have an effect on female labor force participation among conservative protestants. But their economic ideals and behavior are not always consistent. For many women, their conservative ideals about motherhood do not necessarily translate into a traditional family lifestyle where the wife stays at home. This inconsistency between religious ideals and reality indicates that other forces are at work circumventing these long-standing traditional views. Still to be determined are the long-term effects of such inconsistencies on individual believers and on conservative religion in general.

APPENDIX A
Questions Used in Study

FEMPLOY: Which one of the following best describes your employment status?

1 Homemaker (41%)
2 Employed Part-time (25%)
3 Employed Full-time (33%)

FIDEALS: 1) (FIDEAL2) If you were free to do either, would you prefer
                  to…

                  1 Stay home and take care of family and house
                  2 Don't know
                  3 Have a job outside the home

                  2) (FIDEAL1) The most satisfying lifestyle for me would be…

                  1 A marriage in which the husband provides for the family
                    and the wife manages the house and children
                  2 A marriage where both husband and wife work and share
                    household tasks and child care

                  3) (SALMOTH2) Married women with young
                  children should not work outside the home…

                  1 Agree
                  2 Not sure
                  3 Disagree

INTERCORRELATION

	FIDEAL1	FIDEAL2	SALMOTH2
FIDEAL1	1.000	.6869**	.4881**
FIDEAL2	.6869**	1.000	.3562**
SALMOTH2	.4881**	.3562**	1.000

(Minimum pairwise N of cases: 298** - .001)

FRELBEL: 1) (FRELBEL1) God made men and women to be equal in per-
                  sonhood and in value, but different in roles…

                  Strongly Agee (1) to Strongly disagree (5)

                  2) (FRELBEL2) The Bible affirms the principle of male head-
                  ship in the family…

                  Strongly Agree (1) to Strongly Disagree (5)

INTERCORRELATION

	FRELBEL1	FRELBEL2
FRELBEL1	1.000	.6196**
FRELBEL2	.6196**	1.000

(Minimum pairwise N of cases: 306** - .001)

CHURCH: In your church, which of the following types of
                  leadership positions may women hold?

Position	Values
1 Pastor/Minister	3
2 Assistant/Associate Pastor	3
3 Chairperson of Church Board	2

(*Appendix A continued*)

Position	Values
4 Committee/Commission Leader	2
5 Elder	2
6 Deacon	2
7 Deaconess	2
8 Trustee	2
9 Youth Director	1
10 Music/Choir Director	1
11 Sunday School Superintendent	1
12 Adult Sunday School Teacher	1
TOTAL	22

MIDEAL: The most satisfying lifestyle for me would be…

1 A marriage in which the husband provides for the family and the wife manages the house and children
2 A marriage where both husband and wife work and share household tasks and child care

RESPONSE OF HUSBANDS WHOSE WIVES ARE IN THE LABOR FORCE:

Value	Frequency	Percentage
1	77	68%
2	36	32%
	48 (Missing Cases)	

RESPONSE OF HUSBANDS WHOSE WIVES ARE AT HOME:

Value	Frequency	Percentage
1	74	84%
2	14	16%
	25 (Missing Cases)	

FREQUENCIES AFTER ASSIGNING 1 TO MISSING CASES:

Value	Frequency	Percentage
12	24	82%
25	0	18%

PRESCHO: Including yourself, how many individuals in the listed categories live in your household?

1 Do not have children who are 5 years old and under
2 Do have children who are 5 years old and under

FEDUC: Do you have a four year college degree? Do you have a graduate or seminary degree?

1 Less than a college degree
2 Four year college degree only
3 Both college and graduate degree

FAMINC: What was your total family income before taxes
             last year?

Under $10,000
$10,000–14,999
$15,000–19,999
$20,000–29,999
$30,000–34,999
$35,000–39,999
$40,000–49,999
$50,000–59,999
$60,000–74,999
$75,000–99,999
$100,000–149,000
$150,000 or more

NOTES

1. Don Meredith, *Becoming One* (Nashville, TN: Thomas Nelson Publishers, n.d.), p. 156.

2. Peter W. Blitchington, *Sex Roles and the Christian Family* (Wheaton: Tyndale House, 1980), p. 95.

3. Meredith, *Becoming One*, p. 153.

4. Betty DeBerg, *Ungodly Women* (Minneapolis, MN: Augsburg Fortress, 1990).

5. Primary sources for this account of symbolic interactionism are Arnold M. Rose, ed., *Human Behavior and Social Processes* (Boston, MA: Houghton Mifflin, 1962), pp. 11–12; Charles Horton Cooley, *Human Nature and the Social Order* (New York: Scribner's, 1922); and George J. McCall and J.L. Simmons, *Identities and Interactions* (New York: Free Press, 1978).

6. L.W. Hoffman, "The Decision to Work," in *The Employed Mother in America*, eds. F.I. Nye and L.W. Hoffman, (Chicago, IL: Rand McNally, 1963); J.N. Morgan, M. David, W. Cohen, and H. Brazer, *Income and Welfare in the United States* (New York: McGraw-Hill, 1962); A. Thornton, D.F. Alwin, and D. Camburn, "Causes and Consequences of Sex-Role Attitudes and Attitude Change," *American Sociological Review* 48 (1983), pp. 211–227; J.R. Shea, K. Sookin, and R.D. Roderick, *Dual Careers: A Longitudinal Study of Labor Market Experience of Women*, vol. 2, Manpower Research Monograph 21 (Washington, D.C.: Government Printing Office, 1973). Women's Bureau, U.S. Dept. of Labor, *College Women Seven Years after Graduation, Resurvey of Women Graduates—Class of 1957*, in *Bulletin 292* (Washington, D.C.: Government Printing Office, 1966).

7. J. Scanzoni, *Sex Roles, Life-styles, and Childbearing: Changing Patterns in Marriage and Family* (New York: Free Press, 1975).

8. L.W. Hoffman and F. Ivan Nye, *Working Mothers* (San Francisco, CA: Jossey-Bass, 1974).

9. The term "egalitarian" will be used throughout this study to describe those attitudes and behaviors that minimize male-female role differences regarding family and work responsibilities.

10. Wesley Burr, Reuben Hill, F.Ivan Nye, and Ira L. Reiss, eds., *Contemporary Theories about the Family*, vol. 2 (New York: The Free Press, 1979).

11. George Herbert Mead, *Mind, Self, and Society: From the Standpoint of a Social Behaviorist* (Chicago, IL: University of Chicago Press, 1934).

12. Paul H. Chalfant, Robert Beckley, and Eddie C. Palmer, *Religion in Contemporary Society* (Mountain View, CA: Mayfield Pub. Co., 1987), p. 27.

13. Religious beliefs are hypothesized to have direct and indirect effects on female labor force participation. Morgan and Scanzoni ("Religious Orientations") found that religious commitment did not have a strong direct effect on sustained employment, but it did have a strong indirect effect through sex-role attitudes. Both will be examined in the present study.

14. On women in the Christian tradition, see Martha J. Reineke, "Out of Order: A Critical Perspective on Women in Religion," in *Women: A Feminist Perspective*, ed. Jo Freeman (Mountain View, CA: Mayfield Publishing Co., 1989); William M. Newman, "Religion," in *Sex Roles and Social Patterns*, eds. Francis Bordeau, Roger Sennott, and Michael Wilson (New York: Praeger Publishers, 1986); Rosemary Ruether, ed., *Religion and Sexism* (New York: Simon and Schuster, 1973); and her "The Feminist Critique in Religious Studies," in *A Feminist Perspective in the Academy*, eds. E. Langland and W. Gove (Chicago, IL: University of Chicago Press, 1981), 52–66.

15. For a review of the literature, see Kevin Demmitt, *Dual-Earner Families and Conservative Churches: Accommodation and Conflict*, Unpublished doc. diss. (Purdue University, 1990). See also Tim B. Heaton and Marie Cornwall, "Religious Group Variation in the Socioeconomic Status and Family Behavior of Women," *Journal for the Scientific Study of Religion* 28, No. 3 (1989), pp. 283–299; Wade Clark Roof and William McKinney, *American Mainline Religion: Its Changing Shape and Future* (New Brunswick, NJ: Rutgers University Press, 1987); Merlin B. Brinkerhoff and Marlene M. Mackie, "Religious Denominations' Impact upon Gender Attitudes: Some Methodological Implications," *Review of Religious Research* 25 (1984), pp. 365–368; also their "Religion and Gender: A Comparison of Canadian and American Student Attitudes," *Journal of Marriage and the Family* 47 (1985), pp. 415–429; Howard M. Bahr, "Religious Contrasts in Family Role Definitions and Performance; Utah Mormons, Catholics, Protestants and Others," *Journal for the Scientific Study of Religion* 21 (1982), pp. 200–217; and Mary V. Morgan and John Scanzoni, "Religious Orientations and Women's Expected Continuity in the Labor Force," *Journal of Marriage and the Family* 49 (1987), pp. 367–379.

16. Nancy T. Ammerman, *Bible Believers: Fundamentalists in the Modern World* (New Brunswick, NJ: Rutgers University Press, 1987), p. 136.

17. S. Hesselbart, "A Comparison of Attitudes toward Women and Attitudes toward Blacks in a Southern City," *Sociological Symposium* 17 (Fall 1976), pp. 45–68; also A. Thornton and D. Freedman, "Changes in the Sex-Role Attitudes of Women, 1962–1977: Evidence from a Panel Study," *American Sociological Review* 44 (October 1979), pp. 831–42.

18. Roof and McKinney, *American Mainline Religion.*

19. Demmitt, *Dual Earner Families*, p. 16.

20. A. Thornton, D.F. Alwin, and D. Camburn, "Causes and Consequences of Sex-Role Attitudes and Attitude Change," *American Sociological Review* 48 (1983), pp. 211–227; and A. Thornton, "Changing Attitudes toward Separation and Divorce: Causes and Consequences," *American Journal of Sociology* 90 (January 1985), pp. 856–72.

21. Ammerman, *Bible Believers*, p. 137.

22. Fundamentalists and evangelicals are sometimes thought of as different labels describing the same group. These groups must be understood, however, as having both similarities and differences. The differences center around the degree to which believers are willing to get along with the rest of the world. As Ammerman argues (in *Bible Believers*) Evangelicals take a more accommodating stance than do fundamentalists. Scripture is viewed differently; fundamentalists are more likely to view it as literal and to be taken at face value. Evangelicals are more comfortable with ambiguities of interpretation resulting from critical analysis.

23. James Davison Hunter, *Evangelicalism: The Coming Generation* (Chicago, IL: University of Chicago Press, 1987).

24. *Ibid.*, p. 93.

25. *Ibid.*

26. H. Erskine, "The Polls: Women's Role," *Public Opinion Quarterly* 35 (1971), pp. 282–84.

27. Roof and McKinney, *American Mainline Religion*; see also Barbara Hargrove, "Family in the White American Protestant Experience," in *Families and Religions*, eds. William D'Antonio and Joan Aldous (Beverly Hills, CA: Sage, 1983).

28. Burr, Hill, Nye, and Reiss, *Contemporary Theories.*

29. Sar A. Levitan, Richard S. Belous, and Frank Gallo, *What's Happening to the American Family?* (Baltimore, MD: Johns Hopkins University Press, 1988).

30. Women's Bureau, U.S. Department of Labor, "20 Facts on Women Workers," September 1990.

31. Melvin L. Kohn, *Class and Conformity* (Chicago: University of Chicago Press, 1977).

32. Mary R. Jackman and Michael J. Muha, "Education and Intergroup Attitudes: Moral Enlightenment, Superficial Democratic Commitment,

or Ideological Refinement?," *American Sociological Review* 49 (1984), p. 751. For more on the "education as liberation" view, see also Harold E. Quinley and Charles Glock, *Anti-Semitism in America* (New York: Free Press, 1979); and Seymour Martin Lipset, *Political Man* (Baltimore, MD: Johns Hopkins University Press, 1981).

33. H. Holter, *Sex Roles and Social Structure* (Oslo: Universitetsforlaget, 1970); also J. Scanzoni, *Sex Roles, Life-Styles, and Childbearing: Changing Patterns in Marriage and Family* (New York: Free Press, 1975); and J.R. Shea, K. Sookin, and R.D. Roderick, *Dual Careers: A Longitudinal Study of Labor Market Experience of Women*, vol. 2, Manpower Research Monograph 21 (Washington, D.C.: Government Printing Office, 1973).

34. Kohn, *Class and Conformity*.

35. Secondary data provided by the *Christianity Today* Research Department were used for this study. The survey was conducted in January 1990, and was designed to measure the attitudes and theological beliefs of *Christianity Today* subscribers and their spouses regarding female and male roles in church, home, and society. The researchers also wanted to determine the lifestyle/behavior of subscribers and their spouses as it relates to sex roles.

36. The question asks for total income from all sources including the wife's. For our purposes, it was necessary to obtain a measure that would most nearly represent what the family income would have been if she had not contributed to it. It therefore became necessary to create a surrogate variable by estimating the percentage of what the average working female contributes to the family income and subtracting that out of the total. If the wife worked full-time, it was estimated that she contributed approximately 40% to the family income. If the wife worked part-time it was estimated that her contribution was approximately 20%. These estimates were derived from Levitan, Belous and Gallo (*What's Happening*).

37. This model explains 31 percent of the variance in Female Labor Force Participation, compared to the Princeton Fertility Study's 14 variable model that explained 33 percent of the variance (see Marion Gros Sobol, "Commitment to Work," in *Working Mothers*, eds. Lois W. Hoffman and F. Ivan Nye (San Francisco, CA: Josey-Bass, 1974), pp. 63–80). Religion was not a variable used in that study. Thus, using religious variables, a similar amount of variance was explained with fewer variables in the model.

38. Roof and McKinney, *American Mainline Religion*.

II

Exploring New Patterns

7

Religion and Family Ethics

A New Strategy for the Church

Don S. Browning

T he decline of the mainline churches in our society is a phenomenon that has been well documented and widely discussed in a variety of recent books and articles.[1] This decline is deep, and covers nearly every aspect of church life—finances, church membership, confidence, sense of identity, and broader social influence and prestige. I suggest that one of the reasons for this decline—and there are many reasons—is the failure of these churches to develop a strong and commanding family ministry.

Documenting the actual decline of this ministry is difficult to do. It is not difficult to demonstrate that the general public perceives these churches to have retreated from the support and protection of the family; the public further believes the bulwark of energetic family policy has moved to the evangelical and fundamentalist groups, best symbolized, perhaps, by the so-called profamily stance of the Moral Majority.[2] Furthermore, it is now well established in the sociological literature that the denominations that are growing numerically in our society, such as the Mormons, the Assemblies of God, and the Southern Baptists, have strong family emphases.[3] Whether or not the mainline churches have retreated from the family field, they are perceived to be more conflicted, less decisive, and more embarrassed by their family ministries than they once were and than are the more conservative manifestations of the church.

It is my conviction that the mainline churches should recapture leadership in the family field. Or, to say it more defensively, they should not so easily permit the family field to be dominated by the more reactionary conservative and fundamentalist groups of our society. Stated more positively, the complexities of the situation of the modern family require the commitment to honest biblical, historical, theological, and philosophical inquiry; accurate utilization of the social sciences; rigorous ideology critique; and appreciation for certain values of feminism that the liberal churches at least espouse, even though they do not always exhibit them. Recapturing the family field is not only vital to the survival of these churches, it is vital to the fulfillment of an authentic Christian mission.

I am further convinced, however, that, for the mainline churches to do this, they must devise a commanding new family ethic. This new ethic must be flexible enough to relate to a variety of family forms that exist today, but firm enough to both guide and protect the family from the acids of modernization, rapid social change, and the associated drift toward anomic individualism typical of much of contemporary life. On the other hand, it should be an ethic that not only can relate to the families of the congregation and the families of the wider society, it also should apply to the minister's own family, as well as to the way the church itself constitutes a kind of family to its members.

This new family emphasis and strategy should understand that the family constitutes a new and energizing avenue into a variety of wider public issues. A ministry to the family need not end in privatization and a retreat from the church's wider mission to shape the public world. In fact, issues confronting the family can be avenues for linking our so-called personal and intimate relations with the wider issues of education, work, taxation, welfare, medical care, and national defense. Rather than being an obstacle to the public ministry of the church, the family can be a revitalizing avenue to a public ministry—an avenue that joins significant and widely experienced public issues with the vital energies of intimate family affections and commitments.

The idea that the family is an obstacle to the church's public witness may have been an implication of Gibson Winter's influential reinterpretation of Talcott Parsons's sociology of religion. Parsons taught that, in modern societies, secondary institutions such as education, the economy, law, and government differentiate from direct control by religion.[4] This leaves religion with only one institution—the family—that it can directly relate to and shape. Although Parsons believed the church in modern societies still is a carrier at the cultural level of some of the highest values by which society measures itself, its direct influence had narrowed to assisting parents to socialize their children and achieve emotional satisfaction with each other.[5] Whereas Parsons had a rather positive way of stating these things—seeming to say, "Look, the church still has a crucial role in our society"—Winter's evaluation of this alleged narrowing of the church's influence was quite different. In his widely read *The Suburban Captivity of the Churches*, Winter strongly criticized the close association of the church and the residential community (and by implication, the family).[6] He felt that the embeddedness of the church in these communities captured it to parochial and familial concerns and kept it from becoming involved in the larger issues facing the city and the wider public world.[7] From then on, I believe, an implicit split between public and private began to affect the mission strategies of the mainline churches. Family life, sexuality, and intimate relations were seen as part of the private world, and issues of work, legislative matters, education, the economy, and foreign policy were perceived as matters of the public world. It was thought that a church with a heroic mission, either at the local or national level, should address the latter and let the former be more or less a matter of individual Christian preference and lifestyle. For over two decades there has been the implicit assumption in the mainline churches that mission to the public world was somehow antithetical to mission focused on the family. Only gradually has it become clear that family issues and wider public issues—residential-familial issues and issues that relate to the whole city and the wider society—interpenetrate. Sooner or later, all public issues penetrate the family. And conversely, starting with the family, one sooner or later gets to all other public issues. Furthermore, getting to public issues through the immediate and vitally felt experiences of family life may be a strategy for revitalizing and empowering our mission to the wider public world. The public church and the local residential church may have more in common than we have led ourselves to believe.

MODERNIZATION, THE FAMILY, AND THE ETHICS OF AUTONOMY

Two recent programmatic essays by sociologists have presented powerful descriptions of the interaction of religion and the family within the context of modern societies. Furthermore, they have offered suggestions for a future strategy. In contrast to most sociologists, they have used their descriptive and diagnostic work to inform normative proposals of the kind that take them into the realms of ethics and theology.

The essays are by William D'Antonio and Barbara Hargrove.[8] In his presidential address before the Society for the Scientific Study of Religion, titled "The Family and Religion: Exploring a Changing Relationship," D'Antonio demonstrates how both religion and the family have evolved toward serving the values of personal autonomy and individual fulfillment. As recently as thirty years ago, with the publication of Lenski's *The Religious Factor*, there was a clear difference between Catholicism, Judaism, and mainline Protestantism in the way they influenced and shaped the family.[9] Catholics were less inclined to divorce, had larger families, were more oriented around the extended family, less socially mobile, and more conservative in their attitudes toward sexual ethics, contraception, and abortion than were either Protestants or Jews. Protestants and Jews reflected the general social trend typical of modernization that favored personal autonomy and mobility, and saw these values as central for the socialization of their children.[10] According to D'Antonio, within the intervening twenty-five years almost all of these differences have disappeared, and Catholics have moved toward the values of personal autonomy and individualism typical of the mainline Protestant and liberal Jewish groups.[11]

D'Antonio agrees with recent critiques by Bellah and others that the value of individual autonomy has become significantly disconnected from the restraints that, as Tocqueville noticed so astutely, the Protestant ethic provided during an earlier era. Barbara Hargrove, in her essay, "The Church, the Family and the Modernization Process," extends this analysis, and shows how both Western religion, of which liberal Protestantism may be the prototypical illustration, and the family have undergone this persistent drift toward the values of autonomy, individualism, and privatism.[12] Hargrove's essay has the virtue of demonstrating that there are two types of modernization process—the Eastern or Marxist version, and the Western or liberal capitalist version. In contrast to the Western version, with its celebration of the values of individualism and personal autonomy, the Marxist version accentuates the application of technical rationality to social life within the context of communal and corporate values, sometimes of an unbending and rigid kind.

At the end of their articles, both authors call for the church to develop a new strategy that provides a reformulated religious ethic of love to guide the documentable widespread hunger among the young for meaningful and enduring relationships with members of the opposite sex.[13] According to D'Antonio, although autonomy and self-actualization (as Yankelovich and others have also shown) are central values for the young, there is also among them a deep-seated hunger for love.[14] D'Antonio believes that there is a major new mission for the church to address from a religious perspective the meaning of love for contemporary couples and families. Hargrove builds on D'Antonio when she writes, "It would appear, then, that what is called for in the present age is a commitment of religious institutions to an ethic of love as strong as the early Protestant commitment to work, giving theological grounding for loving relationships and institutional examples and support for their maintenance."[15]

At first glance, D'Antonio's and Hargrove's proposals sound either bland, trite, or self-evident. But to conclude this would be to miss the sociological context of their suggestions. For the love that they are proposing is one that takes account of the drive for autonomy implicit in most contemporary love relationships—an autonomy which frequently works to the detriment of the very love relation that the autonomous individual attempts to create. The marriages and families that they are envisioning are not based simply on external institutional commands or dry principles of duty. Rather it is a love that both takes account of but also restructures the contemporary drive for autonomy and self-actualization. Following Foote, D'Antonio defines love as a "relationship between two or more persons that is concerned with the optimal development of each of them."[16] Following her analogy on the liberating potential of the new love ethic with the old Protestant work ethic, Hargrove writes: "As the religious work ethic freed individuals from the externally imposed obligations of the traditional kin group or neighborhood so that they could participate in the economic aspects of modernization, so now a religious love ethic might return them to their families as autonomous persons choosing their own commitments."[17]

Both D'Antonio and Hargrove, in their concepts of love, are struggling to take account of the contemporary drive toward autonomy; both are envisioning a religious image of love that includes, rather than overrides, this contemporary thrust toward autonomy, individuation, and self-actualization. Yet they are attempting to balance this with an equally strong emphasis on a love that is concerned with the autonomy, individuation, and self-actualization of the other. Hence, in a rather unclear and inarticulate way, both are attempting to formulate an understanding of love that includes both autonomy or individuation *and* relatedness.

All of this leads to the question, what kind of ethic is being proposed here, and is it conceivable within a Christian understanding of love?

AUTONOMY AND AN ETHIC OF EQUAL-REGARD

The response of some religious commentators to the emerging ethic of autonomy and self-actualization is to reassert an ethic of duty and self-sacrifice. This is their understanding of both the commands of the Christian faith and the requirements of modern life. This is close to what Robert Bellah and his associates appear to do in their chapter on "Love and Marriage" in *Habits of the Heart*. After examining the various languages of love present in the words of their interviewees, and detecting a widespread utilitarian and expressive individualism, they seem to side with those groups in our society who advocate an evangelical ethic of duty and self-sacrificial giving that is anchored in a larger covenant understanding of the couple's common vocation before God.[18] Although their criticism of the contemporary therapeutic ethic of self-actualization is insightful, it also seems unbalanced. Just as the authors of *Habits* have a difficult time gaining a balanced understanding of the role of the therapeutic in our culture, they also have a difficult time developing an ethic of love that includes within it a place for autonomy, self-actualization, and individuation.

In this respect, the implicit ethics of love in *Habits* is not unlike the ethics of love in much of neo-orthodox theology. For instance, although Reinhold Niebuhr could state a role for the energizing power of eros and self-actualization in the Christian doctrine of love as *agape*, he still believed self-sacrificial love was the meaning of *agape* and the final norm of the Christian life.[19] As Benton Johnson has pointed out, this formulation of love gave mainline Protestantism a moral tone that provided little role for self-affirmation, self-interest, and other values that go into the master value of autonomy.[20] Hence, according to Johnson, at the same time that Western modernization was pushing American society more and more toward the values of autonomy and self-actualization, the social ethic of love promulgated by the church was more and more unable to include a place for these values. When people were searching for a love that included autonomy and self-actualization, they heard from the mainline, socially active churches a screeching ethic of self-sacrificial duty that squeezed out all elements of individual fulfillment and enrichment. Johnson proposes a reformulation of the Gospel message, based on a more optimistic note, and which affirms a constrained and principled autonomy typical of the older religious liberalism that neo-orthodoxy replaced. Although I would not personally want to give up the realistic doctrine of sin that characterized Niebuhr's theology, the remainder of this essay is designed to investigate an ethic of love that both incorporates, extends, and balances some of the suggestions put forth by D'Antonio, Hargrove, and Johnson.

Actually Niebuhr did have a rather positive place in his anthropology for what he called "ordinate" self-concern and self-actualization.[21] He thought, however, that the universal human inability to trustingly confront finitude and anxiety leads us all to become "inordinately" concerned with our security, our autonomy, and our self-actualization. It is this "inordinate" concern, not our ordinate concern, that is our sin. But in spite of this, Niebuhr did formulate his ethics of love around the concept of self-sacrificial love. In contrast to the extreme position of Anders Nygren, who gave no place in *agape* at all for *eros* or self-actualization, Niebuhr believed that *agape* as self-sacrificial love did use—but by transforming—our natural and ordinate energies (*eros*) toward self-concern, self-interest, and self-actualization.[22]

But Niebuhr could never adequately formulate the role of autonomy and self-actualization in a Christian ethic of love. The proof of this can be seen in his continued subordination of love as mutuality to love as self-sacrifice.[23] An ethic of mutuality was, for Niebuhr, a concession that our finite and sinful human condition seems to require, because of our inability to uphold steadfastly and constantly the higher call to self-sacrificial living.[24] An ethic of mutuality always finds a place for self-regard (and the autonomy and self-actualization that self-regard assumes) just as it finds a place for regard for the other. But for Niebuhr, such an ethic of equal-regard for self and other was seen as a concession to the fallenness of history, rather than an essential norm of the Christian life. It is for this very reason that Johnson believed that neo-orthodoxy could not and cannot provide a theology of love that builds into it a legitimate place for self-concern. Niebuhr can talk about ordinate self-concern before the Fall, but seems unable to find a place for it in his doctrine of love after the Fall.

A better formulation of a ethic of love, both theologically and ethically, can be found in the brilliant work of the Belgian, Catholic, moral theologian, Louis Janssens. It also gives expression to the ethic of love that is implicit or explicit in several feminist theologians, such as Judith Vaughan, Judith Plaskow, and Linell Cady.[25] Its main virtue, for the purposes of this essay, is its potential for an ethic of love that can form the basis of a new family strategy for the mainline churches.

Janssens believes that the heart of a Christian ethic of love can be found in the formal structure of the love commandment: "You shall love your neighbor as yourself," which is repeated no less than eight times in the New Testament (Matthew 19:19; 22:39; Mark 12:31,33; Luke 10:27; Romans 13:2; Galatians 5:14; James 2:8). Janssens believes that the fundamental meaning of the principle of neighbor-love is that: "Love of neighbor is impartial. It is fundamentally an equal-regard for every person, because it applies to each neighbor qua human existent."[26] But by "impartial" Janssens does not mean indifferent, nonaffective, or uninterested. In fact, it is just the reverse. Janssens's ethic of love as equal-regard means that we are to take the neighbor's needs and interests with equal seriousness as we take our own. But the reverse is also the case. The principle of neighbor-love tells us to take our own needs and interests as seriously, but no more seriously, as those of the neighbor. Quoting the work of the American theological ethicist, Gene Outka, who has influenced Janssens profoundly, he writes that: "Valuing the self as well as others remains a manifest obligation."[27] For the same reasons one is obligated to value the other constitute the reasons one is to value oneself.

All of this means that, in Janssens's formulation, there is room in the Christian ethic of love for autonomy, ordinate self-concern, and self-actualization, but they can be no more important than the autonomy, self-concern, and self-actualization of the other. Furthermore, a healthy concern for oneself can be a positive guide to empathizing with the needs of the other and promoting the other's growth and enrichment; as we come to know and accept our own needs, we are more able to recognize and accept the needs of the other. This is a formulation that carries further and makes more elaborate the proposals for an ethic of love put forth by D'Antonio and Hargrove—one that combines a concern with autonomy and self-actualization with a dedication to the autonomy and self-actualization of the other.

Yet, if this ethic of love is to be Christian, there must be within it a place for sacrificial love and the way of the cross. But Janssens's formulation reverses the logic of Christian love proposed by Niebuhr. Rather than self-sacrificial love being the norm, as it is for Niebuhr, mutuality in the sense of equal-regard is the normative meaning of Christian love for Janssens. And rather than mutuality being a concession to fallenness, for Janssens it is self-sacrifice that fallenness requires, in an effort to restore the broken mutuality which is itself the goal of the Christian life. Janssens writes: "In short, self-sacrifice is not the quintessence of love…. Self-sacrifice is justified derivatively from other-regard."[28] And for Janssens, other-regard is itself part of the structure of equal-regard and mutuality. Hence, the ethic of self-sacrificial love is required as a transitional ethic, designed to restore unequal and unmutual situations to the true goal of mutuality.

Janssens's formulation of the ethic of love is powerful, and may go to the heart of what D'Antonio and Hargrove are calling for in their plea for a theory of love that takes into account the modern drive for autonomy and self-actualization. They are not making autonomy and self-actualization the end of life, as they are for ethical egoism,[29] what Rieff and Bellah call the culture of the "therapeutic,"[30] or what I have suggested is the implicit ethic of much of humanistic psychology.[31] Janssens interprets the Christian ethic of love to mean that concern for my own autonomy and self-actualization can count as equal—but no more than equal—to the autonomy and self-actualization of the person I love. In addition, I must be as equally concerned with the autonomy and self-actualization of the loved one as I am with my own. Obviously, in this view of love, my autonomy and self-actualization are not ends in themselves, but are constrained and guided by my commitment to equal-regard for the other.

THE FAMILY AND THE ETHIC OF EQUAL-REGARD

Such an ethic may seem attractive at first glance, but also may appear rather abstract and vague upon deeper inspection. This is the case with any attempt to formulate general ethical principles, even the principles governing an ethic of love. General ethical principles never stand alone. In real life they are surrounded by several other ethically relevant dimensions that give these principles life and concreteness. In my other recent writings, I have argued that ethical thinking is in reality quite thick; by this, I mean it consists of several different interpenetrating and mutually qualifying dimensions. General principles, such as the ethic of neighbor-love, are always surrounded by metaphors and narratives (what I sometimes call the visional level of ethical thinking) which project an image of the origins, purposes, and general trustworthiness of life. For instance, in Christianity the story of the life, death, and resurrection of Jesus Christ gives us a model of sacrifice that empowers our need to work hard—indeed to go the second mile—to restore our relationships to mutuality. The theological concepts of grace and forgiveness help us overcome our inordinate self-concern by releasing us from the guilt of past failures and empowering us to renewed efforts to mutuality and equal-regard, even at some sacrifice to ourselves.

In addition to this visional context, principles such as neighbor-love are also informed, at another level, by concepts cataloguing our fundamental human desires, needs, and tendencies. These catalogues (generally quite implicit) of our fundamental wants and needs are theories of what Louis Janssens calls the "premoral good" or the *ordo bonorum*. The premoral good refers to all the ways we use the word good in the nonmoral, in contrast to the moral, sense of the word.[32] Premoral goods are realities inside and outside us that we have a positive response to and believe are worthy of promoting and bringing into heightened realization. Premoral goods are such goods as food, water, pleasure, affection, physical and mental health, joy, friendship, and such cultural values as science, art, technology, and education. We say that food and water are goods because they satisfy our hunger and thirst, but we do not call a loaf of bread or a cup of water a moral thing as such. The same is true of the other premoral goods listed above. Physical and mental health are goods, but we do not say people who are mentally and physically healthy are moral as such, simply because they possess these characteristics. Love as equal-regard is a very formal principle, and can only have living significance when it is informed by a sense for the premoral goods that love deems it worthy to promote in the self and the other. Paul Ricoeur says it well, in commenting on the meaning of the Golden Rule. Ricoeur says that "to do unto others as you would have them do unto you" means "to do *good*" to others as you would have them "do *good* to you."[33] For equal-regard to do its moral task, it must organize and reconcile justly the basic premoral goods of life.

Within the context of the family, guided by the ethic of love developed here, our task becomes not only to exhibit with our loved ones the formal principle of mutuality and equal-regard; it is to inform this equal-regard with a sensibility about the relevant and timely premoral goods that the various members of the family want and truly need. This, of course, becomes the real challenge for an ethic of love for families. Different members of the family need different premoral goods. We do not always know which premoral goods are relevant, either for ourselves or for the others. Sometimes, even if we know which premoral goods are relevant, there may be a scarcity of such goods, and a conflict between goods relevant to more than one member of the family. In addition, there also may be a conflict between the goods relevant to the family and its various members, and the goods needed by others outside the family. To give expression to the ethic of equal-regard, and to demonstrate how it includes but also guides various premoral goods, is not to provide an ethic of the family that is beyond ambiguity. In fact, it is precisely because there always is ambiguity and, indeed, moral failure that a Christian ethic of equal-regard also requires grace. This grace, in turn, empowers us to exert self-sacrificial love in an effort to restore mutuality to our broken and disrupted family relations. But this view of the love ethic at least has the virtue of stating explicitly the way in which one's own autonomy, differentiation, and self-actualization are included within an equal-regard for the autonomy, differentiation, and self-actualization of the other.

SPHERES OF EQUAL-REGARD AND THE LIFE CYCLE

When the ethic of mutuality and equal-regard is supplemented with considerations of the premoral good, then equal-regard begins to look somewhat different, depending upon the spheres of the premoral good to which it is being applied. In fact, one can speak of spheres of equal-regard, paralleling the title of Michael Walzer's *Spheres of Justice*. Equal-regard, of course, is another name for distributive justice, but stated in such a way as to be more applicable to the field of intimate human relationships. I differ with Walzer, however, who believes that concepts of the good are completely historically determined, and therefore quite relative to particular social contexts.[34] Although I agree that they are significantly determined by the evolution of historical traditions, I do believe that goods and needs basic to human life can be discerned at least in part by rational reflection on experience, with a little help, at times, from the psychological, social, and biological sciences. But putting this debate aside, I affirm that Walzer's main point is well taken: equal-regard takes on different meanings depending upon which sphere of premoral good it is trying to justly order. Equal-regard functions differently in the corporate work place, at the public school, at the dinner table at home, and in the marital bed. This is because one is pursuing in these different spheres of life slightly different premoral goods, and will therefore distribute tasks, recognitions, and rewards differently. In fact, we tend to get quite upset, and with reason, when some goods of the family (sexual favors, preferential treatment) get projected into the goods of the school or office. We also become disturbed when the goods of the office or factory (such as technical rationality or the single-mind-ed pursuit of wealth) get projected into the family. Yet, clearly, there are overlapping goods between these spheres. For instance, there is still some sense in which the family is an economic unit. On the other hand, the factory or office needs to find ways to respect its employees and provide for some of their basic physical needs—concerns that are also quite central to the family.

Within the context of the family, there are different premoral goods provided for the children and the parents. This means mutuality and equal-regard look different, depending on whether they are being expressed between the parents, between the parents and the children, between the children, or between the child and the parent. Without moving into all of the complexities of the ways equal-regard and mutuality can work out from these different angles of vision, let me illustrate my point by concentrating on the way they shift in meaning throughout the life cycle of the family. In concentrating on shifting premoral goods at stake at different points in the life cycle, I will be neglecting other institutional and social-systemic influences on our premoral goods, and the way equal-regard effects justice in these changing contexts.

When parents are dealing with infants and very young children, equal-regard and mutuality are both actual and promissory. If one takes seriously the work of Erikson, Kegan, and others on the first years of life, mutuality between parent and infant primarily comes at the level of glance, eye contact, and the nonanxious affirmation of the budding self of the infant.[35] The infant reciprocates with delight, satisfaction, and fleeting moments of I-Thou recognition. Of course, in other ways, the parent-child relation is decidedly nonmutual. The child is tremendously dependent upon the parent, and only gradually develops the skills to be an equal contributor to the family. Hence, equal-regard and mutuality mean, in the parent-child relation, primarily the parent's general willingness, permission, and support for the gradual evolution of their relationship toward the possibility and eventual reality of adult interaction that is marked by these characteristics.

Although mutuality is both partially realized but also promissory in the parent-child relationship, it can become decidedly more fully actualized in the adult relationship between parents and grown sons and daughters. Here mutuality can entail more than simply the mutual delight, affirmation, protection, and enhancement of one another's selfhood. It also can entail mutual consultation on a wide range of cultural, social, and even ethical value issues, as parents and offspring work together to reconstruct experience among changing circumstances.

Mutuality and equal-regard can mean something else again as parents move toward old age. Now parents develop a greater dependency upon their children, not unlike the dependency their sons and daughters once had upon them. Equal-regard can still take the form of mutual respect, but in other areas of premoral good, such as health, living arrangements, or even finances, children may take the initiative and the greater responsibility. Yet the memory of the fuller mutuality that was earlier achieved can still permeate their relationship, even amidst the emergence of new patterns of dependency and initiative.

This is the meaning of Erik Erikson's close juxtaposition of generativity and mutuality as the normative value of the human life cycle. The generative person works to maintain the life cycle, but does so with shifting articulations of mutuality with the young and the old as he or she moves to various age positions in that cycle.[36]

FAMILY ETHICS AND FEMINISM

This ethic of equal-regard and mutuality has much in common with certain expressions of feminist ethics. In addition to the authors mentioned above, the relational ethic of Carol Gilligan and her followers has strong similarities to the ethic of mutuality outlined in the above paragraphs.[37] Although there is an emerging ethic of mutuality in certain quarters of the feminist movement, most feminists have not brought it into the area of family ethics. Therefore, as the Bergers and Jean Bethke Elshtain have observed (and with some sadness), the general public perceives the feminist movement as celebrating the values of autonomy unmitigated by equal-regard. Furthermore, the public perceives feminism to be, on the whole, antifamily.[38] Few feminists use the ethic of mutuality not only to advance the position of women but to advance and strengthen the family as well. Hence, needless resistances have developed against feminism among people who believe they must choose between their dedication to the family and their attraction to the feminist movement. My proposals deal not only with making a rearticulated family policy central to the mainline churches; I recommend as well that this family policy be closely associated with those aspects of feminism that are also struggling to state a positive ethic of autonomy, differentiation, and self-actualization that is mitigated and guided by an ethic of mutuality and equal-regard. This brand of feminism has both much to give to a revitalized family strategy, as well as much to gain from a closer identification with the interests of the family. The mainline churches should be interested in both feminism and the family, and in crafting a creative relation between them within an ethic of mutuality.

AN ETHIC OF LOVE AND FAMILY THERAPY

There are proposals afoot that suggest the church should make an alliance with the family therapy movement to achieve a stronger ministry with families. These proposals raise the question of the moral horizon of the family therapies themselves—whether they are guided by an ethic of mutuality, autonomy, patriarchal authority, or undialectical sacrificial giving. Marie McCarthy has given an intelligent review of the family therapies, locating them along a continuum of implicit ethical value commitments that range from autonomy and self-actualization, to mutuality, to agapic love.[39] Deborah Luepnitz has brought a feminist critique to the moral horizon of the family therapies from the perspective, I think, of an implicit ethic of mutuality significantly informed by the work of Gilligan.[40] In almost all cases, she finds them in some way or other ethically deficient. An example would be Murray Bowen's formulation of "differentiation" as the goal of family therapy in such a way as to overemphasize the qualities of autonomy and initiative.[41] Although there is doubtless a place for these therapies in the ministry of the church, it will be important for their moral value frameworks to be guided by an ethic of love similar to the one advocated here.

These critiques of the ethical horizon of the family therapy movement have a clear relevance to the concerns of this paper. This is especially true when evaluating those proposals urging that the local congregation explicitly use family systems theory in their ministries. The most daring of these proposals can be found in Rabbi Edwin Friedman's *Generation to Generation: Family Process in Church and Synagogue.*[42] Friedman's book primarily addresses the minister or rabbi as leader. The uniqueness of the book is his point that the minister is a leader and potential change agent in three overlapping families—the families that make up the congregation, the congregation as family, and the minister's own family. Friedman argues that the minister should go beyond pastoral counseling, with its emphasis on techniques and psychological knowledge. What is important, he says:

> to changing any kind of "family" is not knowledge of technique or even of pathology but, rather, the capacity of the family leader to define his or her own goals and values while trying to maintain a nonanxious presence within the system.[43]

Friedman's emphasis is clearly on the minister as leader of these three family systems. The power to change a family system rests in the leader's firm self-definition. A firm self-definition resides, for Friedman, in the leader's capacity to maintain an engaged, nonanxious, and "differentiated" self, while making interventions in one or other of these family systems. It is the task of the minister as change agent to help bring about heightened self-differentiation in the members of the family, by using his or her own differentiated self as a tool.[44]

We need not concern ourselves with Friedman's explication of the basic concepts of family systems theory. My main point is to raise the question: What is the implicit ethical content of Friedman's call for a differentiated self in the minister and in the members of his or her three interpenetrating families? The answer is disappointing. The idea of self-differentiation is handled more or less abstractly by Friedman. At times he speaks of the "capacity to remain an 'I' while remaining connected." It is also clear that Friedman wants to develop differentiated family members who remain "connected" not only with their immediate family but with their larger extended family as well. This is the meaning of the phrase "generation to generation" placed in the title of his book. What is lacking in Friedman, however, is an articulated family ethic of mutuality and equal-regard that can give more content to the values involved in the minister's self-definition and in the differentiated selves that should be the goal of the family process. An ethic of mutuality can give a more articulate expression to both the metaphors of "differentiation" (and its implications toward autonomy and self-actualization) and "connectedness" (with its implications toward other-regard). Without a clearer ethical content to Friedman's emphasis on leadership, self-definition, and differentiation, his system can easily drift toward the values of patriarchy or, possibly, toward autonomy and differentiation unmitigated by equal-regard. For Friedman's proposals to work, ministers must be dedicated to an ethic of love as mutuality—one that they can apply not only to the families in their congregations, but to their congregations as families, and finally to their own families as well.

We must remind ourselves, however, that it is one thing to state an ethic that would guide a mission to families, and quite another to develop the concrete initiatives, counseling procedures, and rituals to actually accomplish it. This is the task that stretches before us. The tools of family systems therapy may be of help, but far more important is the development of powerful new rites of passage for young people that address them in their full reality as young men and women. Rather than our more tepid rituals of confirmation, we must discover ways of linking faith with powerful initiation rites. The task is not just to relate the young person to articles of faith, but also to evoke capacities for mutuality and equal-regard in relationships that will someday mature into lifelong commitments. We must have an adequate ethic to guide our ritual processes; that is what this paper has been about. But we also need powerful new ritual processes to implement our ethic of love.

FAMILY ETHICS AND THE PLURALITY OF FAMILY FORMS

One should not conclude an essay on a new family strategy for the mainline churches without assessing this proposal from the perspective of the plurality of family forms which now occupy the sociological scene in Western societies. There are many typologies of family forms to choose from. One proposal distinguishes between families that are closed (highly scheduled and tight boundaries), open (flexible schedule and permeable boundaries), and random (no shared schedule and little boundary). Another economic typology distinguishes among seven types of families—living together, Dinks (dual income with no children), single-parent, two-career (with children), traditionals (working husband with wife at home caring for children), blended (parents and children from previous marriages), and sandwich (middle-aged parents caring for both their own children and their parents).[45] Although the mainline churches may never explicitly sanction couples living together, all of the last six types in the economic list can be the consequence of legitimate, church-blessed marriages functioning more or less within the values of heterosexual covenanted relationships. Even most single parents aspire for this kind of relation once again. These values also can be true of the closed, open, and random family types. Hence, even within the range of explicitly church-sanctioned marriages, the range of family types that can evolve is quite wide.

Yet the ethic of love proposed here can be relevant to all of them, especially if differing premoral goods are taken into account. Mutuality and equal-regard will do their ordering and actualizing tasks somewhat differently for the various family patterns. For example, mutuality means something different for the single parent and, for instance, the Dink. The single parent has no one within the nuclear family unit to work out his or her adult needs for mutuality of intimate friendships. For this reason, the single parent may need to arrange patterns of adult friendship and support to compensate for certain kinds of mutuality which the family unit itself cannot provide. Even though the single parent has to permit and meet the physical and psychological dependencies of growing children, he or she does this within an ethic of equal-regard for the emerging selfhood of the children. Dinks, on the other hand, may have the financial resources to support a wide range of mutual exchanges and enrichments, not only between themselves but with the outside world. On the other hand, they may use these resources to develop more or less autonomous and parallel lives. Hence, the ethic of mutuality is relevant, and will make a difference in how two-career and childless couples actually live out their lives together. Obviously the most complicated and demanding issues pertaining to mutuality would come with the so-called blended family, where highly complicated and separate family histories of affection and tension are brought together into a new synthesis.

With all of these types, the principles of mutuality and equal-regard cannot be applied statically; they must be seen as goals that families grow toward as they go through their family life cycles and as they try to responsibly relate to the outside world. Rather than static images of mutuality, it is better to think of families in terms of evolving histories or pilgrimages of mutuality. The family, as Herbert Anderson and Eric Fuchs have suggested, is an open-ended *project* in mutuality.[46]

FAMILY ETHICS AND PUBLIC ISSUES

In contrast to the impression that Gibson Winter and others helped create in the decades of the 1960s and seventies, a family strategy on the part of the church does not need to preempt its involvement in the wider public world. To the contrary, starting from a family angle of vision, many issues that would seem remote and irrelevant suddenly take on new meaning, and can call forth our deepest energies. New historical and sociological insights are now available showing how the family, in contrast to standard Marxist perspectives, is not always a passive entity molded and sometimes battered by whatever social and material forces are in ascendancy.[47] Writings by Adorno, Mark Poster, the Bergers, and Emmanuel Todd are just a few examples of scholars showing how the family can shape society, as well as be shaped by society.[48] Mutuality and equal-regard, as an ethic for the family, can be a guide for the family as it attempts to shape wider social issues in the area of work, education, taxation, the environment, and even foreign policy.

Work patterns provide the most immediate examples for how this can function. Patterns of work in the public realm must be so structured as to support the mutuality and equal-regard of the family. Without getting into the technical details of specific proposals, this might mean, for example, more flexible work hours, pregnancy leaves, more adequate child care, various tax breaks for children, and so on. It would be possible to give illustrations of a similar kind for other sectors of the public world as well.

Finally, the principles of mutuality and equal-regard, although relevant to the ordering of the internal life of the family, are also pertinent to the family's moral action in the world. Families can only make demands on the public world and on other individuals and families which they, in turn, are willing to have made on them. Hence, families must be willing to live by the reversibility implicit within the principle of equal-regard. Or, to state it more aggressively, the considerations that families demand for themselves they must, in principle, be willing to work hard to realize for other families with similar needs. This is the meaning of equal-regard as applied to relations between families; it entails the willingness to take the needs of other families as seriously as one takes the needs of one's own family. An ethics of equal-regard has a place within it for recognizing special obligations to our own families. This is morally justified, however, only if we work to create a just and equal situation within which others can pursue their special obligations to their families.[49] And within a distinctively Christian context, it would entail the willingness to take meaningful sacrificial action as a family in order to restore the disadvantaged families of a society to a situation of more genuine equality.

NOTES

1. R. Stephen Warner, *New Wine in Old Wineskins* (Berkeley: University of California Press, 1988), pp. 19–30; Robert Wuthnow, *The Restructuring of American Religion* (Princeton: Princeton University Press, 1988), pp. 71–99, 133–240.

2. Brigitte Berger and Peter Berger, *The War over the Family* (New York: Doubleday, 1984), p. 30.

3. Warner, *New Wine in Old Wineskins*, p. 18.

4. See Talcott Parsons's introduction to Max Weber, *The Sociology of Religion* (Boston: Beacon Press, 1967), pp. xix–lxvii.

5. Talcott Parsons, "The American Family: Its Relation to Personality and to the Social Structure," in *Family Socialization and Interaction Process*, eds. T. Parsons and R. F. Bales (New York: Free Press, 1960), p. 16.

6. Gibson Winter, *The Suburban Captivity of the Churches* (New York: Macmillan Co., 1962), pp. 155–66.

7. *Ibid.*, p. 159.

8. William D'Antonio, "The Family and Religion: Exploring a Changing Relationship," *Journal for the Scientific Study of Religion*, 19:2 (1980), pp. 89–102; Barbara Hargrove, "The Church, the Family, and the Modernization Process," *Families and Religions*, eds. William D'Antonio and Joan Aldous (Beverly Hills: Sage Publications, 1983), pp. 21–49.

9. Cited in D'Antonio, "The Family and Religion," pp. 92–93.

10. *Ibid.*, p. 94.

11. *Ibid.*, p. 95.

12. Hargrove, "The Church, the Family, and the Modernization Process," pp. 29–31.

13. D'Antonio, "The Family and Religion," p. 102.

14. See Daniel Yankelovich, *New Rules* (New York: Random House, 1981).

15. Hargrove, "The Church, The Family," pp. 45–46.

16. D'Antonio, "The Family and Religion," p. 101.

17. Hargrove, "The Church, The Family," p. 46.

18. Robert Bellah, *et al., Habits of the Heart* (Berkeley: University of California Press, 1985), p. 97.

19. Reinhold Niebuhr, *The Nature and Destiny of Man*, II (New York: Charles Scribner's, 1941), p. 68.

20. Benton Johnson, "Taking Stock: Reflections on the End of Another Era," *Journal for the Scientific Study of Religion*, 21:3 (1982), p. 195.

21. Reinhold Niebuhr, *The Nature and Destiny of Man*, I (New York: Charles Scribner's, 1941), p. 191.

22. Niebuhr, *The Nature and Destiny of Man*, II, p. 84.

23. *Ibid.*, p. 69.

24. *Ibid.*, p. 82.

25. Linell Cady, "Relational Love: A Feminist Christian Vision," *Embodied Love*, eds. Paula Cooey, Sharon Farmer, and Mary Ellen Ross (San Francisco: Harper and Row, 1987), p. 147. See also Judith Vaughn, *Society, Ethics, and Social Change: A Critical Appraisal of Reinhold Niebuhr's Ethics in the Light of Rosemary Radford Ruether's Works* (New York: University Press of America, 1983); and Judith Plaskow, *Sex, Sin, and Grace: Women's Experience in the Theologies of Reinhold Niebuhr and Paul Tillich* (Washington: University Press of America, 1980).

26. Louis Janssens, "Norms and Priorities of a Love Ethic," *Louvain Studies* 6 (Spring, 1977), p. 219.

27. Gene Outka, *Agape: An Ethical Analysis* (New Haven: Yale University Press, 1972), p. 290.

28. Janssens, "Norms and Priorities", p. 228.

29. William Frankena, *Ethics* (Englewood Cliffs, NJ: Prentice Hall, 1973), pp. 17–18.

30. Philip Rieff, *The Triumph of the Therapeutic* (New York: Harper and Row, 1966), pp. 66–78; Robert Bellah, *et al., Habits of the Heart*, pp. 113–141.

31. Don Browning, *Generative Man* (New York: Dell Publishing Co., 1975), pp. 197–217; also my *Religious Thought and the Modern Psychologies* (Philadelphia: Fortress Press, 1987), pp. 204–237, and *Pluralism and Personality* (Lewisburg, PA: Bucknell University Press, 1980), pp. 149–151.

32. Janssens, "Norms and Priorities", p. 210.

33. Paul Ricoeur, "The Teleological and Deontological Structures of Action: Aristotle or Kant?" Lecture given at the Divinity School, University of Chicago, June, 1987.

34. Michael Walzer, *Spheres of Justice* (New York: Basic Books, 1983), pp. 6–10.

35. Erik Erikson, *Childhood and Society* (New York: W.W. Norton, 1963), pp. 247–251; Robert Kegan, *The Evolving Self* (Cambridge: Harvard University Press, 1982), pp. 113–132.

36. Erikson, *Childhood and Society*, pp. 266–268. See also my *Generative Man* (New York: Dell Publishing Co., 1975), pp. 197–217, my *Religious Thought and the Modern Psychologies* (Philadelphia: Fortress Press, 1987), pp. 204–237; and my *Pluralism and Personality* (Lewisburg, PA: Bucknell University Press, 1980), pp. 149–151.

37. Carol Gilligan, *In a Different Voice* (Cambridge: Harvard University Press, 1982).

38. Brigitte Berger and Peter Berger, *The War over the Family*, pp. 24–25; Jean Bethke Elshtain, "Feminism, Family, and Community," *Dissent* 29 (Fall 1982), pp. 442–449.

39. Marie McCarthy, *The Role of Mutuality in Family Structure and Relationships: A Critical Examination of Selected Options in Contemporary Theological Ethics*. Ph.D. Dissertation, University of Chicago, 1984.

40. Deborah Luepnitz, *The Family Interpreted: Feminist Theory in Clinical Practice* (New York: Basic Books, 1988), p. 42.

41. *Ibid.*, p. 43.

42. Edwin Friedman, *Generation to Generation* (New York: The Guilford Press, 1985), p. 1.

43. *Ibid.*, p. 18.

44. *Ibid.*, p. 27.

45. Eric Schurenberg,"The New Gospel of Financial Planning," *Money* (March 1989), pp. 56–57.

46. Eric Fuchs, *Sexual Desire and Love* (New York: The Seabury Press, 1983), pp. 176–206: Herbert Anderson, *The Family and Pastoral Care* (Philadelphia: Fortress Press, 1984), p. 3040.

47. Frederick Engels, *The Origin of the Family, Private Property and the State* (New York: International Publishers, 1985). That the family is basically passive and a reflection of various social patterns—patriarchy, capitalism, or socialism—is the pervasive thesis of Engels in this classic of the Marxist point of view.

48. Mark Poster, *Critical Theory of the Family* (New York: The Seabury Press, 1978), p. xvii; Emmanuel Todd, *Explanation of Ideology: Family Structures and Social Systems* (Oxford: Basil Blackwell, 1985), pp.1–7; and Brigitte Berger and Peter L. Berger, *The War over the Family: Capturing the Middle Ground* (Garden City, NY: Anchor, 1983).

49. Alan Gewirth, "Ethical Universalism and Particularism," *Journal of Philosophy*, 85:6 (June 1988), pp. 283–302.

8

The Storm and the Light

Church, Family, Work, and Social Crisis in the African-American Experience

Cheryl Townsend Gilkes

T he current relationships among work, family, and the church in the African-American community can be captured in the late Thomas Dorsey's highly favored hymn, "Precious Lord." The petition, "Through the storm, through the night, lead me on to the light," reflects the current social and economic realities facing black families and their current need for leadership from the black church. African-American families are experiencing a storm, and this storm is one of the most significant challenges facing the black church. Observing the depths of the present family crisis, the Carnegie Foundation asked directly, "Black Churches: Can They Strengthen the Black Family?"[1] Given the historical reputation of black churches as the centers and bulwarks and the most critical empowering and mediating institution in the black community, the fact that such questions are being asked points to the changing nature of the society, the changing relationship of black people to the society, and the new and unanticipated pressures facing families.

Although both the family and the church have been called "enduring institutions,"[2] there is a new institutional shape in the urban black community today. The most consistently unemployed and socially isolated exist in unusual concentrations at the center of the cities, while newer concentrations of middle-income African-Americans have regrouped at the outer edges of the ghetto or in its contiguous suburbs. Contemporary African-American churches reflect both of these trends and the realities in between.

Not only has the community reorganized on economic lines, but new challenges have emerged since 1970. New economic and social developments have exacerbated the problems of the ghetto poor, those William Julius Wilson called "the truly disadvantaged."[3] Charles Perrow and Mauro F. Guillen, in their study of the impact of AIDS on New York City, pointed to the current vulnerability of black communities and their institutions of church and family.[4] That vulnerability hinges on the persistently problematic relationship of black people to the economy. They point out that, in addition to a persistent "culture of racism," foreign competition, deindustrialization, and slashed social programs have combined with a sharp rise in poverty to produce the conditions for disaster. Much of the disaster involves the impact of crack (and its associated violence) and AIDS. Wilson, similarly, has pointed to the impact on black family structure of deindustrialization, the production of joblessness, and the increasing economic marginalization of black men. The results, he shows, are a depressed or retarded marriage rate, and the rise in female-headed and impoverished households.[5] The growing crises of the unemployed inner-city poor and the nexus of disaster involving AIDS, crack, and violence are very special conditions challenging the historical strengths of black communities.

The implications for church and family are profound. These current problems are forcing the black church, an institution conscious of its history and its historical relationship to the family, to reexamine the practical applications of its mission and ministry in two directions. First,

Lincoln and Mamiya point out that:

> the major challenge facing a predominantly middle- and working-class
> Black Church is whether it can effectively reach out to the extremely
> deprived members of the truly disadvantaged. While many middle-income
> black church congregations have a few poor members in their midst, recent
> studies like Wilson's point to a major and growing class division in the
> black community with the extremely poor being more and more isolated
> and alienated from even black institutions.[6]

A response to the challenge of the poor and the disadvantaged can build
upon the historic responses of black churches to earlier social crises.
However there is a newer, second challenge, stemming from the growing presence in black churches of persons able to benefit from the gains
of the Civil Rights Movement. Lincoln and Mamiya also point to this,
saying:

> On the other side of the class divide is the challenge presented by the con-
> cerns of the young, black, urban professionals (often called "Buppies"), who
> have been enamored of their newly found education, wealth, and status,
> and like their white counterparts revel in the pursuit of "conspicuous con-
> sumption" and an intensified focus upon self.... The lack of any social or
> communal support system is felt most acutely for African-Americans who
> both live and work in white suburban areas.[7]

This essay examines the relationship between the church and family
in the African-American experience. The church's organizational settings are perhaps the only place where people of all backgrounds and
social classes ask about the condition and the future of the black family.
Not only are sociologists who ask the academic questions found in its
membership, but the women and men who are struggling to organize,
maintain, or reorganize their families are in these same congregations.
Furthermore, the leadership of black churches, particularly its ministers, represents a broad cross section of the black population, often
experiencing in their own immediate or extended families the problems of unemployment, AIDS, teenage pregnancy, violence, crime and
incarceration, alienated men, overburdened women, divorce, and separation. Given the greater prevalence of instrumental, extended, family
networks and the class heterogeneity of black families, even the spatial
reorganization of black communities along class lines does not sufficiently insulate any one segment from the problems of another.[8] This

direct familial involvement is one of the reasons for the angst of the black middle class over the situation of the ghetto poor or underclass.

After a brief look at specific cases in the contemporary church, this chapter focuses on the intersection of the family and church in order to examine the ways in which the crises of social and economic change have shaped and influenced that relationship, particularly in poor communities. The problems of work and the economy have always been in dramatic confrontation with church and family in the African-American experience. This chapter attempts to provide an overview of the relationship between religion and family in African-American life that accounts for this problem. It is both historical and sociological: it utilizes a political and economic history, outlined in terms of crises and discontinuities, as a framework to account for specific configurations of religion and family. It also draws upon insights from my earlier research on community workers, and some preliminary observations from my work on the Sanctified Church (African-American churches in the holiness and pentecostal traditions), and from observations of the intersection of church and family in the working- and middle-class urban congregations with which I am familiar as a Baptist minister.

THE CHURCHES OF "WHAT'S HAPPENING NOW"
Lincoln and Mamiya's landmark study of black churches, the first such large-scale study since the Mays and Nicholson research, reaffirms the historic connection among the church, the family, and economic life, while documenting several new trends and problems. As they point out, certain segments of the black church are experiencing phenomenal growth, especially the megachurches in the African Methodist Episcopal Church (A.M.E.). They point to the explosion in membership among A.M.E. congregations such as Bethel A.M.E. in Baltimore, Ward A.M.E. in Los Angeles, Allen A.M.E. in Queens, and Ebenezer A.M.E. in Fort Washington, Maryland. These churches are similar to congregations in other denominations, such as Mississippi Boulevard Christian Church in Memphis, Tennessee (Disciples of Christ, Christian), Mariners' Temple Baptist Church in New York City (American Baptist), Allen Temple Baptist Church in Oakland, California (Progressive National Baptist), and Trinity United Church of Christ in Chicago, Illinois.[9] While they explain this growth in terms of a "neo-pentecostal" movement, I would argue that these churches are a more recently mainstream expression of core, African-American, Christian traditions made visible by the mobility of large segments of the Sanctified Church and the class reorganization of black communi-

ties.[10] The transformation of these churches is an indication of the changing institutional relationships within the black community and the newer challenges these changes entail.

The transformation has followed a variety of patterns that reflect the shifting economic and spatial configurations of the African-American population. Some of these congregations are older urban churches. Others were previously small, middle-class, black, suburban congregations whose growth came from newly middle-income or geographically mobile black people. In some cases, these were congregations of black people who worked in affluent white suburbs, and who became the nucleus of a black community that experienced very recent growth. In nearly all of the cases with which I am directly familiar, the churches had small, shrinking, middle-class congregations with low birthrates and children who were often geographically mobile, well educated, and more securely middle class. The swift transformation of the church that followed was a transformation from a sedate middle-class style ("the First Church of the Frigidaire") to a more traditionally Afro-Christian one where the vibrant music and charismatic preaching connected with heightened black consciousness and an educated congregation eager for "the Word." Lincoln and Mamiya point out that the membership of these churches:

> consists of a mix of a middle-income working class and middle-class blacks, who make up the majority of traditional A.M.E. membership and some of the black urban poor, the latter tending to be attracted by the informal, less structured, and highly spirited worship services.[11]

The characteristics they describe surely apply beyond the A.M.E. Many new members of these churches are clearly part of what McAdoo calls the "golden cohort." They are a subgroup of the black middle class who are "young male and female professionals, aged 25–35 [in 1981], who delayed childbearing and are concentrating their energies on their careers, …college graduates who are now employed at a salary level equal to that of whites."[12]

One of these churches, Trinity United Church of Christ, was featured in an episode of the Public Broadcasting System's "Frontline." The United Church of Christ is a predominantly white denomination whose Southern black congregations tended to consist of educators affiliated with colleges, for example Fisk, Talladega, Tougaloo, and Dillard, founded by the American Missionary Association.[13] The Northern congregations were sometimes historically abolitionist congregations. Trinity is located on Chicago's south side, and had less than a hundred members when its current pastor was called. At the time of the "Frontline" program, the membership was climbing toward five thousand, and they were raising money to build their second building. Like the pastors of congregations cited by Lincoln and Mamiya, Trinity's pastor is highly educated and dynamic. He articulates the most positive dimensions of African-American nationalism at the same time preaching creative, biblically grounded sermons that appeal to past struggles and current crises. The sermons are informed both by the pastor's undergraduate, graduate, and self-educations in African-American studies, and by graduate theological training. The congregational culture draws on the traditional, the modern, and the shared among African-American Christians, especially in the music and preaching ministries. The pastor must preach to a congregation whose members at some time or another questioned the relevance of Christianity to the black experience and its problems. They are often drawn to the preaching as much for its vitality and biblical groundedness as for its stated relevance to the black experience. Within the congregation there are diverse segments: first-generation Christians whose family alienation from the black church was rooted in the urbanization and migration of their parents and grandparents; former Black Muslims or other nationalists who insist that the pastor make explicit programmatic and sermonic connections with African heritage education; and highly educated "baby-boomer" returnees who seek a combination of traditional African-American religion and biblical/theological sophistication.

Trinity United Church of Christ, like its counterparts in Memphis or Fort Washington, in Maryland or Los Angeles, or in Queens or Lower Manhattan, also draws from those segments of the African-American community who are not so well off and who are not quite so formally educated. They are not quite so visible to the observer on Sunday mornings since, like most African-American churchgoers, they work very hard to dress prosperously in their Sunday best. Although the clothing standards of African-American churches often mask the class position of congregants, occasionally these poorer members are visible, and pastors work hard to challenge the congregations to bridge the class divide. Indeed, the bridging of class boundaries is an important component of the preaching message.

This social mix in the churches of "what's happening now" has brought together a critical mass of people who are conscious about the problems of "the black family," even as they themselves are trying to adjust to new patterns of work and family life shaped by geographic and social mobility and by larger social forces affecting all families. Because of the rapid changes in their lives and in society, they have relocated physically and socially, and are in the process of reworking their connections with the African-American experience. For some members, the nature of their work and family life is such that the church is their only "voluntary association." It is in the church and through the church that all of their connections to the problems of other black people are forged and maintained.

In the PBS episode, Trinity is shown addressing the problems of connecting adolescent males and females with professional role models from the congregation. Conscious of the seeming "destruction" of black youth in the public school system, there are classes which reinforce positive African identity and sociodramas confronting new patterns in race relations. One poignant scene presents a pastoral counseling session where a church member is helped to assert his personhood and spirituality against the forces of depersonalization and racism in his work setting. Because the church is blessed with a substantial middle-income membership, the congregation is also able to stock the food bank of a small "storefront church" across the street. Ironically, this congregation, some of whose members drive long distances from the suburbs, must have secure parking lots in order to worship in "the ghetto." This "Frontline" episode ended with a Black History Month worship service in which a ritual explicitly for the black family was conducted. The ritual remembered the African and American pasts at the same time as it addressed the problems and needs of the present and future. Developed by Rev. Dr. Edward Sims (sociologist and Baptist minister), the ritual asserts the continuing need to keep family and church connected if African-Americans are to survive.

In the large megachurches, there is a highly motivated and energetic core of people, many of whom tithe, making it possible for the churches to fund diverse programs and large staffs. Shiloh Baptist Church in Washington, D.C., built and staffed a "Family Life Center," appointing professional social workers and other nonclergy to these important positions. In the case of Ebenezer A.M.E. Church in Fort Washington, Maryland, the assistant pastor developed a social outreach center called "F.O.R.C.E." (Family OutReach Center of Ebenezer) whose ministry confronts the family problems of both the middle class and the poor.

These black megachurches have had to redefine their notion of ministry and crisis. With the changing class structure of the black community, they have found themselves ministering to a "new middle class" that exhibits problems which parallel other middle class families. At the same time, there are distinctive problems grounded in a legacy of inequity, racial discrimination, and higher-than-average labor force disruption. To minister to the newly middle income or middle class in black churches is to serve on a class frontier, with all of the problems that frontiers present in terms of instability, crises, and lack of rules.

Not all older urban congregations have had the good fortune of the megachurches. They have not experienced the combination of demographic fortune, exceptionally talented and imaginative pastors, growth in new middle-class membership, and the reclamation of traditional Afro-Christian worship which have produced these explosively large congregations. In contrast to the crowded, vibrant, and urgent scene at Trinity and her sister "megachurches," there is a group of black churches that is struggling for its existence. These churches have been, in certain ways, highly successful, and their success has confronted them with a need to change their mission or go out of existence. These churches are established older congregations whose stable membership was part of the settled working class or the traditional, black, middle class—Frazier's "black bourgeoisie."[14] Within these congregations, the members managed to educate a substantial proportion of their youth, and many of their children and grandchildren are part of the "golden cohort" found in the newer "megachurches." However, as the young people of the church have left for schools and new jobs, they have not been replaced from within the congregation.

In fact, the membership of these churches has become increasingly older, and the ministries of the church have had to reflect this fact. The various clubs and auxiliaries of the church are controlled by elderly members who are trapped in the inner city and are afraid of the youth in their neighborhoods. As they have retreated to housing for the elderly, they see the deterioration in their community as services become increasingly difficult to secure. Others of them have moved to better locations, and no longer live in the neighborhood. Their fear of the neighborhood, and urban life in general, means they are unable to support evening and weekday programs unescorted. Indeed, in a growing number of congregations, the majority of the membership lives in surrounding communities.

Thus the ministry of the church to the local community and the ministry of the church to the congregation become increasingly divergent. The family emergencies that are representative of the current problems facing poor black families may occur in the members' family networks, but these do not confront the congregation regularly and directly. The nephew who is arrested, or the grandson who is shot, or the granddaughter who is pregnant is not present to confront the congregation immediately. The pastor knows about the situation and responds—conducting the funeral, visiting the hospital with his or her parishioner, dedicating or christening the infant with AIDS, or going to the detention center on grandmother's behalf. However, the hard-won respectability of this older and more sedate congregation is maintained at the price of secrecy and denial about the actual proximity of social problems to their own lives.

Since these older churches are often surrounded by communities in crisis, their outreach programs do confront contemporary problems, but they are the problems of nonmembers. For these older congregations, meals for the homeless and the elderly are important. In the congregation where I work, the food program serves a population of nonmembers. Because the homeless are disproportionately male, one finds a unique collection of settled, respectable, elderly men and women sitting down to eat with a group of unattached and unemployed younger men whose occasionally rough ways can be intimidating. Unless these congregations are able to engage in direct outreach to the surrounding community, they find their memberships shrinking.

Unlike some urban white congregations, black churches usually do not have endowments to offset shrinking membership bases. According to Lincoln and Mamiya, only 2.2 percent of black churches have any kind of endowment income. They write: "The finding on endowment income is significant because it points to the fact that very few black churches have any endowment income to sponsor programs."[15] With shrinking incomes, grants supporting community service projects become an important source of support, enabling these churches to maintain, or even improve, their physical plants. Sometimes such congregations will share their buildings with newer immigrant congregations of Hispanic, Korean, or Haitian worshippers.

In these churches, like black churches generally, male participation is relatively low. Women represent approximately seventy-five percent of church memberships. More affluent churches have larger male memberships (because two parent black families are much more affluent), but the Holiness and Pentecostal congregations (the "Sanctified Church") have congregations sometimes over ninety percent female. Despite the fact that the most significant, black, male leaders historically have come from the church, the black church currently only attracts one out of five black males, as compared to one out of four white males.[16] This deficit is viewed by most women as a social problem, and some churches specifically reach out to draw in men. In a number of churches this is done through Men's Fellowships or Laymen's Organizations. In one of the black megachurches, the pastor has "engaged in an aggressive campaign to bring men, especially those from 20 to 60 years old, into his church. Week after week he delivers a powerful message that church is where black men belong."[17]

This absence of black men has been explained alternately and concurrently by their overinvolvement with the criminal justice system, their higher mortality rates, their shame at unemployment and impoverishment, and their alienation from the historic relationship between black women and the pastor. Some have even argued that the lack of diverse role models for young men in the church has also alienated men, since being religious outside the role of the pastor is not seen as "manly."[18] (Ironically, the exclusion of women from the pastoral role and women's exploitation of other opportunities such as Women's Day has led to the presentation of diverse professional role models for women.) Although this campaign to recruit men is seen by some as an overreaction that undercuts the empowerment of women, the director of women's ministries in St. Paul Community Church in Brooklyn New York explicitly connects the problem of men with the problem of black families, stating: "When you build black men, you build strong families and strong communities, [and] you can't complain about that."[19]

The current problems faced by black churches as they confront the problems of "the black family" are tied to a consciousness, a history, and a political economy that make the crisis of families generally a more problematic and painful one in black communities. The "black family" has been seen as a social problem both within and outside the black community, with the bulk of research focusing on its difference/deviance from white families.[20] In order to appreciate the impact of contemporary structural changes on the relationship between churches and families, it is important to examine the historical relationship between church and family in the context of American economic history.

CHURCH AND FAMILY: A HISTORY OF ENDURANCE

Heiss has noted that African-Americans are the only ethnic group whose family life is constantly explained in terms of events a century distant.[21] The relationship between the black family and history is both ideological and practical. The relationship between the family and church can only be understood historically, and that historical continuity is part of the contemporary church's self-understanding as it shapes its ministry. The history of African-Americans is a history of economic exploitation, and responses to economic exploitation have traditionally been shaped in the overlapping settings of church and family. The history of changing church structures and organizations can be tied to problems of economic change. Accordingly, some social science analyses of the family stress the importance of the role of religion[22] and analyses of religion often highlight the family.[23] Their intersection and interdependence can also be heard in congregational anecdotes and sermon illustrations.

In their comprehensive history of the African-American experience, Berry and Blassingame analyze the church and family together, calling them "enduring institutions." They point out:

> The family and the church enabled blacks to endure American racism, slavery, segregation, violence, and oppression. Indeed, these institutions provided the foundation for personal identity, communal strength, individual triumphs in the face of overwhelming odds, creative and rewarding lives, and pride. The autonomous black community drew much of its ideology from and created much of its distinctive culture in the institutions nurturing the young, sustaining the spirit, and arming against caste and prejudice. Heroic and tragic in its dimensions, the history of black institutions is a story of a struggle....[24]

Their term "enduring" suggests an ability to survive while undergoing stress, suffering, and misfortune. There is a persisting continuity, in spite of many and varied pressures to disappear. After a lengthy discussion of the history of the African-American family and the importance of women in that history, Berry and Blassingame conclude: "Much of the strength of the black woman and the Afro-American family can be attributed to their roots in the black church."[25]

For African-Americans in the United States, conflict has historically defined the relationship between the structures of work and power and the institutions of religion and family. More than any other group in New World slave societies, Africans and their descendents in the United States had their family lives uniquely exploited for the purposes of perpetuating slavery. At the same time, that same family served as an important bulwark of resistance. Enslavement meant that African-Americans lived on the edge of crisis. From the end of the eighteenth century until Emancipation, families were repeatedly disrupted through sale and relocation. As a result, definitions of kinship and community obligations included strategies for sanctifying marriages, dissolving marriages when partners were lost, and encouraging companionate and parental responsibilities. In the context of slavery, black and white families were assigned very specialized and different functions. White families were assigned the task of reproducing a ruling/owning class, and black families were assigned the task of reproducing a class of property. Law, custom, and coercion assigned these families opposing interests reflecting their places in society. Each group possessed different and opposing ideas about the role of family, the roles of women within families and community, and the organization and practice of religious experience.

Slave churches were better defended than families as institutional entities. They emerged as a self-governing setting for resistance and for personal integration. When one views the traditional functions of the family—education, social placement, conferral of identity and status, socialization, regulation of reproduction, transmission of tradition, customs, and values, economic cooperation—church and household at times overlapped in fulfilling the functions of the family. It is this tradition of overlap that is a critical source of strength for African-Americans, as individuals and as a group. It has been a principle force in the construction of a culture of resistance.

Two-thirds of the history of African-American family and religious life has been spent in slavery. Observers such as Webber note that, during that time, churches conferred status on individuals and placed them in society, and families operated as sites of intensive religious socialization. He focuses explicitly on the problem of socialization in the slave-quarters community. He points out that the narratives and oral histories of former slaves point to their mothers and other relatives as the people from whom they learned prayers and religious perspectives.[26] Members of the community, confronted with enforced separation from spouses who were sold away, also depended upon the church to declare their marriages dissolved.

The visible and invisible churches of the slave South were also the places which helped to construct and maintain personal integrity. In her novel, *Beloved*, Toni Morrison introduces "Baby Suggs," a character constructed from the true story of the slave Margaret Garner and her mother-in-law, "a professor of religion."[27] Morrison's character travels around, without benefit of ordination urging black people to love themselves and to express fully the depths of their suffering. The individual/personal religious experience was encouraged—largely by family members. The corporate/communal experience of the church was the organizational context into which these "babies" were received by their "water mothers" and "water fathers," whose job it was to instruct them in religious thought and practice. Howard Thurman, a theologian who grew up close to his slave heritage, described a process of religious socialization in which these church *parents* taught new members how to pray and to "raise a hymn."[28]

The church has often been a setting in which the metaphor of family has governed the relationships among black people. The titles of address—"brother," "sister," "mother," "daughter," and "son"—reinforce an ethic of kinship as the guiding norms for intraethnic ties. Family titles, such as "brother," "sister," and "church mother," and the importance of the term "church home" also underscore the interrelatedness of church and family. Most black congregations are gatherings of family networks, and the support of kin and congregation combine to sustain people into their old age.[29]

Not only is the metaphor of family important for socialization into the church, but the metaphorical and practical dimensions of family became important in each successive dislocation affecting the black community. According to Wallace Charles Smith, a church mission rooted in the paradigm of family was always the key to the church's success. He argued:

In its missionary outreach the black church modeled a concept of sufferers reaching out to fellow sufferers.... Reaching out was inclusive. Slavery did not permit the luxury of male chauvinism. Men, women, and children suffered equally; so the church reached out comprehensively. Single mothers, orphans, widows, and widowers were all sought out to come as they were. The inclusiveness was possible because of the family paradigm. Evangelism in the black context was not just a church growth scheme; it was the adopting of someone from some other family into one's own family.[30]

When slavery ended, African-Americans moved around the South, seeking to reconstitute their families by finding those relatives who had been sold away. Churches became the settings in which people made appeals for information about kinfolk, and the "adoptionist ethic," as Smith calls it, continued.

African-American churches also attempted to enforce models of family life, particularly regarding the role of women in the family. Paula Giddings describes women who were disfellowshipped from churches in conflicts involving their husbands and family authority.[31] Freedman's Bureau records attest to these women's resistance to husbands who sought to beat them into submission. Frazier later argued that these attempts at female subordination were largely unsuccessful.[32] The relative egalitarianism of the slave community survived this renegotiation of family and religious roles.

The critical area of cooperation between church and family, however, was in the area of education. The early leadership class was a religiously based class of "preachers and teachers," men and women who taught and pastored in the Southern rural and urban communities immediately after the Civil War. During Reconstruction, many pastors saw their role as that of educators, addressing directly the problems of family life. The African Methodist Episcopal Church appointed ministers throughout the South with this specific charge. They preached in such a way as to encourage self-reliance and education.

Throughout the South, following the Civil War, freed men and women attempted to renegotiate their work relationship. The emergence of the sharecropping system, a system in which work was organized among family units, was the result of this struggle. It was not the total freedom that black people sought, but neither was it the reenslavement the former master class wanted. Jacqueline Jones describes a life during this period as one of almost unrelieved drudgery, in oppressed and alienated households. The church, however, appears as an alternative and empowered setting for African-American communities.[33] The ideological, economic, interpersonal, and leadership dynamics of the church combined with its role as a refuge and vehicle for social uplift in order to insure that "church and family structures became closely interlocked and highly interdependent."[34]

As urbanization progressed, first in the South and later as part of Northern migration, the church was carried to these new settings. Part of that movement involved the rise of the Sanctified Church, which explicitly appealed to family images and networks as the basis of church organization. Women's employment, particularly as household domestics, moved to the cities at an earlier and more rapid rate than did men's, and the church was one of those settings where women could recreate and reconstitute community. In the Church of God in Christ, the new formal office of "church mother" emerged. In other churches, the role of church mother was a prominent informal role. Often women were the founders of churches, which then sent "home" for male pastors. This period of transformation may be the root of the disproportionate female majorities in black urban churches, particularly in the Sanctified Church. These churches were first and foremost communities of women, who then called (hired) their male pastors.

The most dramatic social dislocation since slavery was the "great migration" to northern cities beginning during the First World War. With this shift in residence of nearly forty percent of the black population, a substantial proportion of the black population entered the industrial structure. Churches were again an important institution for the reorganization of community life. Churches became important training grounds for leadership and important resources for recruiting workers for war industries during both world wars. Again the church emerged as a setting for family networks to reorganize themselves. One important piece of church organization that emerged during this period was the auxiliary or club, based on state or county of origin—the Alabama Club, Macomb County Club, and the like. Such groups provided a means of integration for people in large, already-established churches. In addition, new churches were organized in the storefronts of black communities—churches organized in response to the alienation felt in the new, Northern churches, and often organized by families or members of a Southern community to maintain the integrity of family and friendship ties and worship traditions.

Not only were the churches a community and organizational focus, but they also interacted with family life to provide the norms and ideologies necessary for effective family formation. This was Frazier's argument concerning the role of the church as an agency of social control. Billingsley concurred.[35] When the Moynihan Report issued its accusatory analysis of black families and their differences from the dominant white population[36], researchers such as Billingsley, Scanzoni, and others discovered that the focus on the differences could be overdrawn. According to Scanzoni's 1960s study, the church was an important component in the preparation for family life and in the fulfillment of their family-role obligations. For many black people, the church was "a 'structural bridge' between the family and entrance into the larger society [and]...provide[d] resources supplemental to their families."[37]

It is possible to read the history of the African-American experience as a succession of dislocations affecting the relationship between work and family. These dislocations can be traced to specific economic upheavals and transformations, such as the growth of slavery, the end of slavery, the reorganization of Southern agriculture (sharecropping), urbanization, and Northern migration to industrial markets. The church provided the organic connection that bound socially and geographically dislocated individuals and families together into meaningful communities. The importance of the church was such, argues Scanzoni, that, "regardless of a family's location in the class structure," families used religion as a means to success and achievement. They stressed the importance of religious training for its socioethical teaching, which meant taking or sending their children to Sunday School.[38] Willie points to class differences in church involvement, but concludes that: "Those who are faithful in church attendance are completely enveloped by the religious system...."[39] Even with the nationalist critique of the 1960s that the Christian church represented "the religion of the white man," the church remained a center of community and individual expectation. It is this state of interdependence between church and family that makes the decline in the church's influence among members of the ghetto poor, or underclass, such a challenge. The destructive consequences of the past two decades are better appreciated in light of this earlier overlap among church, family, and community.

The current problems of "the truly disadvantaged" have resurrected the earlier debates over "the black family." Contemporary debates over the relationship between African-Americans and the political economy have again raised questions about the organization and efficacy of their families. Questions are specifically aimed at the problems of people identified as the underclass or ghetto poor, who suffer from joblessness, diminished opportunities for marriage, and social isolation.[40] With the dominance of conservative voices in political and public policy circles, strategies are proposed which are aimed at the perceived problems of black families, particularly problems of teenage pregnancy, perceived male irresponsibility, and chronic welfare dependency. While some would argue that perhaps the earlier response to the Moynihan Report by black scholars and liberal whites dampened necessary responses to the problems of the black family, I think that such an explanation is too simple. The damage black families absorbed during two 1970s recessions, and from which many never recovered, represents a dislocation unlike any experienced previously.

These current concerns about the African-American family immediately raise questions about indigenous community organizations and resources, especially the church. In spite of the rise of new organizations, the role of the church is still central. Black and white people in human services agencies still attest to their dependence upon churches when state resources are inadequate. The histories of religion and family, when taken together, seem to indicate that the organization with the most vulnerability is the family. At some times and under some conditions, survival in the black community has required investment of energy and resources so that church life could substitute for family. Such a substitution is currently happening in the area of day care, food programs, counseling, shelter, housing, and parent education. As some observers note, however, the problems facing the contemporary poor require more than the church can give. In the face of the current crisis, large-scale state responses are essential.

CONCLUSION: A CONTINUING RESPONSE TO CRISIS

Although a highly politicized debate over the nature, source, and intensity of black family problems has persisted since the mid-1960s, there is more agreement than ever among community leaders and social scientists that poor black families are facing the most protracted crisis ever. Part of the problem has been directed to issues concerning "the underclass," that segment of the population that is concentrated in the poorest census tracts of inner cities and plagued by joblessness, social isolation, and a deteriorating social order.[41] What has made the crisis of the underclass particularly poignant are the large numbers of women and children affected by the economic crises giving rise to the underclass. Although the crisis has been framed in terms of male joblessness, Malveaux demonstrates that cycles and downturns have affected women as dramatically as men.[42] With their higher unemployment rates, black women, when laid off, find work more slowly than men. It is women who fill the pews of African-American churches, and it is women who have been most vulnerable to the ravages of the crack epidemic, with its risk of damaged babies and AIDS.[43]

These new challenges limit the role that ideologies about family play as organizational metaphors in African-American churches. Family is a wonderful organizational metaphor as long as one is inside the circle. But how do the strangers of the underclass, who have never joined the church family and have no "church home," get in? The increased disjuncture between community boundaries and religious boundaries—a trend that can be labeled secularization—is an important new dimension in the current problems facing contemporary African-Americans.

Pastoral theologian Wallace Charles Smith has called for a conscious reclamation of some of the historic strengths of the church and family relationship, as a way to meet contemporary problems and correct some wrongs within the community. In the face of the disjunctures of class restructuring and secularization, he recommends an aggressive program that reasserts the adoptionist role of the black church. He insists that preaching, classroom education, counseling, and community organizing are essential components for this approach to the black family. In addition, at the community level, the problem of the family needs to be approached in terms of economic development (jobs, equity, and the end of consumerism), housing, public education, and programs for youth.

In the interplay among historical strengths and contemporary crises, the family and the church still need to be considered together as cooperating adaptive mechanisms in an unfair society. The retreat of the state and the failure of social policy make this reintegration all the more essential.[44] For both black and white Americans, contemporary family life represents an adaptation to an economy that has subordinated all other institutional arrangements to the needs of advanced capitalism. All families are in trouble, and indicators of trouble identified among African-American families during the mid-1960s have become the current realities of many others.[45] Marian Wright Edelman, describing the problems of the American family as a context for understanding the particularities of black families, argued:

> The American family crisis is not just a black family crisis. Both public and private sector neglect and anti-family policy have contributed to a downward spiral for families and children, black and white.... In some respects (education, income of two-parent families, women's earnings, child nutrition, infant mortality) black rates have been improving and narrowing the gap between whites—or were doing so until the budget cuts and the near-depression of the early 1980s. In certain other respects the gap has been narrowing because blacks have been standing still while whites are slipping backward.[46]

Social institutions are the interfaces of social organization and culture. It is within social institutions that the frameworks for roles and statuses are structured. As societies increase in complexity, institutions become more elaborate, and roles and statuses become more compartmentalized and specialized. Work, family, and religion represent institutional spaces in which human beings act or complete tasks related to physical and psychic survival. They also represent the spaces in our lives where the meanings surrounding self and others are constructed. Although work and business institutions represent the dominant forces in our lives, Bellah and his associates have pointed out that religion and family, along with other settings in community life, are the social spaces where individuals negotiate meaning and identity.[47]

Church, family, voluntary association, neighborhood, and subculture are the places which Berger termed "mediating structures" to denote "those institutions which stand between the individual in his private sphere and the large institutions of the public sphere." Such structures are necessary under social conditions where the institutions which exercise massive and overwhelming power in individual lives are divorced or separated from the settings of everyday life in which action and meaning are combined, that is, where there is "a dichotomy... between the megastructures and private life."[48]

For minority groups in modern societies, the relationship between individuals and "megastructures" is complicated and confounded by a context of explicit exploitation and racial hostility. The racial-ethnic foundations of American social structure have led Robert Blauner to distinguish between colonized and immigrant minorities.[49] The presence in society of colonized groups, people of color, was coerced in a way that tied their racial identity to a specific sphere of work, subordinated their family structures to the needs of that economic sector, and excluded them from political participation. For such groups, family, religion, and subculture are essential, not only as mediating structures, but also as oppositional or countercultural structures. In a context of racial oppression, a truly interstitial role, as implied by the term "mediating," could be counterproductive. It is within the community life of the colonized group that family, religion, and local community become structures which provide identity and meaning, while at the same time those structures enable the construction of a culture of resistance. Within a culture of resistance, individuals may learn to reject the humiliating definitions of the self and the group present in the dominant culture. Here they can formulate alternative pathways to economic survival and political empowerment. It is the construction of alternatives for survival and growth that best characterizes the current mission of African-American churches. Their interrelationship with families has been threatened by the current crisis, but reconstructing that relationship is essential for survival. These alternatives must be the light for families struggling through this seemingly overwhelming storm.

NOTES

1. Carnegie Corporation of New York, "Black Churches: Can They Strengthen the Black Family?" *Carnegie Quarterly* 33, No. 1 (1988), pp. 1–9.See also C. Eric Lincoln and Lawrence Mamiya, *The Black Church in the African-American Experience* (Chapel Hill: Duke University Press, 1990).

2. Mary Frances Berry and John W. Blassingame, *Long Memory: The Black Experience in America* (New York: Oxford University Press, 1982); also Lincoln and Mamiya, *The Black Church*.

3. William Julius Wilson, *The Truly Disadvantaged: The Inner City, The Underclass and Public Policy* (Chicago: University of Chicago Press, 1987).

4. Charles Perrow and Mauro F. Guillen, *The AIDS Disaster: The Failure of Organizations in New York and the Nation* (New Haven: Yale University Press, 1990), p. 160.

<ol start="5">
<li>Wilson, The Truly Disadvantaged; also his "Studying Inner City Dislocations: The Challenge of Public Agenda Research," American Sociological Review 56, No. 1 (1990), pp. 1–14.</li>
<li>Lincoln and Mamiya, The Black Church, p. 269.</li>
<li>Ibid., p. 271.</li>
<li>On instrumental extended family networks, see Dennis P. Hogan, Ling-Xin Hao, and William L. Parish, "Race, Kin Networks, and Assistance to Mother-Headed Families," Social Forces 68, No. 3 (1990), pp. 797–812.</li>
<li>Lincoln and Mamiya, The Black Church, pp. 385–388.</li>
<li>Cheryl Townsend Gilkes, "Together and in Harness: Women's Traditions in the Sanctified Church," Signs: Journal of Women in Culture and Society 11, No. 4 (1985), pp. 678–699.</li>
<li>Lincoln and Mamiya, The Black Church, p. 386.</li>
<li>Hariette Pipes McAdoo, "Transgenerational Patterns of Upward Mobility in African-American Families," in Black Families, 2nd Edition, ed. Hariette Pipes McAdoo, (Beverly Hills, CA: Sage Publications, 1988), p. 149.</li>
<li>A. Knighton Stanley, The Children is Crying: Congregationalism among Black People (New York: Pilgrim Press, 1979).</li>
<li>E. Franklin Frazier, The Black Bourgeoisie: The Rise of a New Middle Class (New York: Free Press, 1957).</li>
<li>Lincoln and Mimiya, The Black Church, p. 255.</li>
<li>Ari L. Goldman, "Black Minister Recruits More Men for the Church," New York Times, July 5, 1990, p. B2.</li>
<li>Goldman, "Black Minister Recruits"; also Jonny Ray Youngblood, The Conspicuous Absence and the Controversial Presence of the Black Male in the Local Church, Unpublished D.Min. thesis (Dayton, Ohio: United Theological Seminary, 1990).</li>
<li>James Tinney, "The Religious Experience of Black Men," in Black Men, ed. Lawrence E. Gary (Beverly Hills, CA: Sage Publications, 1981), pp. 269–276.</li>
<li>Goldman, "Black Minister Recruits".</li>
<li>Jerold Heiss, The Case of the Black Family: A Sociological Inquiry (New York: Columbia University Press, 1975); also Linda M. Chatters, M. Belinda Tucker, and Edith Lewis, "Developments in Research on Black Families: A Decade Review," Journal of Marriage and the Family 52 (November 1990), pp. 993–1014.</li>
<li>Heiss, The Case of the Black Family.</li>
<li>Herbert Gutman, The Black Family in Slavery and Freedom, 1750–1925 (New York: Pantheon Books, 1976); also Robert Hill, The Strengths of Black Families: A National Urban League Research Study (New York: Emerson Hall Publishers, Inc., 1972).</li>
<li>J. Deotis Roberts, Roots of a Black Future: Family and Church (Philadelphia, PA: Westminster Press, 1980); also Wallace Charles Smith,</li>
</ol>

The Church in the Life of the Black Family (Valley Forge, PA: Judson Press, 1985).

24. Berry and Blassingame, *Long Memory*, p. 70.

25. *Ibid.* p. 92.

26. Thomas L. Webber, *Deep Like the Rivers: Education in the Slave Quarter Community, 1831–1865* (New York: W.W. Norton and Co., 1978). See also Gutman, *The Black Family*.

27. Toni Morrison, *Beloved* (New York: Alfred A. Knopf, 1987).

28. Howard Thurman, *With Head and Heart: Autobiography of Howard Thurman* (New York: Harcourt Brace Jovanovich, 1979).

29. Robert J. Taylor and Linda M. Chatters, "Patterns of Informal Support to Elderly Black Adults: Family, Friends, and Church Members," *Social Work* 31 (1986), pp. 432–438.

30. Smith, *The Church in the Life*, p. 18.

31. Paula Giddings, *When and Where I Enter: The Impact of Black Women on Race and Sex in America* (New York: William Morrow and Company, 1984).

32. E. Franklin Frazier, *The Negro Family in the United States* (Chicago: University of Chicago Press, 1939).

33. Jacqueline Jones, *Labor of Love, Labor of Sorrow: Black Women, Work and the Family from Slavery to the Present* (New York: Basic Books, 1989).

34. John H. Scanzoni, *The Black Family in Modern Society* (Boston: Allyn and Bacon, 1971), p. 50.

35. E. Franklin Frazier, *The Negro Church in America* (New York: Schocken Books, 1964), and Andrew Billingsley, *Black Families in White America* (Englewood Cliffs, NJ: Prentice Hall, 1968).

36. Daniel P. Moynihan, *On Understanding Poverty: Perspectives from the Social Sciences* (New York: Basic Books, 1969).

37. Scanzoni, *The Black Family*, p. 126.

38. *Ibid.* p. 287.

39. Charles Willie, *A New Look at Black Families* (Bayside, NY: General Hall, 1976).

40. See Wilson, *The Truly Disadvantaged*, and "Studying inner City Dislocations."

41. Wilson, *The Truly Disadvantaged*.

42. Julianne Malveaux, "The Economic Statuses of Black Families," in *Black Families*, 2nd edition, ed. Harriette Pipes McAdoo, (Beverly Hills, CA: Sage Publications, 1988), 133–46.

43. Ellen Hopkins, "Childhood's End: Crack Babies," *Rolling Stone*, October 18, 1990; also Perrow and Guillen, *The AIDS Disaster*.

44. K. Sue Jewell, *Survival of the Black Family: The Institutional Impact of U.S. Social Policy* (New York: Praeger Publishers, 1988).

45. Daniel Patrick Moynihan, *Family and Nation* (San Diego, CA: Harcourt Brace Jovanovich, 1986).

46. Marian Wright Edelman, *Families in Peril: An Agenda for Social Change* (Cambridge, MA: Harvard University Press, 1987), p. 23.

47. Robert Bellah, *et. al.*, *Habits of the Heart: Individualism and Commitment in American Life* (Berkeley: University of California Press, 1985).

48. Peter Berger, *Facing up to Modernity: Excursions in Society, Politics, and Religion* (New York: Basic Books, 1977), p. 132.

49. Robert Blauner, *Racial Oppression in America* (New York: Harper and Row, 1972).

9

Nurturing and Equipping Children in the "Public Church"

Joseph T. Reiff

All too often it is forgotten that education must rest on an adequate social base. It is impossible to educate people to the values of a nonexistent group. ...Our present catechetics continually put us in the position of telling people, 'Yes, Virginia, there is a church.'[1]

These days children in the U.S. are bombarded with a plethora of images, ideas, and ways of life any time they gaze through what Michael Warren calls the "enormous picture window" of popular culture. Extending the metaphor, he calls the influence of religious education a "peephole" by comparison.[2] Perhaps part of the reason for such a difference in "size" of influence is the widespread confusion over the vision for and role of the church in late-twentieth-century North American society. Ralph A. Keifer's clever appropriation of the famous editorial assurance to young Virginia was written as a Roman Catholic catechetical mandate, but it certainly reflects the general situation in the Protestant mainline as well.

Implicit in the discussion of changing patterns of work, family, and religious faith are two questions among many: What *is* the nature of the church and its relationship to the world in these days? What role can the church and its adult members play in both the nurture of its children in the faith and the equipping of those children for present and future Christian vocation, mission, and ministry?

This paper seeks to answer both questions. To begin with, I claim that the first question for those who would consider the problem of Christian formation of children and adults is simply: What is the church? Asking the question: What kind of persons do we want to form? is unavoidably tied to the prior question: What kind of community are we to be (or is God calling us to be)? Second, for those who see the "public church" as the answer to this last question, this chapter explores some of the problems that parents and other adults within such congregations may face in bringing up children in the Christian faith. I will offer some general reflections on the problem, and then move to some more specific statements about directions for practice in congregations.

These theoretical and practical reflections are supplemented with data from a larger study of St. Paul United Methodist Church, an Atlanta inner city neighborhood congregation.[3] These data were gathered through participant observation and interviews with parents and other adults, as well as my own experience as a member of that congregation from 1986 to 1990. It is situated in a multicultural neighborhood (though gentrification is now a factor), and is a potential "public church" congregation that has undergone a period of renewal since 1985, owing in part to the influx of over 120 "baby-boomer" adults and more than seventy children under the age of thirteen.[4]

THE CHALLENGE FOR THE CHURCH

In truth, Christians are at the very least a "cognitive minority"[5] in the U.S. Many persons who have made a significant commitment to a Christian interpretive framework for life in the world and to a particular community of faith (through their time, regular presence, a portion of monetary resources, creative gifts, and so on) feel trapped into viewing such a commitment as "private." They are afraid to say much about their religiosity to neighbors or coworkers for fear the response will be either open hostility, or perhaps worse, utter indifference. They even have trouble talking with members of their own congregation about their commitment, about the meaning of their faith, about God.

This is the situation described by Wolfgang Schluchter in a 1982 article on the problem of secularization. He offers two theses:

> (1) As far as the world views are concerned, largely completed secularization means that religious beliefs have become subjective as a result of the rise of alternative interpretations of life, which in principle can no longer be integrated into a religious world view. (2) As far as the institutions are concerned, largely completed secularization means that institutionalized religion has been depoliticized as a result of a functional differentiation of society, which in principle can no longer be integrated through institutionalized religion.

On the basis of these claims, he then asks two questions:

> (1) Is there a legitimate religious resistance to secular world views that is more than a refusal to accept the consequences of the Enlightenment?
> (2) Is there a legitimate religious resistance to depoliticization, a resistance that is more than a clinging to inherited privileges?[6]

Thus in bold strokes he paints a portrait that is widely accepted in the academic world. The church has lost authority and power over the society, over persons in the society, and even over persons in the church itself, many of whom might be described as *in* the church but not *of* it. The church has become a service institution, functioning to help *individuals* attain authenticity and transcendental subjectivity.[7] In short, the church has been put to the service of the Enlightenment project.

A few religious educators have focused on this problem. For instance, Charles Foster wrote in 1982:

> My specific concern is the way we respond to the increasing loss of status and place of the Christian community in our larger society. In spite of large church membership and much media attention to some Christian perspectives, our experience is increasingly that of a people no longer in charge.... Many of our symbols, appropriated by the adherents of..."civil religion," have lost their hold on our personal and corporate imagination. Our rituals have been trivialized, and the stories of our heritage have been called sentimental and irrelevant. The blessings of our common life, in other words, often seem superficial and lifeless.[8]

Another writer, discussing the effects of liberalism on Christians, points to a result that comes from this loss of status and place as well: *the diminished ability of Christians to see themselves as a people with a distinctive vision.*[9]

THE "PUBLIC CHURCH": TOWARD A DEFINITION

The "public church" has been proposed as a response to this situation and to Schluchter's questions.[10] As a normative vision for congregations, it offers an alternative to secular worldviews that accept the consequences, if not the assumptions of the Enlightenment. It especially rejects the Kantian claim that any truly "moral" vision for society must leave particular traditions or narratives behind. It also maintains that the rightful place of the church (in both its global and its local forms) and of individual Christians is in all public "spheres," no longer expecting to be in charge, but certainly expecting to be taken seriously as a full partner in the conversation.

The public church is, in James Fowler's phrase, "deeply and particularly Christian." It is primarily a worshipping community that is powerfully formed by the Christian story and tradition, and seeks to live out that identity in the world. It resists any claim that "formation" is necessarily synonymous with "coercion," and it seeks to nurture and equip persons to choose and act out of the Christian faith as a life-centering commitment. It attempts to balance the socializing power of the congregation with a "critical consciousness" that gives individual members perspective on their life together as a community.[11] The public church also lives in the fundamental tension between the need to move beyond the self-protective, self-perpetuating ways of the institutional church and the absolute necessity for institutional form and communal context within which to be such a church.

Firmly rooted in the Christian story and tradition, the public church nonetheless acknowledges that its worldview is one of many, and even recognizes the possibility of other truths that may enrich or help define its faith. This willingness to enter into dialogue with others also enables the public church to be true to its name in the largest sense: to work in cooperation with others for the public good on a local, national, and global scale.

Central to any discussion of this proposal for the church's identity and relationship to the world is the meaning of the word *public*. To what public are we referring? I propose three "publics" for consideration here: the public of the *congregation*, the public of *dialogue and action*, and the public of *human solidarity*. This is not meant to be an exhaustive list, but represents three "publics" upon which congregations can have the most impact.

We begin closest to the center of the life of the church, the *public of the congregation*. In the public church the congregation itself is viewed as a public in which all members can live and practice the faith together as a community. It is in joint, public activity that the congregation gives primary attention to its language, forms of life, particular worldview and presence in the world. Here the story of the community is continually reinterpreted in light of the Christian story, as understood through scripture and tradition, through the individual experiences of members, and through the story and culture of the particular congregation.[12] In so doing, the congregational public functions as a "source of critique over against the stories, conventions, and confirmations of the official publics."[13]

Because the congregation is a public, it belongs to all within it—it is in the "public domain." All are encouraged to be questioning/thinking members of the community with contributions to make, gifts to offer, and a say in the future of the congregation. It is a public in which persons trust each other and are not afraid to explore critically the issues that are important to the life of the community and of the world. It is a place where people can live with the tension of disagreement.

It is from the base of this congregational public that the public church and its individual members can move out into and act in larger publics. In the *public of discussion and action*, the public church can bring "the concerns of biblical religion into the common discussion about the nature and future of our society."[14] Though it believes in a universal, sovereign God,[15] the public church as a human community does not claim to speak from some universal standpoint. Rather it understands itself as one voice among many in a public discourse.[16] At the same time, it speaks and acts (as a congregation and as individuals involved in all facets of life) out of a deep commitment to its interpretation of the Christian vision for life on this earth. Just as it expects to listen to other interpretations, it also expects its own voice to be heard and its actions to be taken seriously. The public church always hears other voices and interprets other actions in light of its own story, but it is also able to have its own position "deepened, broadened, and even corrected by an encounter with the other."[17]

Finally, the public church participates in the *public of human solidarity*. Believing that faith engages the whole of life and is not a private matter, public church congregations and their members are involved in the surrounding world in significant ways, seeking to live in solidarity with the poor, the outcast, the suffering, and to offer hospitality to the stranger. The public church bears critical witness against oppressive structures in society. While firmly rooted in its particular setting as the locus for its mission, such congregations understand their membership in the worldwide community of the living and the dead in Christ, indeed, in the whole human community.[18]

THINKING ABOUT THE PROBLEM

If the kind of church we are talking about is, therefore, conscious of its public, corporate life together and of its place in a larger, pluralistic, public world, then such a church may think and act toward its children in distinctive ways. First, it will act as a corporate whole, not just as a collection of private families. Because of the prevalent view of the family as a refuge, a private domain, or a "haven in a heartless world," parenting and the general nurturing and religious socialization of children is potentially an exclusively *private* matter. Everything that I will say about the role of the public church in the education and formation of children rests on the premise that we are talking primarily about a *corporate* undertaking. Though parents certainly have the main responsibility for their children, in the public church children are a part of the "public domain" mentioned above. This does not mean they are the church's "property." Rather, children are seen as gifts from God entrusted to the entire community.[19]

Second, public churches will recognize that the need to belong to a particular community and the necessity of participating in a pluralistic world are difficult needs to keep in balance. The language of this paper's title, "nurturing and equipping children," underlines the *dual* nature of the public church's endeavor: the importance of providing children a place to belong, significant roles to play as members of the congregation, and deep roots in the Christian faith and story, coupled with the concern to foster in those children an openness to the world around them, an acceptance of diversity, and a commitment to justice. In my experience, most "activist" churches have had limited success at combining strong programs of nurture and support for the needs of members (children included, and sometimes especially[20]) with strong programs of outreach and witness for social justice.

Third, public churches will recognize that the kind of commitment they call for will have to be demonstrated, as much as taught. Congregations and parents in the public church will have to show their children by example that faith is not simply a private matter, but is a public statement of identity. The faith commitments of individuals in a public church are conceived as a way of life, a lens through which all of life is viewed. Such a church is not a "voluntary association" for its members, and its nurture is not a privately chosen service to be consumed. The faith of such a congregation is a significant life-centering commitment. This alone will communicate a great deal to children.[21]

A fourth distinctive in the way a public church will educate its children is that it will value and accept the diversity *they* represent. John Westerhoff makes a strong case for valuing children for who they *are* and viewing them as persons of faith from the beginning.[22] As shall become evident below, the approach to the education of children in the public church reflected here seeks to hold these two concerns in tension: valuing children for who they are, while leading and assisting them to become what they will be in the future.

Fifth, if a public church is to nurture a *particular* vision shaped by the Christian story, it must recognize the enormous power of popular culture. For instance, the omnipresence of television in our lives strengthens our ties to privacy, since TV images serve as easy substitutes for real experience in the world.[23] Included in the public church's "critical consciousness" is a deep awareness (by parents and all adults in the congregation) of popular culture's influence. The congregation will need to undertake specific steps to counter that influence and to foster critical awareness in children.[24]

Sixth, congregations that undertake the task of nurturing and equipping the generation of children growing up in the nineties also need to recognize the particular religious and cultural experiences that have shaped the parents of those children. Most of these parents are baby-boomers, and many of them have questioned (and perhaps still do) commitment to the institutional church. Yet now they feel more responsibility for that institution and for socializing their children into it.[25] For instance, a father at St. Paul Church began attending in late 1985, professing his agnosticism in the young adult Sunday School class, and declining to join the church. He claimed that he was there because what the church was doing was good for the neighborhood, and he simply wanted to support that. Two years later he and his family joined the church, and have since become heavily involved (he chairs an important committee). He has become more comfortable with membership and participation in such an institution, but he is still ambivalent about the faith that goes with it. He expresses reservations about the "indoctrination" of his two children, wanting to allow them freedom to decide for themselves without being unduly influenced by Christian beliefs. This "tentative openness" (as opposed to "committed openness"[26]) places the "deeply and particularly Christian" side of the public church vision at risk.

In many ways the educational task of the public church is encapsuled in the old saying: "There are two lasting gifts we can give our children: one is roots; the other, wings." The public church models both a deeply particular commitment to the Christian faith as an interpretive framework or "story" from which to view the world and all of life, and an openness to the truth of other beliefs, other interpretive frameworks or stories. *Neither* is easy to foster in children in mainstream Christian churches now; yet the public church attempts to accomplish *both*. Commitment is difficult to achieve in the midst of the multitude of demands on our attention, time, and resources. Genuine openness runs counter to the human desire for some form of absolute truth, and it may be impossible when children (and some adults) lack the developmental capacity to hold possibly conflicting truths in tension.

If the church succeeds in forming such deep particularity in its children and in modeling such an openness to other truths, it faces an added risk: the deeply particular commitment provides the roots; the openness to other truth carries within it the potential for wings to fly away from the interpretive framework in which a child is raised, to adopt another set of truths as a late adolescent or adult. It is with some "fear and trembling" that adults in the public church sponsor their children's introduction to the public of discussion and action.

DIRECTIONS

Congregations that seek to nurture and equip children as members of the public church must first create or acknowledge the public space within their walls, and view children as public persons whose faith, growth, and well-being are concerns of the entire church. Resisting the public-private, masculine-feminine split, public churches view raising, nurturing, and equipping children as a *public* calling which touches the life of all—it is important work.

The task begins in the first of the "publics" we discussed—the congregational public—and continues to focus here during the early years of a child's life. If the congregational public is truly a "public domain," then children will be treated as *bona fide* members of it from birth. When the congregation understands the role of children in their midst, children are able to hear the story, "practice" the faith, and offer their unique gifts. Here they grow their *roots*.

Membership: "Roots"

That children might be full members of the congregational public is contrary to current practice in most denominations. For instance, children who are baptized in the United Methodist Church are called "preparatory members." This is a confusing category, albeit designed to leave children some say in the matter when they are old enough to "accept for themselves" at confirmation. In recent years there has been some discussion of the unification of the rites of infant baptism, confirmation, and communion,[27] which would actually include children as "full" members from the time of their baptism. The congregation, as an ecology of faith, "imputes"[28] full membership (and the intention to follow through on the commitment as a youth and adult) to baptized infants, trusting that, through the combined witness of family and community, they will grow into fully committed faith. Perhaps this rite of initiation would mean more to the children if they waited until adolescence or adulthood, yet what they lose in "direct" experience is replaced by the power of their full and formal inclusion in the congregation from the beginning of life.

If roots in the community of faith are to take hold, children need to be prepared and taught to participate in worship, the central focus of life in the congregational public. Unfortunately, in most congregations worship is almost totally adult-centered, with the "children's sermon" usually sufficing for explicit involvement of children. At St. Paul Church, some parents, wanting their children to enjoy worship and not "grow up hating it" (as perhaps some of the parents did), have taken a *laissez-faire* approach to their children's participation. Some attempts have been made by educational leaders and the program minister to give kindergartners some intentional instruction in worship participation, learning the creed and responses. But the adult focus of worship remains.

Congregations concerned with full inclusion of children will find ways to shift at least a bit toward a "child-centered" end: singing more simple hymns or songs that children know (balanced with the desire to teach them traditional hymns); creating more opportunities for movement, action, and touch in worship (shifting slightly away from the centrality of words in most Protestant worship); providing frequent opportunities for children to offer their gifts in worship, through such things as dance, music, drama, reading the scripture, acting as ushers and acolytes (at St. Paul, the youngest acolytes are first-graders), making banners, helping to prepare the sanctuary for worship; and having an occasional service directed almost exclusively to the experience of children.

The underlying issue here is the way the congregation perceives children's potential for relationship with God. As one writer puts it:

> While I do not wish for less than welcoming, loving, providing security, and fostering healthful development, I also wish that young children *meet God, not just learn about God*. My research indicates this is possible in a worship context appropriate for young children.[29]

In developmental terms, belonging is important to preschool and especially elementary children, whose style of faith has been termed "affiliative."[30] It is important for children to belong to the community or institution, but they also need to know that they belong *in* the larger Christian story and *to* God. The issue in "public" terms is one of access: will adults invite children to know God primarily on adult terms, or will adults take the experiences and faith of children seriously and assist them to know God in terms more accessible and intelligible to them?

Here the concept of "ecology of faith experience" becomes important. Adults who teach Sunday School know that young children often display what James Fowler calls an intuitive-projective faith,[31] with elaborate dreams, fantasies and images of God and God's relationship to them, and that this is all quite real to these children. One of the principal gifts preschoolers have to offer a congregation of adults caught in the "current situation" of a secularized world that doubts the reality of God,[32] is an intuitive-projective *conviction* of God's presence in their lives. Worship that takes the experience of children more seriously, and even allows young children to "testify" to this conviction, gives *adults* access to the power of children's faith experience.

As children grow older, it becomes important to communicate more directly to them that they are members of the congregational public, with significant roles to play, and a *voice* in the decision-making processes of the congregation. Here is an example from St. Paul Church:

> One Sunday morning in the summer Jane Morgan substituted for the regular Older Elementary (Third to Seventh-grade) teacher. She had a lesson planned, but discovered upon arriving that two of the oldest girls had just returned from church camp and were disturbed about two things: (1) in a social responsibility interest group at camp they had learned about the environmental dangers of styrofoam; (2) the group leader had urged them all to take some action, and there were two obvious places where styrofoam is used—churches and McDonald's.
>
> Seeing that this was important to the girls, Jane led a discussion about

what they could do as a class. They decided to write a brief letter/petition to McDonald's, asking them to stop using Styrofoam. This was done, and the two girls who had initiated the discussion read the letter to the congregation during the announcement time in worship that morning, inviting adults to sign the letter. They also decided to present their concerns about the church's use of Styrofoam to the congregation's Administrative Council. Jane took this concern to the council for the class, and the council responded, "We need to let the children help us make this decision."

Two weeks later, the program minister (Frances Marie Knight) and the chair of the missions committee (Paul Barfield) served as guest teachers in the Older Elementary class. Paul had done some checking about comparative costs of styrofoam and paper goods. Paper cold cups were not much more expensive; therefore that would be an easy switch to make, they all agreed. However, styrofoam cups and take-out plates (used to take food from First Sunday lunches to older homebound members in the neighborhood) were *much* cheaper than their cardboard and paper alternatives. Paul explained all of this to the children, helping them to see that the additional costs didn't seem like so much until you multiplied them by several thousand cups a year. He talked a little about some of the environmental issues involved, for instance, efforts now being made to recycle Styrofoam. (Paul had happened to catch a lengthy special report on the Styrofoam issue on [National Public Radio's] "All Things Considered" on the way home from work the previous Thursday. He had joked to Frances Marie, "If I thought God did things like this, I would have said that God had provided!")

The class discussed options: (1) Do nothing; or (2) have everyone bring a personal hot drink cup from home. Problems, such as having to drag cups all over the church building, and washing the cups, were discussed. Hot drinkers were a problem. One child said: "Just let them wash their own cup." Another responded: "But we're Mission Buddies, and I think the Mission Buddies could wash the cups." A third option was to buy cardboard hot cups and have persons make a dime contribution to cover the extra cost each time they use one. The kids preferred option 2, and got excited. "Yea, that's what we'll do. It's all decided!" Paul and Frances Marie helped them see that this was an issue the whole church should decide, since it affected the congregation's life together. The kids then decided to take a poll, and the next Sunday they circulated a chart for people to mark their choice between Options 2 and 3. The overwhelming majority voted to bring personal cups.

The implications of this story for the education of children in a public church are obvious. By taking their concerns seriously, the adults communicated a powerful message to the children involved: "You have a voice in this congregational public, and your concerns are our concerns, too." The children were given an opportunity to "rehearse" for participation in larger publics,[33] and a way of living together in faith in the congregational public was modeled. The importance of experience is crucial here. The public church does not simply *tell* children (in children's sermons, and so on) that they are full and valued members of the congregational public; it also *shows* them, by offering them participatory experience in all facets of congregational life.

The value of experience extends to the publics of *human solidarity* and *discussion and action* as well. Even young children can benefit from their family's volunteer work at a church-sponsored homeless shelter or food bank, or from money-raising for mission projects. Many of the St. Paul Church families who live in the surrounding neighborhood have been there for years because of their commitment to the value of life in a multicultural setting. As one parent put it, "We moved here twelve years ago not to serve or 'do for' the 'underprivileged,' but to live next door to folks who are different from us. Now that we've had kids and they are older, we know that has been good for all of us."[34] Older elementary children and teenage youth are ready to deal in creative and significant ways with the relationship of their faith to popular culture and television, and can make important contributions to neighborhood and community efforts to deal with social problems such as racism and drug abuse. The public church seeks to facilitate dialogue over neighborhood/community issues, and often provides public meeting space for community action and discussion. Imaginative youth leaders can involve youth in such issues in meaningful ways.

Finally, because the public church tries to maintain a critical perspective on both its own congregational public and the larger world in which it lives, and because children are treated as members of the congregation, critical reflection needs to be promoted from early in childhood. If children are discouraged from asking and reflecting on the "Why?" of reality, it is likely they will continue in adulthood to settle uncritically for the status quo.[35]

Letting Them Go: "Wings"

This emphasis on a critical perspective leads us into the other side of the fundamental tension involved in the education and formation of children in the public church. The task is to make them members, incorporate them fully into the life of the congregation, and "school" them in the language, story, practices, passions, and affections of the

Christian faith. Yet at the same time, the congregation has the responsibility to give children the freedom to grow, become who they will be, and offer their gifts along the way.

It is important to be sensitive to the changing needs and perspectives of children as they grow older. The worlds of older children and youth are wider, with more possibilities for activities outside and removed from the congregational public. Increasing awareness of the countercultural or alternative nature of the church's interpretive framework is a natural source of ambiguity and inner conflict for the growing child and adolescent. Other commitments begin to pull at them, and they develop a greater desire to choose their own communities, friends, beliefs. Consider this example:

> Shannon has just turned twelve, and her family has been a part of St. Paul Church for four years. They do not live in the neighborhood, but have chosen to drive from their home some ten miles away in another part of the city. Despite the distance, they worship and participate fully in the life of this congregation because it is where they feel most "at home"—with the theology, practices, and vision of the congregation, with the quality of leadership, and with the significant relationships they have made with other members of the church. For the first three years Shannon felt perfectly at home at St. Paul as well—her participation there was a proud part of her identity, and she knew she belonged.
>
> In the past year, however, she has experienced some confusion and frustration about church. She often feels lost in worship, not understanding what the preacher is saying or other things that are said or done. Her parents have been putting some pressure on her to participate more in the service, but it is harder for her to do now. She is bewildered, and feels as if there is something that she should be understanding that she just isn't getting at all.
>
> It doesn't help that none of her school friends go to St. Paul. She likes the small group of kids her age who have made up the core of older kids in the church for four years, but she never sees them during the week, and she doesn't really have a "best friend" among them, anyway. She has expressed some of this to her parents, but doesn't feel they really understand. They suggested she talk to Frances Marie or James (the pastor) about it, but that is hard, because they almost seem like parents, too.

There are various ways to interpret what is going on in Shannon's life. From the perspective of Fowler's faith development theory, she seems to be in transition between mythic-literal and synthetic-conventional faith.[36] Her cognitive abilities have developed to the point where it is no longer sufficient to know that she *belongs*, and the fact that the belonging was so clear and important to her until recently increases her confusion. She is beginning to evaluate for herself this commitment her family has made, "trying it on" for size and finding that somehow it does not quite fit, though she does not understand why. The sociology of knowledge perspective might add that she is in the process of constructing a larger world than the one she has lived happily in as a child, and the separation of her church and school lives means that the "plausibility structure" for her faith and participation at St. Paul is fairly weak. She does not spend enough time at the church or with a group of friends from the congregation to sustain the "church world" in which she existed a year ago.

There are at least three Christian education theorists who have sought to design appropriate congregational responses to the kind of dilemma toward which Shannon's experience is potentially leading her in the next few years—the struggle for an individuated faith. In fact, each one proposes incorporating the response into the sacramental life of the church. A scheme for such a response might sound like this: the church recognizes an important fact in Shannon's life (and that of her peers) at the age of sixteen or so—she is embarking on a long journey; she is beginning to grow up. Maybe not for a while, but at some point, she will begin to question with a more focused critical power all that has seemed obvious to her about her faith and her belonging in this community. She will leave home, perhaps never to return fully to this congregation again. She has received powerful and deep roots from the church; now the church must publicly offer her wings to explore for herself her faith, the world, and her commitments. This is done formally through what G. Temp Sparkman calls "rites of affirmation"; John Westerhoff suggests a "Doubting Thomas Day" on which to have such a rite, and Robert Browning and Roy Reed propose making confirmation a "repeatable sacrament."[36]

This "letting go" may be the most difficult test of the public church's vision for nurturing and equipping its children, and of its vision of existence as a story-formed and truth-claiming community that nonetheless acknowledges that it is one voice among many in the larger public. Church-sponsored visits to synagogues, mosques, or Hindu temples, accompanied by some study of these other faiths and comparison with Christianity, are one way for older children and youth to develop awareness of this religious and cultural pluralism. Being willing to let children go will become harder as the presence of other religions and worldviews becomes stronger in U.S. culture. This will be the real trial of the public church's "committed openness," as the values and visions of families and communities are tested in the laboratory of child-raising. We can give lip service to specific views, but what do we live out with our children?

On Not Letting Parents Off the Hook

This paper has focused almost exclusively on the role of the congregation in the formation and sponsoring of children in the faith. There will be another place and time for a fuller treatment of the family's role in the public church.[37] But before the end, I do want to offer a brief statement about the role of parents. In *Bringing Up Children in the Christian Faith*, John Westerhoff lists five guidelines for sharing our faith with children:

> We need to tell and retell the biblical story—the stories of the faith— together.
> We need to celebrate our faith and our lives.
> We need to pray together.
> We need to listen and talk to each other.
> We need to perform faithful acts of service and witness together.[38]

Part of the point he makes is that the central role for parents and adults in the church is primarily to *be* Christian with their children. While this may seem like a simplistic statement on the surface, I hear it as centering on the faith of parents—a faith that serves as the central organizing commitment for the lives of parent and family alike.

Perhaps the most crucial way this can be focused, given the family's existence in the midst of the cacophonous demands of the surrounding culture, is around the structuring of *time* in the home. It is too easy for work, school, and television to dictate how families structure their days together. The Christian tradition offers alternatives for the pattern of the year and of the days within it—the liturgical seasons and festivals within them, the weekly pattern of Sunday worship in the congregation, the marking of each day with at least morning and evening prayer. Parents may have some success at marking the seasons (certainly the Advent wreath at home is a start), but the attempt to structure daily life around morning and evening family prayer goes against the very grain of life in U.S. culture. A change that sounds so simple may be one of the most countercultural things a family can do (or fail to do).

Language is also important, and perhaps goes hand in hand with the issue of time, as two of the central tools we have for world construction. The use of the language of faith is no longer supported in the culture at large, if it ever was. Families in the public church ought to be encouraged to make the language of faith public in the home, finding ways to talk about faith in a variety of settings (not only in family times of prayer and celebration). Between the home and the congregation, an "axis" might thus be created to support the use of faith language and the "publicity" of faith—its impingement on all spheres of life.

Finally, an implicit and certainly contestable assumption and "working hope" of this paper is that public church children remain in the same congregation throughout childhood and adolescence. In reality such an experience is becoming more rare. Perhaps another countercultural commitment for parents to consider is the priority of relational, congregational, and community ties over the usual middle-class priority of professional advancement. What would it mean to a family, and what kind of example would it set for the family's children, for parents to let the professional future take a back seat to the primary tie of the public church congregation?

CONCLUSION

In this essentially prescriptive paper, I have tried to paint a portrait of the nurture and equipping of children in what has been called the "public church." My intention has been to generate discussion about two important matters: the need for a clear vision of the church's mission and role in the (arguably) thoroughly secularized climate in which mainline North American Christians exist; and an approach to the Christian formation of children that fits with that vision. Whether or not my ecclesiological prescription and my hypothetical response (*If* this kind of church, *then* what do we do with and how do we relate to children?*) are satisfactory to the reader, it is my hope that they will light a fire under some to carry on the conversation, talking even as we continue to experiment with the kinds of congregations in which children can be nurtured and equipped for being rooted Christians in a very plural and public world.

NOTES

1. Ralph A. Keifer, "Christian Initiation: The State of the Question," Murphy Center for Liturgical Research, *Made, Not Born: New Perspectives on Christian Initiation and the Catechumenate* (Notre Dame, IN: University of Notre Dame Press, 1976), p. 142.

2. Michael Warren, "Facing the Problem of Popular Culture," *Youth, Gospel, Liberation* (San Francisco: Harper & Row, 1987), p. 43.

3. This is the church's actual name. The names of individual church members mentioned in this paper have been changed. The fieldwork was done between December, 1988, and February, 1990.

4. As of April, 1990.

5. Peter Berger, *The Sacred Canopy* (Garden City, NY: Anchor Books, 1969), p. 153.

6. Wolfgang Schluchter, "The Future of Religion," *Religion in America: Spirituality in a Secular Age*, Mary Douglas and Steven M. Tipton, eds. (Boston: Beacon Press, 1983), p. 67.

7. The language of this sentence comes from Rebecca Chopp's presentation on ecclesiology for an August, 1988, consultation for the Rollins Center for Church Ministries' project "Faith and the Practice of the Congregation," at Candler School Theology, Emory University, Atlanta, Georgia.

8. Charles R. Foster, *Teaching in the Community of Faith* (Nashville: Abingdon, 1982), p. 12.

9. Gregory C. Higgins, "The Significance of Postliberalism for Religious Education," *Religious Education*, 84, 1 (Winter, 1989), p. 85. Higgins focuses on George Lindbeck's *The Nature of Doctrine* (Philadelphia: Westminster Press, 1984) and its importance for religious educators. It will be clear to anyone familiar with Lindbeck that my paper is informed by his cultural-linguistic approach to theology. However, I see myself as trying, along with others, to strike a middle ground between that approach and what Lindbeck calls "experiential-expressivism."

10. The brief history of the "public church" concept begins with Martin Marty's book, *The Public Church: Mainline-Evangelical-Catholic* (New York: Crossroad, 1981). In the same year Parker Palmer published his *The Company of Strangers* (New York: Crossroad, 1981). Both books influenced James Fowler's subsequent treatment of the idea, now published in several places. (Palmer does not use the term "public church," but his concern for public life has informed Fowler's definition.) See Fowler's *Faith Development and Pastoral Care* (Philadelphia: Fortress Press, 1987), pp. 24–25; "The Public Church: Ecology for Faith Education and Advocate for Children," pp. 134–137 in Doris Blazer, ed., *Faith Development in Early Childhood* (Kansas City: Sheed and Ward, 1989); and most recently, *Weaving the New Creation: Stages of Faith and the Public Church* (San Francisco: Harper, 1991). Robert Bellah and company discuss the concept in *Habits of the Heart: Individualism and Commitment in American Life* (Berkeley: University of California Press, 1985), pp. 238–249; and in Chapter 6 of *The Good Society* (New York: Knopf, 1991). William Johnson Everett's *God's Federal Republic: Reconstructing Our Governing Symbol* (New York: Paulist Press, 1988) also deals with these issues, especially in Chapter 5 and pp. 182–184.

11. For example, see Thomas Groome, *Christian Religious Education: Sharing*

Our Story and Vision (San Francisco: Harper & Row, 1980), especially p. 122.

12. Stanley Hauerwas's contention that the Christian community's primary call is to be true to its story informs my language here; see "A Story-Formed Community," *A Community of Character: Toward a Constructive Christian Social Ethic* (Notre Dame, IN: Notre Dame University Press, 1981), p. 10. It should be noted that Hauerwas would have some definite disagreements with the "public church" concept. Another important source on the culture of the congregation is James Hopewell, *Congregation: Stories and Structures*, Barbara G. Wheeler, ed. (Philadelphia: Fortress Press, 1987).

13. William Johnson Everett, *God's Federal Republic*, p. 157. His notion of "little publics" informs my discussion of the "public of the congregation."

14. Bellah, *et al.*, *Habits of the Heart*, p. 246.

15. The "sovereign God" language comes from H. Richard Niebuhr's theology, and Fowler uses it in his definition in "The Public Church: Ecology for Faith Education and Advocate for Children," pp. 136–137.

16. Again, this formulation was influenced by Rebecca Chopp's presentation on ecclesiology (see above, n. 7).

17. Richard Osmer, "The Church in Public Life: A New Agenda for Christian Education," unpublished paper, 1986, p. 36.

18. This description draws on language from Johann Baptist Metz, *Faith in History and Society: Toward a Practical Fundamental Theology*, trans. David Smith (New York: Seabury Press, 1980), and Matthew L. Lamb, *Solidarity with Victims: Toward a Theology of Social Transformation* (New York: Crossroad, 1982).

19. A *caveat* is in order here: this does not let parents "off the hook" (more on this below). Charles Foster reminds us that in the past few decades, Protestant religious educators have mostly been frustrated in their attempts to involve the family/parents in significant ways in the religious education of their children. See his "The Changing Family," *Religious Education as Social Transformation*, Allen J. Moore, ed. (Birmingham: Religious Education Press, 1989), pp. 47–48.

20. One St. Paul couple that I interviewed had left another potential public church a few years before because of its virtual failure to provide any nurture for children.

21. Using the language of Phillip E. Hammond ("Religion and the Persistence of Identity," *Journal for the Scientific Study of Religion* 27, 1 (March, 1988), pp. 1–11), this commitment is most likely made by persons who are "High-High" on his grid comparing the strength of involvement in overlapping primary "involuntary" groups and in voluntary secondary groups (pp. 6–7). For public church persons, involvement will probably be high in both areas, but the church as "primary group" will take priority, and will provide the central focus. One problem I have with Hammond's analysis is the use of the word "involuntary" with primary ties. The assumption seems

to be that kinship and ethnicity are the two primary factors in such ties. In my view, public church persons *choose* to make such a primary commitment in their lives. The commitment is certainly voluntary, but it is deeper and more definitive in a person's identity than the word *association* suggests. This is not true for their children, of course, as William Everett reminds us that: "Family worlds are involuntary, at least for the children" (*God's Federal Republic*, p. 156), and this is a source of tension for children who may grow up in a public church (see the example of Shannon, below).

As to how such commitment is promoted by congregations, in Rosabeth Moss Kanter's terms, there is more emphasis on "attaching processes" than on "detaching processes" in the public church (*Commitment and Community: Communes and Utopias in Sociological Perspective* (Cambridge: Harvard University Press, 1972), pp. 70–74 —Nancy Ammerman suggested this line of thinking).

22. John H. Westerhoff III, *Bringing Up Children in the Christian Faith* (Minneapolis: Winston Press, 1980), p. 16.

23. See Neil Postman, *Amusing Ourselves to Death: Public Discourse in the Age of Show Business* (New York: Viking, 1985).

24. For example, families could choose not to have a TV, or could at least intentionally center household time around something other than the TV schedule (see below on the importance of structuring time in families). This is not a question of the total rejection of popular culture, but a need for an interpretive framework, rather than just an uncritical "soaking up like a sponge."

25. This is admittedly a generalization based on my own experience and the experience of many of the baby-boomers at St. Paul Church (confirmed in numerous interviews). For theoretical support for such a generalization, see Robert Wuthnow's treatment of the concept of "generation unit" as it applies to the counterculture of the late sixties and early seventies in "Recent Patterns of Secularization: A Problem of Generations?" *American Sociological Review*, 41 (October, 1976), pp 850–867.

26. See Richard Osmer, *A Teachable Spirit: Recovering the Teaching Office in the Church* (Louisville: Westminster/John Knox, 1990).

27. Robert L. Browning and Roy A. Reed are strong advocates for this. See their *The Sacraments in Religious Education and Liturgy*, pp. 141ff.

28. This idea of "imputing" future intentions to infants in the church is influenced by John Shotter, *Social Accountability and Selfhood* (Oxford: Basil Blackwell, 1984), and his treatment of development from a social psychological perspective. See Part Two, especially pp. 61–89.

29. Sonja M. Stewart, "Children and Worship," *Religious Education* 84, 3 (Summer, 1989), p. 351 (emphasis mine).

30. John H. Westerhoff III, *Will Our Children Have Faith?* (New York: Seabury Press, 1976), pp. 91–96.

31. See James W. Fowler, *Stages of Faith: The Psychology of Human Development*

and the Quest for Meaning (San Francisco: Harper & Row, 1981), Chapter 16.

32. See Craig Dykstra, "The Formative Power of the Congregation," *Religious Education* 82, 4 (Fall, 1987), p. 542. In a footnote, he mentions Edward Farley's concept of "reality loss"—"the loss of a believable sense of the reality of God as a foundation for the community's life."

33. William Johnson Everett speaks of "little publics" as providing "the essential 'off Broadway' experimentation, refinement, and education necessary for the big theaters of the wider public." *God's Federal Republic*, p. 157.

34. An excellent resource in this area is Kathleen and James McGinnis, *Parenting for Peace and Justice* (Maryknoll, NY: Orbis Books, 1981).

35. Among religious educators, Thomas Groome argues most forcefully for critical reflection, or "critical dialectical thinking," and tells a story of one mother's attempt to develop this in her eight-year-old son in *Christian Religious Education*, pp. 237–238.

36. Fowler, *Stages of Faith*.

37. G. Temp Sparkman, *The Salvation and Nurture of the Child of God: The Story of Emma* (Valley Forge, PA: Judson Press, 1983), pp. 34, 109–142, 211–216; John H. Westerhoff III, *Will Our Children Have Faith?*, p. 101; Robert L. Browning and Roy A. Reed, *The Sacraments in Religious Education and Liturgy*, Chapter 10.

38. Fowler deals with this issue in "The Public Church: Ecology for Faith Education and Advocate for Children," ed. Doris Blazer *Faith Development in Early Childhood*, pp. 149ff.

39. John Westerhoff, *Bringing Up Children in the Christian Faith*, Chapter 3.

10

Defense Workers

A Challenge to Family and Faith

Mary Johnson, SND

Bill is a middle-aged engineer, married, and the father of four. He lives in a comfortable home in an upper-middle-class neighborhood in a Southern city, and speaks with obvious pride of the accomplishments of his wife and children. He is well educated, articulate, and compassionate, and has used his talents well over the years in support of family, work, church, and community endeavors.

He is also a lifelong and devout Catholic, involved in his local parish. In what he saw as a natural extension of his faith, he participated in peace marches during Vietnam, and has contributed financially to various justice and peace organizations through the years. His religious principles seemed to demand support for the efforts of these organizations at peacemaking.

At the same time, Bill is earning his livelihood by the design and production of nuclear weapons systems. He makes a very good salary and holds a prestigious position within his organization. He is proud of his work, and feels a sense of patriotic duty. But a series of events eventually lead him to believe that his work is incongruous with his faith. Finally, Bill quits his job.

This chapter will examine the specific case of workers in the defense industry in the United States who, like Bill, have left their jobs for reasons of conscience. We will look especially at the influence religion and family had upon their decision to leave their work.

The data used in this analysis consist of four in-depth interviews conducted in the winter and spring of 1990, and fifteen mail-back questionnaires obtained during the spring of 1990. The nineteen respondents were chosen out of a somewhat larger population of former defense workers. The nineteen were chosen on the grounds that they made their decision based upon religious grounds, rather than solely secular moral reasoning or experience. That is, they cited a religious teaching or principle, or were church attenders or activists in various religious organizations. Others, not included, who acted on moral grounds spoke in humanistic terms and were involved in secular organizations alone.

The names of the respondents were obtained from national listings maintained by religious organizations dedicated to action on behalf of justice and peace. Additional names were obtained through the snowball method, that is, the original respondents were asked to name other former defense workers whose names did not appear on the original listings.

The group of respondents is comprised of eighteen men and one woman. Fourteen are Catholic, two Mennonite, one Quaker, one Episcopalian and one Southern Baptist. Sixteen of the respondents are married, one is single, one widowed, and one divorced. All the respondents except one have children, ranging in number from two to ten. The average number of children is 4.4. The group is well educated: two hold doctorates, five have master's degrees, five have bachelor's degrees, two received some undergraduate education and two are high school graduates or the equivalent. The average age of the respondents is 47.3 years, with the range from thirty-three to sixty-four.

The occupations of the respondents varied considerably. Almost one-third are engineers, and several of them were involved in various aspects of research, design, and analysis. Others performed technical, mechanical, or clerical functions. The group was involved with work on a wide range of systems. Individuals worked on missile, submarine, sonar, radar, satellite, nuclear weapon, and artillery systems.

THEORETICAL FRAMEWORK

What has happened to these defense workers is not unlike a conversion experience. They have moved from one worldview to another, and thus, from one behavior to another, namely their choice of labor. "Conversion" in this sense has been defined by Meredith McGuire as a "transformation of self concurrent with a transformation of one's central meaning system."[1] In this case, the transformation involved exiting a central role in one's life. Therefore, we shall use the analysis of the process of role exit developed by Helen Rose Fuchs Ebaugh in *Becoming an Ex*[2] to trace this particular transformation, its causes, and consequences.

Ebaugh defines role exit as "the process of disengagement from a role that is central to one's self-identity and the reestablishment of an identity in a new role that takes into account one's ex-role." In her study of 185 "exes," Ebaugh examined a wide variety of roles—from ex-nuns to ex-doctors to ex-convicts, from alumni to divorcees to mothers without custody of their children to transsexuals, and many more. Ebaugh argues that a pattern of exiting was found across these diverse occupations and lifestyles, and that this pattern constitutes the process of role exit. The first stage of the process is having doubts about the old identity. That is followed by seeking alternatives, and comes to a climax in a turning point. Finally, the person creates an ex-role that incorporates the old identity as a "former" role. Throughout the process, a number of variables can alter its speed, and the ease with which the transition is made. Those variables include the degree to which the change is voluntary and the person is in control of it, the centrality and duration of the role being left behind, the reversibility of the change, the number of other roles affected, whether the person is part of a group exit, whether the role change is an institutionalized process, the social desirability of old and new roles, and the degree to which the process proceeds in an expected sequence. Within each stage, too, Ebaugh identifies conditions that encourage or discourage the role-exiting process.

Since these defense industry workers have been involved with religious organizations of various sorts, we will pay special attention to the role of those organizations in encouraging or discouraging the process of change. Robert Wuthnow, in his analysis of the restructuring of American religion since the Second World War,[3] argues that "special purpose groups" have grown tremendously in number and variety in the last two decades in this country. These groups historically and contemporaneously have myriad purposes, from prison ministry to Bible study to group therapy. Wuthnow argues that they have the potential to serve as agents either of reinvigoration or of cleavage within the churches. Many of the people studied here have been strongly affected by the special interest groups concerned with peace and justice issues, and we will look for the ways in which various kinds of religious organizations—parishes, larger Church, and beyond—have figured in their faith, lives, and decisions.

Decisions about work are often intertwined with a person's identity as part of a family. Indeed the intersection of work and family has been described as one of "systematic interconnectedness."[4] This interconnectedness manifests itself in myriad ways today, as the definitions of both work and family are broadened to include new forms and functions.[5] We will pay special attention to the various ways in which family and work identities interacted in this role-exiting process.

STAGE ONE: FIRST DOUBTS

From her rich data set, Ebaugh identifies several elements that are critical in the first stage of the role-exiting process. Three are germane to our study. We will examine particular events that gave rise to first doubts, the duration of the doubting process, and the role of significant others.

Ebaugh asserts that: "While the individual may have vague, ill-defined, usually unconscious feelings of dissatisfaction, some event will focus these feelings and make them conscious to the individual."[6] Once doubts have begun, they may go unresolved for varying periods of time—ranging from weeks to years.

A myriad of events figured prominently in the doubting stage of the defense workers, and their doubting processes lasted for varying periods. One man, an active Catholic, who worked as an aircraft engineer for thirty-four years, spoke of struggling for ten years with the question of nonviolence. In his reading, and in discussions with friends he considered to be "good Christians and concerned about violence in general," he grappled with the question of how his work for the military fitted with his belief that Christ was nonviolent. He said: "I started to have pangs of conscience a number of times. Debating back and forth about whether it was essential to have a military, and extending this right down to what's the smallest unit in which you answer violence with violence."

Another engineer, who worked on nuclear weapons systems for eighteen years, described his initial struggle as lasting several years. At an intellectual level, the "head level," he had been involved in peace demonstrations during the Vietnam era and had been a member and financial contributor to several justice and peace organizations, the Fellowship of Reconciliation among them.

A third engineer who worked on the cruise missile system and sonar and radar systems, a job he held for almost ten years, traced his first doubts to *before* he entered the defense industry. His struggle began during his college days. He enjoyed math and science and "figured engineering would be a logical choice to make. Come around to senior year, all my interviews were with defense industries…. So even then I had qualms, but it was all that was being offered." He continued, "I'd said, well, I will take what I can get. So I started working for the defense. And it just, it festered with me for a while. After a few years, I got married, and children came along, and I figured I was locked in now to the defense."

A contract administrator for twenty-three years, who worked on several weapon systems, grappled for five years with the question of whether or not he should remain in or leave the industry. His initial doubts were stirred by the Vietnam War, during which time he was involved in missile sales. "We destroyed many, many villages in Vietnam. And so that began to really bother me…. I ended up in (cruise) missiles, and then I ended up with smart bombs and selling them, and killing hundreds of thousands of people in Vietnam." He continued, "I sold them to Israelis. They used them against the Lebanese. I sold them to the Turks and the Greeks. They used them against each other on Cyprus." His struggle continued into the 1970s. "I remember we got the contract right before the Kent State students were killed. And that really affected me."

It is clear that seeds of doubt come in various shapes and sizes, take root in all kinds of soil, and sprout in due season. In this study, the doubts were precipitated by reading, discussions with friends, involvement in justice and peace organizations, and the impact of major social upheavals such as the Vietnam War and Kent State. It is evident, at this stage, that the respondents began to place what could be seen as individualistic acts, their jobs, into a wider social nexus. Their struggles over time involved an examination of the global consequences of their work lives. Church-related justice and peace groups, in particular, served to raise consciousness about the social dimension of one's labor.

Ebaugh argues that the role of significant others in the exit process is critical. She says: "While the decision to exit is a very personal one, it is inevitably made in a social context and is highly influenced by the reactions of other people. At the stage at which the exiter is first questioning role satisfaction, other people serve a number of functions in the process including reality testing, enhancing the rewards of staying, and suggesting alternatives."[7] By reality testing, she means that significant others can either reinforce or challenge the individual's definition of the situation. But significant others can also make staying more or less attractive, as well as helping doubters to think about things differently. I am especially interested here in the roles played by the respondents' family and religious community.

First, the role of family. In the majority of the nineteen cases, the spouses and children ultimately reinforced the definition of reality put forth by the respondents. The spouses were supportive, with only three exceptions: one spouse never agreed with her husband's decision; another spouse left her husband and the marriage dissolved; and the fiancée of a third man almost broke off the relationship. The others evidenced various levels of support from listening to the respondent's concerns, to attending peace demonstrations with him.

There was not always initial agreement, however, and the greatest area of concern regarding the possible role exit was the most obvious one: family finances, especially college tuition. Spouses and children reminded doubting workers that the realities of current bills and future plans did not coincide with the possibility of an unemployed father. Three of the respondents dealt with this situation by keeping their jobs until they were eligible for early retirement. One of these men left his job when his youngest child reached the age of twenty-three, after all his children had completed college.

Several of the others had children in college at the same time they were struggling with doubts regarding their work. In some cases, the decision to leave directly affected the children's schooling. One man recalled how he and his wife began talking with their four high-school-aged and college-aged children.

> You know when it began dawning on us that something had to be done, we started talking to the kids. We did not have one big family meeting, but we started talking to the kids, "You know, Dad's got this job and there is this problem of conscience, and Dad might not have a job much longer. We don't know what the exact situation is, but we know this, and you kids, the college part especially ,might suffer."

He recalled with pride how they responded.

> Probably the one reaction that I will remember the most is from the second one, who is a pretty determined woman. She is also a little more conservative-thinking politically. Even at that time she said, "I think you are crazy, but go for it." It was obvious that the family bonds were stronger than the principles of any one of us.

The responses of children are among the things that can affect the doubting process, making role exit seem more or less attractive. Another respondent eventually left a job with a salary of eighty thousand dollars, and became immediately involved in working for justice and peace efforts. That dramatic financial loss had consequences for the youngest two of his seven children in particular. "The last two did not get to go to college because I spent all the money on peace. That did not make me too popular, but you know...."

Most of the respondents indicated that financial concerns were uppermost in their thoughts during the doubting stage, and only five of the nineteen respondents indicated that they did not suffer an actual loss of income and/or benefits later. The role of their families at this stage was primarily to remind them of the realities of their commitments, plans, and obligations—all of which would be threatened by the loss of the worker's income.

Because these cases have been selected for their religious content, we already know that religion, in some form, was part of the role-exiting process. For all nineteen respondents, it helped to create the doubts they had about their jobs, motivated them to act, and served to confirm their definition of the situation. The majority of the respondents mentioned Jesus Christ and/or the Christian scriptures as the justification for their doubts concerning their work. One said that he believed that: "It was against the teachings of Jesus Christ, first to blow up the world and yourself." Another said: "I have a strong religious background in the belief of Jesus Christ as the Prince of Peace." A third stated that during the last weeks of his discernment: "A question occurred to me back in 1982 during those several weeks of pain, 'What would Jesus do?' Now when you ask that question, you know, it is always clear."

Three applied scriptural passages to their reality: "I believe threatening to kill my enemies by building bombs, etcetera, is inconsistent with Christ's teaching." Another said: "I believe we are supposed to help the least among us. We are spending billions on bombs while people are starving." And another: "It is wrong to kill, especially for rich, white folks to kill poor folks of color for their own selfish interests."

Several mentioned the social teachings on peace of the Catholic and Mennonite churches as important in their process. Others spoke of the role played by various religious individuals and structures. Two respondents mentioned being inspired by two Catholic bishops who have been strongly identified with the 1983 Catholic Bishops' pastoral letter on peace, *The Challenge of Peace: God's Promise and Our Response*. Several mentioned Catholic priests who were friends of theirs, and who listened to their struggle. Others mentioned members of parish justice and peace groups and prayer and support groups who also listened.

Several religious organizations provided explicit structures of support. The group most often mentioned by the respondents was Pax Christi, the international Catholic peace organization. One respondent received support from a program in his local Episcopal diocese and parish. Also influencing some respondents were local Catholic Worker houses, communities of radical Catholic peace activists who serve the poor and work for non-violence. Peacework Alternatives was a source of important friendships for several doubting workers. This group, which provided a national support network for defense workers, was begun by a Catholic sister, and initially funded by her order and the bishops.

While most of these workers were connected to a wide variety of religious organizations, their connections to church and clergy were not uniformly supportive. On one end of the spectrum, one of the respondents left the defense industry after six years to become a priest and peace activist himself. Another was inspired to leave the industry two months after a priest left the military chaplaincy for reasons of conscience. Others had been inspired by the peacemaking efforts of the Berrigan brothers. But while some respondents received support from the clergy, others did not. They expressed disappointment at the lack of support they felt, and in six cases there was overt conflict, usually with the local parish priest. Some of these priests were military chaplains or in the reserves themselves, and their promilitary opinions tinged the possibility of role exit with the potential of clerical disapproval. When asked if he received support of any kind from a church, one respondent in Nevada replied: "No, my pastor supports the Test Site effort." Another, in Texas, remarked that some groups in his parish did not understand his concerns, and others did not support him. Interestingly, while he had been influenced by his bishop, his own pastor would not support him.

That disparity between local church response and the support provided by other religious organizations is a recurring theme. One respondent recounted the following conversation with his confessor:

[He said] "Well, you know you have to defend your country." I said, "Yes, but this is not even self defense. This is slaughter." He said, "Oh, I mean, you have to think of your family first."

This particular respondent went on to receive "tremendous" support from the Quakers who, in turn, introduced him to Pax Christi, the international justice and peace group within his own Church, which, from within his parish, had been "hard to find." Another respondent talked to his pastor, "who was no help. I mean he listened but he really was not much help." This respondent received his support from a priest friend who is an activist involved in protesting U.S. intervention in Central America, and from a Presbyterian minister who was a draft resister during the Second World War.

We hear the theme again from a respondent who received his support at the soup kitchen run by his local Catholic Worker community. His doubts about his job were influenced by the soup kitchen workers' belief in the sanctity of life. "They believe that no killing is correct. There is no reason for any human life to be taken by another." This respondent received no support, however, from his local parish. In fact, he said: "They were very gung ho military, the American flag flying in the Catholic Church, which it is not supposed to be." The parish seemed to be unaware, too, of the kind of support that is needed to sustain an act that rejects American consumer and material values. This respondent was equally disappointed by his bishop:

> I remember writing a letter, I'm not sure if it was shortly before I left [the job] or right after, but all I got back from the bishop was, "Congratulations on your decision; I'm sure it took you much time to discern this." Not that I was looking for much, but I am concerned for other people that are getting out. If this is the kind of support they are going to give, why would anybody want to leave a job that's there for life. I mean you have the security for life, working for multinationals like GE or RCA or whoever else.

Another respondent did not even mention his struggle to his pastor because "our pastor is a [military] chaplain or was a chaplain anyway. I've often thought sometime it would be interesting to hear some of his views." This respondent got his inspiration and support from a priest dedicated to nonviolence, and from parish groups interested in issues of social justice. Very well read in Catholic social teaching and periodicals reporting on matters related to justice and peace, this respondent had been "involved in discussions on the (peace) pastoral at the church. But there again it was not a group led by a cleric. It was a group of us [laity]."

No clear demarcations can be easily seen within families or churches at this point in regard to their support or lack of support for the defense workers' struggles with conscience. Instead, fault lines can be detected along the way that promise impending quakes along more convoluted lines. Issues of patriotism, peace, social justice, personal conscience, families' wants and needs collide within the hearts and minds of clergy, family members, and the workers themselves; many of whom may be unaccustomed to viewing "a job" through such a multilayered prism.

STAGE TWO: SEEKING ALTERNATIVES
Ebaugh argues that the second stage of the role-exiting process involves seeking alternatives. She states: "Alternative seeking behavior is essentially a comparative process in which alternative roles are eval-

uated in comparison with the costs and rewards of one's current role."[8] She continues: "While the exploration and evaluation of role alternatives is in fact a deliberative and rational process, there are also many spontaneous, nonrational, emotional elements involved." During this stage, the doubter will begin deliberate seeking and weighing of role alternatives, responding to social support or the lack of it from significant others. The person finally, perhaps, realizes his or her freedom to choose, shifts reference group orientations, and engages in role rehearsal for alternative visions of a new self. The sorting and sifting, pulling and tugging of the doubting phase now become focused on evaluating specific alternatives.

In the case of the nineteen defense workers, alternatives, clearly, were limited. In most cases, the alternatives were reduced to three: to remain in one's job doing defense-related work, to remain in the company but move to a job that was nondefense related, or to leave the company altogether. For a few respondents who were near retirement age, a fourth alternative presented itself, namely, to seek early retirement, even though that meant receiving a reduced pension. Given the narrow range of alternatives, the process of seeking and weighing possibilities was also narrowly focussed.

One respondent, who had worked in the same plant for thirty-four years, stated that when he began his career there, no more than twenty-five percent of the work was defense-related. He got to the point, however, where he was spending thirty to forty percent of his time on defense work. He said: "You can always tell a military job because it's got a number on it. They don't give the name of an airplane. It's a blank box, just has a number." As he struggled with his growing commitment to Christian nonviolence, he examined the possible alternative of switching to nondefense work within the same plant.

> I could have possibly switched over, even within the company, gotten into some branch of the company that did a lot, was involved a lot less with the military equipment just because of the nature of the variety of things we made. But I didn't. And I am not patting my back. If I were really courageous, I probably would have done it much sooner.

What he did do was take an early retirement with a reduced pension, a move that was facilitated, he admitted, by the fact that all of his children were out of college and his youngest child had turned twenty-three years old. He said, "You see it was easy for me because I had an income. I didn't have expenses. My children were grown."

Another respondent, in his early forties and an owner of the company, decided on a different tack. He refused to do defense-related work but remained in the company. He remembered:

> What I did ended up being pretty clever, because instead of going in and quitting, I decided it was going to be them getting rid of me. I was not going to walk out. So I simply refused to work on any of the military work anymore, any nuclear work we did. And I walked into the boss's office and told him that.

His boss responded by talking about "people demonstrating, about peaceniks and stuff like that for a minute or two, while he was thinking." The boss finally concluded that the respondent could stay with the company and that a subordinate would take over all the military work.

> At first, this alternative seemed viable, but shortly thereafter it became problematic. It really put me in an odd position at work, because now, this was 1982, the beginning of the recession, not just the beginning, we were in a recession. Times were bad. And we were scraping for work everywhere. And here was the guy primarily responsible for bringing work into the company saying "I am not going to deal with our biggest client, the one we made almost half of our profit from."

This respondent began to feel isolated within the company; he was no longer invited to participate in the daily bridge game. The cross-pressures from his own principles and the interests of his coworkers and company eventually made his compromise alternative untenable.

> We were debating certain jobs, which ones we should take and which ones we shouldn't and some of them were jobs with, that had to do with nuclear weapons systems.... And so here I sat around a table with a decision, being a party to a decision that if I voted my conscience, I'd say we shouldn't go after it because we shouldn't do that type of work...if I do what is best for the company, we should go for whatever we can get.

He lived with that tension for about a year, knowing that his company needed the defense contracts badly. Finally, he said, "I had all I could take of that." He resigned shortly thereafter.

Another respondent tried to explore the alternative of switching to nondefense work within the company.

I did bring it up a couple months before I decided to leave. I told them how I felt and I said "I'll continue working for [the company] but I can't work on any defense related projects." Well, there's nothing but defense. It's ninety-five percent or ninety-six percent defense.

This respondent, with a one-year-old child and a forty-thousand-dollar salary, then "just left (with) no certainty of what I would be doing the next week."

STAGE THREE: THE TURNING POINT

Ebaugh argues that the third stage of the role-exiting process can be characterized as the turning point. She states that a turning point is: "an event that mobilizes and focuses awareness that old lines of action are complete, have failed, have been disrupted, or are no longer personally satisfying and provides individuals with the opportunity to do something different with their lives."[9] Ebaugh contends that there are several types of turning points, and that the turning point serves three functions: announcement of the decision to others, the reduction of cognitive dissonance, and the mobilization of the resources needed to exit.

In the case of some defense workers, there was no discernable turning point which they could remember. One janitor in a defense plant said: "It was time. I could not go no more." One machinist said: "No specific incident. I just found it increasingly difficult to accept the idea of spending the rest of my life doing work that I thought was immoral." And an engineer said:

> I thought I was becoming morally bankrupt. I figured if I could do work for the defense industry, knowing that I didn't think it was correct, then other areas of my moral fiber were being infiltrated…. I just felt I was becoming an immoral person. If you feel something is wrong you have to do something about it. I felt working for the defense industry was really leading me down the wrong road.

For most of the defense workers, however, there was a turning point, either significant events or last straws which moved them to exit their roles. In the cases of four men, corporate strategies moved their companies more deeply into defense work. Another man recalled being confronted by a fellow employee for the alleged hypocrisy of believing in peace but working on defense projects. He quit the next day. One man was inspired by others taking risks, and another was challenged by the United Nations Special Session on Disarmament in 1978.

For another engineer, the 1978 and 1982 U.N. Sessions on Disarmament played critical roles at different stages in his process of exiting. In 1978, during the first session, he visited New York on business, and met a Catholic priest friend whom he visited periodically. The priest had planned to attend a massive prodisarmament demonstration outside the U.N., and he accompanied him. The engineer recalls the event:

At one point there was an explosion (to symbolize the atomic bombings of Japan). We all then fell to the street and lay in the street for five minutes in silence. Me in my business suit…. Now the ironic thing is, on this business trip I had gone up to Groton, Connecticut to call on the people at Electric Boat about our next contract.

The irony of the event did not escape him then, and perhaps played a role in creating his first doubts. He remembers sitting next to a woman on the plane going home and matter-of-factly telling her that "I had called on someone trying to design nuclear weapons in Groton, Connecticut and there I was demonstrating against nuclear weapons in the streets of New York." He continues: "I was talking about it as something funny. But after June, 1982, it was *not* funny. Not at all funny."

June, 1982, marked the second U.N. Session on Disarmament, which this respondent attended with his wife. She had heard of the upcoming demonstration and told him that she was planning to go. He decided that it must be important, and he joined her on the seventeen-hour bus ride. He recalls: "Certainly that was the triggering event because it drove it home to me; what was I doing?" After returning home and agonizing with his wife over the decision to leave, his wife said to him: "I don't know what we are going to do but we have to do something, because we can't go on living like this much longer." This permission, as he calls it, spurred his exiting process on.

Another precipitating event is described by an aircraft engineer. He and his wife attended a two-weekend retreat series on Christian nonviolence. The first weekend, held six months before the other, was an introduction to the scriptural basis of nonviolence. The second weekend, he remembers, was an "invitation to action." On their way home from the retreat, he and his wife discussed his work. He recalled "I said, 'I've got to do something. I can't stay at work.' And she said, 'yes'."

One respondent experienced a backbreaking last straw. He had begun to drink heavily as he was being tormented by the knowledge that his creations were being used against women and children in villages in

Vietnam. At the same time, he struggled with not wanting to lose his seventy-five-to-eighty-thousand-dollar-a-year income. The last straw came for him one day in the words of his doctor, who told him that if he did not stop drinking, cirrhosis of the liver would kill him in six months to a year. "That was the clincher," he said. "That's when I called [my company] and said I wouldn't be back. And they kept me on salary for six months."

STAGE FOUR: CREATING THE EX-ROLE

Ebaugh identifies the fourth and final stage in the process as "creating and adapting to an ex-role once one has actually left." She continues: "The ex-role constitutes a unique sociological phenomenon in that the expectations, norms, and identity associated with it do not so much consist in what one is currently doing but rather stem from expectations, social obligations and norms related to one's previous life."[10] Ebaugh argues that there are six major areas of adjustment that exes must struggle with as they disidentify with their old roles and create their new ones: ways of presenting themselves and their ex status through cuing behavior; learning to deal with social reactions to their ex status; negotiating and establishing intimate relationships; shifting friendship networks; relating to group members and other exes; and dealing with role residual.

Interestingly, while the defense workers did experience shifting friendship networks, and had to learn to deal with social reactions to their ex status, the most glaring dynamic that emerged for these defense workers was something not identified by Ebaugh, a process which I have labelled "the absolution." After leaving a job they had come to see as sinful, several of these workers adopted dramatically different occupations, occupations that were for them strikingly purgative.

One engineer moved from doing development work in an engineering firm which designed nuclear submarines to doing development work for a hospice. He described it as a move "from high-tech to high-touch." He left the hospice after a year to work for a spouse abuse center and a child abuse treatment agency, and explained his exit from his engineering role and entrance into his new social service worker role by saying: "I had been a part of designing a system intended to kill, and now I wanted to do something more life-supportive."

This experience is echoed in the choice of another engineer, who also entered a new role in a caregiving system. This respondent, who took early retirement, became a volunteer in the neurological unit of a chronic disease hospital. He describes what he does there with patients who have difficulty speaking: "Occasionally I will do something as practical as writing a letter or note or help make telephone calls, but mostly I just visit with them." He admits that "being part of that (hospital) community is rewarding."

Another ex-defense worker said: "I promised myself I would work for peace the rest of my life." He then embarked on a journey, with a few family members at a time, to see every Catholic bishop in the United States. He wanted to convince each one to work for disarmament. He recalls: "We'd say we are here to help you and your diocese work for peace against nuclear weapons, because I built them for twenty-three years and I know how terrible war would be."

Other respondents describe equally compelling part-time and full-time work after leaving the industry. One ex-engineer volunteers in a soup kitchen, another researches the arms race and the military-industrial complex, another became a teacher and is involved in church efforts to "abate the tide of pornography, violence and abortion." One respondent has begun graduate work in peace studies, one teaches Christian ethics, and another has several times committed acts of civil disobedience in behalf of peace. And several are involved in local, national, and international justice and peace groups, most religiously affiliated.

CONCLUSIONS

In many ways, these ex-defense workers look like the other exes described by Ebaugh. But in other ways, this particular role exit has its own character. In the case of defense workers, the process of exiting was clearly radicalizing, both for the worker and, sometimes, for family members. It changed far more than just which company issued the paycheck. The fuel that moved the process along was a transformed value commitment, usually inspired by a scriptural or church tenet.

Transformed value commitments have been inspired by humanitarian concerns as well. Melissa Everett[11] has also identified defense workers, along with workers in the military and the intelligence community, who have left comfortable jobs to work for peace. Myron and Penina Glazer[12] have identified people who have "blown the whistle" on corruption in industry and government. Their respondents, too, could no longer act in ways at variance with their value commitments. Social supports are essential for such a profound personal transformation, with all its attendant ramifications. Family is usually immediately presumed to be the source of such support but, as we have seen, religious commitments cannot be ignored.

As doubting defense workers began to weigh their alternatives, they were usually supported by family. Family support did not usually come in the very beginning of the process, however, and family financial considerations were a real caution. More likely present from the beginning was support from some form of religious organization, not usually, however, by the local pastor. The network of "special interest" peace and justice groups, inside and outside parish, congregational, and diocesan structures, was often both the initial source of workers' doubts and the structure of support that helped them through the process. As Wuthnow might have predicted, these groups provided significant sources of religious meaning and belonging, often standing at odds with existing church structures.

Ebaugh points out that the ex-role is always defined in part by the role that is being left behind. In the case of ex-defense workers, new vocations seem to take their meaning from the absolution being sought. The exiting process was transformative of the very definition of work, even of the organizational context in which work is done. The majority moved from a highly structured system, geared toward the production of weapons, to new and often creative endeavors that contained caring and caregiving as constitutive values.

This transformed notion of work, work seemingly more informed by the rules of family and faith than by the rules of production and profit, has produced new and provocative configurations on the societal landscape. New notions of religious structures and networks serve to support and sustain the family and work life of individuals struggling with decisions of conscience. These structures and systems reach far beyond the local church or cleric, and seem to envisage an ethic far broader and deeper than any one issue. The structures and networks seem open to a myriad of individuals, from mechanics to engineers to bishops to janitors. They seem to draw their inspiration from a radical critique contained in the Christian scriptures, a critique ironically not held by all in the very churches many of these individuals frequent.

What might the future hold for these new configurations? Do they have the potential to provide support and challenge for individuals and families who struggle with the contemporary challenge of choosing meaningful and ethically based labor? If we look more closely at the religious organizations that are supporting peace and justice alternatives—and that have played critical roles in the transformative process we have observed here—we may see hints of the values and structures of the future. Clearly, they are communal rather than individualistic. While grounded in certain religious traditions, they seem open to ecu-

menical initiatives on many levels. They value both action for social justice and contemplative reflection. In a variety of ways, they challenge
the secularized, individual-achievement models of work and family we
have inherited. They may also challenge or even threaten more traditional religious institutions. These ex-defense workers may be participating in a restructuring movement much bigger than the restructuring
of their own work, family, and faith.

NOTES

1. See her *Pentecostal Catholics: Power Charisma and Order in a Religious Movement* (Philadelphia: Temple University Press, 1982), p. 49.
2. Chicago: University of Chicago Press, 1988.
3. See his *The Restructuring of American Religion* (Princeton: Princeton University Press, 1988).
4. Joan Kelly, "The Doubled Vision of Feminist Theory: A Postscript to the 'Women and Power' Conference," (*Feminist Studies* 5, No. 1 (1979), pp. 222).
5. Naomi Gerstel and Harriet Engel Gross, eds., *Families and Work* (Philadelphia: Temple University Press, 1987).
6. Ebaugh, *Becoming an Ex*, p. 65.
7. *Ibid.*, p. 75
8. *Ibid.*, p. 87.
9. *Ibid.*, p. 123.
10. *Ibid.*, p. 149.
11. Melissa Everett, *Breaking Ranks* (Philadelphia: New Society Publishers, 1989).
12. Myron Peretz Glazer and Penina Migdal Glazer, *The Whistleblowers* (New York: Basic Books, 1989).

Small Faith Communities in the Roman Catholic Church

New Approaches to Religion, Work, and Family

William V. D'Antonio

It was nearing seven P.M. as friends and members of COMMUNITAS gathered in the home of Paul and Millie Riley. The Rileys were among the founding members of COMMUNITAS (an Intentional Eucharistic Community of Roman Catholics), and their home often served as the locus for the community's important liturgical events. This Ash Wednesday service, including the Mass, had become part of the group's traditions in the seven years of its existence. The Mass would include a special ceremony for making the ashes that would serve to remind the faithful of their mortality, at the beginning of another lenten season. The priest who was presiding was himself a community member, an octogenarian who strongly supported the democratic, sharing ethos of the group. Thus, he saw his role as participant with the others in the Eucharistic celebration.

This group and others like it are known as nonterritorial Intentional Eucharistic Communities (IECs). There are at least seventeen such groups with similar orientations and structures known to exist throughout the United States. They represent one end of a continuum of small Catholic groups[1] that have emerged in the past half-century and that consider themselves still within the Roman Catholic tradition.

These groups appear to share at least one objective, namely, to relate their religious faith to their individual, family, and work lives. They are another in the experiments being described in this book—experiments in creating religious arenas in which work and family, and other "public" and "private" concerns are brought together.

But who are they? What are their origins? What do they do, and how do they attempt to relate their individual, work, and family lives to their faith? What sets them apart from the ordinary Church parish with its Sunday and other rituals?

In Section I, I present a descriptive analysis of sixteen IECs that met in Washington DC in May, 1991, to become acquainted and to share histories. The focus is on how they use the Eucharistic celebration to become engaged and responsible citizens, both of the church and of civil society.

Section II is devoted to descriptions of other small Catholic groups that have arisen in recent years within the United States.[2] A Princeton Religion Research Center (PRRC) report indicated that fifteen percent of American Catholics had attended a religious group meeting (other than regular worship) in the previous two years.[3] These meetings were held in homes or in other places not formally connected with the Church parish buildings. While the percentage of Catholics participating (fifteen percent) was lower than that of Protestants (twenty-seven percent), this figure for Catholics amounts to about eight million people (out of a total Catholic population of about fifty-five million) who had attended at least one such meeting. Moreover, the PRRC data indicated that about half (or four million Catholics) were participating on a regular basis in this kind of nontraditional religious activity. Among both Protestants and Catholics, these groups are being called small faith communities or small Christian communities. The data in the PRRC study do not permit us to link their sample directly with any of the groups to be examined in this chapter. However, the members of the groups I will examine are clearly part of a much larger phenomenon.

In Section III, I will examine the key factors that help explain the emergence of these groups. These factors include the political/civic/ social ethos of American society, the pre- and post-Vatican II teachings of the Roman Catholic Church, changing demographic factors within the Church, the changing educational levels of U.S. Catholics, and changes in the Canon Law of the Church.

I conclude with discussion about research questions raised by the groups/communities described herein, as well as implications for the Catholic Church itself, as a complex social organization that acts to insure its longevity even as it seeks to be a prophetic witness to the teachings of Christ. Will the institutional church welcome this varied effort to link faith with work, family, and individual life? Do small faith communities, in varying degrees, portend changes within or of the church's structure? Will they be welcomed by those who control the church as organization, as have so many other groups in the course of the church's two-thousand-year history? And how do they carry out the message of Christ in the world? These are among the questions to be raised by this paper.

INTENTIONAL EUCHARISTIC COMMUNITIES: FAITH, WORK, AND FAMILY IN A NEW SETTING

On May 17, 1991, 150 members from sixteen intentional eucharistic communities met in Washington DC for a conversation. The members came from as far away as Boulder, Colorado, New Orleans, Louisiana, and Boston, Massachusetts. The two day meeting was called a conversation because each group knew so little about the others. When the idea was first broached within the Washington, DC-based "Communitas," its members were uncertain whether there were more than one or two other such eucharistically oriented, independent Catholic groups in the country. By word of mouth, and through a small article in the independent *National Catholic Reporter* (NCR) newspaper, sixteen such groups wrote to indicate their desire to participate in the conversation.

The conversation held in Washington was designed to allow participants to share their community narratives. Each community had prepared beforehand a formal written history that included explanations of how it handled the following activities:

(a.) governance, that is, decision making, finances, recruitment of new members, facilities, and so on;
(b.) liturgy, explaining the meaning and role of liturgy in their services, liturgy planning, presiders, format, music, community involvement;
(c.) community life, involving the differences between and needs of individuals and families, of the culture and flavor of life within their group;
(d.) social action, including involvement and work with oppressed groups, powerless persons, poverty, homelessness, and so on; and
(e.) faith education, with focus on adult and child education, sacraments, evangelization, and so on.

The communities were, without exception, surprised to find other groups like themselves. Before the call went out for a meeting, most groups knew little or nothing about the existence of others. In subsequent meetings of small faith communities, held in Paris and at Notre Dame University, IECs were found to also exist in several European, Asian and African countries.

At the time of the gathering in Washington, the IECs represented there were on average ten to twenty years old, with one or two a bit older, and a couple less than ten years old. In their written histories, many pointed to the events of Vatican II as the catalyst for bringing them to life, and helping to shape their vision of themselves. A mountain state community said: "[This] Community is a Catholic child of the 1960s. Its mother was the sense of empowerment and challenge to established authority that flourished in America's educated middle classes in movements to end the war in Vietnam and enact environmental legislation. Its father was publication in English of the documents of the Second Vatican Council." Another community noted that "the Civil Rights issues of the early years were a point of unity."

The vision that brought the groups together was and is that of becoming a faith community that engages in Eucharistic celebration to support and enrich each other's personal, familial and work lives, thereby influencing and transforming the larger communities of which they are a part. The Eucharist is, therefore, central. All the groups celebrate the Mass regularly each week. But the liturgical practices of IECs are quite varied and innovative. Many have dialogue homilies, with extensive lay involvement and control of the service. One group described itself as "a community of individuals and families drawn together by a need to worship in an atmosphere in which the Word of God is encountered through communal sharing, prayerful reflection and active participation in the liturgy." Most groups also devote a considerable amount of time and importance to "The Kiss of Peace" part of the liturgy. Participants in the Washington gathering agreed that this part of the liturgy seemed to symbolize community for them, noting that there must be a felt need to reach out, to touch, to hug, to be expressive and to receive warm greetings from others.

But the liturgy is not simply celebrated for its own sake. The attempt of these groups is to link liturgy with life in the larger world. The IECs are defined by their commitment to carry the message of the scriptures into their family, daily work lives, and the larger community. They want to be more than mere spiritual support groups for self-actualization. One community reported: "We find that our coming together as a community to worship Christ provides the spiritual strength to allow us to live our Christian commitments. Many of our members manifest this commitment in participation in Peace movements, Hospice care, support for mentally ill and retarded [people], as well as other areas of concern." Among the concerns of the groups gathered in Washington were world hunger, poverty, and the environment. Some supported day care centers; others had developed programs to serve people with AIDS; others conducted voter registration drives. Another community wrote that "the fulfillment of the Gospel message of justice and equality for all peoples requires us *to serve others*." They went on to say that they have "always had a strong social justice focus, working in both direct ministries to the poor and oppressed in our society, and in political efforts to change the systems which necessitate our services to the poor among us." Still another group reported "an Action for Justice Committee, who work especially on issues of hunger, political and economic oppression." Among all the groups, there was an awareness that it is futile to confront the social problems of our times as isolated individuals. They were also likely to tithe or give larger-than-usual contributions to help support their social action/social justice programs.

The IEC members gathered in Washington reported that their communities were quite self-critical about their social activism. They were constantly asking themselves how much they could or should do to carry the message of the Sunday liturgy into the wider world. They worried about whether their actions were satisfactory, sufficient, or morally responsible. They were aware that most of what they were able to accomplish by way of social action consisted of personal behaviors that might ameliorate the conditions of a few local people but did not constitute efforts to bring about fundamental change in church or in civil society. And there was some awareness that social movements do not always produce the results they might hope for. As an example, they cited their opposition to war and the military in the sixties and seventies, with the ironic result of a Gulf War run by a military almost beyond public scrutiny. They were also sensitive to the threat that controversial issues, such as taking a public stand against U.S. action in the Gulf War, posed for them. They were concerned that such actions might cause internal dissension and also further estrange them from the institutional church.

The center of community life, then, is liturgy that leads to action. But in the midst of their worship and social action, a few of the communities have also succeeded in developing programs that attract and appeal to children. A Midwestern group reported "a Montessori-based catechesis program, which is liturgically and scripturally oriented and is directed by a full-time salaried Catechesis Coordinator, has about 120 children and twenty cathechists." Another community named as one of its central features "a desire *to educate our children* through a positive affirmation of the most central of Church traditions and teachings."

The effort to attract college students and young adults has been less successful, however. Thus, in most cases, the members of IECs are thirty-five years old or older. They are also generally middle to upper middle class, college educated, and financially comfortable, although they do include working class and poor people, and even some recently homeless. They are predominantly white, and their class and ethnic composition generally distinguish them from other types of small faith communities (about which more later). They were, in fact, self-conscious about their middle-class, well-educated status, and disturbed about the amount of economic inequality in the larger world about them.

The vocations of IEC members, however, often reflect their social concern. One community wrote: "As individuals we work hard: nine of us are teachers, six are social workers or counselors, two are nurses, two are doctors, two run a day care center, two are students, two have secretarial/clerical jobs, one is a lawyer and part owner of a small restaurant, one is a newspaper reporter, one works for the diocesan retirement home, etc." The people representing their communities at this conversation were Catholics with a deep faith commitment to lives of service.

They were also Catholics with a highly ambiguous relationship to the authority of the church. On some issues, such as the Bishops' Peace and Economy Pastoral Letters, they would be found supporting the church's positions. But on other issues, such as allowing married priests to resume their priestly functions, ordaining women, and much more lay participation in all facets of church life and governance, they would be found in dissent. Almost without exception, the Church, as a formal institution involving bishops, cardinals, the pope, and the bureaucracy that controls the Vatican, was of limited interest to them. Simply put, if anything, it seemed to impede their efforts to live their faith. They remained in the church for reasons not always clear to themselves. Some admitted they remained simply because they found the liturgy appealing, and liked the friends they had made in their particular community. Others insisted this was their church, that they were part of the people of God, and insisted on being part of the church in the spirit of Vatican II.

Among the most important points of difference between IECs and the official Church is their insistence on democracy. A Midwestern community described itself as "an alternative liturgy [begun] 20 years ago, [that] has developed as a faith community within the parish." Its governing mechanism is "a town hall, a body of the whole Community [that] makes and ratifies all major decisions." There was an awareness in these groups that they might represent the beginnings of a social movement for more democracy within the Roman Catholic Church. And there was growing concern about what the next step might be.[4]

The official relationship of IECs to the church places them at the margins of legitimacy. Each of these groups has declared itself to be an independent, nonterritorial parish, a status long recognized by the church.[5] However, most have no formal written document giving them license to act as a non-territorial parish, although a couple of the IECs were actually formed with the formal approval of the local bishop. Each community selects one or more priests to celebrate Mass and other sacraments with them. And frequently the priest also sees himself as a member of the community and is so treated. IECs hold their services in homes, in rented halls, in church-related buildings, and in at least one case, in a building jointly owned with a Protestant congregation.

That shared building is indicative of the ecumenical spirit of the IECs. In fact, some raise the question of the importance of the word Roman before the word Catholic. Many were no longer sure. There was an appreciation of the historical church and a dread about breaking ties. Still, most were not the least bit uncomfortable about sharing the eucharist with people of other denominations. Their thinking was that Jesus shared bread and wine with apostles who later betrayed, denied, or simply fled from him in fear. Sharing the Eucharist was seen then as a first step toward reconciliation, not the last.

One community summed up their relationship to the church this way:

"We see our Community as being of service to the larger Church by being a model for the formation of other small, lay-led, intentional communities. As we evolve in our understanding of ministry, we feel truly called to expand the definition of who is called to the ordained ministry. We feel truly led by the Spirit of God to explore and nurture our ecumenical roots and to invite back to full communion all those who have drifted to the fringes of the church."

The known number of Catholics who identified themselves as members of these IECs did not exceed three thousand. Thus, this particular type of faith community was but a minute portion of the groups serving the four million found by the PRRC in their national study. But while small in numbers, they represent a new wave of Roman Catholics, valuing their personal autonomy, even as they demonstrate their awareness that autonomy rightly understood requires that they be an interdependent part of community rather than apart from it. Thus, they used their autonomy to find new ways to worship, ways that used the Eucharistic celebration as a catalyst for relating the message of the scriptures to their personal, familial, and work lives.

We turn now to a description of other groups that have emerged as small faith communities within the Catholic Church in recent years.

OTHER SMALL CATHOLIC GROUPS

The groups to be discussed in this section are most clearly distinguished from the IECs by the fact that they are not eucharistically centered. They gather on a weekly or biweekly basis to study the Bible, to discuss the relation between their religion and its teachings and the larger world around them, and/or to discuss ways to help revitalize their parish. Some groups have come into being independent of the parish or any formal church movement, and are in this sense like the IECs in their autonomy. Others have emerged as the result of formal action by the National Council of Bishops (as in the case of the Small Church Based or Ecclesial Communities for the Hispanic peoples), or by action of local bishops (as in the case of the diocesan movements following from the Bishops' RENEW Program, in the aftermath of Vatican II). And some have come into being as the result of the energy and dedication of a priest from Detroit, Michigan, who has developed a small faith community plan as a way of bringing new life to the local parish. We will examine each of these in turn.

Relatively Autonomous Groups

While some Catholics were forming IECs, many more were organizing or joining a wide range of other small groups across the country. McManus reported in 1985, in the *National Catholic Reporter*,[6] on the emergence of small Catholic groups nationwide. He described them as being focused primarily on "prayer life and active justice work." There was and is no central office where one can obtain systematic figures on group membership; nor did the groups themselves maintain figures. However, McManus found evidence that tens of thousands of Catholics were participating regularly in these groups, which at least some thought of as lay communities. He reported that "in many instances, group members trace their roots to the Second Vatican Council and the reforms it spawned, especially the call to study scripture, to develop lay participation and to reach across denominational lines." McManus went on to comment that members "feel comfortable within the Catholic tradition, but they are not constrained by a conventional interpretation of 'church.' They say they do not always look to local clergy, or bishops, for leadership. But they do not necessarily eschew them, either.

Francine Cardman, a theologian at the Weston School of Theology, explained the new thinking of the laity to McManus in these words: "Throughout church history, lay Catholics have expanded the church and formed new religious orders to run hospitals, teach the faith and serve the poor. But they were looking for institutional approval. It was taken for granted that they would be institutionalized." But today, Cardman said, that could not be less important. "It's not necessary that they be formally commissioned or instituted—or even recognized." It is simply that, as McManus concludes: "these Catholics have taken it upon themselves to worship, provide services to the poor and practice their faith as they feel most comfortable"[7]

Again, we see autonomous small groups dedicated to living the scriptures in their daily lives. There are thousands of them, some very informal with very little structure, others organized with nominal ties to religious organizations like the Paulist fathers of Beacon Hill in Boston, who share their center with lay people, working together in religious duties and social justice ministries.[8] The spirit of Vatican II seemed to be a vital motivating factor for them.

Further evidence of newly emerging lay groups can be found in two other organizations sponsored by a combination of lay and clerical leadership: The North American Forum for Small Christian Communities, and the Buena Vista Network of Small Christian Communities.

The Buena Vista Group was formed in 1987, when a married couple from Colorado decided to convene a gathering of interested persons in Buena Vista, Colorado (thus the name of the organization). That first gathering had thirty-three participants sharing their visions of small faith communities as part of the life of the church. Out of the meeting came an organization, a mission statement, and the agreement to communicate via a bimonthly newsletter. Three other national meetings have been held since, with Robert Bellah the keynote speaker at the most recent. There are now more than six hundred dues-paying members in small study groups located in ten regions throughout the country. Inspired by Father Baranowski, whose work is described below, their focus has been "on prayer, sharing, listening, learning and discerning," as a means to enliven parish life. They hope soon to develop their own computer network, with their own bulletin board.[9] And they are also striving to open membership to a wider range of people, especially to the poor, minorities, and to those who would foster a respect for multiculturalism.

The North American Forum was founded in 1986, and is run by Ms. Rosemary Blueher, Director of the Religious Education Office of the Diocese of Joliet, Illinois. She traced its roots to the Civil Rights Movement of the 1950s and 1960s, during which time her family belonged to a nonterritorial parish. She brought that experience to her diocesen job in adult education. She emphasized changing the culture of a parish to make it more vital, bringing it into line with Vatican II ideas. She, too, was greatly influenced by Father Arthur Baranowski's book on small Christian communities within parishes, and developed a model based on many of his ideas. She stated that she saw the parish as a "vehicle to experience community." She worked with pastors because they could be instrumental in establishing the communities she believed parishes needed. At the same time, she tried not to allow pastors to dominate the structure.[10] As of March, 1992, about sixty parishes had become members of the Forum.

The objective of both these groups is to create small communities within parishes, with emphasis on making the scriptures relevant to parish life and beyond. Buena Vista is an autonomous umbrella organization, while the North American Forum has formal if somewhat nominal ties to the Chicago Diocese. The Forum, therefore, represents a middle ground between the very autonomous groups like the IECS and the small faith communities described by McManus, on the one hand, and the efforts now being fostered within the institutional church on the other.

Groups within the Institutional Church

There are three efforts within the Church about which I have information and which are worthy of note here. First is the movement begun by Father Arthur Baranowski; second the movement sponsored by the Catholic bishops to establish small communities within Hispanic parishes; and third, the movement sponsored by diocesan bishops to follow up their RENEW Program with a program to establish small faith communities. I will review each briefly.

Father Baranowski and Small Faith Communities

It is apparent that Buena Vista and the North American Forum both owe much to the work of Father Arthur Baranowski. Pastor of a church in Michigan, Baranowski gradually came to the conclusion that the traditional parish was ineffective. So he set about to restructure the parish, and to make small communities the base of parish life. He managed to get between twenty and twenty-five percent of his own parish involved. Beginning in the mid-1980s, he was freed from his pastoral duties to move about the country working with dioceses in which bishops were willing to allow him to experiment. During a five-year period, ending in 1991, he managed to work with pastors and laity from some six hundred parishes in more than sixty dioceses throughout the country. In a 1989 *National Catholic Reporter* article, Baranowski is described as "the only parish priest with long-term experience with small Catholic communities outside the charismatic movement."[11]

Baranowski's format was to bring a small number of parishoners together, get them to feel at home with one another, and to feel free to speak out and discuss issues openly. The pastor of the parish was to work with the laity, and help them select one of their own number to be the pastoral facilitator. Fr. Baranowski recognized that only about twenty percent of the people in most parishes would be willing to make such a commitment, but believed that parishes could be brought to new life with the aid of such small communities. His book, *Creating Small Faith Communities*[12] explains that, in the third and final stage of development, the group begins to act like a "small church." The group reads the Gospel and attempts to apply it to life. That means asking questions such as: What can I do in the workplace, my family, the parish, the larger society?[13]

Small Communities within the Hispanic Church

The organization of communities in the Hispanic Church in the United States had its origins in the Base Christian Communities (*Comunidades Eclesias de Base*) of Latin America. They were given their initial impetus in the meeting of the Latin American Bishops at Medellin, Colombia, in 1968. The bishops declared a preferential option for the poor, and devised a plan to create small communites of neighbors who would meet frequently to discuss the scripture and relate it to their daily lives.

In 1987 the U.S. bishops adopted their own plan for Small Church-Based Communities, by which they hoped to integrate *barrio* neighbors into the larger church. The SCBCs are scripture- and social-action-oriented, but not Eucharistic in practice.[14] The SCBCs are now sufficiently well-organized that they have national and regional meetings; it is estimated that SCBCs now exist in sixty dioceses. In the Brownsville, Texas, diocese alone, there were reported to be some four hundred

SCBCs, in part due to the strong support given by the bishop. Evidence from Latin America suggests that once formed and well organized, these communities become more autonomous, and look less and less to the clergy and bishops for support.[15]

According to one of their leaders, Leonardo Anguiano of the Mexican American Cultural Center, the SCBCs in weekly meetings use the scriptures to give emphasis to family life and values. They look at their present life reality, and in addition to the scriptures, use newspaper articles, TV stories, and other media stories to help them study, judge, and act. They generally meet in homes, in numbers from twelve to twenty persons. Their small size may be one of their strongest assets. Leaders acknowledged that Hispanics have found the typical Anglo church too big.

Among all the groups noted so far, the Hispanics are by far the most economically deprived. Their leaders make clear that one goal of the SCBCs is to help raise the consciousness of the people. It is hoped that group participation will link them more effectively into the economic system, so that they can derive their fair share of society's economic benefits. The focus is on relating the scriptures to their daily lives so as to lift themselves up, striving to become part of the mainstream of American life, while seeing themselves as parts of larger communities.

The RENEW Program and Small Faith Communities

It would be misleading to suggest that the dynamics that have given rise to the emergence of small faith communities in so many forms were mostly independent of the efforts and interests of the institutional church. Even before the bishops launched the SCBC program with the Hispanic peoples, they had developed a national program called RENEW.

The original idea was the creation of Archbishop Peter L. Gerety of Newark, who was seeking a way to instill the spirit of Vatican II in his parishes.[16] RENEW was begun in 1976, and underwent a stringent review from a bishop's review committee on its tenth anniversary. In the interim, eighty-four of the Church's 183 dioceses had adopted RENEW and "more than 10,000 parishes had enlisted in the three-year course in spiritual rejuvenation."[17] Thus, about two million Catholics have apparently participated in the program. In addition, RENEW programs have been developed in Canada, the British Isles, Australia, Central America, and in parts of Asia and Africa.

The Report of the Bishops' Committee recounted the purposes and strategy of the program:

As conceived by its founders, RENEW was intended to draw people into friendly, open groups where they could talk about their faith and, among other things, read and discuss Scripture, focus on issues of justice, ponder the meaning of the church in their lives and take part in liturgy.[18]

In *Holy Siege*, Kenneth Briggs comments at length on the RENEW movement. He says: "the accent was personal and spiritual, affording Catholics an opportunity to explore their beliefs and experiences honestly and openly with other Catholics, something that many had never done before. Likewise, most had never examined the Scriptures together."[19]

For some critics, all of this had an air of biblical Protestantism about it. The bishops' report praised the movement for having touched the lives of so many people, for helping them to identify spiritual needs, and for providing vital training for lay people. At the same time, the bishops were concerned about its less-than-explicitly Catholic tone. In their words, "basic Christian themes are presented without sufficiently relating them to their specific form as experienced in Roman Catholic tradition and practice."[20] They faulted the RENEW literature for not identifying what was specifically Catholic in the faith process.[21] The Executive Director of RENEW's national office countered: "We are helping people talk about their faith in Jesus. For mainline Christians to do that more comfortably is a great step forward.... Without those underpinnings of faith and trust it's hard to lay an iota of doctrine and morality on people."[22]

RENEW was a three-year parish program, with groups meeting twice a year for periods of six weeks each time. One of the places where the program has been promoted is in Hartford, Connecticut. The Diocesan Pastoral Department has served some five hundred groups in 136 of the diocese's 205 parishes. A majority of the group members were married women over the age of forty-five, and the groups were almost entirely suburban. Archbishop Peter A. Rosazza wrote, in a guidebook for the groups:

> These communities, I believe, can help people live out their faith in a time when the culture hardly supports our values. It is important for lay people to be strengthened so that you can carry out our apostolate in the world. Your apostolate, according to the Vatican Council, must lead directly to the transformation of the world and you do this by the impact you have in charity and justice on the areas in which you live and work.[23]

Of course, hortatory booklets do not a successful program make, and only time and systematic research will tell what effect, if any, this new program for Small Christian Communities will have on parish and personal life.

EXPLAINING THE RISE OF SMALL CHRISTIAN COMMUNITIES

The descriptions in the foregoing parts reveal a wide range of small faith communities emerging in the United States in the years since Vatican II. They range from the highly autonomous Intentional Eucharistic Communities, to other groups with little or no formal affiliation with the institutional church, to the Hispanic SCBCs, the communities formed under the leadership of Father Baranowski, and most recently to those that have emerged out of the bishops' RENEW Program.

There is a tendency to think of these new movements as resulting from Vatican II, and there is no doubt that the reforms put in place by the Second Vatican Council have been very influential. Even as John Paul II attempts to rein in and reduce the impact of Vatican II, it is important to recognize that lay movements independent of the institutional church existed in the United States long before Vatican II gave rise to a new era for the laity.

Perhaps the most significant early movement was that of the Catholic Worker, founded by Dorothy Day and Peter Maurin in the 1930s. It is characterized by houses of hospitality serving the poor in cities throughout the country, and by their radical paper, *The Catholic Worker*. This movement and its impact on American society and intellectuals is ably described and analyzed in the book *Breaking Bread* by Professor Mel Piehl.[24] I need only note here that Dorothy Day and her followers were devoted to bringing about social change through making the Gospel relevant to social issues, from pacifism to hunger.

Precursor to the Present: The Christian Family Movement

A movement closer in time and in membership and social structure to the movements described herein is the Christian Family Movement (CFM), founded in Chicago in the 1940s, during the Second World War. I cite the CFM here in some detail to illustrate that the church, even in periods of history thought by outsiders to reflect its monolithic, authoritarian nature, had room for innovators who had the courage to act. Indeed, if the movements described above reveal anything, it is the importance of individual initiative. Things happened because there were laity willing to go out on their own to form IECs, or priests like Father Baranowski, or bishops like Gerety, who were willing to formulate and promote new programs. Of course, their success has ultimately depended on access to and the willingness of followers, a propitious cultural and structural environment, and their ability to build new structures. CFM has been a case in point, illustrating all of these dynamics. It is now almost fifty years old and into a second generation of family membership.

The roots of the Christian Family Movement (CFM) are found in the thoughts and actions of a Belgian priest, later Cardinal Joseph Cardijn. "In 1912 he founded the Young Christian Workers to work with trade unions and cooperative groups."[25] He developed a method which he labeled simply "Observe, Judge, Act." He urged ordinary people to follow this as their mission, to bring to fruition God's design, to live the Gospels. Eventually Cardijn's idea was developed by Pope John XXIII in his encyclical, *Christianity and Social Progress*. In it John urged that "Observe, Judge, Act" be adopted by families as the ideal way to carry their mission into the world.

In 1943 a Notre Dame alumnus and Chicago attorney Pat Crowley became attracted to Cardijn's idea. In a 1991 interview, his widow Patty recalled the group's beginnings:

> My husband, Pat, had been invited to start a men's group in 1943 called Catholic Action using the technique of "observe, judge, act,"—the method used by Young Christian Workers in Belgium. The group met in my husband's office about every two weeks and talked about social issues.
>
> We'd only been married a short time and I didn't like being separated from him on those nights. So the women started a group. We met separately because in those days the church never heard of husbands and wives meeting together. We often wondered why we weren't meeting together. Pat and I decided to invite a few of these couples to join us for a weekend. And that was the start of the Christian Family Movement (CFM).
>
> Our meetings were very structured. We discussed scripture first. The scripture that most affected our lives and the whole working of CFM was Matthew 25: feed the hungry, give drink to the thirsty. We all began to understand that marriage was more than just the love part, it was what we did together.[26]

From the very beginning, CFM was a lay run organization. By the time of Vatican II there were more than fifty-thousand couples, interacting in small groups of five to six couples each, and found in all but three of the states. CFM members tackled just about every major social issue that came before this country during the last forty years, ranging from racism to nuclear war, poverty and homelessness, family violence, alcoholism and drug abuse. Many supported political candidates like Eugene McCarthy, and some became active in politics as a way of living out their Christian commitments.

CFM continues into the 1990s; included among the members are children of the first generation, as they marry and form families of their own. While no systematic studies are available, Lucey's chronicle of the movement describes a number of the children of CFMers whose career choices were greatly influenced by their family experiences, and other children who had become second generation CFMers themselves.[27] Anthropologist Margaret Mead became interested in CFM in the 1970s, and in an address to a Family Life Conference in Tarrytown, NY, stated that: "CFM provides people a wider context by which they can become acquainted with their husbands and wives and developing a pair who can do all kinds of wonderful things together. The main thing that a couple producing children do is to be the focal point of creating the kind of life for those children which produces the kind of people society needs...."[28] Mead's comment seems as appropriate today as it was almost twenty years ago.

The combination of study, prayer, and action found in CFM is clearly a precursor to the small faith communities that have followed. Likewise the combination of lay leadership and church support would be seen again in post-Vatican II efforts. I find it interesting that nowhere in the literature I have examined, or among the people I have talked with, is CFM mentioned as a forerunner or precursor to the present small faith communities movements that we have described. Yet they are clearly another example of a relatively autonomous, lay-led movement that worked toward the integration of faith in the life of work, family, and the world.

The Coming of Age of the American Catholic Laity

It can now be seen that the movements described above have their roots in events that precede Vatican II, indeed lay the groundwork for the reforms of Vatican II. The Christian Family Movement may be seen as evidence that, by the 1950s, American Catholic laity were being transformed.

In earlier writings,[29] I have reviewed data showing that American Catholics have been demonstrating a growing independence from and criticism of official church teachings and of the autocratic manner of church decision-making. Data on the growth of personal autonomy rather than blind obedience to authority can be traced back to Lenski's *The Religious Factor*,[30] a time when Catholic laity were just beginning to emerge from their immigrant past with its limited educational and occupational backgrounds and experiences. The GI Bill after the Second World War helped propel thousands of Catholics into college and university. The election of John F. Kennedy in 1960 (when Lenski was finishing his book) provided a dramatic lift to the Catholic laity, diminished Protestant concerns about Catholic obedience to Rome, and marked the beginning of the end of Catholic parochialism.

The pronouncements of the Second Vatican Council arrived at an opportune moment. One of the key documents of Vatican II, *On The Constitution of the Church in the Modern World*, finally established the principle of religious liberty and freedom of conscience that was so long struggled for by the American Jesuit priest-theologian John Courtney Murray. This principle acknowledged the right, indeed the responsibility in conscience, to dissent from nondogmatic teachings. Within five years of its promulgation, laity and clergy publicly dissented from Pope Paul VI's encyclical *Humanae Vitae*. Some 650 theologians signed a document questioning the Pope's use of his authority and the reasoning behind his decision.[31] The encyclical had the consequence of raising the question of the authority of the church over the consciences of its members. Polls and surveys taken since *Humanae Vitae* have shown increasing majorities of Catholics opposing the encyclical, denying its validity, and refusing to accept the teaching that the Pope was necessarily infallible on matters of faith and morals.[32]

Greeley and others have concluded that Vatican II and *Humanae Vitae* were the watershed experiences that changed the way Catholics related to the teachings of the church as enunciated by the Pope, cardinals, and bishops.[33] My own reading is that Vatican II with its changes in the liturgy, its affirmation of freedom of conscience, its modification of disciplines (such as ending the rule against eating meat on Friday), and its emphasis on the church as the people of God, moved the church in a moderately progressive direction. Had *Humanae Vitae* been accepted, it would have moved the church back in a much more conservative direction. But a great majority of the laity and many clergy have rejected the attempt.[34] Thus, in reasserting traditional authority, Pope Paul and the leaders supporting him undermined the larger authority structure. They had already opened the way for the laity in the documents of Vatican II, and the windows of change were not to be so easily closed.

Whither the Small Christian Community?

In the United States during the past half-century, the Catholic laity have moved from a narrow parochialism to become a much more open

church, more given to ecumenical activities with Protestant denominations, and given to more lay initiatives, in varying degrees under the official control of the hierarchy, and in some cases relatively free of such
control.

The movement toward small communities has so far involved, in
some degree, about fifteen percent of the laity, with about half that
number (roughly four million Catholics) regularly involved. With the
current Catholic population numbering about fifty-six million, but only
about half of them attending parish Eucharistic services regularly, these
figures suggest that about one in seven regular parishoners have been
involved in small faith communities in recent years.

It seems to be the case that members of the more autonomous groups,
such as IEC, CFM, and the miscellany of groups without much official
designation are generally college-educated, professional, and white-col-
lar, with comfortable incomes. On the other hand, post-RENEW groups
and the groups organized by Father Baranowski are like the average
parish in including members from a wide range of locations on the
income, education, and occupation scales. The Hispanic base communities are more likely to be characterized by working-class, first- or sec-
ond-generation people with limited incomes. The age structure of these
small communities is tipped toward those forty-five and older, largely
but not entirely pre-Vatican II Catholics. Recent studies have shown that
Catholics under the age of forty-five have much lower regular Mass
attendance rates than do those over forty-five.[35] It seems plausible that
they would also be less likely to be involved in small faith communities.

One of the most important features that the small faith communities
have in common is their commitment to a lifestyle that ties work, family, and religion into warm, supportive communities. Given the aggran-
dizing, consumer-oriented, individualistic environment that continues
to characterize American society, the existence of communities with
such commitments suggests that at least some portion of the population can be moved to behavior that is concerned with the larger commonweal.[36]

Regardless of occupation, education, income, or age, an important
ingredient shared in these several movements has been the leadership
and daring of a few individuals. We can say that Vatican II, and in particular the *Constitution on the Church in the Modern World*, was the catalyst for encouraging these new initiatives. But we must also credit the
culture of American society that extols personal autonomy, and that in
the past has encouraged people to organize themselves into voluntary
associations to achieve common goals. In an important sense, these small

faith communities represent a touch of American democracy as understood by Tocqueville.

Reverend Bernard Lee, Director of the Institute for Ministry of Loyola University of the South, and a member of an intentional interdenominational community, organized a "conversation" in March, 1992, that included many of the movements discussed in this paper. In a memo about these small communities, he said:

> One gets the impression from the literature on this topic that "small is beautiful," that the limited size of the group is its most attractive feature. A certain kind of people, who used to be called *Commonweal* Catholics, (now probably *NCR* Catholics) think this is the modern movement for the salvation of the Church itself. Meanwhile, the great majority of U.S. Catholics are probably marginal parishioners who are unmoved by popular fads that come and go.

While it is probable that a high proportion of IEC and CFM members were Commonweal and are now NCR Catholics, the fact that National Catholic Register subscriptions do not exceed fifty thousand suggests that Lee's comment should be seen as a literary allusion to a progressive way of thinking about church, and nothing more. Certainly the Hispanics involved in their small communities do not readily fit the Commonweal or NCR mold.

A more important consideration is whether or not this rather broad-based movement is more than another fad that will soon run its course. This question raises interesting and important research questions.

(1.) Given the apparent success of the Base Christian Communities within the Latin American and now U.S. Hispanic Catholic churches, how important to the continuity of the movement are such variables as occupation, education, and income?

(2.) How important are age and gender across types of communities?

(3.) How important is the factor of lay autonomy? Do people who join more autonomous groups have significantly different orientations to church teachings than do those who join church-sponsored groups?

(4.) Does active participation in small faith communities, whether more or less autonomous, have the effect over time of making participants more or less critical of church teachings, and of how the church is governed? Or does it simply make them less concerned about the church as an institution?

(5.) Has the CFM in any way been a factor in promoting current groups? Was it a training ground for future leadership that has emerged since Vatican II? Or are these independent phenomena?

(6.) What kind of impact have these several movements had:

(a) on the individuals participating in them?

(b) on the parishes of which they are or were members?

(c) on the way the church hierarchy views the laity and such movements?

(7.) Is there any evidence that these movements have had or may have any impact on the culture and social structure of the institutional church?

(8.) Will the Intentional Eucharistic Community become the model for other faith communities, such as those organized or fostered by Fr. Baranowski and his followers? In other words, what is the place of the Mass and the Eucharistic celebration in the life of Catholic small faith communities?

In another context, Peter Blau showed that bureaucracies had built within themselves not necesssarily the seeds of their own destruction, but possibly the seeds of their own transformation.[37] It remains to be seen whether the small faith communities may constitute one such seed, borne by the institutional church, and now possibly in the process of transforming it, in spite of itself.

NOTES

1. In this paper the terms groups and communities are often used interchangeably. All the organizations discussed here are groups; those that members call communities either aspire to or have achieved a high level of integration and a deep sense of commitment to the group and its individual members, along the model of an affective, extended family. At times I will simply use the word group to provide variation, without intending to imply meaning difference.

2. The materials used to provide the data for this paper come from the following sources: (1) My participation in the meeting of the 16 Intentional Eucharistic Communities, held in Washington DC, May, 1991. I have been a member since its founding in 1983 of one of the IECS, and I helped plan and participated in the meeting. Thus, I have copies of all the documents presented by the 16 IECs, as well as notes taken during the meeting. (2) My participation in the meeting held in New Orleans in March, 1992, at which representatives from the groups described herein (except CFM) were present. (3) My membership for 12 years on the Board of the

National Catholic Reporter , a paper known by laity, clergy, and hierarchy as a progressive, independent, Catholic newspaper. I know the writers of the stories from which I have quoted, and have checked the data with other persons in a position to know. (4) My earlier studies of the Christian Family Movement. I have known the Crowleys and other leaders personally, and have been a colleague with one of the founders, Rose Lucey, during my years on the board of the NCR.

To my knowledge, there are no other movements of any size now ongoing in the United States involving Roman Catholics as such. The IECs are the smallest of the SCCs described in this paper. But they also represent the goal that Father Baranowski seeks for SCCs, namely giving new life and meaning to the Eucharistic service (the Mass), and through it, revitalizing parish life.

3. Princeton Religion Research Center, *Report* (Princeton: Princeton Religion Research Center, 1988).

4. The IECs have a good deal in common with the situation found by Wallace in her study of priestless parishes, that is, parishes without resident priest pastors. At the time of her study, Ruth Wallace found some 300 such parishes. She did an intensive study of 20 such, all run by women (see *They Call Her Pastor*, (Albany: State University of New York Press, 1992)). In the face of the growing priest shortage, bishops have begun to select lay persons to act as parish administrators, and so far about 60% of the appointments have been to women.

   In some cases, the bishop has permitted the people of the parish to select their own administrator; in others he has simply appointed someone of his choice. Wallace found that while the bishops retain formal authority over these parishes, there is much opportunity for new lay initiatives.

   Moreover, those parishes that freely controlled the selection/election of the administrator seemed to be more closely knit faith communities than those in which the bishop simply appointed someone. Given that the shortage of priests is expected to become more pronounced in the coming years, this new phenomenon of lay administrators may prove a significant vehicle for change in the institutional church in the United States, among other things producing parishes similar in structure and ethos to those of the IECs. The implications for the role of women in the church are even more intriguing.

5. The Roman Catholic Church has long recognized and given its official sanction to non-territorial parishes, mostly ethnic in nature.

6. Jim McManus, "Small Catholic Groups Emerging Nationwide Based on Prayer Life, Active Justice Work," *National Catholic Reporter*, March 29, 1985, pp. 1, 4–5.

7. *Ibid.*, p. 4.

8. Paulist fathers have been especially active on college campuses, with progressive liturgies and a press that has been exceptionally independent of the institutional church. On the Boston Center, see McManus, "Small Catholic Groups," p. 5.

9. March 6–7, 1992, Loyola University New Orleans Conference on Small Christian Communities; information provided by the National Coordinator for Buena Vista at this Conference and in two telephone interviews.

10. March 6–7, 1992, Loyola University New Orleans Conference on Small Christian Communities.

11. *National Catholic Reporter*, October 6, 1989, p. 8.

12. Arthur Baranowski, *Creating Small Faith Communities* (St. Anthony's Press, 1990).

13. *National Catholic Reporter*, October 6, 1989, p. 9.

14. *Guidelines for Small Church-Based Communities*, Secretariat for Hispanic Affairs, NCCB/USCC, Washington, D.C., 1991, p. 2.

15. Madeleine Adriance, "Agents of Change: The Roles of Priests, Sisters and Lay Workers in the Grassroots Catholic Church in Brazil," *Journal for the Scientific Study of Religion.* 30 (1991), pp. 292–305.

16. The following information is derived from a new book by Kenneth Briggs, *Holy Siege: Twelve Months in the Life of the Roman Catholic Church* (San Francisco: Harper, 1993), and from conversations with and materials supplied by Brother Robert Moriarty (SM), Coordinator of the Department of Small Christian Communities of the Hartford Archdiocese; data were also gathered from documents presented to me by one of the active members of RENEW in New Jersey in its formative years.

17. Briggs, *Holy Siege*, p. 128.

18. Report of the Bishops' Committee, December 30, 1986, p. 547.

19. Briggs, *Holy Siege*, p. 128

20. Bishops' Report, p. 548.

21. Bishops' Report, p. 548, quoted in Briggs, *Holy Siege*, p. 129.

22. Reported in Briggs, p. 130.

23. *QUEST: A Reflection Booklet for Small Christian Communities*, December 16, 1991.

24. Mel Piehl, *Breaking Bread: The Catholic Worker and the Origin of Catholic Radicalism in America* (Philadelphia: Temple University Press, 1982).

25. Rose Marciano Lucey, *Roots and Wings: Dreamers and Doers of the Christian Family Movement.* (San Jose, CA: Resource Publications, 1987), p. ix.

26. From "Vicki Quade interviews Patty Crowley," *SALT*, November/December, 1991, p. 4.

27. *Ibid.*, pp. 3–4.

28. Lucey, *Roots and Wings*, p. 97.

29. William D'Antonio, "Family and Religion: Exploring a Changing Relationship," *Journal for the Scientific Study of Religion.* 19 (1980), pp. 89–104; and "The American Catholic Family: Signs of Cohesion and Polarization," *Journal of Marriage and the Family.* May, 1985, pp. 395–405;

and D'Antonio, *et al.*, *American Catholic Laity in a Changing Church* (Kansas City: Sheed and Ward, 1989).

30. Gerhard Lenski, *The Religious Factor* (Garden City, NY: Doubleday, 1963).

31. For a full discussion of the birth control debate, see Robert G. Hoyt, *The Birth Control Debate* (Kansas City: National Catholic Reporter Publishing Co., 1968).

32. *American Catholic Laity*, esp. chaps. 3, 4, and 5.

33. Andrew M. Greeley, *American Catholics Since the Council: An Unauthorized Report* (Chicago: Thomas More, 1985).

34. *American Catholic Laity*, ch. 4.

35. *American Catholic Laity*, chap. 2; also William V. D'Antonio, "Autonomy and Community: Indicators of Change among the American Catholic Laity," unpublished manuscript presented before the Canon Law Society of America, Cambridge, MA, October 12, 1992. Data obtained from a study commissioned by an independent Catholic association called Catholics Speak Out, located in Hyattsville, MD. The study was carried out by Gallup, and was based on a representative sample of the American Catholic laity.

36. For discussions of the struggle between individualism and commitment in American society, see Bellah, *et al.*, *Habits of the Heart* (Berkeley: University of California Press, 1985); also their *The Good Society*, (New York: Alford A. Knopf, 1991); and Amitai Etzioni, *The Responsive Community, Rights and Responsibilities*, 1 (1) (1991), pp. 2–5.

37. Peter Blau, *Dynamics of Bureaucracy*, (Chicago: University of Chicago Press, 1963).

Religious Innovation in the Mainline Church

House Churches, Home Cells, and Small Groups

Stuart A. Wright

O n a balmy March night in Houston, a small group of twelve people meets in the home of Bill and Anna Seemans.[1] It is a modest home in Heights section of Houston, a typical working-class community. All are members of Church in the City (CIC), an inner-city, nondenominational church founded in 1975. CIC encourages members to participate in these small home groups (called "home cells") that meet during the week. This particular group has been meeting together for over three years. There are six married couples, all in their twenties and thirties. They appear to be very close; members exchange embraces as they enter the Seemans home. There is a smell of coffee wafting from the kitchen, and the atmosphere is casual and warm. One of the men has an acoustic guitar which he extracts from a black leather case. He begins strumming and singing softly as members stroll in with cups of coffee in hand. The couples sit in a circle, some on the floor and others in chairs. The man playing the guitar breaks into song, and the group begins singing spontaneously. The guitarist is an accomplished musician, a former member of a rock band. The song is unfamiliar to me, but hauntingly sweet and deeply moving.

The worship is conducted without any discernible protocol. After a period of approximately fifteen minutes, Bill Seemans solicits personal "faith-building" experiences or events that members would be willing to share with the group. A woman in her mid-thirties describes a behavior change in her daughter she attributes to answered prayer. The details of her emotional struggle are disarmingly intimate and personal. The groups responds warmly, affirming the woman and her explanation. Two other accounts of a similar nature are offered, and the group seems to draw energy from their mutual experiences. Several members make requests of the group for prayer, encouraged by the apparent success of these accounts. Bill leads the group in a collective prayer, and the meeting ends within two hours. As the members depart, their words and actions clearly indicate a strong psychological and emotional bond, and one senses that herein lies a faith community that is very central in the lives of its members.

—

At first glance, there doesn't seem to be anything revolutionary about the events described in this home group meeting. Indeed, some might argue that it is reminiscent of traditional social organization, where neighborhood and church served as key primary groups to foster a sense of community and identity. Yet upon careful reflection, it is the generational rebirth of these social forms by intent and design that warrants closer scrutiny. It is evident to any scholarly observer that this type of phenomenon runs counter to prevailing patterns or trends in contemporary society. While the forces of modernity push us toward centralization, increasing complexity and differentiation, secularization, instrumental relations, and the decline of community, the emergence of home cells and house churches in recent years signals a trend that clearly runs against the tide.

I want to suggest in this chapter that the small group movement or house church movement represents a pattern of "de-differentiation," an effort to counteract the compartmentalizing effects on the institutions of work, family, and faith.[2] The competing and conflicting demands on individuals in the modern world leave us with fragmented lives, neatly divided by institutional spheres of activity. Career or work roles impinge on family concerns, a situation made more apparent by the increased participation of women in the workforce. Institutional religion is increasingly the domain of specialists or credentialed technicians (clerics) who preside over religious bureaucracies. The professionalization of religious leaders enhances the separation of clergy and laity. The separation of the public sphere of work from the private sphere of faith is well documented as a concomitant of modernity.[3]

Emerging alternative forms occurring at the borders of the mainline church appear to provide new linkages to the changing institutions of family and work. Innovative structures have crystallized in recent years that may be seen as *adaptations* to new cultural alignments. As a part of the small group revolution in the church over the last three decades, forms such as home cell groups, house churches, home Bible studies, and neighborhood share groups have become increasingly popular expressions of faith and worship. The array of small groups meeting in homes is identified by various names, but comprises a grassroots movement sharing common principles, goals, and beliefs. Some common themes include a reaction to bureaucratization and impersonal corporate structures that dominate contemporary church organizations, a search for meaningful religious experience, a recovery of community and intimate relationships, and more lay participation, commitment, and decision-making.[4] These themes correspond to shifting needs and patterns of American society, which we shall examine later in the chapter, and help to explain the growth of the Christian house group movement.

Studies of house churches and home cell groups now form a distinct body of literature.[5] Thousands of churches in the U.S. and abroad currently use programs of small group meetings in homes. Some have very highly organized structures and programs detailing membership requisites, goals, policies, and leadership training procedures, and even produce handbooks or manuals. Others are very simple in their form and style.

Though yet to be given the attention it deserves by scholarly researchers or the press, the movement has touched a substantial portion of the population. A study by the Princeton Religion Research Center reveals that twenty-two percent of Americans have attended a religious home group in the previous two years, and approximately half of these (forty-nine percent) are attending on a regular basis. Protestants (twenty-seven percent) are more likely to attend than Catholics (fifteen percent), and the likelihood of regular attendence increases with level of education. George Gallup, author of the study, concludes that small groups meeting in homes may offer critical solutions to declining church membership rates by attracting disaffected members back to the church, and by sustaining current members, particularly college graduates. House churches and home cell groups often appeal to disaffected members who have grown tired of traditional religious practices and programs but still express deep spiritual needs and beliefs. Small groups may also sustain current members by solidifying relationships and enhancing a sense of belonging.[6]

One of the most revealing findings of the study was that a majority of Americans expressed a dissatisfaction with *organizational* issues, while scoring high on religious belief items. Fifty eight percent said most synagogues and churches were "too concerned with organizational issues," an increase from forty-seven percent in 1978, while those who professed a belief in the divinity of Christ increased from seventy-eight percent in 1978 to eighty-four percent in 1988. Moreover, the number of those attending church regularly dropped from fifty-nine percent in 1978 to fifty-six percent in 1988. Thus, while the number of "belongers" declined over the ten-year period between 1978 and 1988, the number of "believers" actually increased. On a typical Sunday, only forty percent of Americans are in church. However, the PRRC study found that sixty percent of Americans may be described as fairly religious. Forty-four percent of the "unchurched" (those not attending a church service in the previous six months) have "made a commitment to Christ," and fifty-eight percent say they would consider returning to church.

If the PRRC study is an accurate portrayal of religious belief and behavioral patterns, it would appear that there is a large pool of disaffected but personally religious people in the population. The sources of disaffection may be linked to the shortcomings of the institutional church, but one must keep in mind that the church itself has been victimized by the forces of modernity. Moreover, the forces that have undermined the effectiveness of the church are also those that may help to explain the evolution of house churches and home cell groups. Let us now examine the characteristics of house church groups and the social conditions that have helped to shape them.

CHARACTERISTICS OF HOUSE CHURCH GROUPS

House church groups are small groups meeting in homes for the purpose of worship, sharing, or teaching.[7] Worship modes are distinctly less formal than in traditional church services. They are characterized by loose patterns of activities that are designed to encourage collective participation according to group needs. In this sense, they serve an entirely different function from formalized, corporate worship.

These differing functions are reflective of the differing architectures of the two places. Sanctuaries are structured around a central platform where a single speaker is featured, engendering passivity and a form of removed observation. Modern church architecture is not designed for face-to-face interaction, fellowship, or dialogue, but for large and even massive audiences. On the other hand, homes are domiciles or "dwelling" places, which tend to be architecturally suited for comfort and psychologically conducive to hospitality, warmth, and openness. The informal surroundings are less intimidating, increasing the likelihood of intimacy and sharing of personal concerns. Studies show that people reluctant to attend a conventional church may be more inclined to explore a house church.[8]

House Church Groups typically average between ten and thirty people, and are intentionally designed to remain small and intimate. Indeed, groups that grow too large are often divided into two separate cells in order to cultivate and sustain the advantages of a small group. This method draws upon a biological model of cell growth in living organisms. The body of Christ, like the literal human organism, achieves growth through cell division and reproduction.[9] And it achieves growth because it successfully creates mutual commitment and a strong sense of community (what Christians call *koinonia*).

The widespread interest in small groups of this type should be understood in the context of increased discontent with secondary, instrumental relations in both church and society. The pervasiveness of secondary groups is a distinct characteristic of modern society, extending even into the bureaucratic organization and operation of religious institutions. House church groups may be viewed as reactions or countertrends that attempt to recover primary group relations, according to W. Widick Schroeder, Professor of Religion and Society at Chicago Theological Seminary:

> The...forces producing urbanization, industrialization and bureacratization are very strong and very pervasive in contemporary America. These forces are rooted in technical reason.... Technical reason fosters the separation of

the spheres of the social order, the segmentalization of social roles, and the evaluation of human beings on the basis of their competencies to perform specified tasks. It encourages the proliferation of secondary relationships and a multiplicity of social groups which are primarily instrumental and affective-neutral.

Human beings cannot live exclusively in such secondary groups, for they have needs for intimacy, sharing, caring, wholistic and integrating relations. These needs are best met in primary groups, and it seems to me that the House Church is exploring one means of fostering such groups.[10]

The development of religious primary groups assumes added significance in the face of larger social and cultural changes engendering what many have called the "eclipse of community." The social and psychological gains of involvement have been demonstrated in various studies of small groups and even small churches.[11]

Another feature of the house church group is its mobility. It is intended to draw people from the local community and the neighborhoods where they live. The house church is accessible, familiar, and convenient. Since the location is not permanent, it can be moved at any time. Often members of the house church or cell group take turns hosting meetings on a rotational basis. The ease with which the house group can be moved makes it well suited to a mobile, urban population. Moreover, as the location changes, it may generate new interest in the neighborhoods of host families, creating a type of "natural evangelism".[12]

A corollary to the house group's mobility is its flexibility. The house church can be changed, revised, or modified at any time. Groups can change the time, place, and frequency of meetings, reorganize for specific ministries, or simply accommodate members with special needs. Here, flexibility rules, rather than tradition. Such flexibility is well suited for working couples and busy families in modern society.

However, the appeal of house church groups appears to cut across many social and demographic categories. A demographic breakdown of house church attenders in the PRRC study is shown in Tables 1 and 2. The data do not reveal any marked concentrations of attenders. Slight differences occur by sex, age, education, marital status, region, and religion. Attenders are more likely to be women (twenty-five percent) than men (nineteen percent). Those between the ages of twenty-five and twenty-nine have the highest rates of attendence (twenty-nine percent). Never-marrieds are least likely to attend (eighteen percent). Westerners (twenty-five percent) and Southerners (twenty-five percent) are more likely than those from the East or Midwest to attend. Protestants have

TABLE 1

**Percent of Persons in Various Demographic Groups Who
Have Attended House Church Group Meetings**

	Attenders	Total No. of Interviews
Total	22%	2556
Sex		
Male	19	1270
Female	25	1067
Age		
18–24	21	288
25–29	26	260
30–49	21	1004
50 & older	22	981
Education		
Less than H.S.	19	603
H.S. grad.	21	979
Some college	29	453
College grad.	22	513
Marital Status		
Married	23	1607
Never married	18	501
Divorced/sep./widowed	24	442
Region		
East	16	611
Midwest	21	614
South	25	835
West	25	496
Religion		
Protestant	27	1497
Catholic	15	732
Other	25	139
Church Status		
Churched	30	1471
Unchurched	11	1067

Source: The Princeton Religion Research Center, *The Unchurched American: 10 Years Later.* (Princeton, NJ: 1988), p. 54.

the highest rates of attendance (twenty-seven percent), and the churched (thirty percent) are roughly three times more likely to attend a house group meeting than the unchurched (eleven percent). Similar patterns emerge for frequent attenders in Table 2.

TABLE 2

Frequency of Attendance Among House Church Goers by Demographic Characteristics

	On a Regular Basis	Occasionally	Once Only	No Opinion	Total No. of Interviews
Total	49%	45%	1%	5%	562
Sex					
Male	42	51	2	5	245
Female	55	41	1	3	317
Age					
18–24	45	52	3	-	57
25–29	49	45	-	6	70
30–49	51	43	1	5	222
50 & older	51	44	-	5	208
Education					
Less than H.S.	46	51	1	2	117
H. S. grad.	45	45	2	8	204
Some college	52	45	1	2	123
College grad.	57	39	-	4	116
Marital Status					
Married	52	41	1	6	376
Never married	36	60	2	2	85
Divorced/sep./wid.	51	47	-	2	100
Region					
East	42	49	2	7	106
Midwest	55	43	-	2	129
South	48	48	-	4	211
West	53	39	2	6	116
Religion					
Protestant	51	43	1	5	398
Catholic	47	46	3	4	112
Other	46	51	-	3	36
Church Status					
Churched	54	42	1	3	438
Unchurched	32	57	2	9	115

Source: The Princeton Religion Research Center, *The Unchurched American: 10 Years Later*. (Princeton, NJ: 1988), p. 55.

National survey data provide an estimate of how widespread this phenomenon is, and just which categories of the population may be most attracted. To get a closer look at the way house church groups operate, this study will draw on case studies in San Francisco, Houston, Albuquerque, and Milwaukee. In-depth interviews with leaders and laypersons were obtained and used to supplement information gathered through participant observation. Secondary sources include handbooks, manuals, conference materials, and other publications. These data were collected originally as part of a research project initiated by the Center for Urban Church Studies between 1983 and 1986.[13] Some follow-up of the research has been conducted on a continuing basis in order to monitor any changes or new directions in the movement. The initial thrust of the project was to identify alternatives to traditional church practices in a rapidly changing, urban world, both in Western industrial nations and in the Third World. Given the clear trends of global urbanization, denominational leaders have expressed some concern over the efficacy of traditional church methods that are grounded largely in nineteenth-century rural society. Thus our inquiry into house churches is informed by issues of social change.

Within the scope of this paper, I will look at these case studies with an eye toward what they may tell us about the institutional integration of work, family, and faith through small groups. I will describe and attempt to explain the role these groups are playing as new generations of religious adherents strive to make their faith relevant to their own worlds—jobs, finances, marriage, children, health, relationships.

INTEGRATION OF FAITH AND CHURCH

Faith may be defined here as the obligation to a set of beliefs and practices pertaining to the sacred. Faith is often embedded in a moral community, but it may be highly personalized or individualistic as well. Faith and church are not synonomous. Churches and denominations are *institutional representations* of faith. Churches become institutionalized through tradition. But when tradition becomes irrelevant or ineffective, the distinction between faith and church widens. Indeed, many contemporary churches were born of sectarian movements, fueled by redisovered faith.

Evidently, this fact is not lost on most Americans. The PRRC study reveals that seventy-eight percent of the American population believe that a person can be a good Christian or Jew without attending church or synagogue. Roof's recent study of religion among baby-boomers finds that ninety-five percent of church dropouts believe it is possible to be a good Christian without attending church, and nearly two-thirds of the dropouts consider themselves to be good Christians.[14]

The tension between faith and church is felt as each new generation must appropriate the traditions it has inherited. Religious institutions have a way of turning experiences of the sacred into inflexible bricks and mortar. But neither the people in them nor the context surrounding them remain unchanged over time. Each new generation of men and women faces the challenge of making their faith meaningful and workable within the worlds they inhabit. To inherit uncritically the religious institutions and practices of the previous generation is not sufficient in a world of changed social, technical, and economic conditions. On the other hand, challenges successfully met serve to intensify commitment, as the new generation of adherents experience firsthand the salience and vitality of their beliefs.

Pioneering efforts to make faith relevant may be seen in the case of the Houston Covenant Church (HCC). The HCC began as an experiment in 1977. Seeking to avoid some the pitfalls of the traditional church, HCC organized around the idea of house churches. The HCC is made up of a network of small groups or flocks headed by house church pastors. Currently, the HCC consists of thirteen pastors and over five hundred members. Most of the ministry to members takes place in biweekly house church meetings. Each house church consists of approximately ten to twelve families. The meetings take place in the home of the house church pastor. The HCC does not own a formal church building or sanctuary. A portion of the church's offerings and tithes go to the salaries of the house church pastors enabling the HCC to maintain the ministry of small groups in an economically viable way. The entire HCC meets three Sundays a month in a rented school building. The only facility the church owns is a modest office building to provide work space for the pastoral staff.

A striking feature of the HCC is the age distribution. Approximately ninety percent of the membership is under the age of forty-five. At a time when the mainline church is experiencing an aging trend, and many churches struggle to attract young and middle-aged persons, such a feature is noteworthy. Comprised largely of baby-boom families, the HCC represents a generational shift, an age cohort experimenting with new configurations and methods of ministry and worship. Part of the HCC's success is attributable to its freedom from tradition and its willingness to create alternative forms that meet member's needs. The church has been able to effectively combine a flexible structure with a strong emphasis on evangelical-charismatic beliefs. There is a firm conviction among the HCC leadership that organization and structure should be malleable, and subordinate to the principal issues of personal faith, family, and community. This idea is underscored by remarks from one of HCC's pastors:

We have flexibility. When you don't have a building, or you don't have a mortgage, you don't have to keep a rigid schedule. Some churches feel like they have to open their building and and keep a schedule or they will lose their identity. They're afraid the people will stop coming. They identify the church with the building.... We build our schedules around our people. In the house churches, we used to meet every week. But that got to be too much of a strain on the families, so we moved it to twice a month. Eighty-six percent of the women in our church now work (outside the home)...and the families weren't getting enough time together. So we cut back on our meetings. But we still have ninety-eight percent attendence at everything we do.

The attraction of young adults to religious bodies of this type marks a shift away from intergenerational, denominational loyalties to what Roof and McKinney call "the new volunteerism."[15] Baby-boomers adopt a consumer orientation to church attendance and membership, making selections based on special individual or familial needs. The most prominent needs identified by Roof and McKinney include a religious education for one's children, and some kind of religious experience that helps them make sense of their own lives. The latter need has become more acute, particularly as the established churches have embraced the corporate model. As any hierarchical, well-organized, managerial enterprise will build alienation, the mainline churches have forfeited a critical function of providing a meaningful religious experience for their members. According to Louis Weeks, Dean and Professor of Church History at Louisville Presbyterian Theological Seminary: "The need is to find the kinds of piety and spirituality to sustain us today in a fashion analogous to the way people were sustained in an informal, family-based church 100 years ago."[16]

In one sense, small groups have always been the essential carriers of faith. The sociological literature on secularization contends that religion thrives in primary groups or community ("*gemeinschaft*"), but deteriorates in modern, industrial society ("*gesellschaft*"), because stable relationships of family, neighborhood, church, and community give way to high rates of geographical and social mobility, increased anonymity, privatization and cultural pluralism.[17] Berger and Luckmann take this a step further, arguing that "religion *requires* a religious community, and to live in a religious world requires affiliation with that community" (emphasis mine).[18] If we pursue this line of thinking, we are left with the following conclusion: while faith and church are not inseparable, faith and community are. Embedded in secularization theory is the notion that religion is inextricably tied to small groups or communities of shared beliefs. If the secularization theorists are correct, then we should hardly be surprised that church renewal, ironically especially among the most modernized segments of society, would come by way of small groups, regardless of what we call them.

Some churches have found the best of both worlds through small groups. They have experienced substantial growth in the overall size of the church while effectively placing their members in small groups called home cells, thus resolving the tension between large, complex organizations and human needs for community. This model is perhaps most dramatically seen in the Yoido Full Gospel Church in Seoul, a church that claims approximately half a million members in over ten thousand home cell groups. Their pastor, Paul Y. Cho, lobbies for the expanding of church into homes, thereby creating affective, familial bonds among cell members, developing plural leadership and promoting lay pastors. Home cell groups form the heart of the church, where the bulk of the pastoral care, teaching, and fellowship inhere.[19]

Partly because of the dramatic church growth enjoyed by Cho's church, his model has enjoyed considerable attention among American churches and denominations. Many American church leaders see the home cell group as a key to church growth and evangelism. For example, the annual National Conference on Small Groups sponsored by Fuller Theological Seminary clearly approaches home cells as a tool for church growth.[20] This model also offers the advantage of being a programmatic extension of a traditional church. It leaves much of the existing organizational structure in place, simply adding a new program or layer of activities.

Small groups, then, seem to provide a way for traditional churches to combine their own institutional strength with the dynamism and intimacy that nurtures faith. While society grows more complex, traditional family functions decline, and the organization of work extends instrumental and technical relations, the church is unsurpassed in the institutional resources for providing care, intimacy, emotional warmth, and spiritual growth. Churches, of course, are not guaranteed a monopoly on religious consumers. Some seekers will be drawn to alternative religious and spiritual groups. Indeed, if the church fails to respond to the increasing dearth of primary group experiences, we might expect to see a sharp increase in new religions.

INTEGRATION OF FAITH AND FAMILY

Contemporary families are different from those of the past. One school of thought among sociologists says that the family has experienced a loss or transfer of traditional functions to other institutions and professions. Educators, physicians, counselors, clergy, social workers, and health care professionals now form pools of technical experts who fulfill many of the functions formerly served by the "traditional" family. The primary function that remains for the family is fulfilling emotional needs, represented by the terms "companionate" or "affectionate" family. Amidst an impersonal, bureaucratic society, the companionate family is conceptualized as a sanctuary, a "haven in a heartless world."[21] While this theory has some merit, the conceptual image of the family as sanctuary is not entirely consistent with the circumstances of many households. Increased divorce rates, single-parent families, family violence, dual-income couples, and the reduced role of parents have left some homes with staggering problems that hardly make them a haven.

Churches have barely begun to respond to these changes in family life. In 1983, Joan Aldous wrote: "Families currently are in such flux that, far from serving with religion as guardians of the social heritage, they are forcing theologians to reexamine long-held positions."[22] Some traditional and adapted functions remain. Families, young parents in particular, often seek out a church that can help them instruct and instill values in their children. Divorced and single parents frequently turn to the church for help to work through emotional distress, loneliness, anger, or depression. Never-marrieds may search out churches to find compatible mates holding similar moral values and religious beliefs. Much of this family-related ministry is done most effectively in small groups.

The effectiveness of small groups organized for special ministries can be maximized in house church groups. Numerous churches and communities we investigated structured their house meetings around such family ministry. St. Andrews Presbyterian Church in Newport Beach, California, sponsors over one hundred "covenant groups," many of which target the special needs and problems of families and individuals. Covenant groups are divided into categories, such as singles, marrieds, mothers with young children, and working women only. Consistent with the principles of cell groups, they are designed to remain small and intimate by limiting membership to twelve persons, and subdividing when their numbers exceed the self-imposed limit. According to Lydia Sarandan, director of the covenant group program, the groups furnish support and fellowship for people with common needs, interests, and goals. Singles or working women are distinct groups that can benefit from sharing and mutual concern, providing a kind of empathy that others may not be able to offer. Some covenant groups have been very successful, exhibiting a life span of over eight years.

Elmbrook Church in Milwaukee coordinates an extensive program of "neighborhood home groups" consisting mostly of intact, baby-boom families. The church currently has forty-five such groups, involving approximately six hundred members, and spread over eight regions of the city. The neighborhood home groups have been the principle carriers of evangelism and pastoral care, covering neighborhoods far removed from the physical site of the church. Elmbrook is well known for these home groups and ministry to families. Each group is structured around a "core group" made up of two couples, or one couple and an individual. All core groups must contain at least one married couple, signifying the centrality of marriage and family. Pastoral coordinator of the groups, John Mackett, comments on the familial support one finds in them:

> If you look at what happens in these groups, the family gets a lot of support in the sense that parents are finding resources…for dealing with the issues related to the family. At one level, we do programs and Bible studies that help parents with family problems, you know, how to raise their kids, how to communicate and show love. And at a very informal level, you have a lot of support from others in the group. You may get a shoulder to cry on, some advice given from someone else who has been through the situation before, and, of course, people can pray for you.

Churches that can offer aid, support, and encouragment to beleagured families in the prevailing climate of heightened individualism stand a good chance of ensuring their own vitality and longevity. The church is one of the few institutions that consciously accommodates the needs and interests that bind parents and children together. In small groups, they are more likely to get the kind of personal attention they require and enjoy the kind of group loyalty and support that enhances openness and expression of familial concerns.

INTEGRATION OF FAITH AND WORK

American cultural traditions define work and achievement in a manner that often promotes isolation, alienation, and self-interest. Bellah and his associates have demonstrated dramatically the cultural contradictions of American life—career versus family, individualism versus community, utilitarianism versus spirituality.[23] Successful work and career roles stipulate certain traits, such as competition, ambition and self-reliance that are important in the marketplace. Competition breeds a desire to gain an advantage over others in business and commerce. Ambition fuels one's efforts to achieve material goods, status and power. Self-reliance reflects an ideal by which the individual reduces dependency on and control by others, thereby obtaining a relative degree of autonomy. Yet the instrumental orientation of the workplace may produce behavior that is destructive both socially and psychologically— socially destructive because "immersion in private economic pursuits undermines the person as citizen,"[24] and psychologically destructive because ambition and self-reliance may result in alienation from family and friends. According to these authors, individuals in modern society lack a wider framework by which to justify a common good and evaluate the limitations of self-interest. In the absence of moderating values and ties to a moral community that constrain the narrow pursuit of achievement and success, behavior is judged only on the basis of personal fulfillment. The criterion for what is "right" or "good" simply becomes what is personally rewarding.

In earlier work, Bellah pointed out that the "utilitarian individualism" that dominates the sphere of work has firm historical roots in the Enlightenment. But in earlier periods of American history, it was tempered by Puritan virtues emphasizing covenant and community. The meaning of work and achievement were tied inexorably to deeply held religious and moral beliefs, engendering justice, charity, self-restraint, hospitality, and civic duty. But in the wake of an increasingly secular society, elements of Puritan beliefs have dissipated, leaving only unfettered individualism.[25] Weber's classic work on the Protestant ethic details the waning influence of the Puritan calling in work as a foreboding spector in modern capitalism. There is no question that Weber recognized as problematic the fate of capitalistic economies without the moral and religious constraints of the Puritan faith.[26]

The workplace today fosters competition, individualism and impersonality, values that exacerbate the problems of modern society and sharply contrast with the kinds of traits conducive to community and family life—trust, love, intimacy, sensitivity, and cooperation.[27] The radical discontinuity between the public and private spheres, between work roles and family roles, imply a socially imposed schizophrenia in order to adapt successfully to the conditions of modern life. Cultural contradictions are only a part of the costs of increased compartmentalization and the diminishing role of religion in the public sphere.

Integration of work roles with faith and family roles poses one of the most critical challenges for the church in the 1990s. Our research suggests that house church groups can function in both preventative and therapeutic modes in this regard. For example, small support groups can warn and discipline their members against unscrupulous tendencies in the workplace (preventative mode). One member of a home cell connected to Church in the City (CIC) made the following comments:

> I believe that if your faith really works, it is going to produce fruit. Faith without works is dead. You have to live it out in every part of your life, not just in church, but on the job, at school, wherever you are.... The people at work know I'm serious about my faith. I prove it by my actions, and some people even watch you real close to see if you are going to slip up. We're all in the same boat here [in the house church group]. It helps that we can come together and hold each other up. You know, admonish each other in the faith.

The shared commitment to religious ideals engendered by house church groups attempts to recover the deeply felt convictions and obligations that accompany moral or ethical behavior. The very fact that such convictions are mutually shared empowers the adherent to balance narrow achievement orientation with matters of faith. In one sense, the recovery of religious community enables the church to exert a moral influence on the marketplace, while increasing the integration of members' faith and work roles.

House church groups may also function in a therapeutic mode. The harshness of the workplace and the long working hours sometimes required can drain physical, emotional, and spiritual resources from families. Demographic trends clearly show steady increases in the number of dual-income couples. Yet dual-income couples are more likely to report fatigue and sexual dysfunction, and spend less intimate time together.[28] There is some literature that suggests this is an artifact of dissatisfaction that is particular to the case of *part-time* working wives. And it is certainly the case that the satisfaction has to be specified by gender and total family income. Add the rigors and demands of parenthood to contemporary working families, and the need for relief is apparent. Our research leads us to the conclusion that churches can best offer resources and support to working families through small groups. When conscientiously designed, house church groups can offer rich emotional and spiritual resources for working parents, burned-out professionals, workaholics, and others struggling with work-related problems.

In some cases, the mutual concern for members in the house groups has been evidenced by financial aid. Church in the City helped to support several families whose breadwinners were laid off during the recession of the mid-1980s. In another case, the Houston Community Church paid the salary of a member whose union was on strike for eight months. The HCC maintains a permanent emergency fund for members' needs, one which is made possible largely because they have no mortgage. Few churches of their size, they argue, could do what they have done.

In less dramatic ways, our research turned up numerous examples of persons who had lost jobs and were aided financially by house church groups. Cho corroborates this pattern of economic assistance in his account of home cells in Korea, citing one case wherein a home cell group helped send a member to college.[29] Face-to-face association, mutual commitment, and shared religious expression are likely to increase a sense of accountability regarding other members' health and welfare. In one respect, the role of "citizen" is recovered, because the individual discovers a strong psychological identification with the community, the natural expressions of which are loyalty, compassion, and charity.

PROSPECTS FOR THE FUTURE

The viability of house church groups seems contingent upon several factors. First, house church groups appear to be most effective when they have linkage to and support from the local church. Autonomous groups are highly precarious and unstable, though they can also be very charismatic. There is a mutual exchange in the adoption of house church groups by the institutional church. House church groups can supply the church with a much-needed infusion of lay enthusiasm and leadership. On the other hand, house church groups can benefit from the support, direction, and resources of the local church. As long as the local church can support and direct house church groups—without suffocating them—such groups remain a viable force.

The demographic base for house church groups appears strong and likely to grow. Those most likely to attend, recall, are those with higher levels of education. The egalitarian and participatory structure of house church groups lends itself to this better-educated segment of the population, a segment destined to grow in the years ahead.

That same well-educated segment of the population may also feel most acutely the compartmentalization house church groups seem suited to overcoming. However, it is still unclear just how dedifferentiating these groups really are. The effects of house church group participation on work and family have been documented in a few cases, but these are still too few and too anecdotal to draw any hard-and-fast conclusions. Measuring attendence is not the same as studying attitudinal and behavioral effects. More research is needed to determine the quality and extent of change among house church group members with regard to family and work roles. Certainly, part of any success that house church groups might enjoy in the future is tied to their ability to realize these objectives.

Finally, there are some indications that baby-boomers are redisovering religion.[30] Given the anti-institutional styles of this age cohort, it seems likely that new spiritual yearnings will produce an increased interest in house church groups. Baby-boomers are better educated than older age cohorts, and as they become parents in larger numbers, they have shown an increase in worship attendence. The aging of the baby boom may well predicate a return to religion, and if previous patterns hold, they will not passively accept conventional arrangements and methods of worship. While they have yet to discover or embrace house church groups in significantly larger numbers than others, we can predict that this generation will engage in the sort of institutional innovation that is represented by these efforts to bring faith into the realm of family—and sometimes work—outside the walls of traditional church structures.

NOTES

1. The names have been changed to preserve anonymity.
2. Coauthors Kirk Hadaway and Francis DuBose and I have described these movements in more detail in *Home Cell Groups and House Churches: Emerging Alternatives for the Urban Church* (Nashville: Broadman, 1987). I am using "de-differentiation" here much as Frank Lechner uses it in describing fundamentalist movements in "Fundamentalism and Sociocultural Revitalization in America: A Sociological Interpretation" (*Sociological Analysis* 46 (3) (1985), pp. 243–260.
3. The effects of professionalizing the clergy have been written about by Thomas Luckmann in *The Invisible Religion* (New York: Macmillan, 1967). Other theorists who have developed these arguments about the relationship between religion and modernity include Peter Berger in *Facing Up to Modernity* (New York: Basic Books, 1978); Berger, with Brigette Berger and Hansfried Kellner, in *The Homeless Mind* (New York: Doubleday, 1974); and Berger with R. John Neuhaus, in *Against the World for the World* (New York: Seabury, 1976); as well as John M. Cuddihy, *No Offense: Civil Reigion and Protestant Taste* (New York: Seabury, 1974); and Neuhaus's *The Naked Public Square* (Grand Rapids: Eerdmans, 1984).
4. See Hadaway, Wright, and DuBose, *Home Cell Groups*, and Stuart Wright and C. Kirk Hadaway, "The House Church Movement: A Typology of

Groups" (paper presented to the meetings of the Religious Research Association, in Knoxville, November, 1983).

5. In addition to the sources on house churches already cited, see Philip Anderson and Phoebe Anderson, *The House Church* (Nashville: Abingdon, 1975); Lois Barrett, *Building the House Church* (Scottdale: Herald Press, 1986); Del Birkey, *The House Church: A Model for Renewing the Church* (Scottdale: Herald Press, 1988); Paul Y. Cho, *Successful Home Cell Groups* (Plainfield, NJ: Logos, 1981), and "Reaching Cities with Home Cells," *Urban Mission*, (January, 1984), pp. 4–14; Francis M. DuBose, "Alternative Church Models for an Urban Society," in Larry L. Rose and C. Kirk Hadaway, eds. *The Urban Challenge* (Nashville: Broadman, 1982), pp. 121–144; Arthur L. Foster, *The House Church Evolving* (Chicago: Exploration Press, 1976); Walter J. Hollenwager, "The House Church Movement in Great Britain" *Expository Time* 86 (1982), pp. 45–47; Charles Olsen, *The Base Church: Creating Community Through Multiple Forms* (Atlanta: Forum, 1973); Robert Raines, *New Life in the Church* (New York: Harper and Row, 1980); Lawrence Richards, *A New Face for the Church* (Grand Rapids: Zondervan, 1970); Ron Sider, *Living More Simply: Biblical Principles and Practical Models* (Downer's Grove: Intervarsity Press, 1980); Howard A. Snyder, *The Problem of Wineskins: Church Structure in a Technological Age* (1975), *Community of the King* (1977), and *Liberating the Church* (1983), all published by Intervarsity Press, Downer's Grove, IL; Joyce Thurmond, *New Wineskins: A Study of the House Church Movement* (Bern: Verland, 1982); and David L. Watson, *The Early Methodist Class Meeting: Its Origins and Significance* (Nashville: Cokesbury, 1985).

6. Princeton Religion Research Center, *The Unchurched American* (Princeton, NJ: 1988).

7. I do not intend to give any attention here to distinctions between types of house groups, since I have done that elsewhere (with Hadaway and DuBose, 1987). I want to use the term "house church group" generically, to include all of the groups we have previously identified.

8. Anderson and Anderson, *The House Church*; along with Francis DuBose, "Alternative Church Models"; and Howard Snyder, *The Problem of Wineskins*.

9. This analogy is developed by Cho, *Successful Home Cell Groups*, and by Richards, *A New Face for the Church*.

10. W. Widick Schroeder, "A Sociological and Theological Critique of the House Church Movement" in Arthur L. Foster, ed. *The House Church Evolving*, pp. 53–54.

11. On small groups, see Hyman and Wright, 1971; Michael Hechter, *Principles of Group Solidarity* (Berkeley: University of California Press, 1987); Cecilia Ridgeway, *The Dynamics of Small Groups* (New York: St. Martin's, 1983); Michael Olmsted and A. Paul Hare, *The Small Group* (New York: Random House, 1978); John H. Marx and Burkhardt Holzner, "Ideological Primary Groups in Contemporary Cultural Movements,

Sociological Focus 8 (4) (1975), pp. 311–329; and Theodore Newcomb, "Stabilities Underlying Changes in Interpersonal Attraction," pp. 82–95 in Richard Ofshe, ed., *Interpersonal Behavior in Small Groups* (Englewood Cliffs: Prentice-Hall, 1973), pp. 82–95. On small churches, see Jackson Carroll, *Small Churches are Beautiful* (New York: Harper and Row, 1977); and Carl Dudley, *Making the Small Church Effective* (Nashville: Abingdon, 1978).

12. Snyder, *The Problem of Wineskins*.

13. See Hadaway, Wright, and DuBose, *Home Cell Groups*.

14. Wade Clark Roof, *A Generation of Seekers: The Spiritual Journeys of the Baby Boom Generation* (San Francisco: Harper San Francisco, 1993).

15. See *American Mainline Religion*, Chap. 2.

16. Quoted in Gerald Renner, "Power Changes at the Mainstream's Helm," *Progressions: A Lilly Endowment Occasional Report* 2 (1) (1990), p. 12.

17. Peter Berger, "Secularization and Pluralism," *Yearbook for the Sociology of Religion* 2 (1966), pp. 73–90; and his *Facing Up to Modernity*; David Martin, *A General Theory of Secularization* (New York: Harper and Row, 1978); and Bryan Wilson, *Religion in a Secular Society* (London: C. A. Watts, 1966).

18. *The Social Construction of Reality* (New York: Anchor, 1966) p. 158.

19. Cho, *Successful Home Cell Groups*, and "Reaching Cities."

20. While the topics covered in the conference are quite far-ranging, the predominant theme, in my judgment, has been church growth. However, the expanding range of subjects each year suggests a direction that is more comprehensive.

21. On shifting functions, see Ernest W. Burgess and Harvey J. Locke, *The Family: From Institution to Companionship* (New York: Macmillan, 1945). On the family as emotional haven, see Christopher Lasch, *Haven in a Heartless World* (New York: Basic Books, 1976).

22. Joan Aldous, "Problematic Elements in the Relationships between Churches and Families," in William V. D'Antonio and Joan Aldous, eds., *Families and Religions: Conflict and Change in Modern Society* (Beverly Hills: Sage, 1983), p. 69.

23. Robert Bellah, *et al.*, *Habits of the Heart* (Berkeley: University of California Press, 1985).

24. Bellah, *et al.*, *Habits*, p. 38.

25. Robert Bellah, *The Broken Covenant* (New York: Seabury, 1975).

26. Max Weber, *The Protestant Ethic and the Spirit of Capitalism* (New York: Scribner's, 1905/1958).

27. See William D'Antonio, "Family Life, Religion, and Societal Values and Structures," in W. D'Antonio and J. Aldous, eds., *Families and Religions*.

28. C. Avery-Clark, "Career Women Most Likely to Suffer from Inhibited Sexual Desire," *Behavior Today Newsletter* 16 (August, 1985), pp. 4–6;

James C. Coleman, *Intimate Relationships: Marriage and Family* (New York: Macmillan, 1988); and George Masnick and Mary Jo Bane, *The Nation's Families: 1960–1990* (Cambridge: M.I.T.-Harvard Joint Center for Urban Studies, 1980).

29. Cho, *Successful Home Cell Groups*.

30. See David A. Roozen, William McKinney, and Wayne Thompson, "The 'Big Chill' Warms to Worship" *Review of Religious Research*, 31 (1990), pp. 314–322; Cheryl Russell, *100 Predictions for the Baby Boom* (New York: Plenum Press, 1987); and Wade Clark Roof, *A Generation of Seekers*.

13

Constructing Women's Rituals

Roman Catholic Women and "Limina"[1]

Mary Jo Neitz

SUMMER SOLSTICE, JUNE 21, 1989

After carefully following the intricate directions, driving through affluent suburbs for what seemed like forever, my companion and I arrived at the modern Unitarian church building where Limina was holding its summer solstice ritual.

People were gathering at 5:30 P.M. The event would begin then with "aperitifs," according to the printed schedule we had received along with the directions. We were taken to a registration desk, where we put the flowers we had been asked to bring in a pail of water. We wrote our names on name tags and were shown to the book exhibit and to a table where soft drinks, beer, and wine were available.

Most of the event took place in two rooms of the church. The ritual itself mostly occurred in the sanctuary. The sanctuary's large, round, center space—cleared out except for an "altar"—featured four large panels (two feet by four) painted with acrylics, depicting Native American women in four stages of the life cycle. The panels stood on a base that raised them about two feet off the ground, which also provided a shelf extending a foot from the panels. On the shelf was a garland of greens with a few daisies woven in. At the back of the room, in a raised area, nine round tables, each seating eight people, had been placed. A light-yellow cloth covered each table, and each had a carafe of iced tea.

About seventy women gathered for the event, ranging from teenagers to an eighty-nine-year-old. The theme of the evening's meeting was the initiation of young girls into womanhood. While we stood in an anteroom next to the sanctuary, the leaders of the ritual told us about the symbolism of the wheel of life. They pointed out connections between three different kinds of rotations: (1) seasons of the year—spring, summer, fall, winter; (2) stages of life cycle—youth, fertile years, midlife and old age; and (3) inner characteristics—temperaments that people are born with.

Tesse, one of the founders, began her opening monologue at about 6:30 P.M. She introduced the symbolism of the wheel, as well as some ideas about Native American spirituality and what it might mean to Americans today. She said that the object of life for Native American traditions was "to walk in beauty," not "to do one's duty." She also said that we needed to learn how to recognize beauty. Tesse suggested that people are now gravitating toward Native American spirituality because of a common concern for the earth, and a sense of connection with this land that shaped our religious and legal traditions and shaped us as Americans.

Cathal, another Limina founder, led a short, guided meditation. She had everyone in the group remember the child within herself—the uninitiated girl. She suggested we bring to mind the names we had been called as children, and shared that she had been called "mouse." Her meditation was gentle and short. She commented that the wheel's correlation of temperament with the season of the year in which a person is born corresponds to what psychologists now say about individuals not coming into the world as a *tabula rasa* to be written on by their parents; rather, at birth we seem to possess a specific personality.

Then Cathal and Tesse divided us into groups, based on where we were born on the wheel. In the symbol system they had borrowed for this ceremony, the four directions correspond with the seasons of the year and with the four elements (fire, earth, water, and air), each of which also stands for a temperament. After describing the temperaments, they asked each participant to identify the one she had been given at birth—according to her month of birth. Then they had us line up according to sign in order to walk in a procession into the sanctuary. This lining up was done with some joking. Cathal personalized this part of the ceremony by recognizing her mother and her sister explicitly when she came to the signs for their seasons.

For the procession they taught us a simple dance step (identified as Ojibwa), and, accompanied by a drum beat, the seventy women entered the sanctuary. As the group began to move into the sanctuary, many of the women who were part of the planning group—and had been bustling about in preparation for the main part of the ritual—transformed themselves, donning ritual decorations, including capes, special jewelry, and elaborate masks made of feathers. As we entered the room, we were given two flowers, and when we walked past the four panels, we placed our flowers on the garland.

Tesse and Cathal walked in together. Tesse wore a basic black dress, black patent leather pumps, and dramatic turquoise jewelry. Her grey hair was cut in a neat, short style, and she wore very little makeup. She looked very much the suburban matron—except for the life-sized, carved, wooden snake wrapped around her neck. She led the procession with an air of confidence, melding her worlds of conventional roles and New Age ritualist.

Once in the sanctuary, the group formed a circle around the panels in the center of the room. The leaders of the evening's ceremony—all wearing symbols of some kind—came forward and gave their gifts to the group, including such things as fire, an ear of corn, water, earth, and the spirit of peace symbolized by a peace pipe.

This was followed by a dance of the wheel. The dance for the element fire was introduced first, with a drum beat and a leaping motion. Then earth was given another drum beat and a low-to-the-ground motion. Fluid body movements to the sound of a xylophone represented water. Air's dance used high hand motions accompanied by a recorder. First the groups embodying each element practiced in turn, then all danced together, each woman supposedly dancing her temperament. When leaders announced that the women could move from one place on the wheel to another one, symbolizing the possibility of change during the life course, many did so.

After dancing, the group broke for dinner. One of the women who had brought a gift to the circle headed each table. They guided the conversation through a set of questions in keeping with the theme of recognizing womanhood. The first set of questions asked about the experience of beginning to menstruate. The second set of questions evoked discussion of a moment when each woman "knew she was a woman."

As a way of introducing us to each other, the facilitator asked the women seated at her table to give their names, and then to "put something in the center of the table," using the wheel symbolism. They suggested that we take a symbol from the dance, or talk about where we were born and where we had moved to on the wheel. The introduction of the subject of menarche (over dinner) began slowly, but each woman told her story.

The facilitators introduced the next question by saying that, although we all experienced menarche, that physical change did not necessarily mark the point at which we became conscious of ourselves as women. Each facilitator asked for the telling of "the internal story," and led in the telling of what had happened inside each person that made her realize that she was a woman—an adult. For some women at the table, stories came immediately to mind. The topic seemed less daunting than that of the previous question.

As we finished the round of questions, Lil, the third founder, asked for the attention of the entire group. She said that with the questions some painful memories had come up, and that maybe the group needed a moment of healing. We held hands with one another while she said a short, impromptu prayer. Although this had not been planned, it was clearly important for some of the women at my table.

This section of the ritual ended with the singing of two songs, the first a rousing song about becoming a wild woman, the second calmer and solemn.

During the first section of the ritual, while the older women talked about their experiences, the initiates sat together at a table by themselves with their own set of questions. They were now asked to come before the group with their mothers and sponsors. Those hoping to be initiated into womanhood in this ritual stood in front of the group, while Lil told an initiation story (in the first person) from a Northwest

Native American tribe. The rest of the women listened attentively from their places at the tables. The story told of a girl being made strong by her grandmother—taught first to run in the sand, and then in the water, and finally to swim. At the time of her first menstruation, the women of her family made a cape of feathers and then a dugout for her. They took the young girl out into the ocean, and she had to swim back, returning to a feast in her honor. The event marked a transformation: she knew that she was now an adult, and ready to have children.

After hearing the story, the women of the group moved into a circle around the girls, and then escorted the girls and their mothers or sponsors to the door of the church. The girls were to run around the building—at first holding hands with their mothers, then breaking away from their mothers and completing the journey on their own. The rest of the women in the group met the girls at the other doorway and formed a "birth canal" through which the girls had to pass.

When all of the girls had returned, now ritually reborn as adult women, everyone once again formed a circle with the girls in the middle. Each girl was given a card with the Limina symbol to wear around her neck, and a candle. Each one took the candle and put it on the altar, with a statement about what she wanted to affirm or ask for from the ceremony. Then the girls danced "the girls' dance," to a song by Madonna that they had chosen for themselves. Toward the end of the song the other women were asked to join in, and everyone danced. At first each person dancing individually, then individuals began to hold hands and to move into a spiral. The ceremony ended with a healing song—sung as a round—and the Limina dance which closes every Limina event. The women present form two circles: an inner circle composed mostly of active Limina participants—including those who had organized and led the evening's event—and an outer circle composed of everyone else. The two circles moved in opposite directions— as the women faced each other and took a forward step, then moved away with a backward step, and, stepping sideways in opposite directions, faced a new person to begin again.

My companion, on the way home, said that the event helped her to feel good about her body and to recover something that she had not gotten from her mother, but wished that she had. The solstice ritual provided a passage for the adolescent girls, but also, as Cathal had suggested early in the evening, provided a passage for the part of each person that was still a young girl needing acceptance.

—

This ritual event brings together women at all stages in the life cycle in a way that celebrates the lives and bodies of women, along with the connections among women—mothers and daughters, women without children, old and young. It celebrates the work of women and all of the ways women bring beauty and wisdom and community to the world around them. Through the work of creating new rituals, Limina women are redefining what it means for them to be women, to be family, to have a work to do in the world.

CHANGING SYMBOLS

Limina rituals are elaborately planned. Although they do have some flexibility, and there are usually some innovations as the event proceeds, much effort goes into designing and scripting an event which combines many experiential modes into what is hoped will be a transformative ritual. Cathal Rich, a visual artist and a psychologist with her own therapy practice, contributes visual art work appropriate to the occasion. Her art works reflect the themes of the ceremony, with images of women drawn from many different cultures. (The summer solstice ritual is unusual in its exclusive reliance on Native American symbolism; several seasonal rituals draw from Celtic feasts, and use symbols from many times and places—from Baubo to bag ladies. See Below.) Music is always part of a Limina ritual, often including contributions by skilled musicians on a variety of instruments. The rituals incorporate movement, as in the dancing that takes place at various times in the summer solstice ritual. Finally, there is always a social component, where food and drink are shared and informal conversations can be enjoyed.

The Limina rituals include a reflective aspect, asking the women present to turn inward and look at themselves. Other parts, however, draw the focus back to the community—the group of women present, and also the wider community. Limina members raise issues that concern them as citizens of the world.

While, for some people, the concept of ritual calls to mind habitual activities, engaged with little reflection on content or meaning, that is not what is meant in this case. Here rituals are actively constructed by the leaders and participants. They are acts of bricolage, using symbols and stories from various times and places, combined in a form that has special meaning for participants. These rituals are part of a larger effort to find symbolic expressions that are both relevant and sacred. During times of rapid social change, "traditional" ritual forms often change, incorporating new experiences and making them holy.

When I studied the Catholic charismatics I was struck, for instance, by new images of God that were very different from those I had grown up with in the pre-Vatican II Roman Catholic church. The charismatics that I knew cultivated "personal relationships" with God. But the God the Father, with whom they spoke on a regular basis, was Daddy-god, not a powerful creator and stern judge, but an affectionate and nurturing parent who "loves you just the way you are." I came to interpret the charismatic renewal as a revisioning of the Catholic God symbols and family norms, in an attempt to bring authoritarian, patriarchal, Catholic families into the twentieth century.[2] I have argued that female charismatics took part in this revision in part because it allowed them to demand considerable change in men's roles. It was not without cost for them, insofar as they accepted the teaching that "wives should be submissive to their husbands." However, the husbands they were "submitting to" defined their roles very differently from how their fathers had.

The founders and participants in Limina are seeking to redefine the symbols of the divine, as well as the daily practices of women, in more radical ways. These women—a large proportion of whom come out of Catholic traditions—are designing and conducting public rituals that seek to explore and express the sacredness of women's lives as they live upon the earth. As I hope to show in this chapter, this effort constitutes a "public work" for these women, whom I see as engaged also in a larger process of redefining the gendered nature of public and private space in our culture.

LIMINA

Limina is a women's spirituality group based in Oak Park, Illinois. Founded by three Irish-American, Roman Catholic women in the mid-1980s, it organizes rituals and workshops that explore "the feminine aspect of the divine, [promote] community among women, and [celebrate] the many forms of womanhood and the changes of our lives and the earth herself."[3] Limina takes its name from the Latin word for threshold. The notion of threshold takes on many meanings for the three founders. They talk about the various passages they observe and celebrate, including the passages through the cycle of a woman's life, from birth to menarche, to maternity, to menopause, to death, and the seasons of the year from winter to spring, to summer, to fall, to winter. They also believe that our society stands at a threshold, of choosing life or participating in the death of all life on the planet.

The three founders have worked together in Catholic social action and community projects for nearly two decades. They helped to start an alternative high school and an alternate Catholic parish in their community. Limina itself came out of retreats and workshops that they organized together, originally under the sponsorship of St. Giles, the alternative Catholic parish where one of them was employed as the liturgist. Later they continued their work together in connection with various colleges in the area. Finally, they became frustrated with having to negotiate with an institutional sponsor each time they had activities they wanted to do, and in 1985 decided to incorporate. In addition to the three founders, in the late 1980s the organization had a twelve-member board and a large membership—fourteen hundred women who had come to at least one event and paid a yearly membership fee (fifteen dollars in 1989).[4]

Limina's ties to the Catholic church are informal and not exclusive. The strongest tie is perhaps the training and decades of experience in liturgical innovation the founders shared as a part of an alternative parish. Many, but not all, of the members are Catholics or ex-Catholics. The board of directors includes two women who are members of Roman Catholic religious orders, and some grant support has come from orders of Catholic sisters. But the board also includes several women who are Quakers, and at least one woman recently ordained as an American Baptist minister. Limina has no official status, and does not present itself as a Roman Catholic organization. It makes no references to any church in its literature, and the founders emphasize the ecumenical nature of the group.

Originally Limina events took place in Catholic spaces—churches, hospital chapels, and Newman centers in the Chicago area—but they no longer do so. Places that had allowed Limina to rent space early on became quite cautious about doing so when the events engendered negative reactions from right-wing Catholic groups. Many of the rituals do employ Catholic symbolism; for example, the Virgin Mary may be present, along with other "goddess" images from different cultures. Insofar as Limina is Catholic, however, it is culturally Catholic rather than institutionally so. While they lack the support of the institutional church, Limina rituals draw women who then draw on their common experiences. Much of their recruiting, in fact, is done through Catholic networks.[5] To the extent that Limina events feel Catholic—and the rituals I have witnessed do feel Catholic to me, although the extent to which this is so depends on the particular ritual—it is because of what the organizers and the participants bring with them, as much as because of specific words or symbols.

CONSTRUCTING RITUALS AND CELEBRATING WOMANHOOD

Limina has had two thrusts. One is to develop rituals and a liturgical cycle that meet the needs of contemporary women. They perform seasonal rituals during the year, and hope one day to be able to publish their formats for others to use. The body of seasonal rituals constitutes a "wheel of the year" or a liturgical calendar, drawing on pre-Christian (as well as Christianized) holidays and symbols. The other thrust is the creation of new symbols and celebrations that work for the empowerment of women in ritual contexts and performances. These events are not part of an ancient liturgical cycle. Yet, like the women's wheel of the year, these rituals are designed to awaken women to the pride and power of belonging to a community of women.

One of the founders speaks here about their original event, "The Goddesses and the Wild Woman":

> [We initiated] a large program—a large event that breaks open new territory. "The Goddesses and the Wild Woman" was a way of opening up a very large spectrum of archetypal feminine…the deep feminine, opening this up with many images, many possibilities. Jean Bolen's book [*Goddesses in Everywoman*] does the same thing. The difference in Limina…is to use the heat of the persons who are present in such an event as transformational energy for them, so that the ritual, and dance, and so on bring the participant to a pitch in which some kind of newness, or some kind of healing thing [takes place]…. It's big enough to touch the soul….
>
> In a container of those who are agreeable to you, supportive of you, ritually…you show that you're giving away the blood, giving away the milk…. You do that in a ritual sense. The fact of it has already occurred. The ritual reintegrates you into the society as being a beloved figure, and not a discard. And being a wise woman. That's how you should come out of such a day's ritual. With those things that are denigrated being transformed into value.

Transforming women's lives has, of course, long been a goal of feminist groups. I talked with Tesse about where she saw Limina in relation to feminism. She said that she did not use the word very much anymore, certainly not as freely as she had in the seventies. Tesse added that she saw herself as part of the women's movement—that the women's movement had saved her life. She said that through it she recovered her self which had been lost in her family. She had belonged to a woman's group for nine years, and that had been central to who she was. What she cared about for Limina, however, was initiating women into the community of women, not whether or not they used the term feminism.

Limina is part of what has been called the women's spirituality movement. If we were to imagine that movement as a spectrum, with Wiccans and Dianic lesbian feminist witches on one end, and liberal groups seeking reforms in the established churches (such as the ordination of women and the integration of women into the existing power structure) on the other end, Limina is somewhere in the middle.[6] As an organization, Limina does not choose to work at reforming the institutional church. One of the founders tells a story that illustrates her priorities. A women's organization associated with the cathedral of a neighboring diocese called and asked her to give a speech on women and the church. She was not sure she wanted to give a speech to the women of the cathedral, and so she told her inviter that she was not really interested in that topic. They discussed what she would be willing to talk about, and she proposed a title she felt would be rejected: "Who is the Goddess? And What Does She Want?" The topic was not rejected, however, and she gave the talk, finding the women surprisingly receptive to what she had to say.

While Limina maintains some distance from institutional church concerns, it also keeps its distance from the most radical wing of women's spirituality. Although their liturgical calendar and symbolism evoke that of neopagan and feminist witchcraft, the leaders of the movement are careful to separate themselves from those who would call themselves witches. Privately, the Limina board members whom I interviewed felt they had learned from and could use material from Wiccan and New Age sources, such as Starhawk's *Spiral Dance* and Vicki Noble's *Motherpeace* tarot deck. Yet they all wanted distance from the label "witch." One board member gave reasons which included both her personal uneasiness with the label, and her feelings that such associations were dangerous for the organization:

> I don't like being called a witch. You know, I—the word witch had a wonderful reputation at one time I think. It was the old women who lived on the boundaries with their herbs and everything, and also it could have been the midwives and all. And that's been given a bad name over time, by men. And priests! We've been called witches. The four of us [the three founders plus the part-time administrator] have been called witches to drive away other women.... In the first couple of years when we went to Catholic places to do our things we almost had pickets. The far right was on our tail for the first two years. We no longer go to Catholic centers to do our work.

The last time we used the Newman Center was two winter solstices ago. And those poor people were put through hell for the weeks before we got there…. They [people protesting Limina's presence] called that center daily. I mean, there's a far right hotline you can call everyday and they tell you what's happening and who to harass! It's been after us for a while now. And we've been labeled witches to keep other women away…. If women go from us to that [Wicca], that's fine. But it frightens women away to be—to be thought of as part of the witch thing, because there's that association. Personally I'd rather not say that we were witches. I mean, we use the term crones. And that's, you know, we feel more comfortable with that.

Limina shares with feminism the goal of empowering women. In conjunction with other groups throughout the spectrum of the women's spirituality movement, Limina seeks to effect such empowerment through transforming rituals, many but not all of which are connected to the liturgical cycle. Limina does not take the radical step of embracing the identity of pagan/witch, yet it has faced more harassment than some groups which do accept that label. Because the most radical women's spirituality groups do not usually perform their rituals in public, they do not draw the criticism that a public group like Limina draws. But Limina's harassment has come primarily from groups of conservative Catholics, who see Limina rituals as threatening. While Limina has tried to distance itself from the Catholic Church, its founders have reputations within Catholic circles as people who have consistently challenged the church from within. Even without intending it, the symbols and rituals they are creating are seen as an implicit (and threatening) call for change.

SYMBOLS OF THE FEMININE DIVINE

When the founders talk about historical roots, they are likely to talk about the "Celtic [catholic] Church" as opposed to either the Roman Catholics or the Celtic pagans.[7] They take the somewhat ambiguous symbol of the triple spiral (Figure 1, below) from the Newgrange site in Ireland as the symbol of the group. This ancient symbol (circa 3,200 BC) of three united in one is believed to have symbolized the Irish triple goddess Brigit to neolithic Celts.[8] Celtic Christians retained the symbol but changed its meaning: for them it stood for the three persons in one God. The women of Limina return it to the older meaning.

Limina's literature claims that the organization is "seeking to reintegrate the feminine aspect of the divine into contemporary life." Combining seasonal changes, women's life cycle changes, Ericksonian

FIGURE 1
Limina Symbol

psychology, and ancient Celtic holidays, Limina founders developed a basic liturgical cycle. (See Figure 2.)

One of the founders talked about the need for such a calendar:

> I think maybe because of our link with menstruation and our link with time, women are, whether they're Catholic or not, have a greater orientation toward wanting that kind of calendar. Also, you know, it's actually in the seasons of the year…it's in the whole of nature. And the [Catholic] Church…based the liturgical calendar on that…. I think in general the reason that [the Limina calendar] is so powerfully affirming and positive is because of the need there. [With regard to menstrual cycles] there's a need there within women to say, "Yes, this is a continuing experience of my life from the time I'm twelve years old till I'm fifty years old." Does one make meaning out of this or does one just say, "you're on the rag?" Is there a spiritual orientation for this? Does one's spirituality include this?

Based on the solar cycle, the Limina calendar, called "Seasons of a Woman's Life," adds layers of meaning, providing a powerful set of symbols for Limina women to draw upon in developing their own spirituality.

Limina interprets the seasonal holidays in a way that blends Catholic and pagan elements. The Catholic Church itself practiced considerable syncretism, especially in absorbing local holidays to fit with its yearly cycles, and local goddesses and gods to fit into the new configuration of father/mother/son and the pantheon of saints.[9] Limina celebrates the summer solstice on or close to June 21. For the winter solstice, they celebrate a ritual which they call "preparing for the winter solstice," closer to December 8. For Roman Catholics, this is the feast day of the

FIGURE 1
The Calendar/Seasons of a Woman's Life

Immaculate Conception of the Virgin Mary. Limina programs for this holiday have included such elements as having someone appear in ritual as Our Lady of Guadalupe, proclaiming her identity with the Great Goddess.

Limina's liturgical season, like that of contemporary neopagan groups, borrows the solar holidays held on the solstices and equinoxes. It also borrows the Celtic feasts traditionally celebrated on the cross-quarter days. These fall exactly between the solstices and equinoxes.[10] Taken together there are eight major holidays, although Limina does not celebrate all of them in a given year. November 1, for example, falls between the fall equinox and the winter solstice. The old Celtic feast was "Samhain" or "Hallows." Christianized, it became "All Saints Day," and was preceded by "All Souls Day."[11] Samhain was a feast of the dead, and the beginning of the new year. For Limina it is a solemn feast, and one where crones—the wise "old" (postmenopausal) women of the community—have been honored. Limina also celebrates another, less-known holiday: February 2, between the winter solstice and the vernal equinox. It is known in various traditions as Brigit's Day, or Candlemas, or Imbolc; but at Limina, it is Ground Hag's Day. For Celtic pagans and Christians it was a traditional time of purification and healing, bringing hope with the coming of light and spring. May 1, between the vernal equinox and the summer solstice, is Beltane in the Celtic calendar. Although the Catholic Church claimed May Day as a feast for Mary, in recent years this has been a time when Limina has looked at gender relations, sometimes preparing programs with men. In 1990, for example, they held a "Beating the Beltane Blues" gathering, with the intention of recognizing a history of pain, but also anticipating a future in which reconciliation is possible.[12]

In celebrating these holidays, Limina draws on connections between the Celtic and solar holidays and the holidays many Limina participants remember from their Roman Catholic childhoods, connections that exist because the early church incorporated so many pagan holidays into its own liturgical cycle. At the same time, Limina transforms the holidays by connecting them specifically to the cycles of women's lives. Limina founders hope that this will also contribute to the transformation of women's lives by helping them to recognize the sacred in their ordinary experiences.

Another symbol, the Wildwoman, is less clearly derived from ancient traditions, and more the invention of two Limina founders, Lil Lewis and Cathal Rich. Symbol systems that celebrate women's life cycle events often seem to focus on images of women as fertile and nurturing. In the Christian tradition, the Virgin Mother holding her plump infant son exemplifies this image: women as mothers can be Madonna-like. Among mainstream neopagans we also find emphasis on images of young and beautiful goddesses. The dominant images of women are images of "maidens" and "mothers." The third stage, that of the post-menopausal woman, or the crone, is one that is less common but of increasing interest to women in the Goddess movement.[13] Lil Lewis's Wildwoman is the crone, but this crone is more than the bringer of death.

Limina's first performance was based on the symbol of the Wildwoman. Her creator, Lil Lewis, connects her with Baubo in the Demeter-Persephone story: Baubo was the old woman who met Demeter after she had been mourning the loss of her daughter. In the myth, Baubo moons Demeter, and Demeter laughs. Distracted from her sorrow Demeter then notices that without her attention the fields have turned to stubble. In addition, Lewis sees the old women of the fairy tales as models for the Wildwoman.[14] In the visual image produced by Cathal Rich the wise woman is connected to the earth and the heavens; she wears the stole of the priest/ess, but her stole of corn, grapes, and roses comes from nature. She is dancing in a mud puddle from which a flower blooms. She carries in her hand a frying pan, which is in place of the traditional witch's cauldron, and is woman's instrument of transformation: with it she "cooks," transforming raw nature in the process.

While the Wildwoman is beloved by many of Limina's members, in recent years she has been supplemented by other figures, especially images of women of color. Limina women have been challenged to carry their message of affirmation of women into communities beyond their original Irish Catholic base. A dream of some of the women who saw the first Wildwoman performance was to take Limina presentations into prison populations. The founders recognized that, in order to meaningfully expand their base in this way, they also needed to expand their imagery. They set about learning about goddesses of color, collecting visual material, and working with the bureaucracy to get permission to offer Limina programs to women within the Metropolitan Corrections Center. They raised money to produce their "Goddesses of Color" programs on video, and the first screenings occurred in 1993.

In addition, summer solstice celebrations feature Native American imagery. The initial summer solstice using this theme is described at the beginning of this chapter, but Limina leaders have continued to hone their production. Current borrowings are attributed to specific cultures, and are done with more awareness of the controversies that exist about the appropriation of Native American spirituality by whites. Starting in 1991, the Mescalero Apaches' initiation ritual, *na ih es*, has shaped Limina's summer solstice ritual. In an article in the newsletter, Tesse Donnelly explains what they are doing and why:

> When our situation as women in a wilderness weighs heavily on our hearts, it is encouraging to retell for ourselves and our daughters the story of the Mescalero *na ih es*. The Mescalero Apache have had the creativity and resilience to recover and restore a ceremony forbidden for many years by the laws of the United States. Perhaps we can do the same....
>
> At the Limina Solstice festival, we tell the story of the Apache girl's initiation, rooted in the myth of Changing Woman, to encourage us in our own forgotten story.... We "quote" from the ceremony in our own brief

ritual in the same spirit as film makers pay homage to admired predecessors by "quoting" them in their films.[15]

In addition to borrowing from Native American women, the images of African and Asian goddesses and women featured in the "Goddesses of Color" project have begun to diffuse through other Limina programs, as well as in their art-work—such as the yearly solstice cards designed by Cathal Rich and available for purchase by members. All of this is part of the cultural milieu that Limina provides. The message of affirmation continues, but the images used to convey it are still in flux.

LIMINA, WOMEN, AND THEIR FAMILIES

As a women-only group, Limina may be thought to draw women away from their families.[16] On the contrary, Limina supports women's traditional family roles, but it does not do so exclusively. In the first place, while they are based on traditional seasonal holidays, Limina rituals do not compete directly with the usual family celebrations. For example, although Imbolc/Candlemas was incorporated into the Christian calendar, it is not a holiday most modern Christians observe. We may recognize "Ground Hog's Day" as a folk tradition, but it requires little from us. When Limina appropriates this holiday, the ancient roots are real, but the reclaiming of it for a women's ritual takes nothing from the family lives of participants. Similarly, Limina avoids conflict with traditional Christmas and New Year's family obligations by celebrating "Preparing for the Solstice" (rather than the actual winter solstice). This holiday in early December nurtures members by giving them a time for themselves, and by connecting them to the broader world outside their families at a time when family responsibilities can be overwhelming.

In addition, Limina rituals affirm ties between mothers, daughters, and sisters. In women's spirituality, the words sister, daughter, maiden, mother, crone, are metaphoric. They stand for idealized relationships between women. Yet one of the striking things about the Limina rituals I have observed is the presence of women related by blood. Women's rituals, as celebrated by Limina, seem to strengthen matrilineal ties. At the summer solstice described above, the theme was the coming of young girls into womanhood and the celebration of menarche. That year there were fifteen teenage girls being initiated. Many were the daughters of regular Limina participants. But some of the daughters had brought mothers who were not members. Middle-aged Limina participants were there with their mothers and sisters. Although the summer solstice ritual is about separation, it affirms bonds between mothers and daughters.

In Limina's interpretation, the community of women represents the ways that it is valuable for women to share their individual experiences as they pass through the life cycle: the liminal moment in a passage ritual illuminates knowledge that one woman shares with another, from the maiden to the crone as well as from the crone to the maiden. Each seasonal ritual focuses on a particular place in the life cycle, but the emphasis is on passage. The summer solstice ritual described at the beginning of this chapter is an example. Mothers and daughters who are struggling with issues of separation (as well as the impact of the age grading of this society) find affirmation in a ceremony where separation is symbolically achieved. Each acknowledges the autonomy of the other as they both acknowledge their common participation in the community of women.

Limina rituals celebrate mothers, daughters, sisters, and grandmothers as coparticipants in the community of women. Yet membership in the community of women is not dependent upon the fulfillment of these particular roles, and the roles themselves are seen in a multifaceted way. Family roles are honored and validated, without mandating them. We are in a time in which women face "hard choices" about work and family roles, and experience conflicted emotions as they attempt to perform these roles. Regardless of their choices and circumstances, many women feel defensive about their inability to live up to their own expectations and what they imagine to be the expectations of others.[17] Limina rituals provide a context in which family roles are connected to other roles of women in the community. Women for whom motherhood is currently a central role share the space with other women who have never married or had children—in Limina this includes "wise women" who are Sisters, women members of religious orders who have made careers as social activists. An intentionally inclusive vision of a "community of women" recognizes women's family roles, and attempts to place those roles in a broader context. It assumes that women's work has a public as well as a private meaning.

PUBLIC RITUALS AND WOMEN'S WORK

In an obvious way, a calendar based on the cycles of a woman's life affirms mothering and childbearing, as well as the passages into and out of those states. It makes sacred these parts of women's lives: the traditional work of women is made sacred. Yet Limina's rituals go beyond this, just as Limina's leaders have gone beyond conventional definitions of those traditional roles in their own lives. In addition to celebrating the maiden and the mother, they celebrate the mature woman, who is past childbearing and has the time and energy and wisdom to work for others, "bearing the world" as their calendar describes it. They also celebrate the crone, the hag, the older woman.

Doing this in public rituals has another effect. It says that these passages are not private biological matters to be ignored, or at least hidden, by the civilized woman, but that they have collective meaning within the community of women. Tesse Donnelly said to me: "I believe women must always have a role in public life and—and that every woman needs a work, but not every woman needs a job." Feminist theorists have written about how the traditional dichotomy between the public and the private has been a powerful source of women's inequality.[18] One way to understand the importance of these rituals is to see them as the "public work" of these women, aimed at breaking down such distinctions and promoting equality.

Liberal feminists suggested that the subordination of women through the dichotomy between public and private life could be dismantled by the entry of women into the public arenas which have been the domain of men. Radical feminists argued that the "personal is political." They argued that the public power of males, including the state, was heavily involved in the continuing subordination of women in areas believed to be most private, such as sexual relations and the family. Socialist feminists argued that in fact the public and private domains were intimately connected, and that women's work in families reproduced the labor that was required for other labor to take place.

The Limina women, through their practices, are also criticizing and dismantling the dichotomy between public and private. Their challenge in the domain of religious symbols has special significance, given the churches' collaboration in restricting women to the private domain. Rather than advocating that the only solution is to enter male domains, these women are calling for a reevaluation of the feminine and the creation of feminine symbols and rituals.

In a sense then, these women are using a liturgical mode to affirm a definition of work that is quite different from that found in the world at large. It is at odds with the notion that the value of one's work is defined by the size of one's paycheck. Yet it also does not find a refuge in "woman's nature"; it only partly supports a traditional definition of women's work. Limina women seek to develop a criterion for evaluating meaningful work based on the contribution it makes to the common good, and the common good here extends beyond the household.

Other studies of women who have taken on "public work" as activists and community leaders have demonstrated that those women's concerns were originally generated by issues they faced as mothers. Cheryl Gilkes, in her study of Black women community leaders, states: "The problems they faced in helping to support and educate their families were transformed from private troubles to public issues."[19] In her study of low-income Black women and Latinas who had paid work as community activists, Nancy Naples found that the women did not distinguish between their paid and unpaid work. She argues that the distinction between the public and private does not make sense of what they do.[20]

The middle-class, Irish Catholic, suburban women who make up the majority of Limina leaders and founders are situated differently from women studied by Gilkes and Naples, but their community work originated in similar sources: their personal concerns about local institutions, such as schools and churches.[21] For all of these women, becoming an activist meant going beyond traditional definitions of women's work. The women studied by Gilkes and Naples remained focused primarily on the exigencies of living in a particular, geographically defined community. However, for the Limina women, most of whom live in more affluent neighborhoods, community came to be defined in a more abstract way, as the community of women. While Limina in part constitutes such a community, the members see themselves as part of a movement to recover and create the community of women. It is for this reason that the summer solstice initiation ritual, which symbolically brings a new group of young women into the larger community of women, is perhaps the most institutionalized of Limina events.

CONCLUSION

Limina offers a redefinition of family and work in its creative reenactment of women's experience through public rituals. The status of the new symbols is, of course, contested in the public realm. Such "public works" are not entered into without considerable risk. This is especially true in the highly polarized realm of today's Catholic Church. Nevertheless, Limina women continue to challenge the boundaries between public and private domains. And in doing so they enact new relations between family, faith, and work.

NOTES

1. I would like to thank Nancy Ammerman for her keen editorial guidance on several drafts of this chapter. Patricia Monaghan and Peter Mueser also

read drafts, and provided useful comments. I am grateful to members of Limina who spent time with me, sharing their insights into the organization and the women's spirituality movement.

2. See Mary Jo Neitz, *Charisma and Community*, especially pp. 122–152.

3. Cited in Limina publications.

4. I heard about Limina from various Chicago area friends. One friend knew someone who had attended a ritual, and got me a copy of the newsletter. Another friend sent me a copy of a newspaper story about the group. By the time I decided to write about Limina for this book, a poet whom I had met at a women's spirituality conference moved to Chicago and joined the Limina board. She introduced me to the founders and executive secretary of the organization. Most of the fieldwork for this project was done in 1989. That year I interviewed two of the three founders, the executive secretary, and three other board members. I also attended rituals, and spoke informally with other members, as well as subscribing to the newsletter. I have not attended any Limina events since December of 1991. Since that time I have kept in touch through occasional telephone calls as well as through the newsletter, which I continue to receive.

5. Among the women I have met and talked with in 1989, over 80% had Catholic backgrounds. It is possible that the longer Limina exists the more variation there will be among the women who attend its events.

6. The women's spirituality movement has produced a number of works by feminist theologians. For readings in this area, see Carol Christ, *The Laughter of Aphrodite* (San Francisco: Harper and Row, 1987); Carol Christ and Judith Plaskow, *Womanspirit Rising* (San Francisco: Harper and Row, 1979); Naomi Goldenberg, *The Changing of the Gods: Feminism and the End of Traditional Religions* (Boston: Beacon Press, 1979); Rosemary Ruether, *New Woman/New Earth: Sexist Ideologies and Human Liberation* (New York: Seabury, 1975); Elizabeth Schussler Fiorenza, *In Memory of Her: A Feminist Theological Reconstruction of Christina Origins* (New York: Crossroads, 1983); and Charlene Spretnak, ed., *The Politics of Women's Spirituality: Essays on the Rise of Spiritual Power Within the Feminist Movement* (New York: Doubleday, 1982). For sociological description of the women-church end of the continuum, see Diana Trebbi, "Women-Church: Catholic Women Produce an Alternative Spirituality," in Thomas Robbins and Dick Anthony, eds., *In Gods We Trust: New Patterns of Religious Pluralism in America*, rev. ed. (New Brunswick: Transaction Publishers, 1991), pp. 347–351; and Ruth Wallace, "Bringing Women In: Marginality in the Churches," *Sociological Analysis* 36 (4) (1975), pp. 291–303. For a discussion of feminist and neopagan wicca and the relations between them, see Mary Jo Neitz, "In Goddess We Trust," in *In Gods We Trust*, pp. 353–371.

7. The women who are members and who come to Limina's rituals include women from both ends of this continuum. Some members are also participants in other groups which explicitly identify as Wiccan or witches circles. Members also include a few women who, in the late seventies,

when it seemed like a possibility, had prepared for ordination in the Roman Catholic Church.

8. Marija Gimbutas, *The Language of the Goddess* (San Francisco: Harper and Row, 1989), p. 97.

9. For examples, see Pamela Berger, *The Goddess Obscured: The Transformation of the Grain Protectress from Goddess to Saint* (Boston: Beacon Press, 1985).

10. One source that Limina founders used in drawing up their calendar was Starhawk's *The Spiral Dance* (San Francisco: Harper and Row, 1979). For more information about the contemporary neopagan movement, see Margot Adler, *Drawing Down the Moon* (Boston: Beacon Press, 1986).

11. In our time, All Hallows Eve has become Halloween.

12. The fourth cross-quarter-day feast from the old Celtic calendar is Lammas, on August 1. To my knowledge this has not been appropriated by Limina women.

13. In neopagan theology the goddess has three phases, the mother, the maiden, and the crone, corresponding to the phases of the moon.

14. Lil Lewis, the original Wildwoman, left Limina in 1990. Other women, however, have continued to play her part in Limina programs since that time.

15. Tesse Donnelly, "Gender and Celebration: A Welcome to Womanhood," *Limina Newsletter*, Spring 1992, p. 3.

16. Limina occasionally has events that are open to men as well as women, to which members can bring male partners. The founders state that they do not see themselves as opposed to male participation, but that at this point in their development they are called to focus on women. For a more general discussion of the tensions women in women's spirituality groups experience in relation to the exclusion of men, see Mary Jo Neitz, "Feminist Spirituality Groups and Men: Views of Women Inside and Outside of Organized religion," paper presented at the Meetings of the Society for the Scientific Study of Religion," in Alexandria, VA, 1992.

17. Kathleen Gerson's study of the baby-boom generation, *Hard Choices* (Berkeley: University of California Press, 1985), shows that women's choices regarding whether or not they had children or were employed were determined less by the expectations they had for themselves than by constraints imposed by their marriage and job opportunities. However, regardless of what they were doing in their own lives, Gerson found that the women had to do "ideological work" in order to rationalize for themselves the positions in which they found themselves. In the process they often came to denigrate the choices that other women had made.

18. See, for example, Carole Pateman, "Feminist Critiques of the Public/Private Dichotomy," in S.I. Bem and G.F. Gaus, eds., *Private and Public in Social Life* (New York: St. Martins Press, 1983), pp. 281–303; Michelle Rosaldo, "Women, Culture and Society: A Theoretical View," in *Women, Culture and Society* (Palo Alto: Stanford University Press, 1973),

pp. 17–42; Michelle Rosaldo, "The Use and Abuse of Anthropology," *Signs* 3, (1980), pp. 389–417.

19. Cheryl Townsend Gilkes, "Holding Back the Ocean with a Broom: Black Women and Community Work," in LaFrances Rogers Rose, *The Black Women* (Beverly Hills: Sage, 1980).

20. Nancy Naples, "Activist Mothering: Cross-Generational Continuity in the Community Work of Women from Low-Income Urban neighborhoods," *Gender and Society* 6, (1992), pp. 441–463.

21. Limina's leaders are middle class women with college educations. Yet for women in this society, class position is often precarious. If we look at the leaders of the organization, we find that one's activist career has been financially supported by her husband. Another, with young children, is not currently working outside her home, but she does the administrative work for Limina, which benefits from her skills and previous experience working full-time as the paid administrator of a nonprofit organization. One experienced downward mobility after a divorce, when she became the sole support of her children, and another became the main provider for her family when her husband became disabled. I do not have complete information on the women who come to Limina gatherings, but occupations such as teacher, sales worker, and student were common among the women I met.

14

Couples at Work

A Study of Patterns of Work, Family, and Faith

William Johnson Everett
with Sylvia Johnson Everett

I don't know, we enjoy being with each other. It's fun to work together. It has been for us. Now that might be an old-fashioned answer or something, but we enjoy being together. You know, I couldn't have done this by myself, and she couldn't have done it by herself. And it is something, you look back and see where you came from, where you're at now and where you're planning on going. You know, there's kind of a surprise in that. We've accomplished a lot.

—A Farm Couple

SHE: To me it is real important to work together. It is part of what I believe in. If you're not really working with your partner, then are you really sharing your life? If you don't have common goals, especially that are outside the personal or romantic, then I think that the relationship has a hollowness to it, whereas a commitment of our lives to a common purpose, is very valuable.... I would feel the same way if we were farmers.

HE: Even though we said we were going to start a theater and work together—I didn't understand what that meant, and it was only through doing it that I came to understand the real implications of what that means.... I didn't know it was that unusual, it just seemed like the thing we were supposed to do, because we were together, and we're soul mates, and part of being soul mates, I think, means continuing to try to come to an understanding of that. What does it mean when souls comingle? I don't think it is something to be considered lightly or to be sloughed off. I think we are supposed to be active in trying to understand that, just as we feel it.

—Arts Directors

Work and family are the center of most people's lives. Work and family are not only the sources of our livelihood, but also the source and expression of some of our deepest values. They are crucibles as well as manifestations of our faith. The various forms of this faith are the subject of this chapter.

By "faith" we mean the ultimately trustworthy relationships by which we live. Faith is not simply a set of beliefs or propositions. It is not simply a set of values. It is more like an image of fundamental relationships. Faith is our pattern of deepest fidelity.[1] With that definition, many of the controversies of our day can be seen as matters of faith—the right order of parenthood and coupling, the right to abortion, the right way to organize the economy and to educate children. "Right religion" and "right family and work" are inextricably matters of faith in our sense.[2]

In examining changing patterns of work and family, we are therefore also examining changing patterns of faith. This study focuses on a particular pattern for combining work and family—that in which a couple work together. It is based on interview and questionnaire data colected in 1988. It explores the patterns of trustworthy relationship underlying this pattern of life, in an effort to see its possible implications for religious life, especially for its symbolism and organization.

THE OIKOS IMAGE

We use the ancient Greek word *oikos* to talk about the ensemble of faith, work, and family, including its bond to the land.[3] The oikos, which we usually translate as "house," actually embraced all of these components. In the ancient world, and in most traditional societies today, these elements are fused together. The history of our own civilization, however, has seen them differentiate from one another, even to the point of fragmentation and hostility.[4] In the process, we have been left with no English word for talking about them as a system. To recapture that systemic sense, we use the term *oikos*. Our *oikos* is the way we put work, family, and faith together, whether as persons or as a society. It is also a powerful and emotionally rooted image of how things *ought* to be. People tend to act and to evaluate life in terms of images they have of how the *oikos* should be put together. A particular *oikos* pattern shapes the way people spend their time and energy. It expresses the sense of durable relationship and right order standing at the center of our faith image. This study therefore focuses on the *oikos* images informing the lives of couples who work together.

It is these images which legitimate how we arrange our lives and our institutions. They deeply affect the way institutions, especially religious institutions, justify themselves. Acceptable patterns of sacred order are closely tied to the emotionally resonant patterns of our *oikos*. In addition, the governing images grounded in work and family help legitimate patterns of organization in politics, education, and health care, as well as the church. Images of this strength endure across time. Churches, for instance, bear with them governing images based on the *oikos* patterns of previous eras. But churches can also—through events of conversion or deep spiritual formation—reshape the *oikos* images people bring to them. Sometimes people consciously try to reshape the rest of life according to religiously legitimated *oikos* images, just as images that come from other times and institutions may shape the life of family or church. This complex interplay of fundamental images shapes the way we put our lives together.

OIKOS TYPES

Oikos images can be categorized in several ways, two of which are central for this study. First, *oikos* images can be placed along a spectrum between a fusion of components and fragmentation. We call this the *spatial* dimension of the *oikos*. Second, *oikos* images can be examined in terms of the way the participants arrange and govern their relationships. This is the *relational* dimension.

The Spatial Dimension

Oikos patterns vary in terms of the "distance" among the components of work, family, faith, and land. At one end we have the *fused oikos* typical of traditional agrarian society, in which the family is a productive economic unit bound together on the same land. Moreover, their faith is a set of ancestral loyalties tightly bound to working the land. In the *tight oikos*, family, work, and land are still tied together, while religion has become somewhat independent. Religious organizations are likely, however, to follow the pattern of family relations. This pattern, most familiar to us in the family farm, has been typical of most of our society until the end of the nineteenth century.

The *open oikos* represents a further differentiation, in which work and family are separated from each other. Schools usually emerge in order to help children pass from the family sphere to the work sphere. In the nineteenth century, this pattern took on a form which we call the *split oikos*, in which the separated spheres of work and family were divided between men and women. The husband worked outside the home, and the wife took care of the domestic sphere. Religion was split between them, with the male taking over most formal leadership, and the female supervising religious instruction and matters of the spiritual life.

As women have now moved into the workplace on an increasingly equal footing, more and more functions are moving out of the household—funerals, birth, food preparation, manufacture of personal items, entertainment, care of the elderly and sick, and so forth. We call this pattern of intense differentiation the *fragmented oikos*. This *oikos* pattern has become, at least in some sectors, a cultural norm in our society.

The Relational Dimension

The other distinctions to be made regarding these basic governing images have to do with relationship and authority patterns. There appear to be three basic types—hierarchical, organic, and egalitarian.

The *hierarchical* pattern is one in which one person is the final authority in the relationship. This can take a strong form, in which one party controls the others in every aspect, or a more limited form, in which one person controls only the key decisions affecting the group. Most of the hierarchies we know have been male-dominant.

The *organic* pattern, often neglected in research, is one in which the activity of the group is divided up by functions. Decision-making and command are not as salient, because the members of the group do what is demanded by the task of the moment. The work, not a person, controls the group. Within each function, individuals exercise considerable autonomy in fulfilling their tasks. In some forms, they all participate in performing each function, as when members of a farm family all turn out for the harvest. In others the work is divided up into interdependent but distinct functions, with individuals assigned to each. This pattern occurs not only in farm families but also in small family-run businesses.

In the *egalitarian* pattern the members stand on a roughly equal footing, and negotiate tasks and policies. They form agreements about their common life. They may reshape these agreements when one or more of the parties feels it necessary. Here the group is controlled by the outcomes of communication, persuasion, and negotiation. This image has become dominant in the open and fragmented *oikos* as it is experienced in American culture today.

THE **OIKOS** SHIFT AND THE INTIMACY DILEMMA

North Atlantic societies have gradually shifted from a fused or tight *oikos* to an open or fragmented one. When women began to be accommodated in the workplace, there was, however, no change in the split *oikos* image that operated with sharp distinctions between work and family. This economic base enabled women to press for greater gender equality and to pursue the ideals of equality, persuasion, public participation, and genuine citizenship; but it has also created a fundamental strain in our life.[5] This strain in the *oikos* can be identified as a conflict between the intimate communication assigned to marriage and the individualistic career expectations of our economy. People are told that their marriage depends on intense communication, but they are not allowed to place their common work at the center of that communication. Thus, marriage comes to be a leisure activity divorced from work. Moreover, parents are estranged from the process of passing on their values, usually expressed in their work, to their children. Religious institutions exist increasingly in the leisure sphere, with their values also detached from the work-family connection.

The couple who work together present an alternative to this pattern—one in which the values of marriage and those of work are combined in one operation. In one sense, this arrangement seeks to preserve the values of the tight or fused *oikos*. On the other hand, it may provide an opportunity for the expression of the egalitarian values of the open and fragmented economy. Couples who work together, then, present a peculiar crucible for the refinement of basic *oikos* images, one which might have critical significance for religious symbolism and organization, as well as for family and economic life.[6]

THE STUDY

Through "snowball" sampling, we have slowly accumulated a list of over 130 couples, located throughout the U.S., who work together. We sent each couple a questionnaire, and we received forty-nine responses. We also conducted twenty in-depth interviews with couples close enough to Atlanta to visit in person. Both the questionnaires and the interviews sought to identify the governing *oikos* images arising in the lives of couples who work together. By "working together," we mean that the couple interact more than fifty percent of their work time and/or produce more than fifty percent of their income in this manner. We identified some initial couples through newspaper accounts, friends, and colleagues, and one advertisement in a trade magazine. We then let that list snowball through subsequent referrals from couples responding to our questionnaire. We sought out as great a variety of occupations and backgrounds as possible, especially in our interview group. Since no one knows how many couples actually work together or what defines them, it is not possible to say whether our sample is a truly representative one. The few students of this phenomenon estimate that between one-half and one and a half million couples fulfill these criteria.[7]

In particular, we wanted to explore three types of questions.

The Context. What are the economic, educational, familial, geographic and religious characteristics of these couples? What economic structures foster or impede them?

The Oikos Images. Why do they try to put their lives together this way? Are they building on inherited patterns? Are they value-driven and idealistic, or are they a devising a pragmatic response to their circumstances? What types of oikos images (spatial and relational) are present with these couples, and how do they structure the way the spouses interact? What are the sources or key supports for these images? What kind of explicit or implicit spirituality is allied with them? What are the advantages and disadvantages couples have found in this pattern?

Institutional Ramifications. What implications do these patterns and experiences have for the workplace and economy? What changes do they imply for marriage and family? What are the relationships between these patterns and religious symbolism and organization? What kinds of religious involvement and values do they foster or undermine? How might churches and other religious organizations deal with these alternative patterns?

EXPLORING THE CONTEXTS

Where Are the Couples at Work? The majority of our forty-nine questionnaire respondents were self-employed in some way. Thirty-one operated their own businesses—three couples in farming, eighteen had a business firm, three a franchise, six had professional practices, and one couple were artists. Fifteen were nonprofit entrepreneurs or professionals, generally employed by churches as pastors or by educational institutions. Four couples were corporate employees with professional training.

Most worked in small-scale organizations and settings. Half were in work organizations of less than seven people, with even fewer people in their immediate work area.

As we expected, we were unable to find any couples sharing standard jobs in large corporations. The exceptions are the few professionals employed by corporations. We do know that some corporate job-sharers exist, but they are rare indeed. The opposition between the corporation and couples is near universal—unless, of course, they own the corporation, as many couples do.

What Are Their Common Characteristics? These couples, on average, were quite well educated. Their educational levels ranged from high school to doctoral degrees, along with certificates in the arts and skilled trades. Twenty-seven of the men had graduate or professional degrees, as did fourteen of the women. All men had studied beyond high school, as had all but three of the women. On average, the males had a few years more schooling than the females. Though education may not in itself produce couples at work it may contribute greatly to the capacity for economic autonomy, which seems critical to the development of a couple-career path.

The couples we discovered ranged in age from people in their late twenties who had worked together only six months to couples in their late sixties, one of which had worked together thirty-five years. The couples had from zero to nine children. Their gross incomes ranged from twenty thousand to over a hundred thousand dollars, with an average of about sixty thousand dollars, placing them solidly in the upper middle class.

Ethnically, the vast majority were Euro-Americans (ninety-two percent), especially from the British Isles (sixty-seven percent)—not surprising, given the concentration of the study in the Southeast. The remainder included African-Americans and Hispanics.[8]

The religious affiliations we discovered covered a broad range, from Methodists (eighteen percent) and Presbyterians (fourteen percent) through Episcopalians (eleven percent), Baptists (eight percent), "Evangelical Protestants" (seven percent), and Jews (three percent). Eighteen percent checked "none," with "other" counting for another fourteen percent of the sample. Compared to the general population, Baptists are under-represented, and Episcopalians, "nones," and "others" are somewhat overrepresented. We believe this denominational distribution is reflective of the entrepreneurial and professional class where these couples are found. It also appears to be the result of changes that have taken place since childhood. Several reported childhood religious affiliations, but said they had none now. And most mainline denominational categories were more strongly represented among childhood affiliations than among current ones. However, nonaffiliates, Episcopalians, and "other" (Unity, Meher Baba, "New Age," and the like) have increased over reported childhood affiliations. Thus, the religious dynamics reflect two central features of these couples—their preponderance in the professional and entrepreneurial classes, and their affinity with novel, freshly constructed frameworks of meaning and relationship.

EXPLORING THE **OIKOS** IMAGES

Why Are They Working Together? While in some cases couples could identify ancestors who worked together, all but one had simply invented their own work together rather than inheriting it. This ran contrary to our expectation that ancestral images, largely from farming, would find reexpression in modern form. Among those ancestors who had worked together, half were in small business, one fourth in farming, and one fourth in professional life. Thus, the farm experience was not as important as entrepreneurship in shaping these couples' contemporary *oikos* patterns and images.

People cited a number of different reasons for originally working together: to meet financial need or opportunity (thirty-five percent), to have mutual support in their work (twenty-nine percent), and to maintain their common interests (twenty-seven percent). Eighteen percent launched their common effort because they worked well together. Only two couples listed domestic flexibility (child care, household equity) as a prime motivator, although the advent of children precipitated the decision for a number of couples. Couples with a more hierarchical *oikos* image tended to concentrate on financial reasons. Those with organic images supplemented financial reasons with companionship values, while more egalitarian couples concentrated on common interest, synergy, and companionship. This seems to indicate that egalitarian couples emphasize the importance of the direct, interpersonal, couple relationship, while for the others the values of household and children are more important.

When asked why they were *still* working together, "synergy" rose from eighteen percent to thirty-six percent of the reasons, with common interest dropping sharply, and financial need dropping slightly. Thus, common interest and financial need seemed to form a kind of foundation or prerequisite. Once that was established, these couples found out, contrary to common cultural myths, that they *can* work together quite well. As a couple in real estate put it:

HE: Well, we had the dream of being together, but it wasn't work related.
SHE: Although I remember you telling me years before that you had always wanted to work in real estate with your wife. You don't remember that? I remember you saying that. And, of course, at that time I was working on the base. I never dreamed about really working with him, particularly in real estate, but I do remember him saying that.
HE: She always said she couldn't work with me.
SHE: That's right. I really… I'm surprised we can work together…. He is so bossy, really and truly. And so am I. And I thought that we probably would have great difficulty working together, although we get along well. I guess we have such a division of things, I never really thought about it that way until you had [us answer] the questionnaire, but we kind of separate things so that we get along better. But I thought that we would have great difficulty because I'd want things my way and he'd want his way, you know.

On balance these couples have found working together very rewarding. It is this discovery that sustains their work arrangement. The widespread belief that spouses cannot work together may well be a cultural myth to justify the split *oikos* that has little basis in people's actual capacities and tested experience.

How Are They Integrating Life? How are they integrating work with family and spirituality? We expected to discover that couples who work together have a tight or even fused *oikos* structure: not only are they working and living together, but they tend to have an intense involvement in this work as an expression of their key values. We expected that couple careers would be a contemporary expression of the tight *oikos* of our agrarian past.

The findings, however, indicate that these arrangements today clearly bear the mark of the open and fragmented *oikos*. Taking together the responses to a number of questions, we found that their *oikos* structure was on average more open than tight (average of 1.63 on a scale of 1 to 2). What was striking in the survey and interviews is that our respondents tend generally to be very couple-centered, and less embedded in a wider set of relations. Instead of being "tight," their world is *focused*. Moreover, it is focused on the *couple* and their construction of an *oikos* suited to their needs, rather than on the family as a transmitter of the values and patterns of a wider community.

The *oikos* of these couples is a *voluntarily constructed* pattern to achieve particular personal and couple goals. It is a part of the pluralism of our society, and seems to thrive only in the most autonomous and entrepreneurial sectors of the culture. Because they felt they were making it up as they went along, many couples felt their common work had just "happened."

> HE: This business just happened. The way it happened is totally unexplainable. Martha started it just to have something to play with. It grew, and her mother came in, and it grew some more, and her mother got out. I think that one of our biggest pitfalls in the four and a half or five years that we've been doing this is that our growth has been totally unplanned for the most part. We have developed business plans and tried to do annual budgets like all good businesses are supposed to do. Even when we sit down and do those, it's, like, "how do we get that?"

While this improvisational character of the *oikos* made life exciting, it also often created considerable strain and demanded frequent attention to the way they made decisions and carried out tasks.

How Are They Relating To Each Other? Three key questions were used to identify the relational dimension of a couple's *oikos* image—questions about their image of their work relationship, about their spirituality image, and about their formal position descriptions. We discovered that the organic *oikos* image was central for work relations, while egalitarian themes dominated their spirituality, and were slightly more prominent in their formal position descriptions. We expected to see the organic pattern of work relationships, because of its familiarity from agrarian life. However, the combination of organic and egalitarian themes was even stronger than we expected.

Since there were not significant variations among the couples in spiritual images and position descriptions, we used the image of their work relationship to distinguish them. Thus we found four couples with hierarchical images, thirteen with egalitarian images and thirty-two with organic images of their life together. The organic patterns have, however, maintained some of the traditional hierarchical elements. This was especially apparent in the tendency of husbands to control big decisions and represent the couple's enterprise to the outside world. This pattern persisted regardless of whether the couple professed hierarchical values or egalitarian ones. One wife in a largely egalitarian structure put it this way:

> I don't know, it's just that we've always, I mean I've always felt—now I know the young people don't look at it this way—but I've always felt, like, that he should make the decisions. You know, I can make them, but I would rather that he make them.

In its more organic version, the man is the public face of sales, interpretation, external contracting, and the like. The wife takes care of the inside work of financial records, office management, and internal monitoring. As a wife in a complex entrepreneurial partnership put it:

> I'm a good inside person, he's a good outside person, and once he gets the customers then they get taken care of very well.

It is important to see what others have also suspected, that hierarchy is not so much a matter of command and submission as of public and private spheres of influence. This pattern persists in our sample, though against a more egalitarian value scheme.

There was a striking regional variation in the couples' work images. Almost none of the respondents from outside the Southeast had any hierarchical components. They had fewer organic images as well, and were heavily egalitarian in their composition. This marked difference clearly shows that regional cultures are still very powerful, especially those shaping basic relational images and patterns.

When asked to describe their pattern of coworking, there was considerable preference for "team" and "director/assistant," with "council" as an important additional image. When we asked them to speak to particular role images within this overall pattern, we found great complexity in the way some couples would share a great many roles, others dividing roles up more clearly. Some emphasized the importance of common goals in dividing up work:

> He: Rather than setting out tasks—this is your task, and this is my task.... We don't do much about "are you doing fifty percent or am I doing fifty percent." That's not really the issue. The issue is more around our goal.

Others depend on an immediate need and a common knowledge of their whole operation.

> That is a big advantage, the fact that she knows everything that goes on and I know everything that goes on.... I mean I can go—I don't have to worry about anything here and she can do the same thing because there's nothing about it that she don't know.... If she's taking care of it, I leave it alone. If I'm taking care of it, she leaves it alone.

Despite the preponderance of organic images and patterns in their day-to-day activity, the *formal positions* claimed by these couples were more likely egalitarian or hierarchical. They designated their formal positions as partners, coprofessionals, and frequently in terms of corporate designations (president, vice president, secretary, treasurer). In these terms eighteen were egalitarian, eighteen were hierarchical, and thirteen were organic. Thus, the public face of their work tends not to reflect their felt working reality. Officially, our public culture and official language are generally either hierarchical or egalitarian. The bureaucratic corporation and political democracy dominate our imagery. The organic reality of the *oikos* known by many people is effaced, creating considerable tension between the self-understanding of these couples and other people's perceptions of them. What is experienced as an organic division of labor that fits their own individual gifts and needs is translated into hierarchical job titles. Indeed, they themselves may be at a loss for words to describe how they work together.

The values of equal dignity and recognition, also strong among these couples, can create feelings of resentment about this imposition of hierarchical assumptions. As one wife in a strongly egalitarian partnership put it:

SHE: From my perspective, I think there are two things at work. One is, I think, the very male patriarchal world we live in. Like, I'm the cofounder of the theater, and people refer to "Robert Barnard's Theater" all the time. Depending on how emotionally stable I am feeling, that may hurt. Like, am I invisible here? On the other hand, if you look at me as a human being, I am not particularly aggressive or outspoken, I think I am those things privately, but in large groups, I am shy. And so if I am feeling strong and confident in myself, then I don't have a problem with that. I feel like it is a complementary thing. If we were both shy, what would happen? We would both be invisible. So I think part of it is the structure and part of it is my own personal personality. So sometimes I feel bad about that and other times I say well why not, that's perfectly okay. But also...he had a name for himself, before I even met him. So it was like a marketing or PR tool, and frankly, I don't enjoy that, that public exposure as much.

This tension of public and private roles dominated the list of dissatisfactions we shall examine later.

Not surprisingly, the "organic" division of labor between these husbands and wives includes about twice as many hours of housework for women as for men.[9] Egalitarian couples exceeded organic and hierarchical couples by only a small margin in their sharing of household work hours. Here, as with dual career couples, women have moved into public life, but men have not moved into much of the private world.

Age was more complexly related to *oikos* images than we expected. Older couples do tend to have hierarchical images and younger couples organic ones. However, among retired couples who had taken up a new work together, we found very strong egalitarian motifs. Their couple values shaped their work, rather than work shaping their relation. In this case, their relative freedom from job expectations and job-derived income enabled them to express their underlying sense of equality more directly in their work.

This finding offsets the impression that younger people are more individualistic and egalitarian. In fact, they may be much more oriented to building a joint pattern rather than simply fulfilling their potential as individuals.[10] Younger couples often reported that they tried to do everything together as equals before settling on a more organic but nevertheless negotiated pattern. As a ministerial couple put it:

> For us, what has been crucial here is to get some separation in job descrip-
> tion. But early on we were sort of trotting around together as a team, and
> we found that that really wasn't the best use of time. And so we tried to
> separate out some paths, both for some good use of time and also for some
> sort of accountability to the profession as well.

Each age group has been shaped not only by the values of their cohort culture, but also by their current stage in the life cycle. It seems that the more intensely they are involved in their common work, the more organic their image (or, when one is taking the lead, the more hierarchical). When their work demands less of them, as in the middle years and retirement, more egalitarian values can come into play.

What Is Their Spirituality? "Spirituality" signifies the root orientations behind people's images and values. Any *oikos* pattern has a spiritual dimension in this sense. The tight or fused oikos, for instance, lay at the heart of most of our traditional religious symbolism. In this symbolism, the patriarchal fused *oikos* was reinforced by the religious images of Christ's rule over the church (his bride), "her" children, and the church's lands and corporation. The church also exercised control over marriage and family, through which most economic and governance power was exercised. The open *oikos*, however, tends to emphasize the direct relation of believers to God, usually through the guidance of the Holy Spirit or an immediate grasp of God's Word. This kind of symbolism has usually reinforced personal autonomy in marital, economic, and political matters.

We asked people to consider a number of classic spiritual images of relationships—such as cocreator, friend, Abraham and Sarah, Mary and Joseph, and servants of God—as well as less obviously religious ones, such as soul mates. Some of our respondents chose explicitly Biblical or Christian images. Others were more general. Some people were very explicit about their spirituality, while others were more indirect.

Overall, people chose much more egalitarian spiritual images than were present in their work. Of the forty-five responding to both questions, forty-one chose egalitarian spiritual images, three chose organic, and one chose a hierarchical spiritual image; whereas eleven chose egalitarian work images, thirty-one organic images and three hierarchical ones. Almost all respondents also reported that their domestic and intimate relationships were more egalitarian than their work relationship. We also found that the more ecstatic or mystical the spiritual image, the more egalitarian the couple. It is not too surprising that an egalitarian spirituality corresponds more closely to people's intimate life and their felt equality than to work, since the privatization of religion is a signal aspect of the fragmented *oikos* of modernized societies.

The strongest link between work images and spiritual images was in the relationship between a spirituality based on rational principles and ethics and a more hierarchical and/or task-oriented *oikos* pattern and image.[11] These differences were also related to gender. More men than women (twenty-eight compared to twenty-two) checked "ethical values" as crucial for their spirituality, whereas women more frequently checked "Holy Spirit" (nineteen women to twelve men). This in turn seems to be tied to gender-based work patterns. Women who were coentrepreneurs and couples with hierarchical and organic *oikos* images were more likely to emphasize "ethical values" as the source of their spirituality. This may occur because men tend to have the public role of dealing with decisions affecting the general public. They are therefore trained to think abstractly about values. Women, with their traditional assignment to the inner and private sphere, have a spirituality of particular affections and less publicly rational dynamics. Women also chose more "other" patterns (twelve to six), reflecting, we think, the possibility that their creativity has been channelled into cultural and religious realms, since they were traditionally excluded from the world of public work. Thus, they tend to be more sophisticated and innovative in spiritual matters.

What Were their Satisfactions and Dissatisfactions? By far the biggest satisfaction in working together was the cultivation of greater mutuality (seventy-one percent). Couple values are decisive here. Working together, as some couples stressed in interviews, made them respect each other more and discipline themselves for better communication. This communication was also a source of professional support. In the words of a ministerial couple:

> HE: ...this is a new form of ministry, and we're individuals, but we're more than the sum of each person separately.... I've learned a lot about myself by being in partnership. So it may be that first we have gained a partnership and in that we have the space and the freedom to explore who we are.
> SHE: Well, it's [a big advantage] having a trained spouse that you could go [to] and either with a sermon or a pastoral care issue, who understands, who's had the same training and is a colleague and you could go and say, "I need help with this issue. Help me brainstorm about this part

of my sermon." That's wonderful to be able to have that support and somebody who understands ministry....

The focus on the couple that we have already seen is also apparent in the satisfactions they report. Only two couples put high regard on creating something to pass on to their children. In fact, the more egalitarian the values of the couple, the fewer children they had. For a number of couples, however, involving their children in their work was an important way of passing on family values and skills for dealing with the public, even at an early age. Some also emphasized that their work pattern enabled them to integrate their lives more satisfactorily than wass possible in the corporation.

This very focusing of the *oikos*, however, requires extra attention to differentiating work and family more consciously. Some couples reported that, though they were able to pursue the goal of having more time together, they also found themselves forced to have too much time together. They were often searching for an optimum balance between togetherness and apartness. Fourteen of the couples reported dissatisfaction over the relation of the private and public sectors of their lives. Being equally involved in everything tended to break down sectoral boundaries. In a tight or fused *oikos*, those boundaries tend to disappear. Many of these couples were actively engaged in redrawing them, establishing clear rules about work and family spheres. For many of them work problems easily seeped into every conversation and activity. Listen to how one couple developed this awareness:

> SHE: I know our son used to fine us a quarter at the dinner table if we would bring up anything about our patients. I think that really helped us because...he wanted his time and he didn't want all these people floating into it. But I think even before that we were working pretty hard to get distance between the office and the home.... I think that was more of the case when we were less sure of ourselves professionally, so we were seeking more assurance personally about it. I think that as we have become more confident and skilled professionally it is, like, "I don't need to deal with this." You can put those boundaries around it, and look the other way and not worry about it.

The advice books on working together spend a good deal of time emphasizing a self-imposed differentiation between the two spheres, something these couples had to develop for themselves. While this *focused oikos* centers on the priority of the couple relationship, it still experiences and needs considerable differentiation.

A number of couples found it difficult to move back and forth between the organic/hierarchical values of their work endeavors and the egalitarian values of their spiritual, emotional, intimate, and domestic life. This applied to their relationship as couples, as well as to their roles as parents. Many felt that women kept lower boundaries between these two spheres, and operated out of a single image in their various roles. As one husband put it:

> Mary has always been the love center of whatever we did. Whether or not she even worked there, she was always the one who understood the human dynamics that would play in the company. And we have always—and in each company we did it better—created a family environment. It was an extension of our family.

Separating out or integrating these dynamics is even more complex in the two-generation family business. In the words of one father in a family firm:

> This is probably the toughest part of a family operation. We have two sons here in the business, and the final responsibility of this operation lies with me. You can't have but one manager. You can't have but one person who is guiding the situation. Now at the same time, one has to try to keep a balance. I have a relationship with my wife here at the office, and I have a relationship with the boys. But here at the office, its not a cold business relationship, but in the end it does have to be a business relationship, and I can't let emotion or let my heart get too involved sometimes with dealing in a businesslike way with her or with the boys. Now whether this is inherent in a woman or a mother, she probably is a mother first. And that may not be exactly fair, because she is so objective when it comes to numbers. But it does get sort of wrapped up, mixed up together, it's hard to separate. We have two sons. We love them the same.... But I have to consider them as employees, at a certain point, rather than just sons. It comes to certain situations where I can't treat them equally.

Here we can clearly see the complex dynamics involved in balancing hierarchical work images, egalitarian couple dynamics, and parental care. Each couple in such a situation has to develop their own pattern for dealing with these points of potential strain as well as mutual reinforcement.

"Couple stress" was a reported dissatisfaction from nineteen of the respondents. Hierarchical patterns tended to increase this stress. This may be due to the stress of the more financially oriented pursuits of these couples. It may also arise from the stress of hierarchy itself, which typically leaves the dominant person feeling lonely and the subordinate person resentful. Some of this tension may well result from the enormous demands of their work, with some couples reporting sixty to sixty-five work hours per week. In other cases it seems to have occurred because they tend to become isolated from nonwork friends and pursuits. The *oikos* patterns of these couples are often so demanding (especially for the entrepreneurs) that they seem to exclude many other engagements. Involvement of children has to be a very conscious part of the enterprise, or else the couple's work tends to cut heavily into parental time. While this tension was recognized by many couples, they were generally unwilling to adjust their *oikos* to overcome it.

IMPLICATIONS FOR THE WORKPLACE

The modern corporation required a radical separation of work from family. Rules against nepotism crystallized this separation. Work would be ruled by rational, nonfamilial norms. The family would be governed by love, emotion, and particular bonds. While increasing numbers of corporations have had to abandon explicit commitment to their antinepotism policies (they violate EEOC regulations against gender discrimination), actual changes in employment are minimal.[12]

The primary reason for inertia at this point is because work is still defined in rational units performed by individuals. Job-sharing in any form is still a marginal phenomenon, though its benefits have been clearly identified.[13] A number of couples spoke about the opportunity to combine their creative powers as a major reason for choosing to work together. In spite of such benefits, almost no corporations employ couples who are job-sharers.

Our inquiry reveals two possible avenues for change in this respect. One involves the professionalization of work. We did identify work-sharing in corporations employing professionals—the churches, journalism, the media. Their relative autonomy and the structure of the work make possible job-sharing by professional couples. Secondly, we found that franchise businesses not only attract couples, but in one case find them the best choice for franchise operation.[14] The more the large corporation devolves in the direction of subcontracting and franchising, the more opportunities for couples will be created.

Some of the couples developed joint work because the husband left his corporation in order to have more control over his life, especially his basic work values. Sometimes this dissatisfaction with the corporation was augmented by the couple's desire to have more flexibility in ordering their domestic and parental lives. In the face of values like these, corporations are beginning to adopt more flexible approaches to work time, not to mention career paths, as people seek a better balance in their lives.[15]

There are clearly certain niches in the economy where couples can pursue their desire to have a tighter or more focused integration of their life so that it can conform more closely to their own values. While there are ways that corporations could change to accommodate these desires and values, such change will come slowly, if at all. If it does, it will have to occur as part of a basic value shift in our culture, one which seeks to preserve personal autonomy but balance it with the needs for enduring bonds of mutual support and transmission of viable *oikos* patterns to the next generation.

IMPLICATIONS FOR MARRIAGE AND FAMILY

We have been exploring an *oikos* pattern which is focused on the couple who work together. It reflects not only the egalitarian commitments arising in the spouses' spiritual life and self-conception, but also the organic patterns arising in the way they work together. It is a couple held together not only by intimacy but also by work. This makes the marriage as much a public institution as it is a private refuge. In one woman's words:

> I think it is exciting that our relationship has its personal part, its romantic part, and all of that is also in the public and in the community. I just feel that that is good, rather than just sitting out in our little house in the suburbs someplace, and maybe we have a child or whatever, but there is no social responsibility involved in that partnership.

Thus, the civic qualities of respect and argument play a greater role here. This emphasis came from many couples in a variety of ways. In the words of a couple operating a consulting firm:

> SHE: We're very tolerant with each other. I think we're definitely two different types of people, but with great respect for the other.
> HE: First as individuals, you know in individual respect, human respect. And then professional respect as well.
> INTERVIEWER: Has that changed over the period of years?
> HE: I think it's matured a lot. I mean I feel like it's matured to the point

where we can now disagree on something and discuss it, where in the early days if we disagreed it was too emotional and we couldn't discuss it.

In succinct form a farm couple put it this way:

HE: Well, it's really easy. All it takes is that you love and respect one another and then you just don't have a problem.

SHE: There is no problem. I mean I respect what he does, and he respects what I do. You know, we've been married thirty-six years and we just never have had no problems. I guess people think we're not telling the truth when we say that, but there is no problem, you know, what else can I say?

The respect of these couples is one earned through concrete achievements in the workplace. It is not the respect that derives from the status they occupy by nature of their sex or role as mother or father.

Inasmuch as the couple itself is the focus of this *oikos*, the spouses move away from the individualism of the dual-career couple. The couple's sense of "we-ness" is reinforced by their work, rather than threatened by it. This does not necessarily mean that these couples will be less prone to divorce. The values of dignity, respect, and fair play are necessary for intimate communication and tend to enhance marriage. But the enhancement gained through joint work might have only a marginal impact on the divorce rate, since workplace strains alone can also deeply aggravate weaknesses in the couple's relationship. An inquiry into these dynamics demands further research.

The couple focus we have seen here also means that this *oikos* arrangement is not primarily intergenerational. It is not a "mom and pop" operation, since parenthood is not its focus; coupling is. It is a "his and hers" operation in two senses. Each spouse is seeking fuller expression in socially and publicly recognized terms. That is its individual side. It is also "his and hers" in that the whole operation is shared. To a high degree the couple have at least psychological co-ownership in the operation. That is its couple side. They represent their enterprise to a public world. Here are just two versions of that widespread theme:

There are two of us who are doing the same work. You don't have to pull the plow by yourself. It's like being in two places at once.

So there is an advantage of working together, the fact that the two of us know what's going on and she can deal with these people as well as I can. In fact, a lot of these people call me "Mr. Ruth Burns!"

In this sense these couples evidence a significant variation on the individualism so much vaunted and maligned in American life. It is life lived in intimate relationship, not merely through direct emotional communication, but through the public instruments of work. Marriage here expresses itself not only in the bedroom, but in the board or work room as well. The couple shares a publicly recognized world, which in turn shapes their marriage. This is what gives the organic shape to their relationship. They are related to each other through their work, as well as through their personalities, emotions, and, frequently, children. In this sense, American culture may actually be a culture of couples rather than of individuals. Its purported individualism may actually mask a pervasive desire for coupling that is an even more important dynamic in American life.[16]

These couples also raise up for us a public vocation for couples that lasts longer than that of raising children. Since the historic separation of work and family, raising children and perhaps maintaining a home have been the chief means by which a couple could have what we call a *marital vocation*. While the home (and perhaps several pets) can last a marital lifetime, children grow up. What worldly expression and confirmation of marriage can hold people together in a world, and give them a basis for communication, struggle, and mutual appreciation? It is this need for some form of marital vocation which is being addressed by these couples. It is a need which our society does not address and indeed suppresses or trivializes. Meeting that need, it seems to us, can do much to strengthen the intimate bonds that give so much of life its vitality.

IMPLICATIONS FOR RELIGIOUS INSTITUTIONS

Christianity and Judaism continue to bear an ambiguous relationship to these developments. On the one hand, their traditional symbolism of male dominated hierarchy has reinforced the split *oikos* of the public male and the private female. On the other hand, they are also the bearers of egalitarian images of spiritual friendship and equal participation in the divine life. Both of these have been mediated by family life, and will continue to be so.

In our study we found that the more egalitarian the couple, the less involved they are with religious institutions and with traditional religious symbolism. Egalitarian couples were less likely even to respond to the religious questions. In substantial part, this seems to arise from the way churches are associated with symbols of hierarchical order. It may also arise from the perception that churches exist more to pass on traditional values to the next generation than to help today's adults, especially couples, invent new patterns for their lives. Moreover, these couples are very busy people. They have no time for the committees and volunteer work required for maintaining religious institutions. The church or synagogue does not play a big part in their life on either symbolic or organizational grounds.

The split *oikos* provided womanpower for religious life in nineteenth-century America. Today that pool of volunteers is rapidly evaporating. Today's couple needs private leisure time to cultivate the communication not possible during the workweek. Weekend religious activities compete for that time. In the words of one woman:

> I think it is really important, and I really like the quiet time at church, and the music and stimulation. But any time we tried to get involved in the church...you go two times and they want you to take on the youth group or you feel obligated with things like that. And we just don't have enough time. Sunday mornings is really about our only downtime. It is like we go, and just get what I want out of the situation, I don't have much left over to give back.

If churches are to find volunteers they will have to find them among retired couples rather than younger housewives. The organization of church work and activity has to adjust to people's dominant *oikos* patterns.

Moreover, these couples tend to want a more intense focus on the symbolic and worship life of the church. In worship they find a structured and insulated hour for personal reflection—regardless of what may be pronounced from the pulpit. That is, we got the impression that social relationships and community work are not what these couples want from religion. They want development and confirmation of their distinctive spiritual life. The church provides this opportunity, especially in public worship. However, few churches provide worship that draws on egalitarian or organic symbols that would be relevant to the *oikos* of these couples. They are at once more spiritual, then, but also more institutionally alienated.

Support for couples who work together offers a way that churches could meld their traditional concern for a more tightly integrated *oikos* with an equally compelling commitment to the equality arising in the call of men and women to a shared public life. By lifting up the option of combining work and family, the church can also counteract the historic tendency to confine its mission to the realm of female domesticity. By adjusting its symbolism and ritual as well as its program and personnel along these lines, it can be a place where men and women deal jointly with the interconnected dynamics of work and family. That twenty-one percent of our sample are clergy couples may indicate a skewed sample, but it also may indicate that the churches are one of the few places where this *oikos* pattern can be sustained. It may also mean that this is a group who will inevitably recast religious symbolism in their direction.

The question is whether religious leaders will shape religious symbolism to appeal to the organic and egalitarian patterns of the couples we have met, or to the hierarchical ones pervasive in the corporations maintaining the split or fragmented *oikos* of the last century. It may well be that when religious groups have sought to be more egalitarian, they have actually reinforced the individualism of separate spousal careers, with its attendant strains, rather than the organic bonds of couples seeking to integrate work and family more closely. Church-sponsored day care centers, for instance, may simply support the dominant split between work and family, just as most marriage enrichment programs ignore the work-family interface. This is not to say that the *oikos* split between public men and private women is the only alternative to these arrangements. Here we have tried to explore the lives of people taking another route. At this point, religious institutions need to move beyond the individualism of the old, split *oikos* and its modern egalitarian counterpart, to legitimate other patterns that honor both the equality of people and their need for deep relationship in marriage and work.

NOTES

1. This view is worked out in considerable systematic detail in William Johnson Everett, *Blessed Be the Bond: Christian Perspectives on Marriage and Family* (Philadelphia: Fortress Press, 1985; Lanham, MD: University Press of America, 1990).

2. For exemplary discussions, see William V. D'Antonio and Joan Aldous, eds., *Families and Religions: Conflict and Change in Modern Society* (Beverly Hills, CA: Sage Publications, 1983). For one example of changing family symbolism in religion, see Mary Jo Neitz, *Charisma and Community: A Study of Religious Commitment within the Charismatic Renewal* (New Brunswick, NJ: Transaction Books, 1987), Chap. 5.

3. We have developed this language over the past six years through the *oikos* Project on Work, Family and Faith, based in Atlanta. For one exploration of these connections, see William Johnson Everett, "*oikos*: Convergence in Business Ethics," *Journal of Business Ethics* 5 (1986), pp. 313–325.

4. This simplified picture of family history needs to be augmented by the resurgent work in this field by, among many others, J. E. Goldthorpe, *Family Life in Western Societies: A Historical Sociology of Family Relationships in Britain and North America* (Cambridge: Cambridge University Press, 1987), especially Chaps. 2, 4, and 10. See also Martine Segalen, *Historical Anthropology of the Family* trans. J. C. Whitehouse and S. Matthews (Cambridge: Cambridge University Press, 1986); Carl Degler, *At Odds: Women and the Family in America from the Revolution to the Present* (New York: Oxford University Press, 1980); Herman Lantz, Martin Schultz, and Mary O'Hara, "The Changing American Family from Pre-industrial to the Industrial Period: A Final Report," *American Sociological Review*, 42 (1977), pp.406–421; Leonard Sweet, *The Minister's Wife: Her Role in Nineteenth-Century American Evangelicalism* (Philadelphia: Temple University Press, 1982); Virginia Tufte and Barbara Myerhoff, eds., *Changing Images of the Family* (New Haven: Yale University Press, 1979); Michael Young and Peter Willmott, *The Symmetrical Family* (New York: Pantheon, 1973).

5. For key discussions of the general phenomenon of two-earner couples see Joan Aldous, ed., *Two Paychecks: Life in Dual-Earner Families* (Beverly Hills, CA: Sage, 1982); Norma A. Heckman and Rebecca and Jeff Bryson, "Problems of Professional Couples: A Content Analysis," *Journal of Marriage and the Family*, 39 (1977), pp. 323–330; Jeane Herman and Karen K. Gyllstrom, "Working Men and Women: Inter- and Intra-role Conflict," *Psychology of Women Quarterly*, 1 (1977), pp. 319–30; F. S. and D. E. Hall, *The Two-Career Couple* (Reading, MA: Addison-Wesley, 1979); Rosanna Hertz, *More Equal than Others: Women and Men in Dual-Career Marriages* (Berkeley: University of California Press, 1986); Jane C. Hood, *Becoming a Two-Job Family* (New York: Praeger, 1983); Janet G. and Larry L. Hunt, "Dilemmas and Contradictions of Status: The Case of the Dual-Career Family," *Social Problems*, 24 (1977), pp. 407–416; Rosabeth Moss Kanter, *Work and Family in the United States: A Critical Review and Agenda for Research and Policy* (Beverly Hills, CA: Sage Publications, 1977); Hannah Papanek, "Men, Women and Work: Reflections on the Two-Person Career," *American Journal of Sociology*, 78:4 (January 1973), pp. 853–872; Joseph H. Pleck, *Working Wives/Working Husbands* (Beverly Hills, CA: Sage, 1985); G. Wade Rowatt and Mary Jo Rowatt, *The Two-Career Marriage* (Philadelphia: Westminster, 1980); Mary G. Taylor and Shirley F. Hartley, "The Two-Person Career: A Classic Example," *Sociology of Work and Occupations*, 2:4 (November 1975), pp. 354–372; David N. Ulrich and Harry P. Dunne, Jr., *To Love and Work: A Systemic Interlocking of Family, Workplace and Career* (New York: Brunner/Mazel, 1986); Patricia Voydanoff, ed., *Work and Family: Changing Roles of Men and Women* (Mountain View, CA: Mayfield Publishing Co., 1984).

6. For specific discussion of couples who work together, see Frank and Sharan Barnett, *Working Together: Entrepreneurial Couples* (Berkeley: Ten Speed Press, 1988); R. B. and J. B. Bryson, and M. H. and B. G. Licht, "The Professional Pair: Husband and Wife Psychologists," *American Psychologist*,

31 (1976), pp. 10–17; Cynthia F. Epstein, "Law Partners and Marital Partners," *Human Relations*, 24 (1971), pp. 549–564; Lenore Hoffmann and Gloria DeSole, eds., *Career and Couples: An Academic Question* (New York; Modern Language Association, 1976); Arlene Krupa, with Chris Kirk-Kuwaye, *Couple-Power: How to be Partners in Love and Business* (New York: Dodd-Mead, 1987); Thomas A. Lyson, "Husband and Wife Work Roles and the Organization and Operation of Family Farms," *Journal of Marriage and the Family*, 47:3 (August 1985), pp. 759–764; Linda McKiernan-Allen and Ronald J. Allen, "Colleagues in Marriage and Ministry," in *Women Ministers*, ed. Judith L. Weidman, new and expanded ed., (San Francisco: Harper and Row, 1985), pp. 207–220; Sharon Nelton, *In Love and in Business: How Entrepreneurial Couples are Changing the Rules of Business and Marriage* (New York: John Wiley & Sons, 1986); Fran Pepitone-Rockwell, ed., *Dual Career Couples* (Beverly Hills, CA: Sage Publications, 1980); E. M. Rallings and David J. Pratto, *Two-Clergy Marriages: A Special Case of Dual Careers* (Lanham, MD: University Press of America, 1984); Rhona and Robert N. Rapoport, eds., *Working Couples* (New York: Harper & Row, 1978); Elyse and Mike Sommer, *The Two-Boss Business: The Joys and Pitfalls of Working and Living Together—And Still Remaining Friends* (New York: Butterick, 1980); John P. and Nancy Jo Kemper von Lackum, *Clergy Couples* (New York: National Council of Churches, 1979).

7. See Barnet, *Working Together*, pp. xxvii–xxviii, and Nelton, *In Love and in Business*, p. 12.

8. Unfortunately, when asked to describe their ethnic origins, couples frequently responded "middle class" or "suburban mainline," or else had a mixed and forgotten ancestry, making it practically impossible to discern linkages between ethnicity and *oikos* patterns, though, on the basis of our interviews, we believe there are important connections here.

9. See, most recently, Arlie Hochschild, *Second Shift* (New York: Viking Press, 1989).

10. In Daniel Levinson's terms, they are climbing the ladder at this point. See his *The Seasons of a Man's Life* (New York: Ballantine Books, 1979).

11. This connection between rational ethical principles and task-oriented images would surely not have surprised Max Weber. See *The Protestant Ethic and the Spirit of Capitalism* (New York: Charles Scribner's Sons, 1958).

12. For example, Suzanne Pingree, *et al.*, "Anti-Nepotism's Ghost: Attitudes of Administrators Toward Hiring Professional Couples," *Psychology of Women Quarterly*, 3:1 (Fall 1978), pp. 22–29. More recently, many academic institutions have developed special contracts for couples. Other organizations are developing more refined rules to enable couples to work in the same corporation or department.

13. Fred Best, *Work Sharing: Issues, Policy Options and Prospects* (Kalamazoo: W.E. Upjohn, 1981); Gretl S. Meier, *Job-Sharing: A New Pattern for Quality of Work and Life* (Kalamazoo: W.E. Upjohn Institute for Employment

Research, 1979), pp. 134–147; Maureen McCarthy and Gail Rosenberg, *Work Sharing Case Studies* (Kalamazoo: W.E. Upjohn, 1981); Barney Olmstead and Suzanne Smith, *The Job Sharing Handbook* (Berkeley: Ten Speed Press, 1983).

14. For instance, the Norrell Corporation, a temporary employment franchise system, reported to us that, as of 1989, 28% of their franchises were owned by couples, with actual operation of franchises by couples approaching 50%. Couples are their primary source of owner-operators.

15. Fred Best, *Flexible Life Scheduling: Breaking the Education-Work-Retirement Lockstep* (New York: Praeger, 1980); Sheila Kamerman and Alfred Kahn, *The Responsive Workplace* (New York: Columbia University Press, 1987); Bureau of National Affairs, *Work and Family: A Changing Dynamic* (Washington: BNA, 1986); and Ann Harriman, *The Work/Leisure Trade Off: Reduced Work Time for Managers and Professionals* (New York: Praeger, 1982).

16. In their book *Habits of the Heart: Individualism and Commitment in American Life* (Berkeley: University of California Press, 1985), Robert Bellah and his associates struggle with the problem of balancing the need for more individual equality in marriage with the desire for forms of commitment that might simply reinstate familial hierarchies (Chap. 4)

BIBLIOGRAPHY

Adriance, Madeleine. 1991. "Agents of Change: The Roles of Priests, Sisters and Lay Workers in the Grassroots Catholic Church in Brazil." *Journal for the Scientific Study of Religion* 30 (3): 292–305.

Aldous, Joan. 1983."Problematic Elements in the Relationships between Churches and Families." In *Families and Religions*, edited by Joan Aldous and William V. D'Antonio. Beverly Hills: Sage, pp. 67–80.

———, ed. 1982. *Two Paychecks: Life in Dual-Earner Families*. Beverly Hills, CA: Sage.

Aleshire, Daniel. 1989. "Family Life and Christian Spirituality." *Review and Expositor* 86 (2): 209–214.

Alwin, Duane. 1886. "Religion and Parental Child-Rearing Orientations: Evidence of a Catholic-Protestant Convergence." *American Journal of Sociology* 92 (2): 412–440.

Anderson, Herbert. 1984. *The Family and Pastoral Care*. Philadelphia: Fortress Press.

Anderson, Philip and Phoebe Anderson. 1975. *The House Church*. Nashville, TN: Abingdon.

Argyle, M. and B. Beit-Hallahmi. 1975. *The Social Psychology of Religion*. Boston: Routledge & Kegan Paul.

Avery-Clark, C. 1985. "Career Women Most Likely to Suffer From Inhibited Sexual Desire." *Behavior Today Newsletter* 16 (August): 4–6.

Bahr, Howard M. 1982. "Religious Contrasts in Family Role Definitions and Performance; Utah Mormons, Catholics, Protestants and Others." *Journal for the Scientific Study of Religion* 21: 200–217.

Bahr, H.M. and K. Goodman. 1981. "Divorce." In *Utah in Demographic Perspective: Regional and National Contrasts*, edited by H.M. Bahr. Provo, UT: Brigham Young University, Family and Demographic Research Institute.

Bahr, Howard and Bruce Chadwick. 1985."Religion and Family in Middletown." *Journal of Marriage and the Family* 47 (2): 407–414.

Baldwin, Wendy and Christine Nord. 1984. "Delayed Childbearing in the U.S.: Facts and Fictions." *Population Bulletin* 39(4). Washington, D.C.: Population Reference Bureau.

Baranowski, Arthur. 1988. *Creating Small Faith Communities*. Cincinnati, OH: St. Anthony's Messenger Press.

Barnett, Frank. 1988. *Working Together: Entrepreneurial Couples*. Berkeley, CA: Ten Speed Press.

Barrett, Lois. 1986. *Building the House Church*. Scottdale: Herald Press.

Barrish, Gerald and Michael R. Welch. 1980. "Student Religiosity and Discriminatory Attitudes Toward Women." *Sociological Analysis* 41(1): 66–73.

Bayer, Alan E. 1975. "Sexist Students in American Colleges: A Descriptive Note." *Journal of Marriage and the Family*, May, 391–96.

Bellah, Robert N. 1975. *The Broken Covenant*. New York: Seabury.

Bellah, Robert, Robert Madsen, William M. Sullivan, Ann Swidler, and Steven M. Tipton. 1991. *The Good Society*. New York: Alfred A. Knopf.

———. 1985. *Habits of the Heart: Individualism and Commitment in American Life*. Berkeley: University of California Press.

Berger, Brigitte and Peter L. Berger. 1983. *The War Over the Family*. New York: Doubleday.

Berger, Peter L. 1966. "Secularization and Pluralism." *Yearbook for the Sociology of Religion* 2: 73–90.

———. 1977a. *Facing Up to Modernity: Excursions in Society, Politics, and Religion*. New York: Basic Books.

———. 1977b. "In Praise of Particularity: The Concept of Mediating Structures." In *Facing Up to Modernity: Excursions in Society, Politics, and Religion*. New York: Basic Books, Inc., pp. 130–147.

Berger, Peter L., Brigitte Berger, and Hansfried Kellner. 1974. *The Homeless Mind*. New York: Doubleday.

Berger, Peter L. and Hansfried Kellner. 1975. "Marriage and the Construction of Reality." In *Life as Theater*, edited by Dennis Brissett and Charles Edgley. Chicago: Aldine, pp. 219–233.

Berger, Peter L. and Thomas Luckmann. 1966. *The Social Construction of Reality*. New York: Anchor Books.

Berger, Peter L. and Richard John Neuhaus. 1976. *Against the World for the World*. New York: Seabury.

Berk, Sarah F., ed. 1980. *Women and Household Labor*. Beverly Hills: Sage.

Berry, Mary Frances and John W. Blassingame. 1982. *Long Memory: The Black Experience in America*. New York: Oxford University Press.

Best, Fred. 1981. *Work Sharing: Issues, Policy Options and Prospects*. Kalamazoo: W.E. Upjohn.

———. 1980. *Flexible Life Scheduling: Breaking the Education-Work-Retirement Lockstep*. New York: Praeger.

Bianchi, Suzanne. 1990. "America's Children: Mixed Prospects." *Population Bulletin* 45 (1, June). Washington, D.C.: Population Reference Bureau, Inc.

Billingsley, Andrew. 1968. *Black Families in White America*. Englewood Cliffs, NJ: Prentice Hall.

Birkey, Del. 1988. *The House Church: A Model for Renewing the Church*. Scottdale: Herald Press.

Birnbaum, J.A. 1975. "Life Patterns and Self-Esteem in Gifted Family-Oriented and Career-Committed Women." In *Women and Achievement: Social and Motivational Analyses*, edited by Martha Mednick, Sandra Tangri and Lois Hoffman. Washington: Hemisphere Pub.

Blau, Peter. 1963. *The Dynamics of Bureaucracy*. Chicago: University of Chicago Press.

Blauner, Robert. 1972. *Racial Oppression in America*. New York: Harper and Row.

Blitchington, Peter W. 1980. *Sex Roles and the Christian Family*. Wheaton: Tyndale House.

Blood, W.G. and D.M. Wolfe. 1969. *Husbands and Wives: The Dynamics of Married Living*. Glencoe, IL: The Free Press.

Bock, E. Wilbur and M. L. Radelet. 1988. "The Marital Integration of Religious Independents: A Reevaluation of its Significance." *Review of Religious Research* 29 (3): 228–241.

Bowen, W.G. and T.A. Finegan. 1969. *The Economics of Labor Force Participation*. Princeton, NJ: Princeton University Press.

Briggs, Kenneth. 1993. *Holy Siege: Twelve Months in the Life of the Roman Catholic Church*. San Francisco: Harper.

Brinkerhoff, Merlin B. 1984a. *Family and Work: Comparative Convergences*. Westport: Greenwood.

———, ed. 1984b. *Work, Organizations, and Society*. Westport: Greenwood.

Brinkerhoff, Merlin B. and Kathryn L. Burke. 1980. "Disaffiliation: Some Notes on 'Falling from the Faith.'" *Sociological Analysis* 41 (1): 41–54.

Brinkerhoff, Merlin B. and Marlene M. Mackie. 1985. "Religion and Gender: A Comparison of Canadian and American Student Attitudes." *Journal of Marriage and the Family* 47: 415–429.

———. 1984. "Religious Denominations' Impact on Gender Attitudes: Some Methodological Implications." *Review of Religious Research* 25 (4): 365–378.

Bromley, David G., Anson Jr. Shupe, and Donna Oliver. 1982. "Perfect Families: Visions of the Future in a New Religious Movement." In *Cults and the Family*, edited by Florence Kaslow, and Marvin B. Sussman. New York: Hawthorn Press.

Browning, Don. 1987. *Religious Thought and the Modern Psychologies*. Philadelphia: Fortress Press.

———. 1980. *Pluralism and Personality*. Lewisburg, Penn.: Bucknell University Press.

———. 1975. *Generative Man*. New York: Dell Publishing.

Browning, Robert L. and Roy A. Reed. 1985. *The Sacraments in Religious Education and Liturgy*. Birmingham: Religious Education Press.

Bryson, R.B., J.B. Bryson, M.H. Licht, and B.G. Licht. 1976. "The Professional Pair: Husband and Wife Psychologists." *American Psychologist* 31: 10–17.

Bumpass, L.L. and J.A. Sweet. 1972. "Differentials in Marital Instability, 1970." *American Sociological Review* 37: 754–66.

Bureau of National Affairs. 1986. *Work and Family: A Changing Dynamic*. Washington: Bureau of National Affairs.

Burgess, Ernest W. and Harvey J. Locke. 1945. *The Family: From Institution to Companionship*. New York: Macmillan.

Burr, Wesley, Reuben Hill, F.Ivan Nye, and Ira L. Reiss, eds. 1979. *Contemporary Theories About the Family*, Vol. 2. New York: The Free Press.

Cady, Linell. 1987. "Relational Love: A Feminist Christian Vision." In *Embodied Love*, edited by Paula Cooey, Sharon Farmer, and Mary Ellen Ross. San

Francisco: Harper and Row.

Caplow, T. and H. M. Bahr, et. al. 1982. *Middletown Families*. Minneapolis: University of Minnesota Press.

Center for Applied Research in the Apostolate. 1980. *Women and Ministry*. Washington: Center for Applied Research in the Apostolate.

Carnegie Corporation of New York. 1988. "Black Churches: Can They Strengthen the Black Family?" *Carnegie Quarterly* 33 (1): 1–9.

Carroll, Jackson W. 1977. *Small Churches are Beautiful*. New York: Harper and Row.

Carroll, Jackson W. and David A. Roozen. 1975. *Religious Participation in American Society: An Analysis of Social and Religious Trends and Their Interaction*. Multilith. Hartford, CT: Hartford Seminary Foundation.

Chalfant, Paul H., Robert Beckley, and Eddie C. Palmer. 1984. *Religion in Contemporary Society*. Palo Alto, CA: Mayfield Pub. Co.

Chancey, David. 1983. "The House Church." *Missions USA*, January/February, 57–58.

Chatters, Linda M., M. Belinda Tucker, and Edith Lewis. 1990. "Developments in Research on Black Families: A Decade Review." *Journal of Marriage and the Family* 52 (November): 993–1014.

Chaves, Mark. 1991. "Family Structure and Protestant Church Attendance: The Sociological Basis of Cohort and Age Effects." *Journal for the Scientific Study of Religion* 30: 501–515.

Cho, Paul Y. 1984. "Reaching Cities with Home Cells." *Urban Mission*, January, 4–14.

———. 1981. *Successful Home Cell Groups*. Plainfield, NJ: Logos.

Christiano, Kevin. 1986. "Church as a Family Surrogate: Another Look at Family Ties, Anomie, and Church Involvement." *Journal for the Scientific Study of Religion* 25 (3): 339–354.

Chusmir, Leonard H. and Christine S. Koberg. 1988. "A Look at Sex Differences in the Relationships Between Religious Beliefs and Work-related Attitudes." *Journal of Social Behaviour and Personality* 3 (1): 37–48.

Clapp, Steve. 1984. *The Third Wave and the Family: The Church Family Braces for Change*. Champaign: C–4 Resources.

Coleman, James C. 1988. *Intimate Relationships, Marriage and Family*. New York: MacMillan.

Cooley, Charles Horton. 1922. *Human Nature and the Social Order*. New York: Scribner's.

Cuddihy, John. 1978. *No Offense: Civil Religion and Protestant Taste*. New York: Seabury.

D'Antonio, William V. 1985. "The American Catholic Family: Signs of Cohesion and Polarization." *Journal of Marriage and Family*, May, 395–405.

———. 1983. "Family Life, Religion, and Societal Values and Structures." In *Families and Religions*, edited by Joan Aldous and William D'Antonio. Beverly Hills: Sage, pp. 67–80.

————. 1980. "The Family and Religion: Exploring a Changing Relationship." *Journal for the Scientific Study of Religion* 19 (2): 89–104.

D'Antonio, William, *et al.* 1989. *American Catholic Laity in a Changing Church*. Kansas City: Sheed and Ward.

D'Antonio, William V. and Joan Aldous. 1983. *Families and Religions: Conflict and Change in Modern Society*. Beverly Hills: Sage Publications.

D'Antonio, William V., William M. Newman, and Stuart A. Wright. 1982. "Religion and Family Life: How Social Scientists View the Relationship." *Journal for the Scientific Study of Religion* 21 (3): 218–225.

Daly, Mary. 1968. *The Church and the Second Sex*. New York: Harper and Row.

Davidson, James D., Dean Knudsen, and Stephen R. Lerch. 1983. "Involvement in Family, Religion, Education, Work and Politics." *Sociological Focus*, January, 13–36.

Davis, James A. and Tom Smith. 1990. *General Social Surveys, 1972–1990*. Machine-readable data file. Chicago, IL: National Opinion Research Center.

Degler, Carl. 1980. *At Odds: Women and the Family in America From the Revolution to the Present*. New York: Oxford University Press.

Demerath, N.J., III. 1965. *Social Class in American Protestantism*. Chicago: Rand McNally.

————. 1961. "Social Stratification and Church Involvement: The Church-Sect Distinction Applied to Individual Participation." *Review of Religious Research* 2: 146–154.

Demmitt, Kevin. 1990a. "The Accommodation of Dual-Earner Families in Conservative Protestant Churches." Paper presented at the annual meetings of the Society for the Scientific Study of Religion. Virginia Beach, November.

————. 1990b. *Dual-Earner Families and Conservative Churches: Accommodation and Conflict*. Unpublished doc. diss, Purdue University.

Demos, John. 1979. "Images of the American Family, Then and Now." In *Changing Images of the Family*, edited by V. Tufte and B. Myerhoff. New Haven, CT: Yale University Press.

Dempewolff, J.A. 1974. "Some Correlates of Feminism." *Psychological Reports* 34 (April): 671–76.

DeVaus, David A. 1984. "Workforce Participation and Sex Differences in Church Attendance." *Review of Religious Research* 25 (3): 247–256.

DeVaus, David and Ian McAllister. 1987. "Gender Differences in Religion: A Test of the Structural Location Theory." *American Sociological Review* 52 (52): 472–481.

Douglas, Ann. 1977. *The Feminization of American Culture*. New York: Knopf.

DuBose, Francis M. 1982. "Alternative Church Models for an Urban Society." In *The Urban Challenge*, edited by Larry L. Rose and C. Kirk Hadaway. Nashville: Broadman, pp. 121–144.

Dudley, Carl S. 1978. *Making the Small Church Effective*. Nashville: Abingdon.

Dudley, R.L. and M.G. Dudley. 1986. "Transmission of Religious Values from Parents to Adolescents." *Review of Religious Research* 28: 3–15.

Dudley, Roger L., Patricia B. Mutch, and Cruise Robert J. 1987. "Religious Factors and Drug Usage Among Seventh-Day Adventist Youth in North America." *Journal for the Scientific Study of Religion* 26 (2): 218–233.

Dykstra, Craig. 1987. "The Formative Power of the Congregation." *Religious Education* 82 (4): 530–546.

Ebaugh, Helen Rose Fuchs. 1988. *Becoming an Ex*. Chicago: University of Chicago Press.

Edelman, Marian Wright. 1987. *Families in Peril: An Agenda for Social Change*. Cambridge, MA: Harvard University Press.

Elshtain, Jean Bethke. 1982. "Feminism, Family and Community." *Dissent* 29 (Fall): 442–449.

Engels, Frederick. 1985. *The Origin of the Family, Private Property, and the State*. New York: International Publishers.

Epstein, Cynthia F. 1971. "Law Partners and Marital Partners." *Human Relations* 24: 549–64.

Erikson, Erik. 1963. *Childhood and Society*. New York: W. W. Norton.

Erskine, H. 1971. "The Polls: Women's role." *Public Opinion Quarterly* 35: 282–84.

Etzioni, Amitai. 1991. *The Responsive Community: Rights and Responsibilities* 1 (1): 2–5.

Everett, William Johnson. 1990. *Blessed be the Bond: Christian Perspectives on Marriage and Family*. Lanham, MD: University Press of America.

———. 1988. *God's Federal Republic: Reconstructing Our Governmental Symbol*. New York: Paulist Press.

———. 1986. "Oikos: Convergence in Business Ethics." *Journal of Business Ethics* 5: 313–25.

Exter, Thomas. 1990. "Demographic Forecasts: Married with Kids." *American Demographics* 55 (February).

Fairchild, Roy and John C. Wynn. 1961. *Families in the Church: A Protestant Survey*. New York: Association.

Firebaugh, Glenn and Kenneth E. Davis. 1988. "Trends in Anti-Black Prejudice, 1972–1984: Region and Cohort Effects." *American Journal of Sociology* 94: 251–272.

Fishbein, Martin and Icek Ajzen. 1975. *Belief, Attitude, Intention and Behavior: An Introduction to Theory and Research*. Menlo Park, CA: Addison Wesley Pub. Co.

Fishburn, Janet. 1991. *Confronting the Idolatry of Family: A New Vision for the Household of God*. Nashville, TN: Abingdon Press.

Foster, Arthur L. 1976. *The House Church Evolving*. Chicago: Exploration Press.

Foster, Charles R. 1982. *Teaching in the Community of Faith*. Nashville: Abingdon Press.

———. 1989. "The Changing Family." In *Religious Education as Social Transformation*, edited by Allen J. Moore. Birmingham: Religious Education Press.

Fowler, James. 1991. *Weaving the New Creation: Stages of Faith and the Public Church*. San Francisco: Harper.

———. 1989. "The Public Church: Ecology for Faith Education and Advocate for Children." In *Faith Development in Early Childhood*, edited by Doris Blazer. Kansas City: Sheed and Ward.

———. 1987. *Faith Development and Pastoral Care*. Philadelphia: Fortress Press.

———. 1981. *Stages of Faith: The Psychology of Human Development and the Quest for Meaning*. San Francisco: Harper and Row.

Frankena, William. 1973. *Ethics*. Englewood Cliffs: Printice Hall.

Frazier, E. Franklin. 1964. *The Negro Church in America*. New York: Schocken Books.

———. 1957. *The Black Bourgeoisie: The Rise of a New Middle Class*. New York: Free Press.

———. 1939. *The Negro Family in the United States*. Chicago: University of Chicago Press.

Friedman, Edwin. 1985. *Generation to Generation*. New York: The Guilford Press.

Freudiger, P. 1983. "Life Satisfaction Among Three Categories of Married Women." *Journal of Marriage and the Family* 45 (1): 213–219.

Fuchs, Eric. 1983. *Sexual Desire and Love*. New York: Seabury Press.

Fukuyama, Yoshio. 1961. "The Major Dimensions of Church Membership." *Review of Religious Research* 2: 154–161.

Garland, Diana S. Richmond. 1989. "An Ecosystemic Perspective for Family Ministry." *Review and Expositor* 86 (2): 195–208.

Gary, Lawrence E., Editor. 1981. *Black Men*. Beverly Hills, CA: Sage Publications.

Gee, Ellen M. 1991. "Gender Differences in Church Attendance in Canada: The Role of Labor Force Participation." *Review of Religious Research* 32: 267–273.

Gerson, Kathleen. 1985. *Hard Choices: How Women Decide About Work, Career, and Motherhood*. Berkeley: University of California Press.

Gerstell, Naomi and Harriet Gross. 1984. *Commuter Marriage*. New York: Guilford.

Gewirth, Alan. 1988. "Ethical Universalism and Particularism." *Journal of Philosophy* 85 (6, June): 283–302.

Giddings, Paula. 1984. *When and Where I Enter: The Impact of Black Women on Race and Sex in America*. New York: William Morrow and Company.

Gilkes, Cheryl Townsend. 1985. "Together and in Harness: Women's Traditions in the Sanctified Church." *Signs: Journal of Women in Culture and Society* 11 (4): 678–699.

Gilligan, Carol. 1982. *In a Different Voice*. Cambridge: Harvard University Press.

Glenn, Norval D. 1987a. "Social Trends in the United States: Evidence from Sample Surveys." *Public Opinion Quarterly* 51: S109–S126.

———. 1987b. "The Trend in 'No Religion' Respondents to U.S. National Surveys, Late 1950s to early 1980s." *Public Opinion Quarterly* 51: 293–314.

Glick, Paul. 1984. "American Household Structure in Transition." *Family Planning Perspectives* 16: 205–211.

Glock, Charles, Benjamin Ringer, and Earl Babbie. 1967. *To Comfort and to Challenge: A Dilemma of the Contemporary Church*. Berkeley, CA: University of California Press.

Glock, Charles and Rodney Stark. 1965. *Religion and Society in Tension*. Chicago, IL: Rand, McNally and Company.

Goldman, Ari L. 1990. "Black Minister Recruits More Men for the Church." *New York Times*, July 5, B2.

Goldscheider, C. 1971. *Population, Modernization, and Social Structure*. Boston: Little, Brown.

Goldscheider, Calvin and Frances Goldscheider. 1988. "Ethnicity, Religiosity, and Leaving Home: The Structural and Cultural Basis of Traditional Family Values." *Sociological Forum* 3: 525–547.

————. 1986. "Moving Out and Marriage: What Do Young Adults Expect?" *American Sociological Review* 52: 278–285.

Goldscheider, Frances and Celine Lebourdais. 1987. "The Falling Age At Leaving Home, 1920–1979." *Sociology and Social Research* 70: 99–102.

Goldthorpe, J.E. 1987. *Family Life in Western Societies: A Historical Sociology of Family Relationships in Britain and North America*. Cambridge: Cambridge University Press.

Greeley, Andrew M. 1985. *American Catholics Since the Council: An Unauthorized Report*. Chicago: Thomas More.

————. 1979. "The Sociology of American Catholics." *Annual Review of Sociology* 5: 91–111.

————. 1978. "Religious Musical Chairs." *Society* 15 (4): 53–59.

————. 1976. *Catholic Schools in a Declining Church*. Kansas City: Sheed and Ward.

————. 1972. *Unsecular Man*. New York: Schocken Books.

Greif, Geoffrey, L. and Alfred Demaris. 1990. "Single Fathers with Custody." *Families in Society* 71 (5): 259–266.

Groom, Thomas. 1980. *Christian Religious Education: Sharing Our Story and Vision*. San Francisco: Harper and Row.

Gutman, Herbert. 1976. *The Black Family in Slavery and Freedom, 1750–1925*. New York: Pantheon Books.

Hadaway, Kirk and Penny Marler. 1990. "A Retest and Extension of Nash's 1968 'A Little Child Shall Lead Them.'" Unpublished manuscript. Hartford, CT: Hartford Seminary.

Hadaway, C. Kirk, Stuart A. Wright, and Francis M. DuBose. 1987. *Home Cell Groups and House Churches: Emerging Alternatives for the Urban Church*. Nashville: Broadman.

Hadden, Jeffrey. 1983. "Televangelism and the Mobilization of a New Christian Right Family Policy." In *Families and Religion: Conflict and Change in Modern Society*, edited by W. D'Antonio, and J. Aldous. Beverly Hills, CA: Sage

Publications.

———. 1969. *The Gathering Storm in the Churches: the Widening Gap between Clergy and Laymen*. Garden City, NJ: Doubleday.

Hall, F.S. and D.E. Hall. 1979. *The Two-Career Couple*. Reading, MA: Addison-Wesley.

Hall, Robert L. and Carol B. Stack. 1982. *Holding on to the Land and the Lord: Kinship, Ritual, Land Tenure and Social Policy in the Rural South*. Athens, GA: University of Georgia Press.

Hammond, Phillip E. 1992. *Religion and Personal Autonomy: The Third Disestablishment in America*. Columbia: University of South Carolina Press.

———. 1988. "Religion and the Persistence of Identity." *Journal for the Scientific Study of Religion* 27 (1): 1–11.

Harding, Vincent. 1987. "Toward a Darkly Radiant Vision of America's Truth." *Cross Currents* 37 (1): 1–32.

Hargrove, Barbara. 1989. *The Sociology of Religion*. 2nd edition. Arlington Heights, IL: Harlan Davidson.

———. 1985. "Gender, the Family, and the Sacred." In *The Sacred in a Secular Age*, edited by Phillip E. Hammond. Berkeley: University of California Press, pp. 204–214.

———. 1983a. "The Church, the Family, and the Modernization Process." In *Families and Religions*, edited by Joan Aldous and William D'Antonio. Beverly Hills: Sage, pp. 21–48.

———. 1983b. "Family in the White American Protestant Experience." In *Families and Religions*, edited by Joan Aldous and William D'Antonio. Beverly Hills, CA: Sage.

Harriman, Ann. 1982. *The Work/Leisure Trade Off: Reduced Work Time for Managers and Professionals*. New York: Praeger.

Harris, Louis. 1987. *Inside America*. New York: Vintage Books.

Hart, Stephen. 1986. "Religion and Changes in Family Patterns." *Review of Religious Research* 28 (1): 51–70.

Hastings, Adrian, ed. 1991. *Modern Catholicism: Vatican II and After*. New York: Oxford University.

Hauerwas, Stanley. 1981. "A Story-Formed Community." In *A Community of Character: Toward a Constructive Christian Social Ethic*. Notre Dame: Notre Dame University Press, pp. 9–35.

Hayghe, Howard. 1986. "Rise in Mothers' Labor Force Activity Includes Those With Infants." *Monthly Labor Review*, February, 43–45.

Heaton, Tim B. and Marie Cornwall. 1989. "Religious Group Variation in the Socioeconomic Status and Family Behavior of Women." *Journal for the Scientific Study of Religion* 28 (3): 283–299.

Heaton, Tim B. and Kristen L. Goodman. 1985. "Religion and Family Formation." *Review of Religious Research* 26 (4): 343–359.

Hechter, Michael. 1987. *Principles of Group Solidarity*. Berkeley: University of California Press.

Heckman, Norma A., Jeff Bryson, and Rebecca Bryson. 1977. "Problems of Professional Couples: A Content Analysis." *Journal of Marriage and the Family* 39: 323–30.

Heiss, Jerold. 1977. "Social Traits and Family Attitudes in the U.S." *International Journal of Sociology of the Family* 7 (2): 209–225.

———. 1975. *The Case of the Black Family: A Sociological Inquiry*. New York: Columbia University Press.

Henley, N.M. and F. Pincus. 1978. "Interrelationship of Sexist, Racist, and Homosexual Attitudes." *Psychological Reports* 42 (February): 83–90.

Herberg, Will. 1955. *Protestant, Catholic, and Jew*. Garden City, NJ: Doubleday and Company.

Herman, Jeane and Karen K. Gyllstrom. 1977. "Working Men and Women: Inter- and Intra-role Conflict." *Psychology of Women Quarterly* 1: 319–330.

Hertel, Bradley. 1988. "Gender, Religious Identity, and Work Force Participation." *Journal for the Scientific Study of Religion* 27 (4): 574–592.

Hertel, Bradley R. and Michael Hughes. 1987. "Religious Affiliation, Attendance, and Support for 'Pro-Family' Issues in the U.S." *Social Forces* 65: 858–882.

Hertel, Bradley R. and Hart M. Nelsen. 1974. "Are We Entering a Post-Christian Era? Religious Belief and Attendance in America." *Journal for the Scientific Study of Religion* 13: 409–419.

Hertz, Rosanna. 1986. *More Equal than Others: Women and Men in Dual-Career Marriages*. Berkeley: University of California Press.

Hesselbart, S. 1976. "A Comparison of Attitudes Toward Women and Attitudes Toward Blacks in a Southern City." *Sociological Symposium* 17 (Fall): 45–68.

Hester, Michael. 1989. "A Theology for Family Ministry." *Review and Expositor* 86 (2): 161–174.

Hewlett, Sylvia, A. S. Ilchman, and J. J. Sweeney. 1986. *Family and Work: Bridging the Gap*. Cambridge, MA: Ballinger.

Higgins, Gregory C. 1989. "The Significance of Postliberalism for Religious Education." *Religious Education* 84 (1): 85.

Hill, Reuben. 1971. "Modern Systems Theory and the Family." *Social Information* 10: 7–26.

Hill, Robert. 1972. *The Strengths of Black Families: A National Urban League Research Study*. New York: Emerson Hall Publishers, Inc.

Hobart, Charles W. 1974. "Church Involvement and the Comfort Thesis in Alberta." *Journal for the Scientific Study of Religion* 17: 107–127.

Hochschild, Arlie. 1989. *Second Shift*. New York: Viking Press.

Hoffman, L.W. 1963. "The Decision to Work." In *The Employed Mother in America*, edited by F.I. Nye and L.W. Hoffman. Chicago: Rand McNally.

Hoffman, L.W. and F. Ivan Nye. 1974. *Working Mothers*. San Francisco, CA: Jossey-Bass.

Hoffmann, Lenore and Gloria DeSole, eds. 1976. *Career and Couples: An Academic Question*. New York: Modern Language Assn.

Hogan, Dennis P., Ling-Xin Hao, and William L. Parish. 1990. "Race, Kin

Networks, and Assistance to Mother-Headed Families." *Social Forces* 68 (3): 797–812.

Hoge, Dean and Jackson W. Carroll. 1978. "Determinants of Commitment and Participation in Suburban Protestant Churches." *Journal for the Scientific Study of Religion* 17 (2): 107–127.

Hoge, Dean, G. Pegtrillo, and E. Smith. 1982. "Transmission of Religious and Social Values from Parents to Teenage Children." *Journal of Marriage and the Family* 44: 569–580.

Hoge, Dean and David Polk. 1980. "A Test of Theories of Protestant Church Participation and Commitment." *Review of Religious Research* 21: 315–329.

Hoge, Dean and David Roozen. 1979. "Research on Factors Influencing Church Commitment." In *Understanding Church Growth and Decline: 1950–1978*, edited by Dean Hoge, and David Roozen. New York: Pilgrim Press.

Hollenweger, Walter J. 1982. "The House Church Movement in Great Britain." *Expository Time* 86: 45–47.

Holmes, Steven A. 1991. "Unlikely Union Arises to Press Family Issues." *New York Times*, May 1, A12.

Holter, H. 1970. *Sex Roles and Social Structure*. Oslo: Universitetsforlaget.

Homola, Michael, Dean Knudsen, and Harvey Marshall. 1988. "Status Attainment and Religion: A Reevaluation." *Review of Religious Research* 29 (3): 242–258.

Hood, Jane C. 1983. *Becoming a Two-Job Family*. New York: Praeger.

Hopewell, James. 1987. *Congregation: Stories and Structures*, edited by Barbara G. Wheeler. Philadelphia: Fortress Press.

Hopkins, Ellen. 1990. "Childhood's End: Crack Babies." *Rolling Stone*, No. 589, October 18, 66.

Hout, Michael and Andrew Greeley. 1987. "The Center Doesn't Hold: Church Attendance in the United States, 1940–1984." *American Sociological Review* 52: 325–345.

Hoyt, Robert G. 1968. *The Birth Control Debate*. Kansas City: National Catholic Reporter Publishing Co.

Huber, Joan and Glenna Spitze. 1981. "Wives' Employment, Household Behaviors, and Sex-Role Attitudes." *Social Forces* 60: 150–169.

Hunsberger. Bruce and L.B. Brown. 1984. "Religious Socialization, Apostasy, and the Impact of Family Background." *Journal for the Scientific Study of Religion* 23 (3): 239–251.

Hunt, Janet G. and Larry L. Hunt. 1977. "Dilemmas and Contradictions of Status: The Case of the Dual-Career Family." *Social Problems* 24: 407–416.

Hunt, Richard A. and Morton B King. 1978. "Religiosity and Marriage." *Journal for the Scientific Study of Religion* 17 (4): 399–406.

Hunter, James Davison. 1987. *Evangelicalism: The Coming Generation*. Chicago: University of Chicago Press.

———. 1983. *American Evangelicalism: Conservative Religion and the Quandary of Modernity*. New Brunswick, NJ: Rutgers University Press.

Iannaccone, Laurence R. and Carrie A. Miles. 1990. "Dealing with Social Change: The Mormon Church's Response to Change in Women's Roles." *Social Forces* 68 (4): 1231–1250.

Ihinger-Tallman, Marilyn and Kay Pasley. 1987. *Remarriage*. Newbury Park, CA: Sage Publications.

Jackman, Mary R. and Michael J. Muha. 1984. "Education and Intergroup Attitudes: Moral Enlightenment, Superficial Democratic Commitment, or Ideological Refinement?" *American Sociological Review* 49: 751–769.

Jackson, Jaquelyne Johnson. 1983. "Contemporary Relationships Between Black Families and Black Churches in the United States." In *Families and Religions*, edited by J. Aldous and W. D'Antonio. Beverly Hills: Sage, pp. 191–220.

Jacquet, Constant H., Jr., ed. 1990. *The Yearbook of American and Canadian Churches*. Annual edition. Nashville, TN: Abingdon Press.

Janssens, Louis. 1977. "Norms and Priorities of a Love Ethic." *Louvain Studies* 6 (Spring).

Jaynes, Gerald David and Robin M. Williams, Jr., eds. 1989. *A Common Destiny: Blacks and American Society*. Washington, D.C.: National Academy Press.

Jeffrey, Kirk. 1972. "The Family as Utopian Retreat From the City: The Nineteenth Century Contribution." In *The Family, Communes, and Utopian Societies*, edited by S. TeSelle. New York: Harper and Row.

Jewell, K. Sue. 1988. *Survival of the Black Family: The Institutional Impact of U.S. Social Policy*. New York: Praeger Publishers.

Johnson, Barry L., Susan Eberly, James Duke, and Deborah Sartain. 1988. "Wives' Employment Status and Marital Happiness of Religious Couples." *Review of Religious Research* 29 (3): 259–270.

Johnson, Benton. 1987. "Is There Hope for Liberal Protestantism?" In *Mainstream Protestantism: Its Problems and Prospects*, edited by Dorothy Bass, Benton Johnson, and Wade Clark Roof. Louisville: Committee on Theological Education of the Presbyterian Church (U.S.A.), pp. 13–26.

———. 1982. "Taking Stock: Reflections on the End of Another Era." *Journal for the Scientific Study of Religion* 21 (3).

Johnson, M.A. 1973. "Family Life and Religious Commitment." *Review of Religious Research* 14: 144–150.

Johnson Robert A. 1980. *Religious Assortative Marriage in the US*. New York: Academic.

Johnson, Suzanne. 1989. *Building Community with First Generation Christians in a Twentieth Century New York City Context*. Unpublished D.Min. thesis. Dayton, OH: United Theological Seminary.

Jones, E.F. and C.F. Westoff. 1979. "The End of 'Catholic' Fertility." *Demography* 16: 209–217.

Jones, Jacqueline. 1989. *Labor of Love, Labor of Sorrow: Black Women, Work and the Family From Slavery to the Present*. New York: Basic Books.

Kamerman, Sheila B. 1979. "Work and Family in Industrialized Societies." *Signs* 4: 632–650.

Kamerman, Sheila and Alfred Kahn. 1987. *The Responsive Workplace*. New York: Columbia University Press.

Kanter, Rosabeth Moss. 1977a. *Men and Women of the Corporation*. New York: Basic.

———. 1977b. *Work and Family in the United States: A Critical Review and Agenda for Research and Policy*. Beverly Hills, CA: Sage Publications.

———. 1972. *Commitment and Community: Communes and Utopias in Sociological Perspective*. Cambridge: Harvard University Press.

"Keeping the Faith." 1987. *Frontline*. Public Broadcasting Service.

Kegan, Robert. 1982. *The Evolving Self*. Cambridge: Harvard Unversity Press.

Kemper von Lackum, John P. and Nancy Jo Kemper von Lackum. 1979. *Clergy Couples*. New York: National Council of Churches.

Keifer, Ralph A. 1976. "Christian Initiation: The State of the Question." In *Made, Not Born: New Perspectives on Christian Initiation and the Catechumenate*. Notre Dame: University of Notre Dame Press.

Kieren, Dianne K. and Brenda Munro. 1987. "Following the Leaders: Parents' Influence on Adolescent Religious Activity." *Journal for the Scientific Study of Religion* 26 (2): 249–255.

Klatzky, Sheila. n.d. *Patterns of Contact with Relatives*. Washington: ASA Rose Monographs.

Kohn, Melvin L. 1977. *Class and Conformity*. Chicago: University of Chicago Press.

Korman, Sheila K. 1983. "The Feminist: Familial Influences on Adherence to Ideology and Commitment to a Self-Perception." *Family Relations* 32: 431–439.

Krupa, Arlene and Chris Kirk-Kuwaye. 1987. *Couple-Power: How to Be Partners in Love and Business*. New York: Dodd-Mead.

Kunz, Philip R. and Stan L. Albrecht. 1977. "Religion, Marital Happiness, and Divorce." *International Journal of Sociology of the Family* 7 (2): 227–232.

Ladner, Joyce A. 1988. "The Impact of Teenage Pregnancy on the Black Family: Policy Directions." In *Black Families*, edited by Harriette Pipes McAdoo. Beverly Hills, CA: Sage Publications.

LaHaye, Timothy. 1982. *The Battle for the Family*. Old Tappan, NJ: Fleming H. Revell.

———. 1980. *The Battle for the Mind*. Old Tappan, NJ: Fleming H. Revell.

Lamb, Matthew L. 1982. *Solidarity with Victims: Toward a Theology of Social Transformation*. New York: Crossroad.

Lampe, P.E. 1981. "Androgyny and Religiosity." *Women's Studies* 4 (1): 27–34.

Lantz, Herman, Martin Schultz, and Mary O'Hara. 1977. "The Changing American Family from Pre-industrial to the Industrial Period: A Final Report." *American Sociological Review* 42: 406–421.

Lasch, Christopher. 1991. *The True and Only Heaven: Progress and Its Critics*. New York: W.W. Norton.

———. 1977. *Haven in a Heartless World: the Family Besieged*. New York: Basic

Books.

Laslett, Barbara. 1973. "The Family as a Public and Private Institution: An Historical Perspective." *Journal of Marriage and the Family* 35: 480–492.

Lawton, Kim A. 1991. "Giving Black Families a Boost." *Christianity Today* 35 (9): 38–39.

Lazerwitz, Bernard. 1960. "Some Factors Associated With Variation in Church Attendance." *Social Forces* 39: 301–309.

Lechner, Frank J. 1985. "Fundamentalism and Sociocultural Revitalization in America: A Sociological Interpretation." *Sociological Analysis* 46 (3): 243–260.

Lehrer, Evelyn L. and Marc L. Nerlove. 1986. "Female Labor Force Behavior and Fertility in the U.S." *Annual Review of Sociology* 12: 181–204.

Leinberger, Paul and Bruce Tucker. 1991. *The New Individualists: The Generation after the Organization Man*. New York: Harper.

Lenski, Gerhard E. 1963. *The Religious Factor*. Garden City, New York: Doubleday.

———. 1953. "Social Correlates of Religious Interest." *American Sociological Review* 18: 533–544.

Leser, C.E.V. 1969. *Economic Techniques and Problems*. Griffins' Statistical Monographs and Courses, Vol. 20. London: Griffin.

Levinson, Daniel. 1979. *The Seasons of a Man's Life*. New York: Ballantine Books.

Levitan, Sar A., Richard S. Belous, and Frank Gallo. 1988. *What's Happening to the American Family?* Baltimore, MD: Johns Hopkins University Press.

Lincoln, C. Eric and Lawrence Mamiya. 1990. *The Black Church in the African American Experience*. Chapel Hill: Duke University Press.

Lindbeck, George. 1984. *The Nature of Doctrine*. Philadelphia: Westminster Press.

Lipman-Billumen, J. 1972. "How Ideology Shapes Women's Lives." *Scientific American* 266 (January): 33–42.

Lipset, Seymour Martin. 1981. *Political Man*. Baltimore, MD: Johns Hopkins University Press.

———. 1965. "Religion in America: What Religious Revival?" *Columbia University Forum* 11 (2, Winter).

Lopata, Helen. 1970. "The Social Involvement of American Widows." *American Behavioral Scientist* 14: 41–57.

Lucey, Rose Marciano. 1987. *Roots and Wings: Dreamers and Doers of the Christian Family Movement*. San Jose, CA: Resource Publications.

Luckmann, Thomas. 1967. *The Invisible Religion*. New York: Macmillan.

Luepnitz, Debra. 1988. *The Family Interpreted: Feminist Theory in Clinical Practice*. New York: Basic Books.

Lynd, Robert and Helen Lynd. 1937. *Middletown in Transition: A Study in Cultural Conflicts*. New York: Harcourt, Brace & World.

Lyson, Thomas A. 1985. "Husband and Wife Work Roles and the Organization and Operation of Family Farms." *Journal of Marriage and the Family* 47 (3, August): 759–764.

Mace, David and Vera Mace. 1978. "The Marriage Enrichment Movement: Its History, Its Rationale, and Its Future Prospects." In *Toward Better Marriages: The Handbook of the Association of Couples for Marriage Enrichment (ACME)*, edited by L. Hopkins *et al.* Winston-Salem, NC: Assn. of Couples for Marriage Enrichment.

Malveaux, Julianne. 1988. "The Economic Statuses of Black Families." In *Black Families*, 2nd Edition, edited by Harriette Pipes McAdoo. Beverly Hills, CA: Sage Publications, pp. 133–46.

———. 1981. "Shifts in the Occupation and Employment Status of Black Women: Current Trends and Future Implications." Conference on Black Working Women. Berkeley, CA: University of California.

Marcum, J.P. 1981. "Explaining Fertility Differences Among U.S. Protestants." *Social Forces* 60: 532–543.

"Marketing Tools Alert." 1990. *American Demographics* 1 (July).

Marler, Penny. 1992a. "Churches Must 'Make Family' in '90s." *The Witness* 74: 6–9, 16.

———. 1992b. "Lifestyles and Religious Tastes of the Protestant New Class." Paper presented to the Society for the Scientific Study of Religion, Washington, D.C., 1992.

Marler, Penny and Kirk Hadaway. 1992. "New Church Development and Denominational Growth (1950–1988): Symptom or Cause?" In *Research in the Social Scientific Study of Religion*, Vol. 4, edited by M. Lynn, and D. Moberg. Greenwich, CT: JAI Press.

Marler, Penny and David Roozen. 1993. "From Church Tradition to Consumer Choice: The Gallup Surveys of the Unchurched American." In *Church and Denominational Growth*, edited by David Roozen, and C. Kirk Hadaway. Nashville, TN: Abingdon Press.

Martin, David. 1978. *A General Theory of Secularization*. New York: Harper and Row.

———. 1967. *A Sociology of English Religion*. London: S.C.M. Press.

Marty, Martin. 1981. *The Public Church: Mainline—Evangelical—Catholic*. New York: Crossroad.

Marx, John H. and Burkhardt Holzner. 1975. "Ideological Primary Groups in Contemporary Cultural Movements." *Sociological Focus* 8 (4): 311–329.

Masnick, George and Mary Jo Bane. 1980. *The Nation's Families: 1960–1990*. Cambridge: M.I.T.-Harvard Joint Center for Urban Studies.

Mason, K. and L.L. Bumpass. 1975. "U.S. Women's Sex Role Ideology, 1970." *American Journal of Sociology* 80 (March): 1212–1219.

McAdoo, Harriette Pipes. 1988. "Transgenerational Patterns of Upward Mobility in African-American Families." In *Black Families*, 2nd Edition, edited by Harriette Pipes McAdoo. Beverly Hills, CA: Sage Publications.

———, ed. 1981. *Black Families*. Beverly Hills, CA: Sage Publications.

McAdoo, Harriette Pipes and John Lewis McAdoo, eds. 1985. *Black Children: Social, Educational, and Parental Environments*. Beverly Hills, CA: Sage

Publications.

McCall, George J. and J.L. Simmons. 1978. *Identities and Interactions*. New York: Free Press.

McCarthy, J. 1979. "Religious Commitment, Affiliation, and Marriage Dissolution." In *The Religious Dimension*, edited by Robert Wuthnow. New York: Academic.

McCarthy, Marie. 1984. *The Role of Mutuality in Family Structure and Relationships: A Critical Examination of Selected Options in Contemporary Theological Ethics*. diss. University of Chicago.

McCarthy, Maureen and Gail Rosenberg. 1981. *Work Sharing Case Studies*. Kalamazoo: W.E. Upjohn.

McCready, W.C. 1972. *Faith of Our Fathers*. diss. University of Illinois.

McCurley, Donna and Robbie Sharp. 1977. *The Effect of Economic Development, Birthrate, and Religious Ideology on the Participation of Women in the Labor Force*. New Orleans: Tulane University Press.

McCutcheon, Alan L. 1988. "Denominations and Religious Intermarriage: Trends Among White Americans in the Twentienth Century." *Review of Religious Research* 29 (3): 213–227.

McGinnis, Kathleen and James McGinnis. 1981. *Parenting for Peace and Justice*. Maryknoll: Orbis Books.

McGuire, Meredith. 1982. *Pentecostal Catholics: Power, Charisma and Order in a Religious Movement*. Philadelphia: Temple University Press.

McKiernan-Allen, Linda and Ronald J. Allen. 1986. "Colleagues in Marriage and Ministry." In *Women Ministers*, edited by Judith L. Weidman. San Francisco: Harper and Row, pp. 207–220.

McManus, Jim. 1985. "Small Catholic Groups Emerging Nationwide Based on Prayer Life, Active Justice Work." *National Catholic Reporter*, March 29, 1, 4, 5.

Mead, George Herbert. 1934. *Mind, Self, and Society: From the Standpoint of a Social Behaviorist*. Chicago, IL: University of Chicago Press.

Meier, Gretl S. 1979. *Job-Sharing: A New Pattern for Quality of Work and Life*. Kalamazoo: W.E. Upjohn Institute for Employment Research.

Meredith, Don. n.d. *Becoming One*. Nashville, TN: Thomas Nelson Publishers.

Metz, Johann Baptist. 1980. *Faith in History and Society: Toward a Practical Fundamental Theology*, translated by David Smith. New York: Seabury Press.

Moberg, David O. 1962. *The Church as a Social Institution*. Englewood Cliffs: Prentice-Hall.

Morgan, J.N., M. David, W. Cohen, and H. Brazer. 1962. *Income and Welfare in the United States*. New York: McGraw-Hill.

Morgan, Mary Y. and John Scanzoni. 1987. "Religious Orientations and Women's Expected Continuity in the Labor Force." *Journal of Marriage and the Family* 49: 367–379.

Morrison, Toni. 1987. *Beloved*. New York: Alfred A. Knopf.

Mortimer, J., R. Hall, and R. Hill. 1978. "Husband's Occupational Attributes and Constraints on Wives' Employment." *Sociology of Work and Occupations* 5:

285–313.

Mosher, William D. and Gerry E. Hendershot. 1984. "Religious Affiliation and the Fertility of Married Couples." *Journal of Marriage and the Family* 46 (3): 671–677.

Moynihan, Daniel Patrick. 1986. *Family and Nation.* San Diego, CA: Harcourt Brace Jovanovich.

———. 1969. *On Understanding Poverty: Perspectives from the Social Sciences.* New York: Basic Books.

Mueller, Charles W. and Weldon T. Johnson. 1975. "Socioeconomic Status and Religious Participation." *American Sociological Review* 40: 785–800.

Nash, Dennison. 1968. "A Little Child Shall Lead Them: A Statistical Test of an Hypothesis That Children Were the Sources of the American 'Religious Revival.'" *Journal for the Scientific Study of Religion* 7: 238–240.

Nash, Dennison and Peter Berger. 1962. "The Child, the Family, and the 'Religious Revival' in Suburbia." *Journal for the Scientific Study of Religion* 2: 85–93.

Neitz, Mary Jo. 1987. *Charisma and Community: A Study of Religious Commitment Within the Charismatic Renewal.* New Brunswick, NJ: Transaction Books.

Nelsen, Hart M. 1981. "Religious Conformity in an Age of Disbelief: Contextual Effects of Time, Denomination, and Family Processes upon Church Decline and Apostasy." *American Sociological Review* 46: 632–640.

———. 1980. "Religious Transmission Versus Religious Formation: Preadolescent-parent Interaction." *Sociological Quarterly* 21: pp. 207–18.

Nelsen, Hart M. and Raymond H. Potvin. 1981. "Gender and Regional Differences in the Religiosity of Protestant Adolescents." *Review of Religious Research* 22: 268–285.

Nelton, Sharon. 1986. *In Love and in Business: How Entrepreneurial Couples are Changing the Rules of Business and Marriage.* New York: John Wiley & Sons.

Neuhaus, Richard John. 1984. *The Naked Public Square.* Grand Rapids: Eerdmans.

Newcomb, Theodore. 1973. "Stabilities Underlying Changes in Interpersonal Attraction." In *Interpersonal Behavior in Small Groups,* edited by Richard Ofshe. Englewood Cliffs, NJ: Prentice-Hall, pp. 82–95.

Newman, William M. 1986. "Religion." In *Sex Roles and Social Patterns,* edited by Francis Bordeau, Roger Sennott, and Michael Wilson. New York: Praeger Publishers.

Niebuhr, Reinhold. 1941. *The Nature and Destiny of Man.* New York: Scribners.

Niemi, Richard, John Mueller, and Tom Smith. 1989. *Trends in Public Opinion: A Compendium of Survey Data.* New York: Greenwood Press.

Nock, Steven L. and Paul Kingston. 1988. "Time with Children: The Impact of Couple's Work-Time Commitments." *Social Forces* 67: 59–85.

Olmstead, Barney and Suzanne Smith. 1983. *The Job Sharing Handbook.* Berkeley, CA: Ten Speed Press.

Olmsted, Michael and A. Paul Hare. 1978. *The Small Group*. New York: Random House.

Olsen, Charles. 1973. *The Base Church: Creating Comunity Through Multiple Forms*. Atlanta: Forum.

Oppenheimer, Valerie. 1982. *Work and the Family: A Study in Social Demography*. New York: Academic Press.

Orr, J. and F.P. Nichelson. 1970. *The Radical Suburb*. Philadelphia: Westminster.

Outka, Gene. 1972. *Agape: An Ethical Analysis*. New Haven: Yale University Press.

Palmer, Parker. 1981. *The Company of Strangers*. New York: Crossroad.

Pancoast, Diane. 1990. "A Network Focus for Family Ministry." In *The Church's Ministry With Families*, edited by D. Garland, and D. Pancoast. Dallas, TX: Word Publishing.

Papanek, Hannah. 1973. "Men, Women and Work: Reflections on the Two-person Career." *American Journal of Sociology* 78 (4, January): 853–72.

Parsons, Talcott. 1960. "The American Family: Its Relation to Personality and to the Social Structure." In *Family Socialization and Interaction Process*, edited by T. Parsons and R. F. Bales. New York: Free Press, pp. 3–33.

———. 1952. "Sociology and Social Psychology." In *Religious Perspectives in College Teaching*, edited by H.N. Fairchild, *et al*. New York: Ronald Press Co., pp. 286–337.

Pepitone-Rockwell, Fran, ed. 1980. *Dual Career Couples*. Beverly Hills, CA: Sage Publications.

Perrow, Charles and Mauro F. Guillen. 1990. *The AIDS Disaster: The Failure of Organizations in New York and the Nation*. New Haven: Yale University Press.

Piehl, Mel. 1982. *Breaking Bread: The Catholic Worker and the Origin of Catholic Radicalism in America*. Philadelphia: Temple University Press.

Pingree, Suzanne, *et al*. 1978. "Anti-Nepotism's Ghost: Attitudes of Administrators Toward Hiring Professional Couples." *Psychology of Women Quarterly* 3 (1, Fall): 22–29.

Plaskow, Judith. 1980. *Sex, Sin, and Grace: Women's Experience in the Theologies of Reinhold Niebuhr and Paul Tillich*. Washington: University Press of America.

Pleck, Joseph H. 1985. *Working Wives/Working Husbands*. Beverly Hills, CA: Sage Publications.

———. 1978. "Men's Family Work: Three Perspectives and New Data." *The Family Coordinator* 28: 481–488.

———. 1977. "The Work-Family Role System." *Social Problems* 24: 417–427.

Plutzer, Eric. 1988. "Work Life, Family Life, and Women's Support of Feminism." *American Sociological Review* 53: 640–649.

Porter, Judith and Alexa Albert. 1977. "Subculture or Assimilation? A Cross-cultural Analysis of Religion and Women's Role." *Journal for the Scientific Study of Religion* 16 (4): 345–359.

Poster, Mark. 1978. *Critical Theory of the Family*. New York: Seabury.

Postman Neil. 1985. *Amusing Ourselves to Death: Public Discourse in the Age of*

Show Business. News York: Viking.

Princeton Religion Research Center. 1988a. *Princeton Religion Research Center Report*. Princeton Religion Research Center.

———. 1988b. *The Unchurched American: Ten Years Later*. Princeton: PRRC.

———. 1980. *Religion in America: 1979–1980*. Princeton: PRRC.

Preister, S. 1982. "Social Change and the Family: An Historical Perspective with Family Impact Assessment Principles for Catholic Charities." *Social Thought* 8: 3–21.

Quest: A Reflection Booklet for Small Christian Communities. 1991. Hartford, CT: Archdiocese of Hartford.

Quinley, Harold E. and Charles Glock. 1979. *Anti-Semitism in America*. New York: Free Press.

Raines, Robert. 1980. *New Life in the Church*. New York: Harper and Row.

Rallings, E.M. and David J. Pratto. 1984. *Two-Clergy Marriages: A Special Case of Dual Careers*. Lanham, MD: University Press of America.

Rapoport, Robert N. and Rhona Rapoport, Eds. 1978. *Working Couples*. New York: Harper and Row.

Reineke, Martha J. 1989. "Out of Order: A Critical Perspective on Women in Religion." In *Women: A Feminist Perspective*, edited by Jo Freeman. Mountain View, CA: Mayfield Publishing Co.

Renner, Gerald. 1990. "Power Changes at the Mainstream's Helm." *Progressions: A Lilly Endowment Occasional Report* 2 (1): 11–12.

Rhodes, A. Lewis. 1983. "Effects of Religious Denomination on Sex Differences in Occupational Expectations." *Sex Roles* 9 (1): 93–108.

Richards, Lawrence. 1970. *A New Face for the Church*. Grand Rapids: Zondervan.

Ricoeur, Paul. 1987. "The Teleological and Deontological Structures of Action: Aristotle or Kant?" Lecture. University of Chicago Divinity School, June.

Ridgeway, Cecilia. 1983. *The Dynamics of Small Groups*. New York: St. Martin's.

Rieff, Philip. 1966. *The Triumph of the Therapeutic*. New York: Harper and Row.

Riley, M. 1983. "The Family in an Aging Society." *Journal of Family Issues* 4: 439–454.

Ritzer, George. 1988. *Sociological Theory*. New York: Alfred A. Knopf.

Robbin, Jonathan. *PRIZM (Potential Rating Index for Zip Markets)*. Alexandria, VA: Claritas Corporation.

Roberts, J. Deotis. 1980. *Roots of a Black Future: Family and Church*. Philadelphia, PA: Westminster Press.

Roberts, Keith. 1984. *Religion in Sociological Perspective*. Chicago: Dorsey Press.

Roof, Wade Clark. 1993. *A Generation of Seekers*. San Francisco: Harper.

———. 1987. "The Third Disestablishment and Beyond." In *Mainstream Protestantism: Its Problems and Prospects*, edited by Dorothy Bass, Benton Johnson, and Wade Clark Roof. Louisville: Committee on Theological Education of the Presbyterian Church (U.S.A.), pp. 27–37.

———. 1978. *Community and Commitment: Religious Plausibility in a Liberal Protestant Church*. New York: Elsevier.

Roof, Wade Clark and Dean Hoge. 1980. "Church Involvement in America: Social Factors Affecting Membership and Participation." *Review of Religious Research* 21: 405–426.

Roof, Wade Clark and William McKinney. 1987. *American Mainline Religion: Its Changing Shape and Future*. New Brunswick, NJ: Rutgers University Press.

Roof, Wade Clark and Jennifer L. Roof. 1984. "Review of the Polls: Images of God among Americans." *Journal for the Scientific Study of Religion* 23: 201–215.

Roozen, David A. 1979. *Church Attendance From a Social Indicators Perspective: An Exploration Into the Development of Social Indicators of Religion From Existing National Data*. Unpublished dissertation. Atlanta, GA: Emory University.

Roozen, David A., William McKinney, and Wayne Thompson. 1990. "The 'Big Chill' Generation Warms to Worship: A Research Note." *Review of Religious Research* 31 (3): 314–322.

Rose, Arnold M., ed. 1962. *Human Behavior and Social Processes*. Boston: Houghton Mifflin.

Rowatt, G. Wade, and Mary Jo Brock Rowatt. 1980. *The Two-Career Marriage*. Philadelphia: Westminster.

Ruether, Rosemary. 1981. "The Feminist Critique in Religious Studies." In *A Feminist Perspective in the Academy*, edited by E. Langland, and W. Gove. Chicago: University of Chicago Press, pp. 52–66.

———. 1975. *New Woman, New Earth*. New York: Seabury Press.

———, ed. 1973. *Religion and Sexism*. New York: Simon and Schuster.

Ruether, Rosemary Radford and Rosemary Skinner Keller. 1981. *Women and Religion in America, Vol. 1: The Nineteenth Century*. San Francisco: Harper and Row.

Russell, Cheryl. 1987. *100 Predictions for the Baby Boom*. New York: Plenum Press.

Sandomirsky, Sharon and John Wilson. 1990. "Processes of Disaffiliation: Religious Mobility Among Men and Women." *Social Forces* 68 (4): 1211–1230.

Scanzoni, John H. 1975. *Sex Roles, Life-Styles, and Childbearing: Changing Patterns in Marriage and Family*. New York: Free Press.

———. 1971. *The Black Family in Modern Society*. Boston: Allyn and Bacon.

Schaller, Lyle. 1991. "The Disappearing Pillars." *Net Results* 7 (February): 8–11.

Schluchter, Wolfgang. 1983. "The Future of Religion." In *Religion and America: Spiritual Life in a Secular Age*, edited by Mary Douglas, and Steven M. Tipton. Boston: Beacon Press.

Schroeder, W. Widick. 1976. "A Sociological and Theological Critique of the House Church Movement." In *The House Church Evolving*, edited by Arthur L. Foster. Chicago: Exploration Press, pp. 53–58.

Schurenberg, Eric. 1989. "The New Gospel of Financial Planning." *Money* (March) 18 (3): 54–58.

Segalen, Martine. 1986. *Historical Anthropology of the Family*, translated by J.C.

Whitehouse and S Matthews. Cambridge: Cambridge University Press.

Sekaran, Uma. 1986. *Dual-Career Families*. San Francisco: Jossey-Bass.

Shea, J.R., K. Sookin, and R.D. Roderick. 1973. *Dual Careers: A Longitudinal Study of Labor Market Experience of Women*. Vol. 2. Manpower Research Monograph 21. Washington, DC: Government Printing Office.

Sherrill, Lewis J. 1937. *Family and Church*. New York: Abingdon.

Shotter, John. 1984. *Social Accountability and Selfhood*. Oxford: Basil Blackwell.

Sider, Ronald J. 1980. *Living More Simply: Biblical Principles and Practical Models*. Downer's Grove: Intervarsity Press.

Smith, Ralph E. 1979a. "The Movement of Women into the Labor Force." In *The Subtle Revolution: Women at Work*, edited by R. E. Smith. Washington: Urban Institute, pp. 1–20.

———. 1979b. *Women in the Labor Force in 1990*. Washington: Urban Institute.

Smith, Wallace Charles. 1985. *The Church in the Life of the Black Family*. Valley Forge, PA: Judson Press.

Snyder, Howard A. 1980. *Liberating the Church*. Downer's Grove: Intervarsity Press.

———. 1977. *Community of the King*. Downer's Grove: Intervarsity Press.

———. 1975. *The Problem of Wineskins: Church Structure in a Technological Age*. Downer's Grove: Intervarsity Press.

Sobol, Marion Gros. 1974. "Commitment to Work." In *Working Mothers*, edited by Lois W. Hoffman and F. Ivan Nye. San Francisco: Josey-Bass, pp. 63–80.

Sobel, Mechal. 1979. *Trabelin' On: The Slave Journey to an Afro-Baptist Faith*. Westport, CT: Greenwood Press.

Sommer, Elyse and Mike Sommer. 1980. *The Two-Boss Business: The Joys and Pitfalls of Working and Living Together—And Still Remaining Friends*. New York: Butterick.

Sparkman, Temp. 1983. *The Salvation and Nurture of the Child of God: The Story of Emma*. Valley Forge: Judson Press.

Specht, D.A. 1975. "On the Evaluation of Causal Models." *Social Science Research* 4: 113–133.

Stacey, Judith. 1990. *Brave New Families: Stories of Domestic Upheaval in Late Twentieth Century America*. New York: Basic Books.

Stanley, A. Knighton. 1979. *The Children is Crying: Congregationalism Among Black People*. New York: Pilgrim Press.

Stark, Rodney and William Sims Bainbridge. 1985. *The Future of Religion: Secularization, Revival and Cult Formation*. Berkeley: University of California Press.

Stewart, Sonja M. 1989. "Children and Worship." *Religious Education* 84 (3): 350–366.

Strommen, M.P. 1963. *Profiles of Church Youth*. St. Louis: Concordia.

Stryker, Robin. 1981. "Religio-Ethnic Effects on Early Career." *American Sociological Review* 46 (2): 212–231.

Sweet, James A. 1970. "Family Composition and the Labor Force Activity of

American Wives." *Demography* 7: 195–209.

Sweet, Leonard. 1982. *The Minister's Wife: Her Role in Nineteenth-Century American Evangelicalism*. Philadelphia: Temple University Press.

Swidler, Ann. 1986. "Culture in Action: Symbols and Strategies." *American Sociological Review* 51: 273–286.

Tamney, Joseph and Stephen Johnson. 1983. "The Moral Majority in Middletown." *Journal for the Scientific Study of Religion* 22 (2): 145–157.

Taylor, Mary G. and Shirley F. Hartley. 1975. "The Two-Person Career: A Classic Example." *Sociology of Work and Occupations* 2 (4, November): 354–372.

Taylor, Robert J. and Linda M. Chatters. 1986. "Patterns of Informal Support to Elderly Black Adults: Family, Friends, and Church Members." *Social Work* 31: 432–438.

Thomas, Darwin L., ed. 1988. *The Religion and Family Connection: Social Science Perspectives*. Provo: Brigham Young University Religious Studies Center.

Thomas, Darwin L. and Gwendolyn C. Henry. 1985. "The Religion and Family Connection: Increasing Dialogue in the Social Sciences." *Journal of Marriage and the Family* 47 (2): 369–479.

Thornton, Arland. 1988. "Reciprocal Influences of Family and Religion in a Changing World." In *The Religion and Family Connection*, edited by Darwin Thomas. Brigham Young University: Religious Studies Center.

———. 1985. "Changing Attitudes Toward Separation and Divorce: Causes and Consequences." *American Journal of Sociology* 90: 856–72.

Thornton, A., D.F. Alwin, and D. Camburn. 1983. "Causes and Consequences of Sex-role Attitudes and Attitude Change." *American Sociological Review* 48: 211–227.

Thornton, A. and D. Freedman. 1982. "Changing Attitudes Toward Marriage and Single Life." *Family Planning Perspectives* 14: 297–303.

———. 1979. "Changes in the Sex Role Attitudes of Women, 1962–1977: Evidence From a Panel Study." *American Sociological Review* 44 (October): 831–42.

Thurman, Howard. 1979. *With Head and Heart: Autobiography of Howard Thurman*. New York: Harcourt Brace Jovanovich.

Thurmond, Joyce. 1983. *New Wineskins: A Study of the House Church Movement*. Bern: Verland.

Tilly, L.A. and J.W. Scott. 1978. *Women, Work, and Family*. New York: Holt Rinehart, and Winston.

Tinney, James. 1981. "The Religious Experience of Black Men." In *Black Men*, edited by Lawrence E. Gary. Beverly Hills, CA: Sage Publications, pp. 269–276.

Todd, Emmanuel. 1985. *Explanation of Ideology: Family Structures and Social Systems*. Oxford: Basil Blackwell.

Troeltsch, Ernst. 1931. *The Social Teaching of the Christian Churches*, translated by Olive Wyon. New York: Macmillan.

Tufte, Virginia and Barbara Myerhoff, eds. 1979. *Changing Images of the Family*.

New Haven, CT: Yale University Press.

Turner, Pauline. 1985. "Religious Aspects of Women's Role in the Nicaraguan Revolution." In *Women, Religion, and Social Change*, edited by Yvonne Yazleck Haddad and Ellison Banks Findly. Albany: State University of New York Press.

Ulbrich, Holley and Myles Wallace. 1984. "Women's Work Force Status and Church Attendance." *Journal for the Scientific Study of Religion* 23: 341–350.

Ulrich, David N. and Harry P. Dunne, Jr. 1986. *To Love and Work: A Systemic Interlocking of Family, Workplace and Career*. New York: Brunner/Mazel.

U.S. Bureau of the Census Current Population Reports, Series P–20, No. 447. 1990a. *Household and Family Characteristics: March 1990 and 1989*. Washington, DC: U.S. Government Printing Office.

———. Current Population Reports, Series P–20, No. 445. 1990b. *Marital Status and Living Arrangements: March 1989*. Washington, DC: Government Printing Office.

———. Current Population Reports. 1988. *Projections of the Population of the United States by Age, Sex, and Race: 1988 to 2020*. Washington, DC: U.S. Government Printing Office.

———. Current Population Reports, Series P–20, No. 106. 1960. *Household and Family Characteristics: March 1960*. Washington, DC: U.S. Government Printing Office.

———. Current Population Reports, Series P–20, No. 33. 1950. *Marital Status and Household Characteristics: March 1950*. Washington, DC: U.S. Government Printing Office.

———. 1980. "1980 Demographic Profile Report." Ithaca, NY: National Planning Data Corporation, Online Demographic Data Management and Reporting System.

———. Special Demographic Analysis, CDS–80–8. 1984. *American Women: Three Decades of Change*. Washington, DC: U.S. Government Printing Office.

———. 1990. *The Statistical Abstract of the United States: 1990*. 110th Edition. Washington, DC: U.S. Government Printing Office.

U. S. Department of Labor Women's Bureau. 1990. *20 Facts on Women Workers*. Washington, DC: U.S. Dept. of Labor: Women's Bureau.

———. 1971. *Working Women and Their Family Responsibilities: United States Experience*. Washington, DC

———. 1966. *College Women Seven Years After Graduation, Resurvey of Women Graduates—Class of 1957*. In *Bulletin 292*. Washington, DC: Government Printing Office.

Valentine, Bettylou. 1978. *Hustling and Other Hard Work: Life Styles in the Ghetto*. New York: Free Press.

Vaughn, Judith. 1983 *Society, Ethics, and Social Change: A Critical Appraisal of Reinhold Niebuhr's Ethics in Light of Rosemary Radford Ruether's Works*. New York: University Press of America.

Verhof, Joseph, Elizabeth Douvan, and Richard Kulka. 1981. *The Inner American: A Self-Portrait from 1957 to 1976*. New York: Basic Books.

Voydanoff, Patricia, ed. 1984. *Work and Family: Changing Roles of Men and Women*. Mountain View, CA: Mayfield Publishing Co.

Wagner, Melinda Bollar. 1991. *God's Schools: Choice and Compromise in American Society*. New Brunswick, NJ: Rutgers University Press.

Wahlstrom, Billie J. 1979. "Images of the Family in the Mass Media: An American Iconography?" In *Changing Images of the Family*, edited by V. Fufte, and B. Myerhoff. New Haven, CT: Yale University Press.

Waite, Linda, Frances Goldscheider, and Christine Witsberger. 1986. "Non-family Living and the Erosion of Traditional Family Orientations Among Young Adults." *American Sociological Review* 51: 541–554.

Wallace, Ruth. 1992. *They Call Her Pastor*. Albany: State University of New York Press.

———. 1989. "Bringing Women In: The ACSS/ASR Story." *Sociological Analysis* 50 (4): 409–413.

———. 1975. "Bringing Women In: Marginality in the Churches." *Sociological Analysis* 36: 291–303.

Walzer, Michael. 1983. *Spheres of Justice*. New York: Basic Books.

Warner, R. Stephen. 1993. "Work in Progress Toward a New Paradigm for the Sociological Study of Religion in the United States." *American Journal of Sociology* 98 (5, March): 1044–1093.

———. 1988. *New Wine in Old Wineskins*. Berkeley: University of California Press.

Warren, Michael. 1987. "Facing the Problem of Popular Culture." In *Youth, Gospel, Liberation*. San Francisco: Harper and Row.

Watson, David Lowes. 1985. *The Early Methodist Class Meeting: Its Origins and Significance*. Nashville: Cokesbury.

Webber, Thomas L. 1978. *Deep Like the Rivers: Education in the Slave Quarter Community, 1831–1865*. New York: W.W. Norton and Co.

Weber, Max. 1905/1958. *The Protestant Ethic and the Spirit of Capitalism*. New York: Scribner's.

———. 1922. *The Sociology of Religion*. Boston: Beacon Press.

Weigert, Andrew and Ross Hastings. 1977. "Identity Loss, Family, and Social Change." *American Journal of Sociology* 82 (6): 1171–1185.

Weiss, Michael J. 1988. *The Clustering of America*. New York: Harper and Row.

Welter, Barbara. 1973. "The Cult of True Womanhood: 1820–1860." In *The American Family in Social-Historical Perspectives*, edited by M. Gordon. New York: St. Martin's Press.

Westerhoff, John H. 1980. *Bringing Up Children in the Christian Faith*. Minneapolis: Winston Press.

———. 1976. *Will Our Children Have Faith*. New York: Seabury Press.

Whitehead, Barbara Defoe. 1992. "A New Familism?" *Family Affairs* 5 (1–2, Summer).

Willie, Charles. 1976. *A New Look at Black Families*. Bayside, NY: General Hall.

Willits, Fern K. 1988. "Religion and Well-Being: Men and Women in the Middle

Years." *Review of Religious Research* 29 (3): 281–294.

Wilson, Bryan. 1966. *Religion in a Secular Society*. London: C.A. Watts.

Wilson, John. 1978. *Religion in American Society*. Englewood Cliffs, NJ: Prentice-Hall.

Wilson, William Julius. 1990. "Studying Inner City Dislocations: The Challenge of Public Agenda Research." *American Sociological Review* 56 (1): 1–14.

———. 1987. *The Truly Disadvantaged: The Inner City, the Underclass and Public Policy*. Chicago: University of Chicago Press.

Windsor, Pat. 1989. "Roving Priest Advocates Small Faith Communities." *National Catholic Reporter*, October 6, 8, 9.

Winter, Gibson. 1962. *The Suburban Captivity of the Churches*. New York: Macmillan.

Wright, Stuart A. and C. Kirk Hadaway. 1983. "The House Church Movement: A Typology of Groups." Paper presented at the annual meetings of the Religious Research Association. Knoxville, Tenn., November.

Wuthnow, Robert. 1988. *The Restructuring of American Religion*. New Jersey: Princeton.

———. 1976a. *The Consciousness Reformation*. Berkeley: University of California Press.

———. 1976b. "Recent Patterns of Secularization: A Problem of Generations?" *American Sociological Review* 41: 850–867.

Yankelovich, Daniel. 1981. *New Rules: Searching for Self-Fulfillment in a World Turned Upside Down*. New York: Random House.

Yinger, J. Milton. 1977. "A Comparative Study of the Substructures of Religion." *Journal for the Scientific Study of Religion* 16: 67–86.

———. 1970. *The Scientific Study of Religion*. New York: Macmillan.

Young, Michael and Peter Willmott. 1973. *The Symmetrical Family*. New York: Pantheon.

Youngblood, Jonny Ray. 1990. *The Conspicuous Absence and the Controversial Presence of the Black Male in the Local Church*. Unpublished D.Min. thesis. Dayton, Ohio: United Theological Seminary.

Ziegenhals, Gretchen E. 1991. "Black Values, Families, and Churches." *The Christian Century* 108 (16): 509–511.

Zimmerman, Carle C. 1973. "Family and Religion." *Social Science* 48: 203–215.

INDEX

Elshtain, Jean Bethke, 169

employment, effects on religiosity, 88–89, 95–99, 113–117

empty-nesters, 8, 32, 34, 40, 43, 44, 45

Episcopalians, 33, 47, 142; and pacifism, 220, 225

equal-regard, ethic of, 163–76

Erikson, Erik, 168–69

Erskine, H., 142

"ethic of commitment," 3

ethics, 157–76

evangelicals. *See* Protestantism, evangelical; women, evangelical

Everett, Melissa, 233

executives, young corporate, 4

Fairchild, Roy, and John C. Wynn, 6, 33

faith, church as institutional representation of, 269–72; definition of, 269; and family, 272–74; and work, 274–77

family: blended, 9, 37, 70–72, 77, 173; changing, 27–30, 62–64, 142; without children, 32 (*see also* children, couples without); in the church, 204 (*see also* Protestantism, family/church dynamic in); as church consumers, 8, 37, 38, 42–45, 48, 50–52 (*see also* consumerism); concern about, 17; divorced, 9, 273 (*see also* divorce); dual-income, 276 (*see also* women, full-time employment of; women, in workforce); ethics, 157–74; extended, 14, 30, 52, 171; individualism within, 63–63, 68, 76; influence of, on work, 221–22, 223–25, 234–35; ministry to, 158–62, 170–74, 272–74; models of, 2–5, 11, 77, 172–73; nostalgia about, *see* nostalgia; privatization of,

158–60; single-parent, *see* parenting; therapies, 170–72; traditional nuclear, 5, 7–12, 17, 67, 77 (*see also* women, evangelical); nontraditional, 7, 8, 12; differences between traditional and nontraditional, 23–60, 123–36; values, 2–4, 32, 62, 68, 135 (*see also* values, traditional). *See also* African-American, family

family surrogate theory, 46

family systems theory, 170–72

feminist: critique of separation between public and private, 300; ethics, 169, 170; movement, 10, 11, 158, 291–93; witches, 292

feminists, 7, 13; and religiosity, 123–35

fertility rates, 11

Firebaugh, Glenn, and Kenneth E. Davis, 90, 98, 104, 110

Focus on the Family, 24

Foote, 161

Foster, Charles, 201

Fowler, James, 202, 208, 211

Frazier, E. Franklin, 184, 189, 191

Freeman, D., and A. Thornton, 140

Friedman, Rabbi Edwin, 170–71

Fuchs, Eric, 173

Fukuyama, Yoshio, 82

fundamentalism, 138; and change, 141; and the family, 158. *See also* conservatives

Gee, Ellen M., 84, 85

gender: differences, 83, 93, 318; equality, 3, 117, 126, 132–33; relationship to work and religion, 81–84, 123–35; roles, 11, 123–35, 138–48; space, 77

Gerson, Kathleen, 124

ghetto poor. *See* underclass.

Giddings, Paula, 189

Gilkes, Cheryl, 301

population change, 26, 38
Poster, Mark, 173
pregnancy, teenage, 1
premoral goods, 166–69, 172
Presbyterians, 142
privatism, 160–62, 200–01. *See also*
    public, split between, and private;
    autonomy; individualism
"Protestant principle", 63
Protestantism: and change, 13, 23,
    78; and church attendance, 33,
    124 (*see also* church attendance);
    clergy, 27; declining, 27, 157–58;
    dropping out of, 68–69, 74, 82;
    evangelical, 24, 34, 158 (*see also*
    women, evangelical); family/
    church dynamic in, 28, 33–40, 46,
    48, 51; fundamentalist, 141(*see
    also* fundamentalism); mainline,
    13, 14, 24, 34, 157–74, 199–218;
    ministries, 12, 43 (*see also* family,
    ministry to); small group meet-
    ings, 15–16, 17, 238, 261–81; and
    traditional families, 8, 50 (*see also*
    family, traditional nuclear)
public: church, 158–60, 202–18;
    issues and relationship to family,
    173–74; split between, and pri-
    vate, 6, 158–60, 300–01, 319–21
    (*see also* religion, linking public
    and private; religion, privatized)
Puritan values, 275

Quakers, 220, 226, 290
Quayle, Dan, 62

racism, 14, 178, 183
Reed, Roy, and Robert Browning, 212
Reformation, 63
reincarnation, 73
religion, 5, 7; declining, 116 (*see also*
    Protestantism, declining); drop-
    ping out of, 68–69; effects of, on
    idealized self, 140–43; institution-

al, and baby-boomers, 14, 72,
    77–78 (*see also* baby-boomers, and
    distrust of institutions); institu-
    tional, and change, 15, 77–78,
    269–70; institutional, vs, priva-
    tized, 9, 10; institutional, and
    socialization of children, 16; insti-
    tutional, and women's participa-
    tion in, 133–34; linking public and
    private, 13, 15, 17, 238, 154,
    275–77; non-Western, 77; priva-
    tized, 9, 10, 63, 74, 129, 135; as
    women's work, 6
religiosity: and employment, 9–10,
    82, 89; and gender-roles, 140; pas-
    tiche style, 73; as shaped by family
    and work, 82, 89–90, 324–26 (*see
    also* women, impact of work on
    religiosity of); and traditional fam-
    ilies, 9
religious education, 12
RENEW, 17, 248–50
retirement, 31
Ricoeur, Paul, 166
Rieff, Philip, 165
Ringer, Benjamin, Charles Glock, and
    Earl Babbie, 46–48
rites: of initiation, 207; of passage,
    171–72, 299
ritual, 16, 72, 183; women's,
    283–304
role exit theory, 220–35
Romanticism, 26
Roof, Wade Clark, 269; and William
    McKinney, 84–88, 99, 109, 115,
    140, 142, 271
Roozen, David A., 33; and Penny
    Long Marler, 45
Rosazza, Archbishop Peter A., 249

Sanctified Church, 180–81, 185, 190
Scanzoni, John H., 139, 191
Schaller, Lyle, 42
Schluchter, Wofgang, 201–02

Wilson, William Julius, 178
Winter, Gibson, 159, 173
witchcraft, 16, 292–93
women, 61; clergy, 12, 326; confined to private sphere, 6–7; and divorce, 124–25; and education, *see* education; and egalitarian ideals, 10, 123–35; empowerment of, 3; evangelical, 137–51; full-time employment of, 84, 114–17, 125, 128, 130–31, 141; at home, 4, 6, 82, 84, 141–42, 307; ordination of, 124, 142; in positions of church leadership, 142–43, 190; religiosity of, 9–10, 83–85, 123–35; rituals, *see* ritual; single, *see* singles, women; spirituality movement, 292; and traditionalist ideals, 10, 123–35; impact of work on religiosity of, 65–66, 85–98, 113–17; in workforce, 2–12 *pas-*

sim, 27, 30, 123–33, 137–54, 307–09
workforce hypothesis, 9–10, 83–117
working-class: and child care, 12; families, 6; and participation in organized religion, 82; and religious individualism, 66
working couples, 16, 305–29
working parents, 1, 4, 66, 173
workplace: changing, 3–5; as secular danger, 27, 274–77
World War: I, 47, 190; II, 27, 47, 82, 86, 221
Wuthnow, Robert, 124, 221, 234
Wynn, John C., and Roy Fairchild, 6, 33

Yankelovich, Daniel, 3, 67, 161
Young Christian Workers, 251
youth groups, 25, 39–41
"Yuppies," 62, 66

CONTRIBUTORS

Nancy Tatom Ammerman is Associate Professor of Sociology of Religion at Candler School of Theology, Emory University. In 1995, she will join the faculty at Hartford Seminary, in the Center for Social and Religious Research. She is the author of *Bible Believers: Fundamentalists in the Modern World* and *Baptist Battles: Social Change and Religious Conflict in the Southern Baptist Convention*. More recently, in a project funded by the Lilly Endowment, Nancy has been investigating the responses of local congregations to social changes in their communities.

Don S. Browning is the Alexander Campbell Professor of Ethics and the Social Sciences at the University of Chicago Divinity School. His most recent book is *A Fundamental Practical Theology: Descriptive and Strategic Proposals*. As director of the Religion, Culture, and Family project, funded by the Lilly Endowment, Don has been giving a great deal of attention to the changes in family life he writes about here.

William V. D'Antonio is Professor Emeritus, University of Connecticut, and Adjunct Research Professor at the Catholic University of America. In 1991, he completed nine years as Executive Officer of the American Sociological Association. Bill has written extensively about American Catholic life, including *American Catholic Laity in a Changing Church*, coauthored with Dean Hoge, James Davidson, and Ruth Wallace. He has also written numerous articles on religion and family and coedited (with Joan Aldous) *Families and Religions: Conflict and Change in Modern Society*.

William Johnson Everett is Professor of Christian Ethics at Andover Newton Theological School. He is the author of several books, including *Blessed Be the Bond: Christian Perspectives on Marriage and Family*. With his wife Sylvia, he has developed the oikos Project on Work, Family and Faith, a program of research and adult education which informs the research reported in this book. In 1991 to 1992, he conducted research in India and Germany on the relation of religious organizations to the development of modern federal republics.

Lyn Gesch is a graduate student in Sociology at the University of California at Santa Barbara, anticipating completion of the Ph.D. degree in 1996. She is focusing on changing understandings of gender and the challenges they pose to institutional religion.

Cheryl Townsend Gilkes is the John D. and Catherine T. MacArthur Associate Professor of African-American Studies and Sociology at Colby College. She also serves as Associate Minister of the Union Baptist Church in Cambridge, Massachusetts. She earned the Ph.D. degree in 1979 from Northeastern University, and has published widely on the religious experience of African-American women. Recent articles have appeared in *Women of Color in the United States* and in *A Troubling in My Soul: Womanist Perspectives in Evil and Suffering*.

Charles Hall is Assistant Professor of Sociology at Prescott College in Prescott, Arizona. Having received the Ph.D. degree from Purdue University in 1993, he is currently involved with the Crossroads Program at the Center for Public Justice, a program that attempts to integrate religious principles with public policy. He is the author of a monograph on "Homosexuality and Public Policy."

Bradley R. Hertel is Associate Professor of Sociology at Virginia Polytechnic Institute and State University. He is continuing to do research on the relationship between religion and social structure, especially relationships between labor force participation and religion, about which he writes in this volume. In addition, Brad is involved in a long-term study of the division of labor among Hindu priests and their assistants in northern India.

Mary Johnson, SND, is Associate Professor of Sociology and Religious Studies at Emmanuel College in Boston. She received the Ph.D. degree in 1993 from the University of Massachusetts, and is working on a book that will take up the stories of the defense workers she describes in her essay in this volume, asking how cultural institutions affect occupational choices.

Penny Long Marler is Assistant Professor of Religion at Samford University in Birmingham, Alabama. Having received the Ph.D. degree from the Southern Baptist Theological Seminary in 1991, she has written several articles on recent changes in family and religious life. She was also codirector, with Kirk Hadaway, of a study, funded by the Lilly Endowment, examining "marginal members" among Protestants. Among the articles from that study is a major reexamination of church attendance patterns published in the *American Sociological Review*. She is working on a book on the spirituality of the unchurched.

Mary Jo Neitz is Associate Professor of Sociology and Women Studies at the University of Missouri. She specializes in the study of culture, religion, gender, and qualitative methodologies and is the author of *Charisma and Community: A Study of Religious Commitment within the Charismatic Renewal*. She is also coauthor of *Culture: Sociological Perspectives*. Mary Jo's most recent research examines contemporary neopaganism.

Joseph T. Reiff is Assistant Professor of Religion at Emory and Henry College in Virginia. A 1992 Ph.D. graduate from Emory University, Joe is working on a book describing the congregation that is the subject of his essay in this volume.

Wade Clark Roof is J. F. Rowny Professor of Religion and Society at the University of California at Santa Barbara. He is coauthor of *American Mainline Religion: Its Changing Shape and Future*, and, more recently, the author of *A Generation of Seekers: The Spiritual Journeys of the Baby Boom Generation*.

Stuart Wright is Associate Professor of Sociology at Lamar University in Beaumont, Texas. He has been an NIMH Research Fellow at Yale University (1984–1985) and is coauthor of *Home Cell Groups and House Churches*. His most recent work is editing a collection of essays and research reports on the Branch Davidians and their encounter with the federal government. It is titled *Armageddon in Waco*.